# SOUL EATER

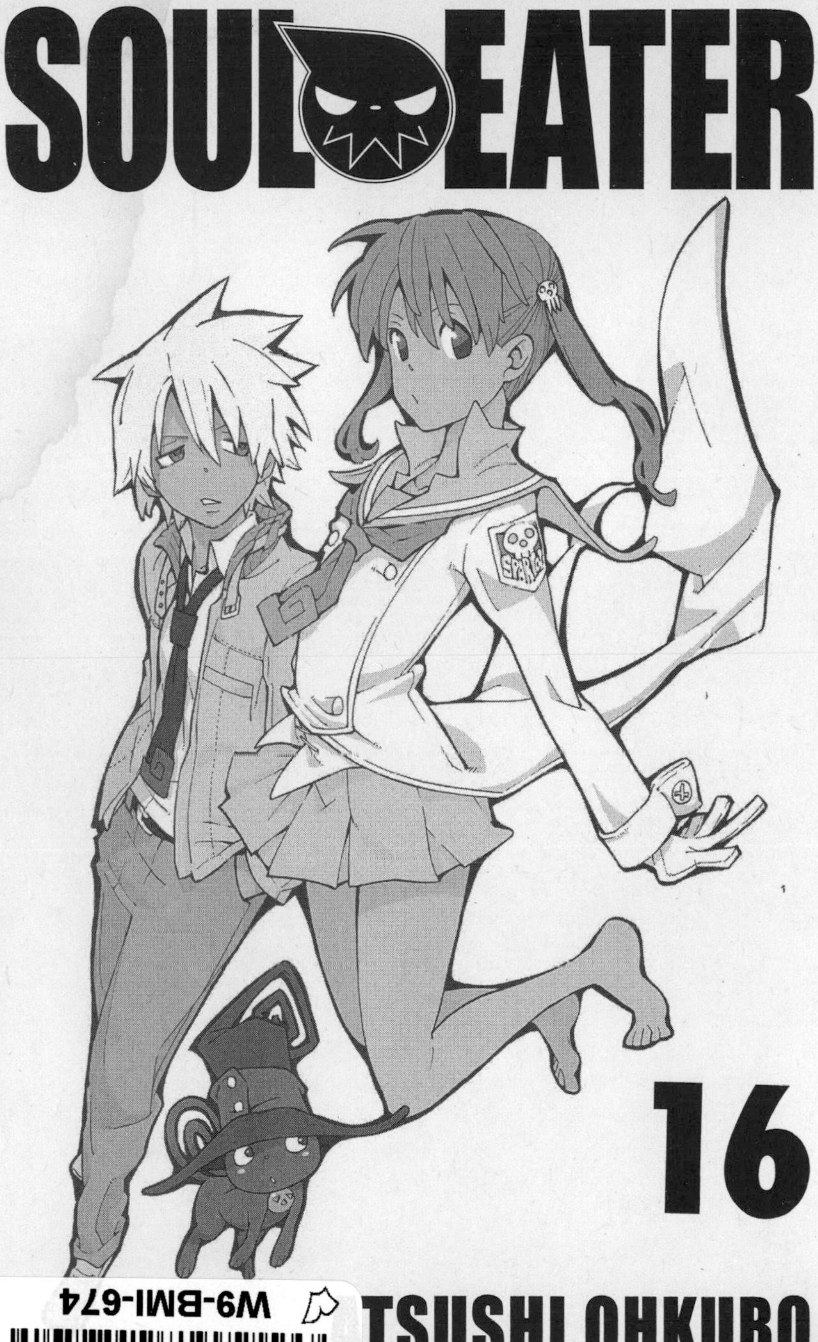

16

ATSUSHI OHKUBO

# SOUL EATER

vol. 16

by ATSUSHI OHKUBO

# This is the new SOUL resonance

# SOUL EATER 16

# CONTENTS

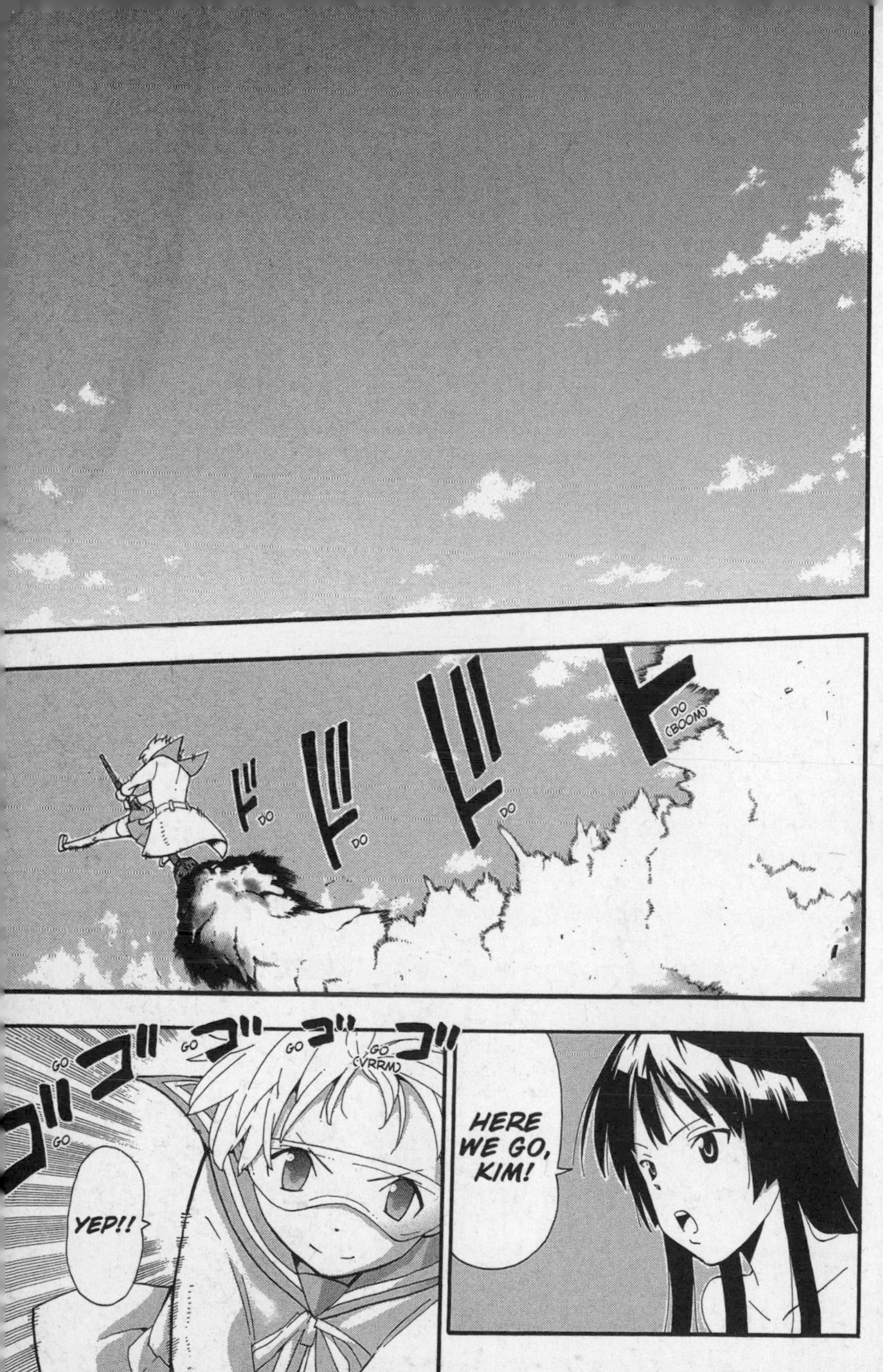
DO (BOOM)
DO
DO
DO
HERE WE GO, KIM!
GO (VRRM)
GO
GO
GO
GO
YEP!!

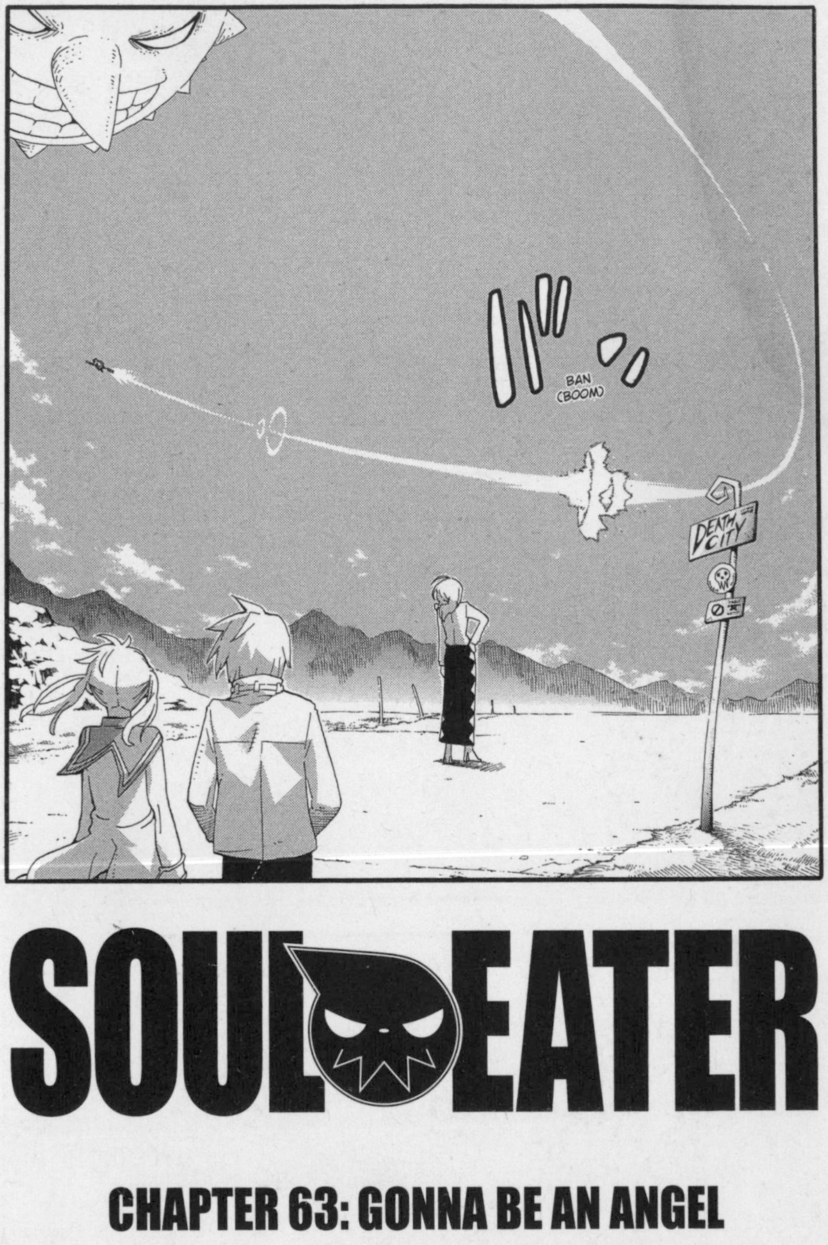
BAN
(BOOM)
DEATH CITY

# SOUL EATER

## CHAPTER 63: GONNA BE AN ANGEL

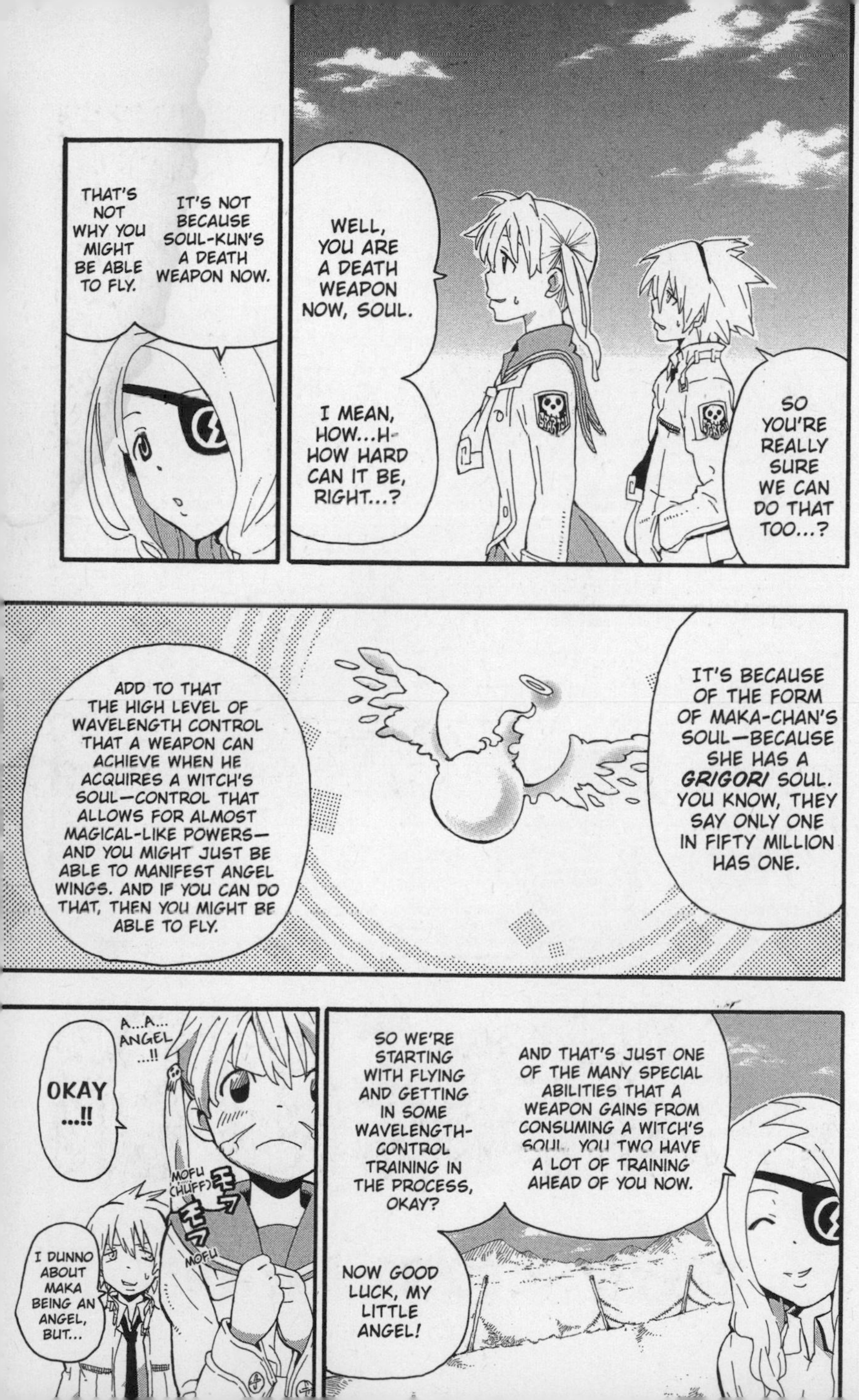
SO YOU'RE REALLY SURE WE CAN DO THAT TOO...?
WELL, YOU ARE A DEATH WEAPON NOW, SOUL.
I MEAN, HOW...H-HOW HARD CAN IT BE, RIGHT...?
IT'S NOT BECAUSE SOUL-KUN'S A DEATH WEAPON NOW.
THAT'S NOT WHY YOU MIGHT BE ABLE TO FLY.
IT'S BECAUSE OF THE FORM OF MAKA-CHAN'S SOUL—BECAUSE SHE HAS A *GRIGORI* SOUL. YOU KNOW, THEY SAY ONLY ONE IN FIFTY MILLION HAS ONE.
ADD TO THAT THE HIGH LEVEL OF WAVELENGTH CONTROL THAT A WEAPON CAN ACHIEVE WHEN HE ACQUIRES A WITCH'S SOUL—CONTROL THAT ALLOWS FOR ALMOST MAGICAL-LIKE POWERS—AND YOU MIGHT JUST BE ABLE TO MANIFEST ANGEL WINGS. AND IF YOU CAN DO THAT, THEN YOU MIGHT BE ABLE TO FLY.
AND THAT'S JUST ONE OF THE MANY SPECIAL ABILITIES THAT A WEAPON GAINS FROM CONSUMING A WITCH'S SOUL. YOU TWO HAVE A LOT OF TRAINING AHEAD OF YOU NOW.
SO WE'RE STARTING WITH FLYING AND GETTING IN SOME WAVELENGTH-CONTROL TRAINING IN THE PROCESS, OKAY?
NOW GOOD LUCK, MY LITTLE ANGEL!
A...A... ANGEL...!!
OKAY...!!
MOFU (CHUFF) モフ
モフ MOFU
I DUNNO ABOUT MAKA BEING AN ANGEL, BUT...

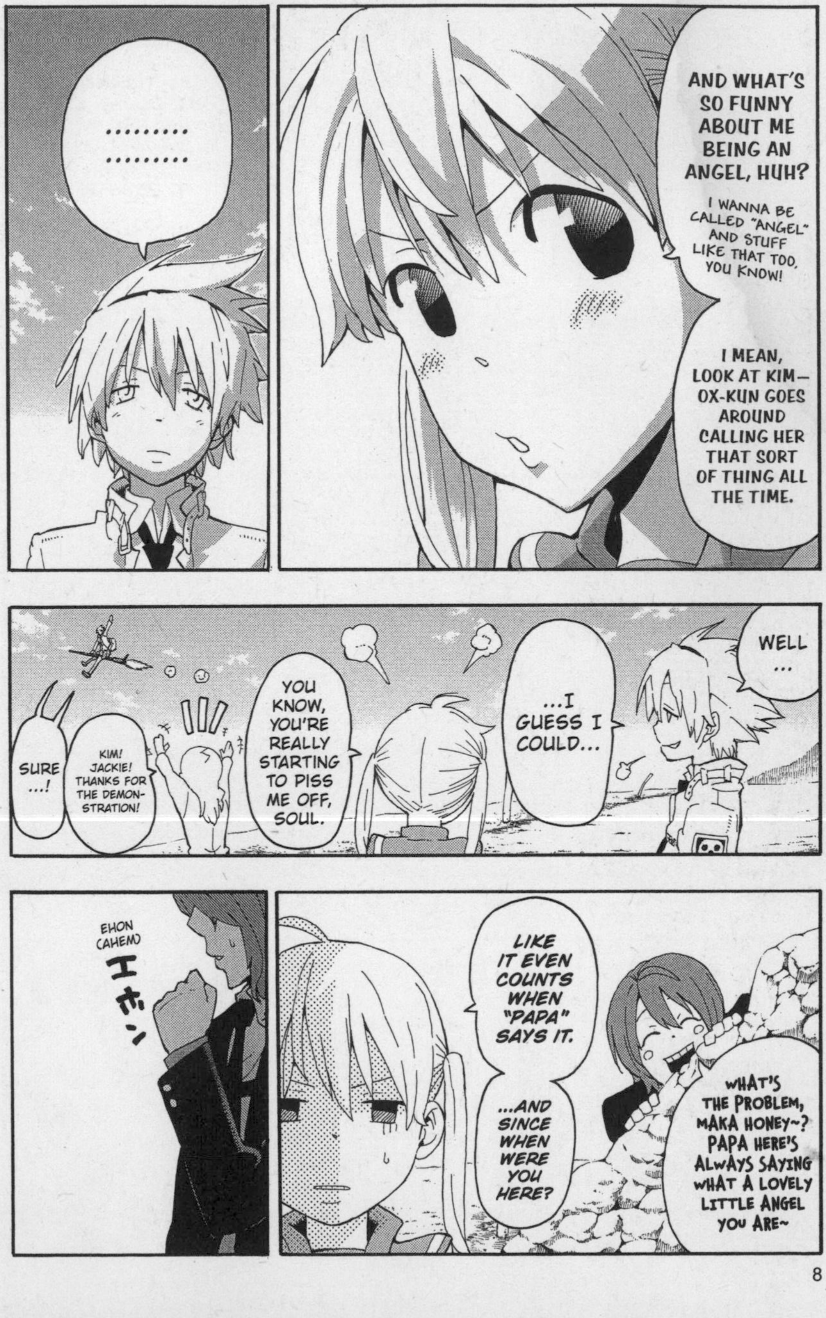
AND WHAT'S SO FUNNY ABOUT ME BEING AN ANGEL, HUH?
I WANNA BE CALLED "ANGEL" AND STUFF LIKE THAT TOO, YOU KNOW!
I MEAN, LOOK AT KIM—OX-KUN GOES AROUND CALLING HER THAT SORT OF THING ALL THE TIME.
.........
.........
WELL ...
...I GUESS I COULD...
YOU KNOW, YOU'RE REALLY STARTING TO PISS ME OFF, SOUL.
KIM! JACKIE! THANKS FOR THE DEMONSTRATION!
SURE ...!
WHAT'S THE PROBLEM, MAKA HONEY~? PAPA HERE'S ALWAYS SAYING WHAT A LOVELY LITTLE ANGEL YOU ARE~
LIKE IT EVEN COUNTS WHEN "PAPA" SAYS IT.
...AND SINCE WHEN WERE YOU HERE?
EHON (AHEM)
エホン

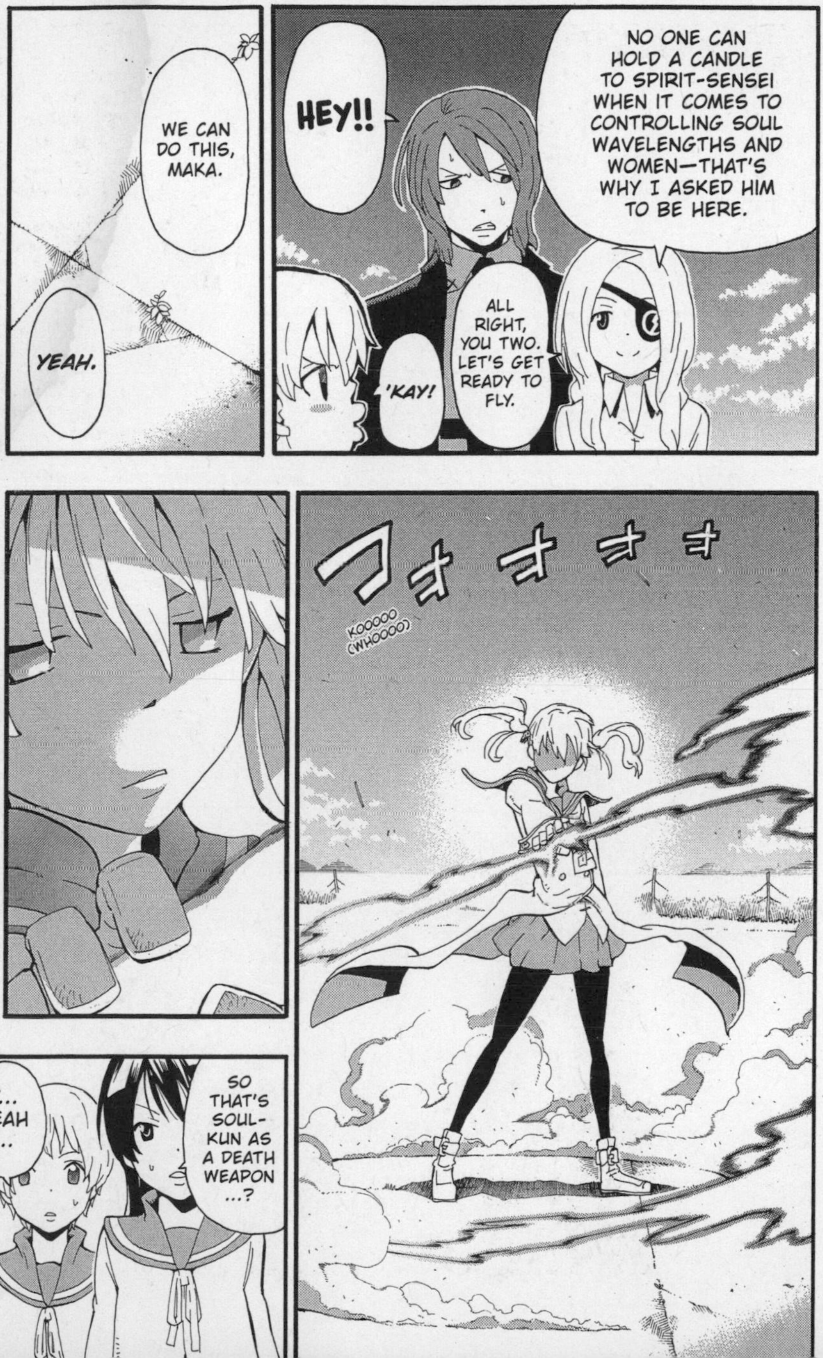
NO ONE CAN HOLD A CANDLE TO SPIRIT-SENSEI WHEN IT COMES TO CONTROLLING SOUL WAVELENGTHS AND WOMEN—THAT'S WHY I ASKED HIM TO BE HERE.
HEY!!
ALL RIGHT, YOU TWO. LET'S GET READY TO FLY.
'KAY!
WE CAN DO THIS, MAKA.
YEAH.
フォオオオオ
KOOOOO (WHOOOO)
SO THAT'S SOUL-KUN AS A DEATH WEAPON ...?
Y... YEAH ...

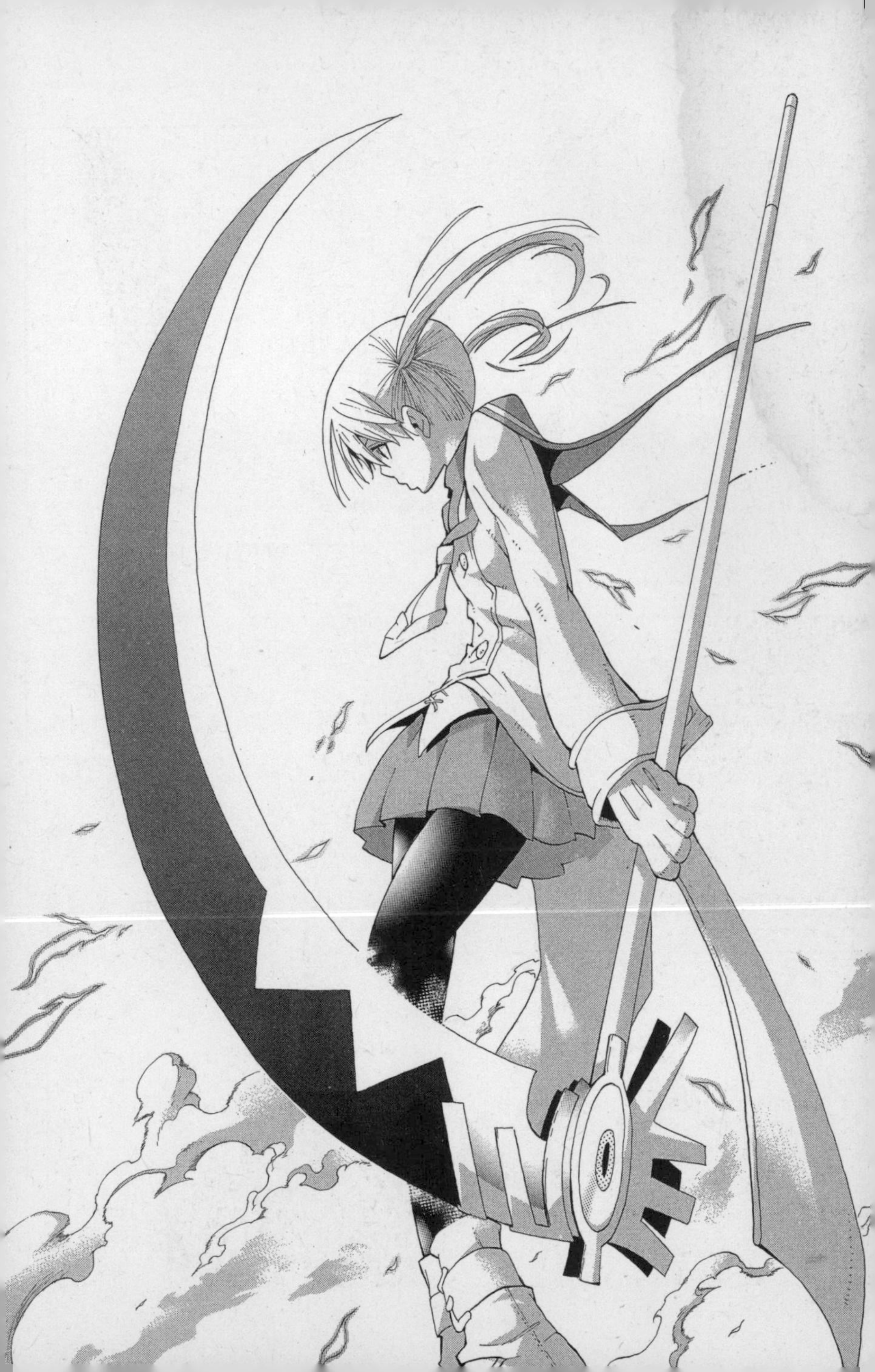

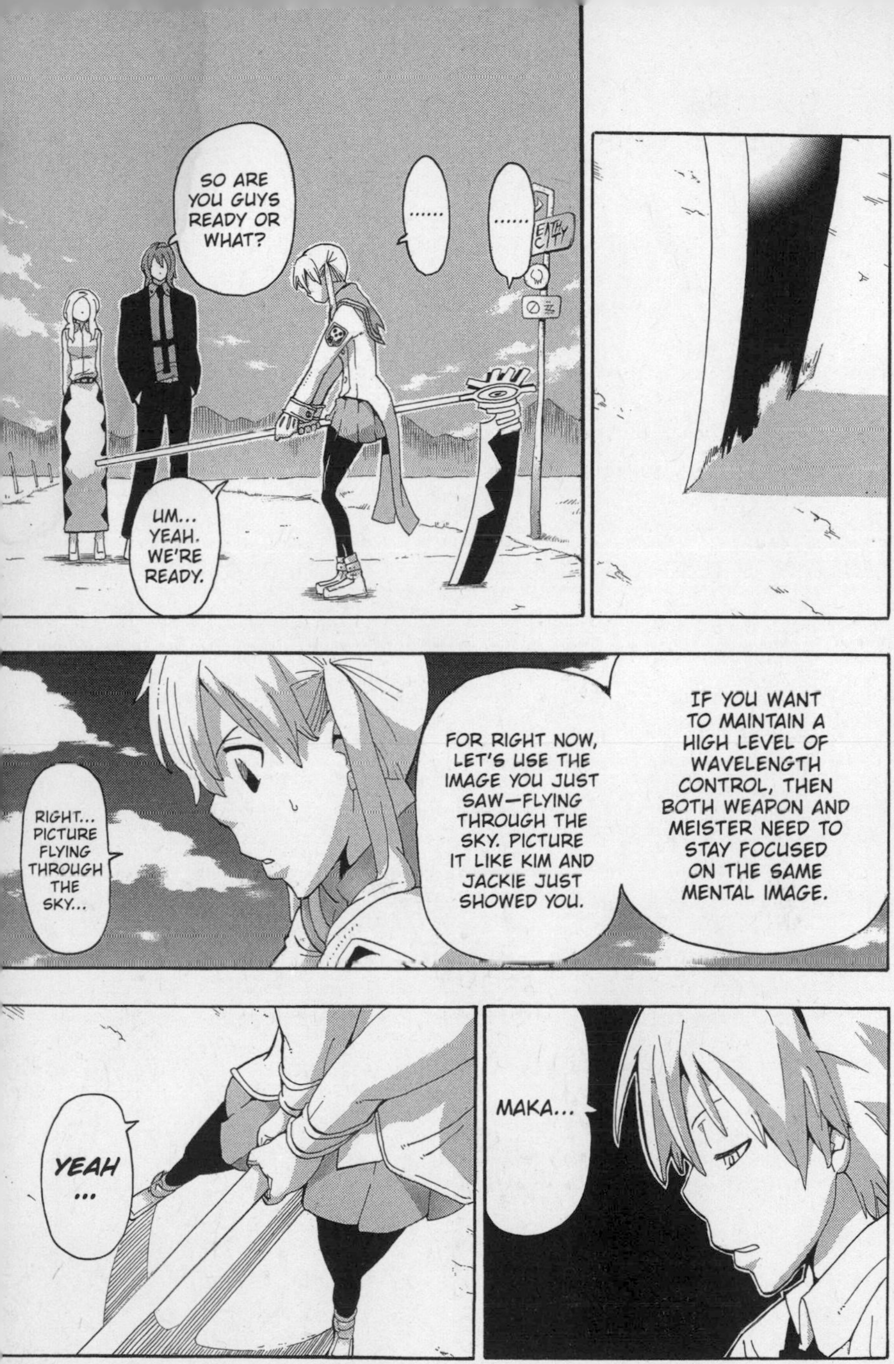
......
......
SO ARE YOU GUYS READY OR WHAT?
UM... YEAH. WE'RE READY.
IF YOU WANT TO MAINTAIN A HIGH LEVEL OF WAVELENGTH CONTROL, THEN BOTH WEAPON AND MEISTER NEED TO STAY FOCUSED ON THE SAME MENTAL IMAGE.
FOR RIGHT NOW, LET'S USE THE IMAGE YOU JUST SAW—FLYING THROUGH THE SKY. PICTURE IT LIKE KIM AND JACKIE JUST SHOWED YOU.
RIGHT... PICTURE FLYING THROUGH THE SKY...
MAKA...
YEAH ...

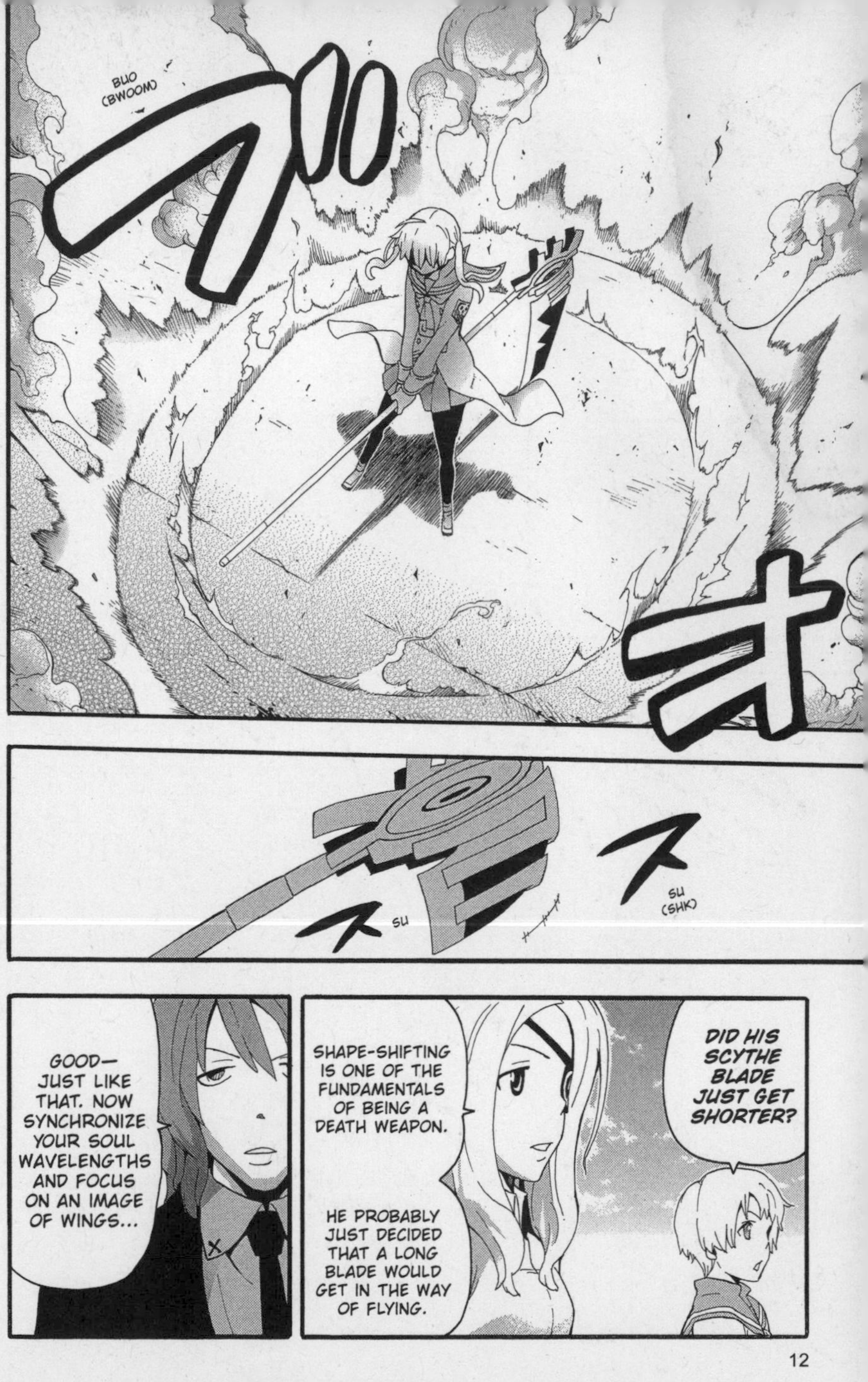
BUO (BWOOM)
SU (SHK)
SU
DID HIS SCYTHE BLADE JUST GET SHORTER?
SHAPE-SHIFTING IS ONE OF THE FUNDAMENTALS OF BEING A DEATH WEAPON.
HE PROBABLY JUST DECIDED THAT A LONG BLADE WOULD GET IN THE WAY OF FLYING.
GOOD—JUST LIKE THAT. NOW SYNCHRONIZE YOUR SOUL WAVELENGTHS AND FOCUS ON AN IMAGE OF WINGS...

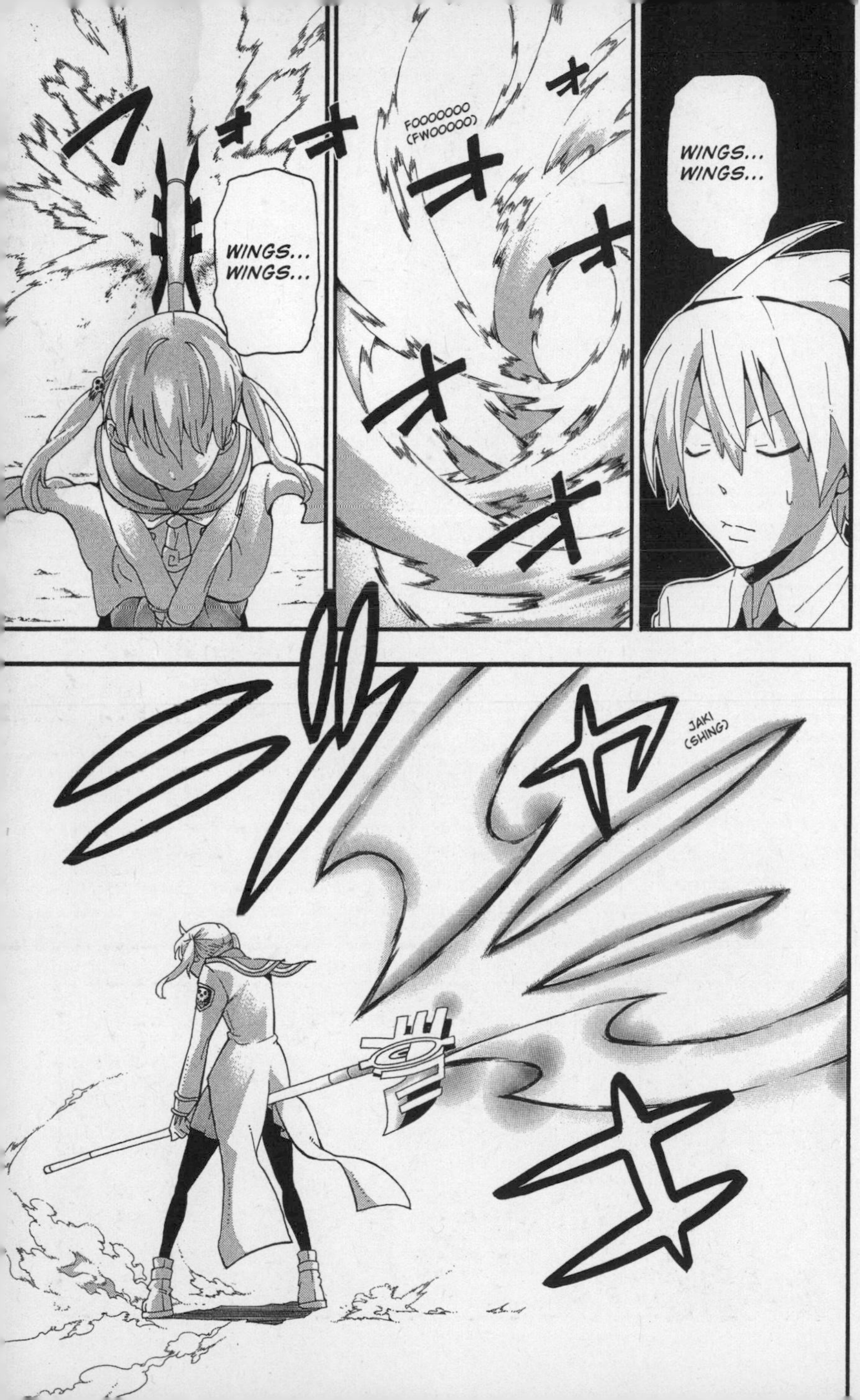
WINGS... WINGS...
FOOOOOOO (FWOOOOO)
WINGS... WINGS...
JAKI (SHING)

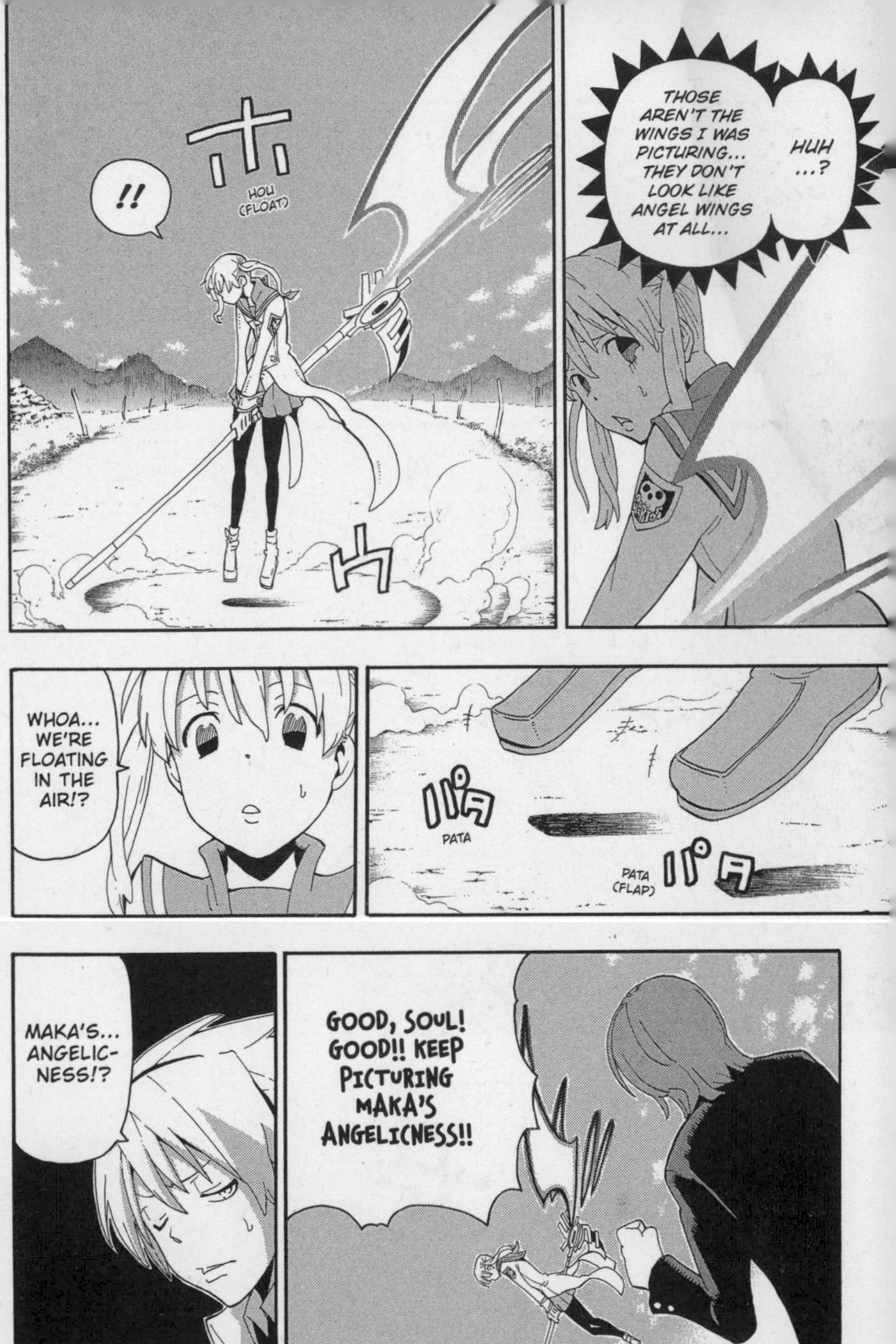
HUH ...?
THOSE AREN'T THE WINGS I WAS PICTURING... THEY DON'T LOOK LIKE ANGEL WINGS AT ALL...
HOU (FLOAT)
!!
パタ
PATA (FLAP)
パタ
PATA
WHOA... WE'RE FLOATING IN THE AIR!?
GOOD, SOUL! GOOD!! KEEP PICTURING MAKA'S ANGELICNESS!!
MAKA'S... ANGELIC-NESS!?

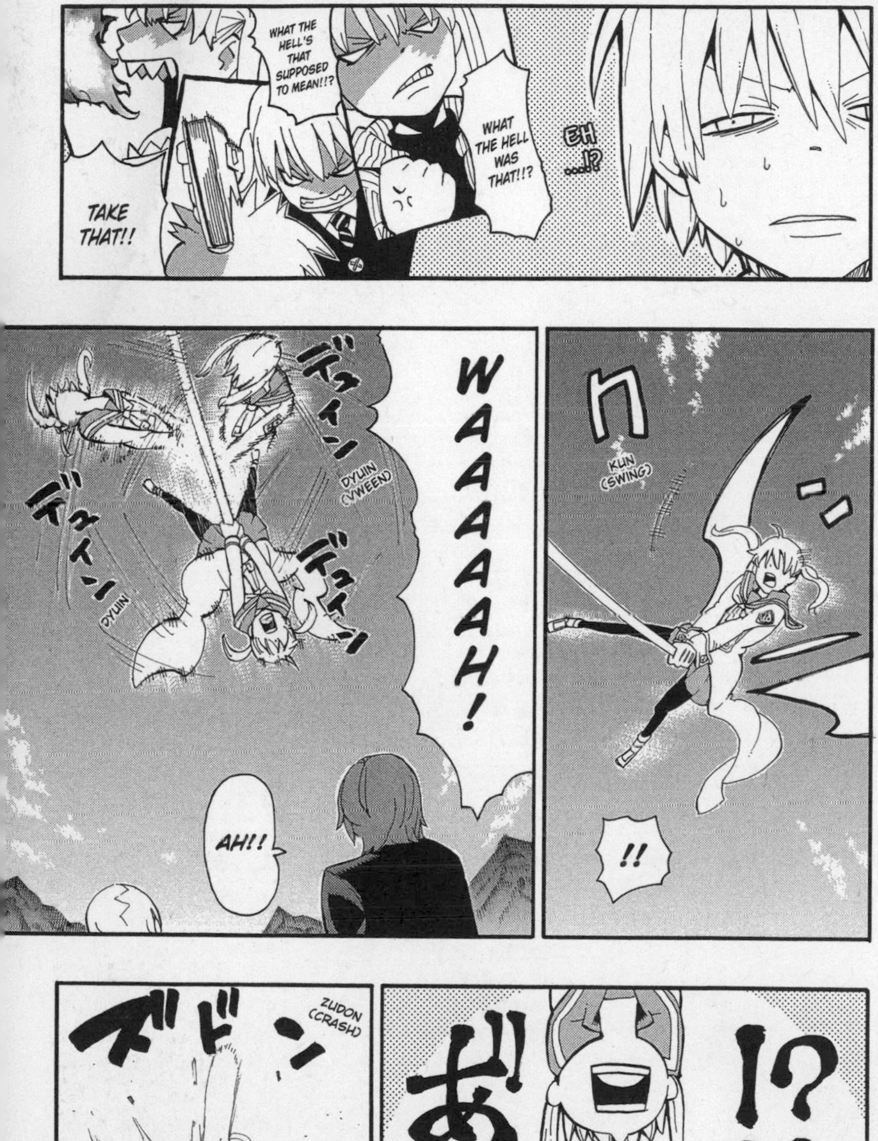
EH ...!?
WHAT THE HELL WAS THAT!!?
WHAT THE HELL'S THAT SUPPOSED TO MEAN!!?
TAKE THAT!!
KUN (SWING)
!!
WAAAAAAAH!
DYUIN (VWEEND)
DYUIN
AH!!
あ!!?
HUNH!!?
ズドン
ZUDON (CRASH)

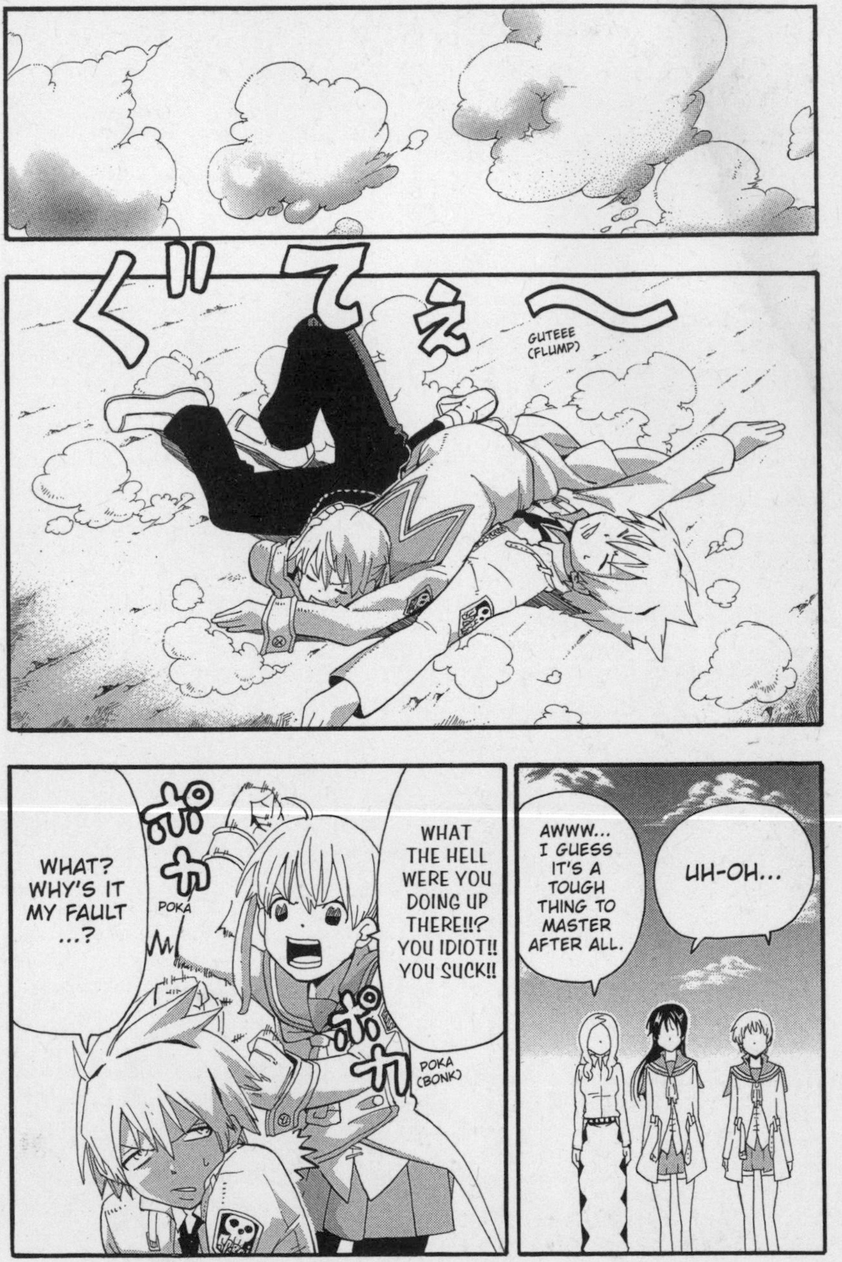
ぐてぇ~
GUTEEE (FLUMP)
UH-OH...
AWWW... I GUESS IT'S A TOUGH THING TO MASTER AFTER ALL.
WHAT THE HELL WERE YOU DOING UP THERE!!? YOU IDIOT!! YOU SUCK!!
ポカ
POKA
ポカ
POKA (BONK)
WHAT? WHY'S IT MY FAULT ...?

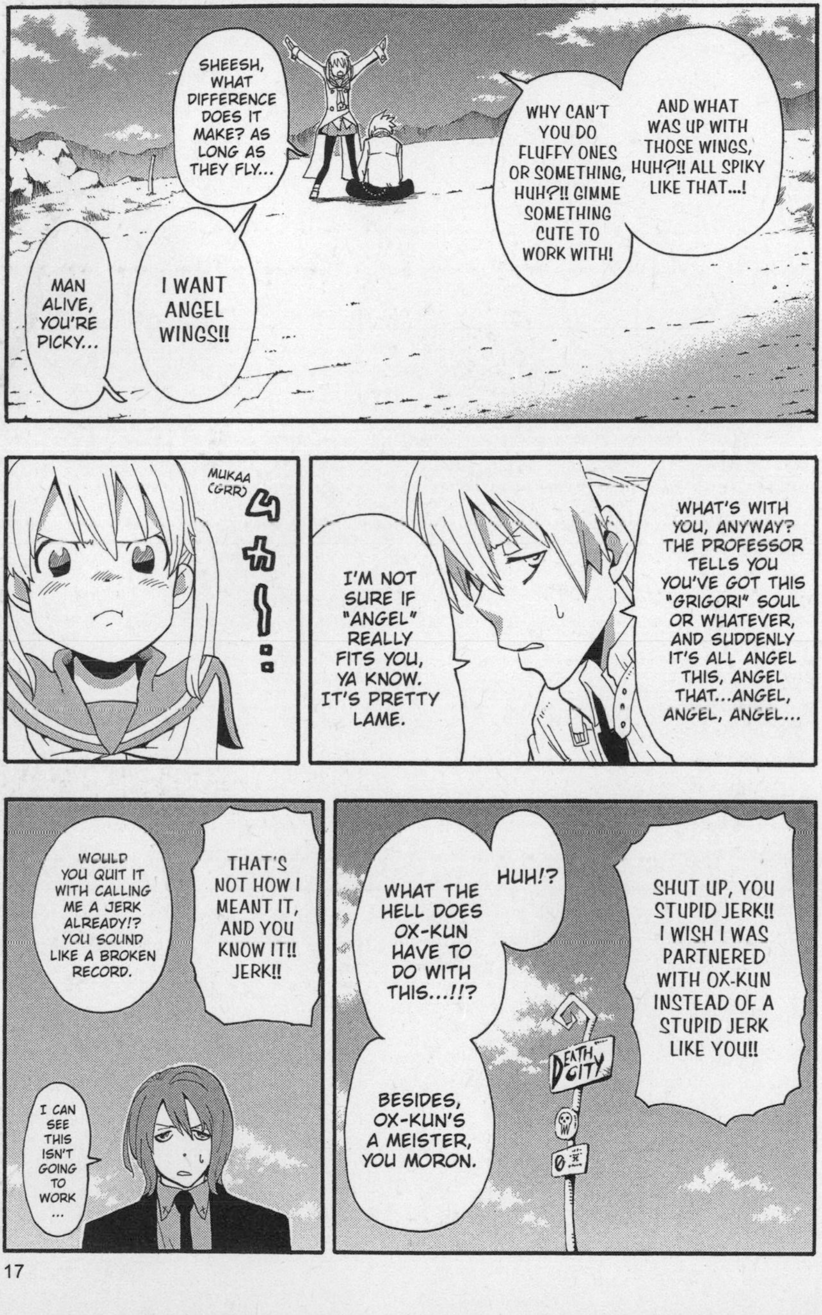
AND WHAT WAS UP WITH THOSE WINGS, HUH?!! ALL SPIKY LIKE THAT...!
WHY CAN'T YOU DO FLUFFY ONES OR SOMETHING, HUH?!! GIMME SOMETHING CUTE TO WORK WITH!
SHEESH, WHAT DIFFERENCE DOES IT MAKE? AS LONG AS THEY FLY...
I WANT ANGEL WINGS!!
MAN ALIVE, YOU'RE PICKY...
WHAT'S WITH YOU, ANYWAY? THE PROFESSOR TELLS YOU YOU'VE GOT THIS "GRIGORI" SOUL OR WHATEVER, AND SUDDENLY IT'S ALL ANGEL THIS, ANGEL THAT...ANGEL, ANGEL, ANGEL...
I'M NOT SURE IF "ANGEL" REALLY FITS YOU, YA KNOW. IT'S PRETTY LAME.
MUKAA (GRR)
SHUT UP, YOU STUPID JERK!! I WISH I WAS PARTNERED WITH OX-KUN INSTEAD OF A STUPID JERK LIKE YOU!!
HUH!?
WHAT THE HELL DOES OX-KUN HAVE TO DO WITH THIS...!!?
BESIDES, OX-KUN'S A MEISTER, YOU MORON.
DEATH CITY
THAT'S NOT HOW I MEANT IT, AND YOU KNOW IT!! JERK!!
WOULD YOU QUIT IT WITH CALLING ME A JERK ALREADY!? YOU SOUND LIKE A BROKEN RECORD.
I CAN SEE THIS ISN'T GOING TO WORK ...

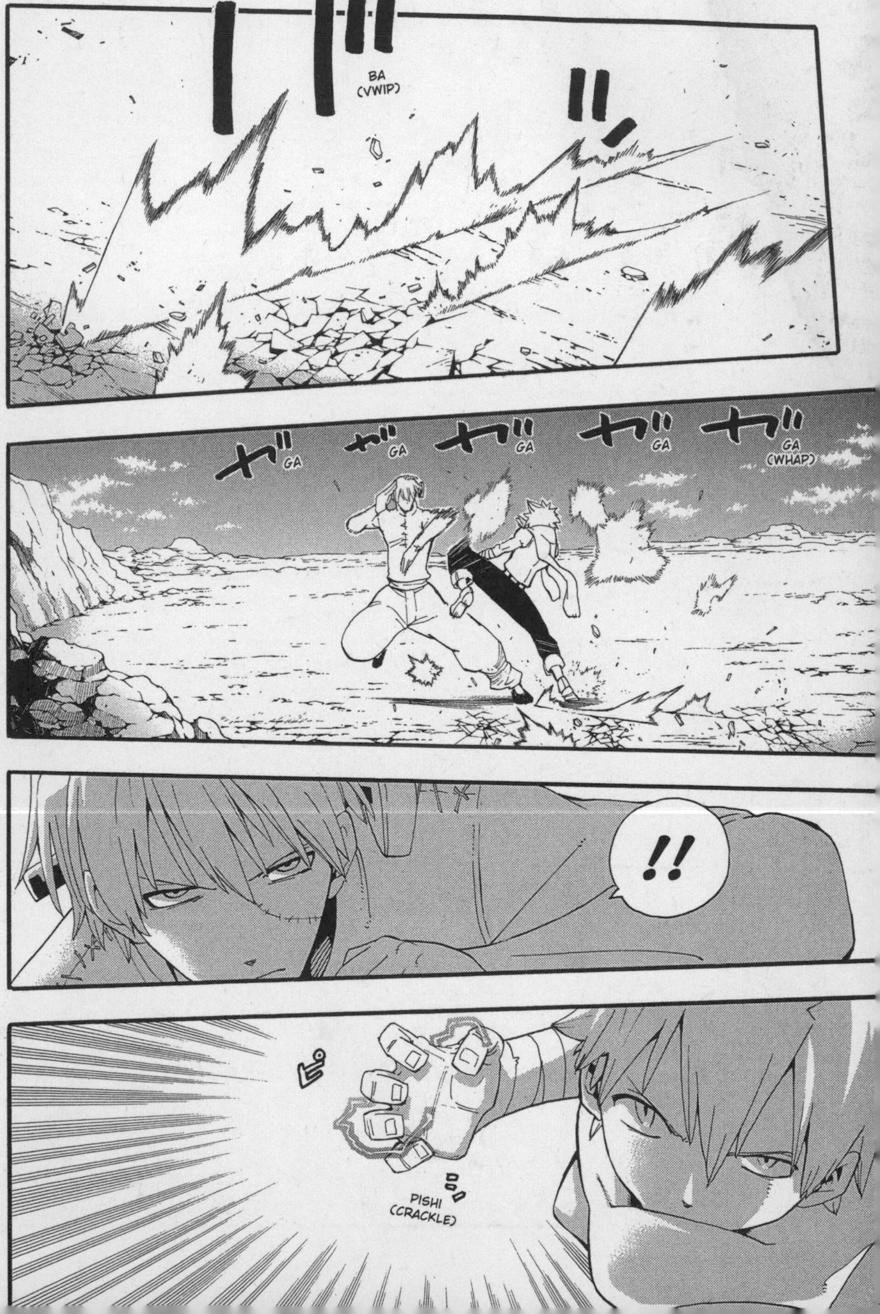
BA
(VWIP)
GA
GA
GA
GA
GA
(WHAP)
!!
PISHI
(CRACKLE)

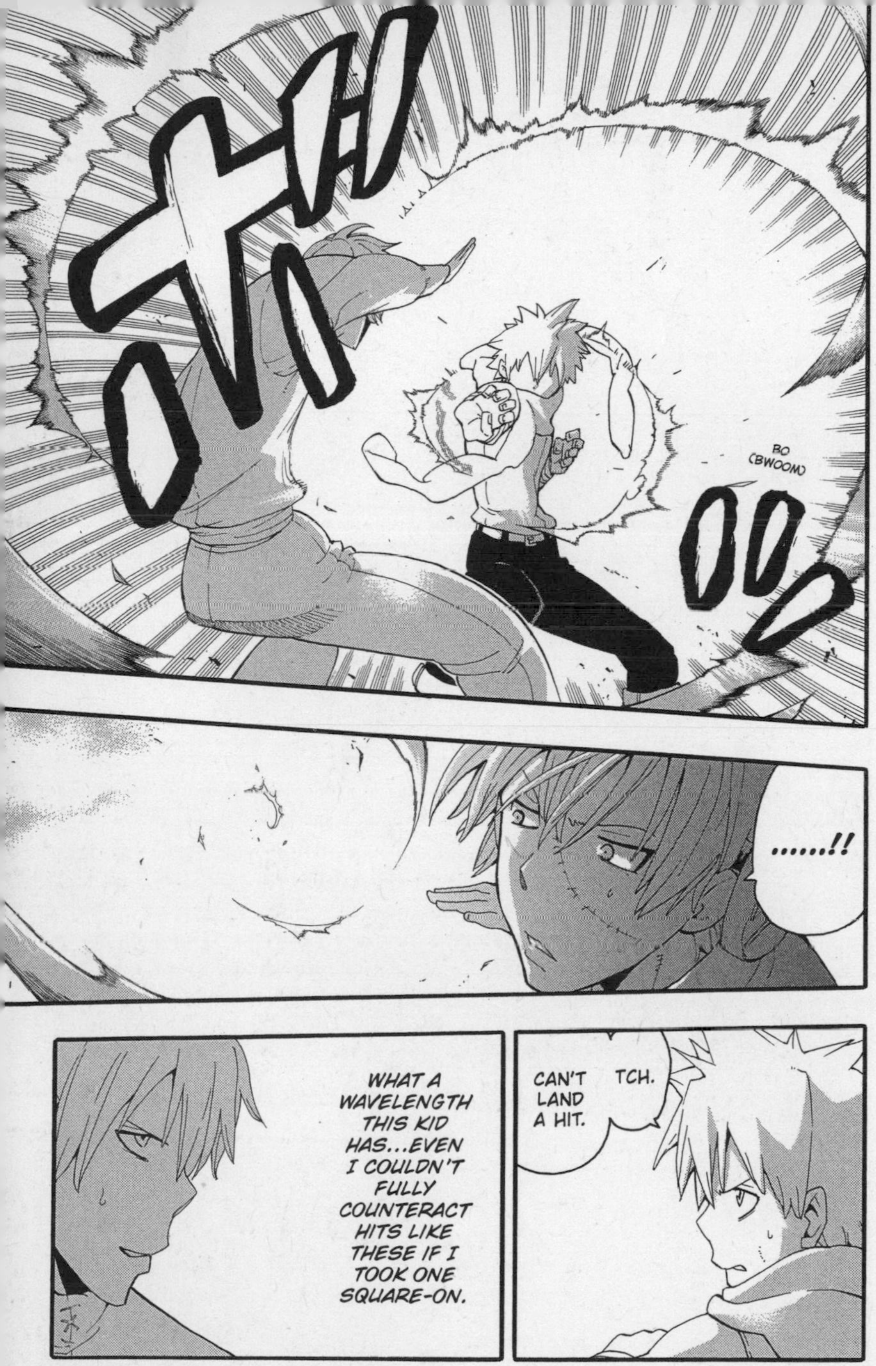
BO
(BWOOM)
......!!
TCH.
CAN'T LAND A HIT.
WHAT A WAVELENGTH THIS KID HAS...EVEN I COULDN'T FULLY COUNTERACT HITS LIKE THESE IF I TOOK ONE SQUARE-ON.

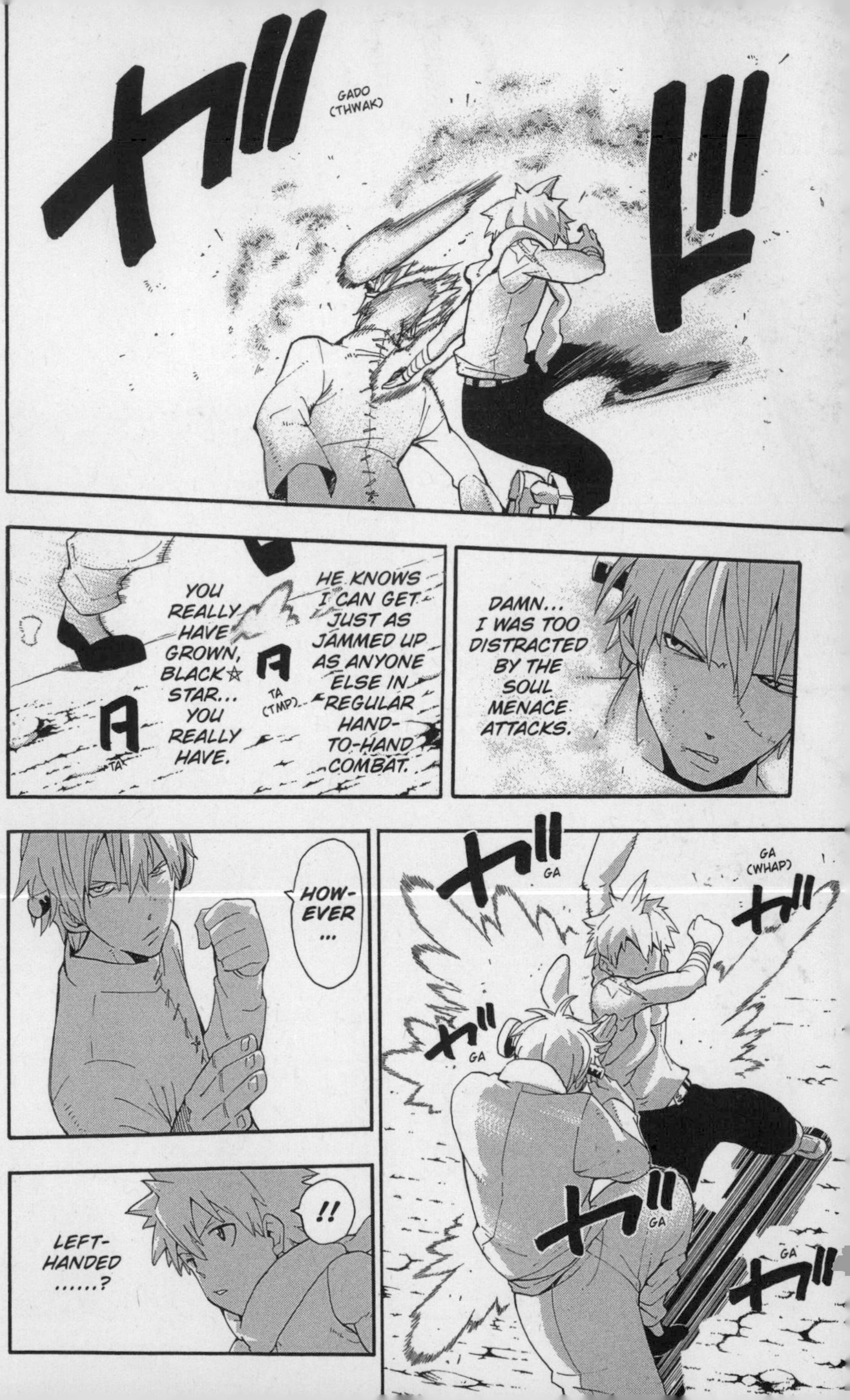
GADO
(THWAK)
DAMN... I WAS TOO DISTRACTED BY THE SOUL MENACE ATTACKS.
HE KNOWS I CAN GET JUST AS JAMMED UP AS ANYONE ELSE IN REGULAR HAND-TO-HAND COMBAT.
TA
(TMP)
YOU REALLY HAVE GROWN, BLACK☆STAR... YOU REALLY HAVE.
TA
GA
(WHAP)
GA
GA
GA
GA
HOW-EVER ...
!!
LEFT-HANDED ......?

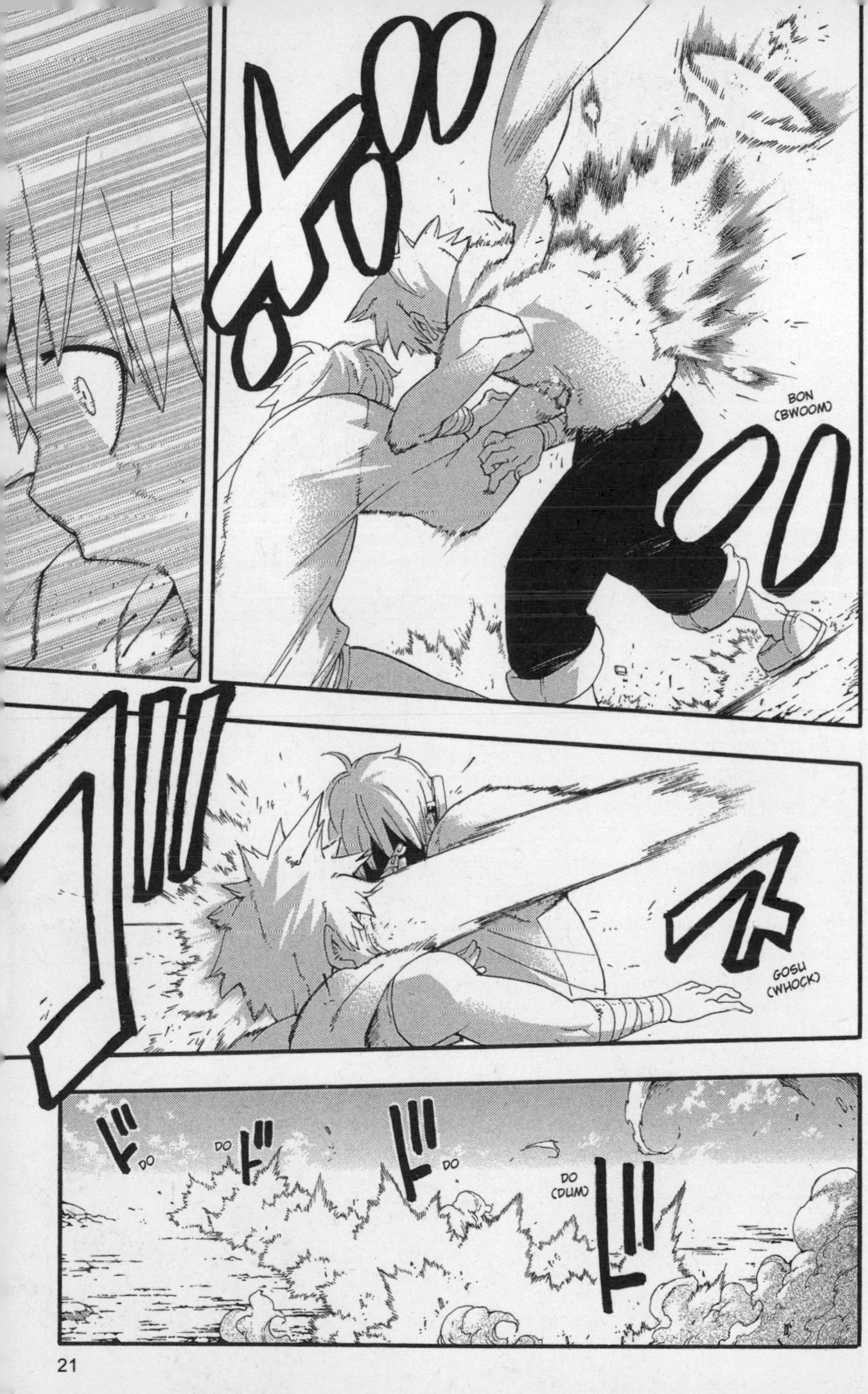
BON
(BWOOM)
GOSU
(WHOCK)
DO
(DUM)
DO
DO
DO

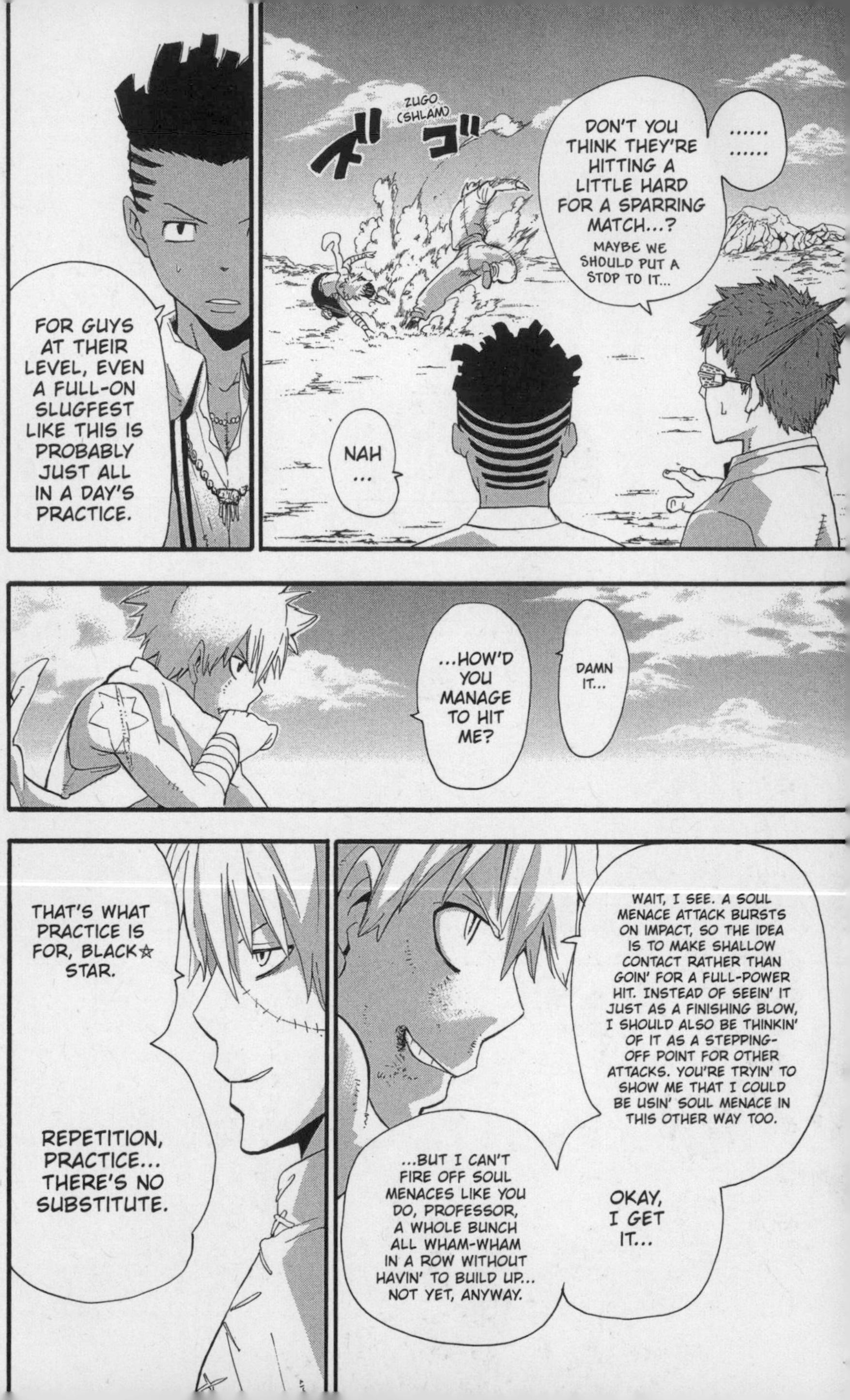
......
......
DON'T YOU THINK THEY'RE HITTING A LITTLE HARD FOR A SPARRING MATCH...? MAYBE WE SHOULD PUT A STOP TO IT...
ズゴ
ZUGO (SHLAM)
NAH ...
FOR GUYS AT THEIR LEVEL, EVEN A FULL-ON SLUGFEST LIKE THIS IS PROBABLY JUST ALL IN A DAY'S PRACTICE.
DAMN IT...
...HOW'D YOU MANAGE TO HIT ME?
WAIT, I SEE. A SOUL MENACE ATTACK BURSTS ON IMPACT, SO THE IDEA IS TO MAKE SHALLOW CONTACT RATHER THAN GOIN' FOR A FULL-POWER HIT. INSTEAD OF SEEIN' IT JUST AS A FINISHING BLOW, I SHOULD ALSO BE THINKIN' OF IT AS A STEPPING-OFF POINT FOR OTHER ATTACKS. YOU'RE TRYIN' TO SHOW ME THAT I COULD BE USIN' SOUL MENACE IN THIS OTHER WAY TOO.
OKAY, I GET IT...
...BUT I CAN'T FIRE OFF SOUL MENACES LIKE YOU DO, PROFESSOR, A WHOLE BUNCH ALL WHAM-WHAM IN A ROW WITHOUT HAVIN' TO BUILD UP... NOT YET, ANYWAY.
THAT'S WHAT PRACTICE IS FOR, BLACK☆STAR.
REPETITION, PRACTICE... THERE'S NO SUBSTITUTE.

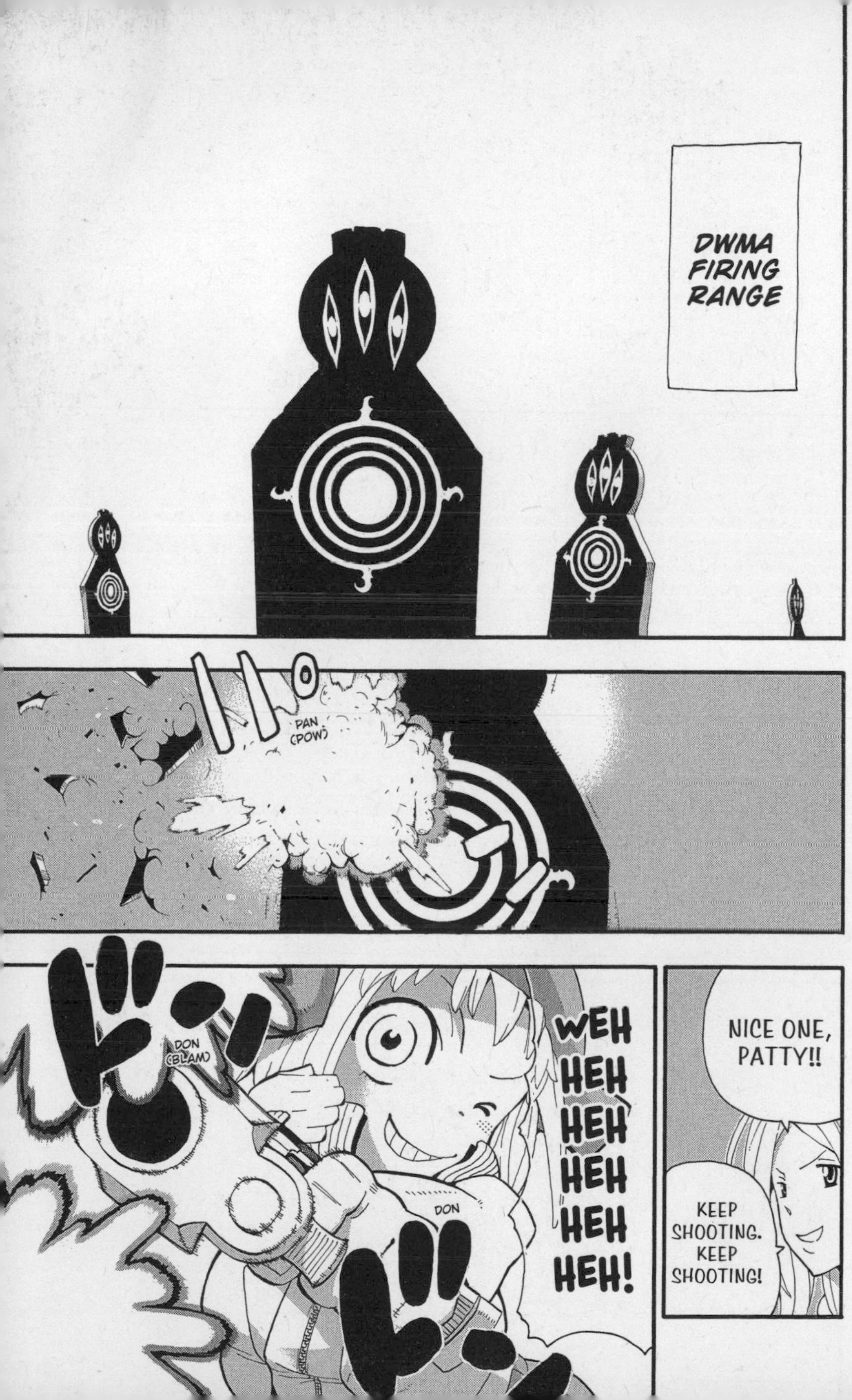

DWMA FIRING RANGE
PAN (POW)
NICE ONE, PATTY!!
KEEP SHOOTING. KEEP SHOOTING!
WEH HEH HEH HEH HEH HEH!
DON (BLAM)
DON

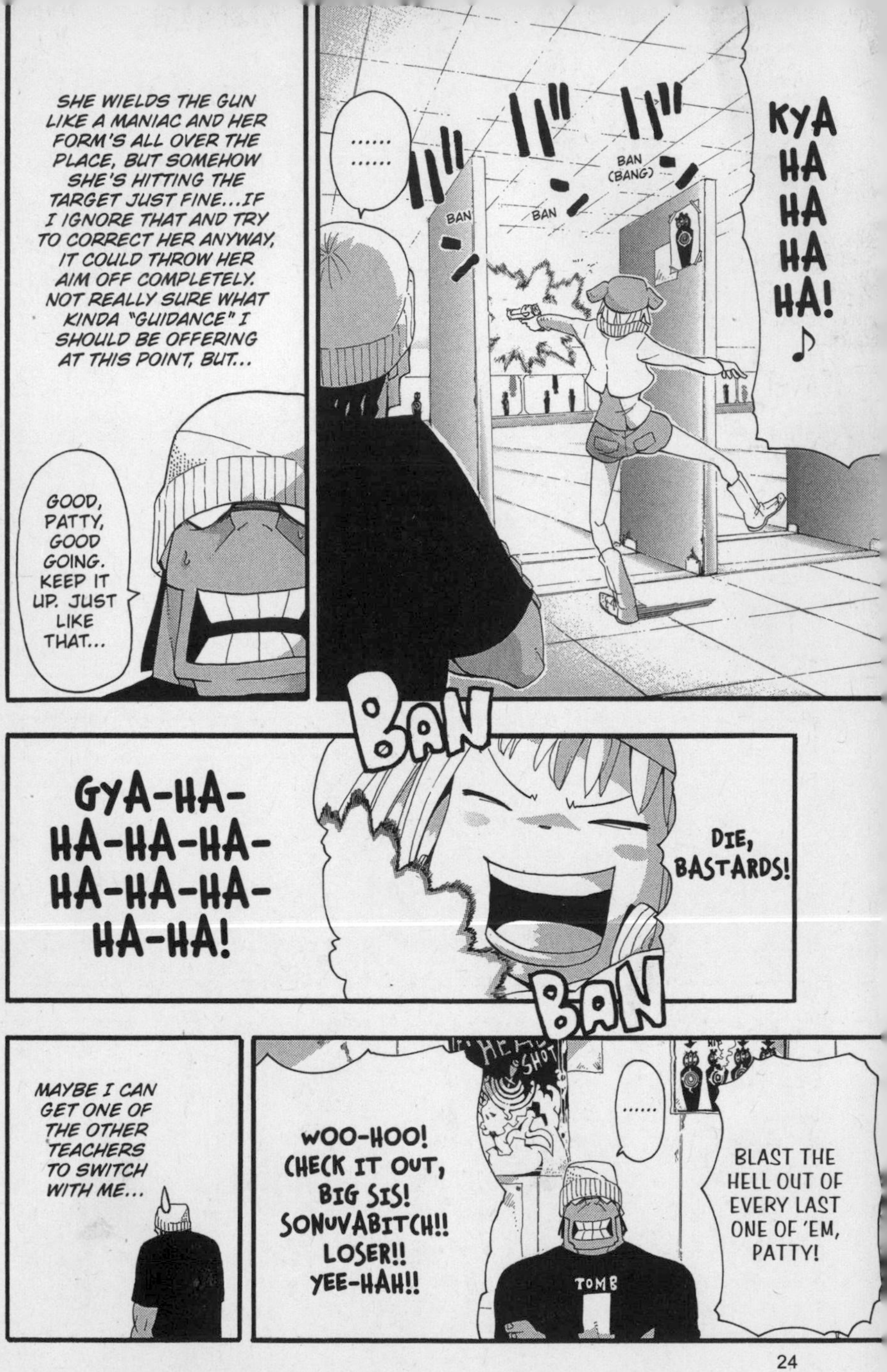
KYA HA HA HA HA! ♪
BAN (BANG)
BAN
BAN
...... ......
SHE WIELDS THE GUN LIKE A MANIAC AND HER FORM'S ALL OVER THE PLACE, BUT SOMEHOW SHE'S HITTING THE TARGET JUST FINE...IF I IGNORE THAT AND TRY TO CORRECT HER ANYWAY, IT COULD THROW HER AIM OFF COMPLETELY. NOT REALLY SURE WHAT KINDA "GUIDANCE" I SHOULD BE OFFERING AT THIS POINT, BUT...
GOOD, PATTY, GOOD GOING. KEEP IT UP. JUST LIKE THAT...
BAN
DIE, BASTARDS!
GYA-HA-HA-HA-HA-HA-HA-HA-HA-HA-HA!
BAN
BLAST THE HELL OUT OF EVERY LAST ONE OF 'EM, PATTY!
......
WOO-HOO! CHECK IT OUT, BIG SIS! SONUVABITCH!! LOSER!! YEE-HAH!!
TOMB
MAYBE I CAN GET ONE OF THE OTHER TEACHERS TO SWITCH WITH ME...

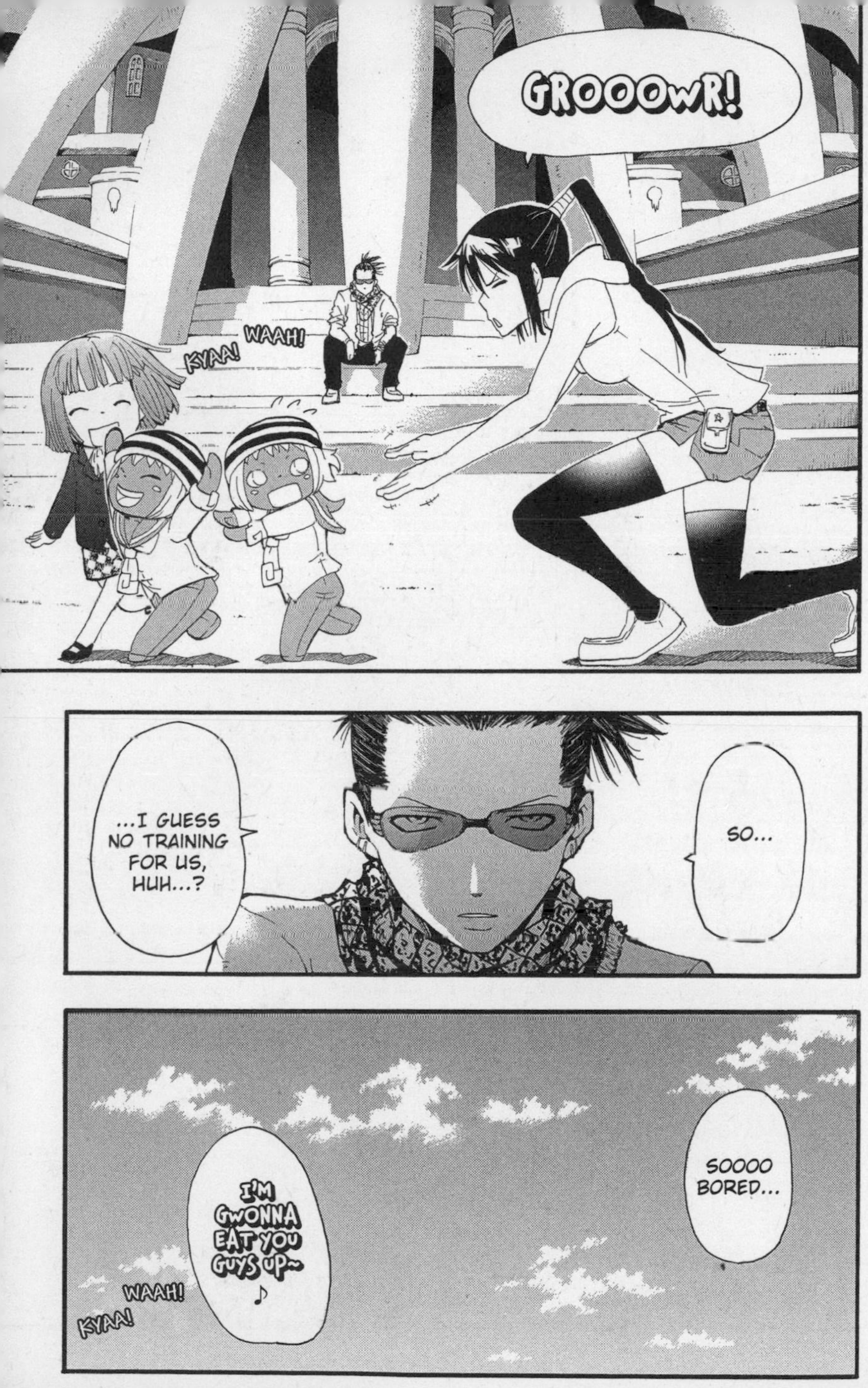
GROOOWR!
WAAH!
KYAA!
SO...
...I GUESS NO TRAINING FOR US, HUH...?
SOOOO BORED...
I'M GWONNA EAT YOU GUYS UP~ ♪
WAAH!
KYAA!

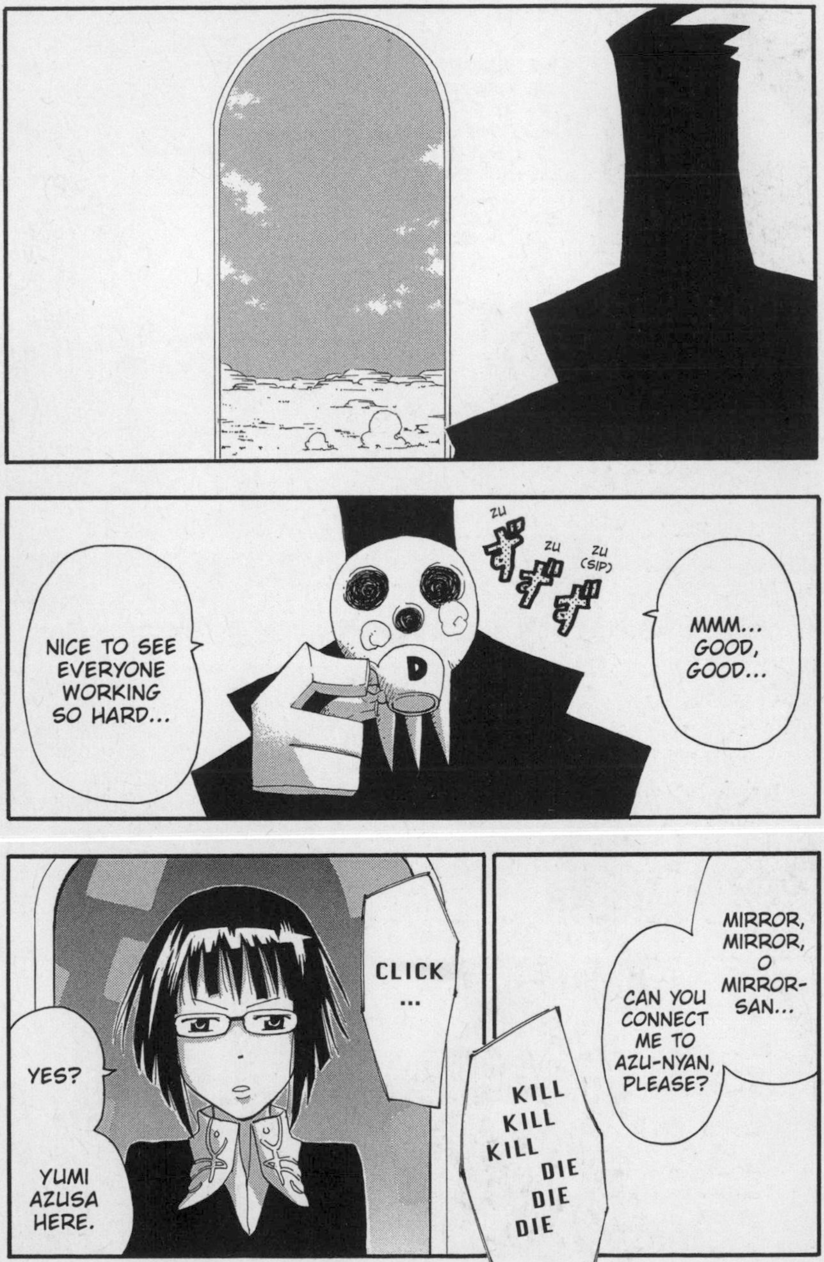
ZU
ZU
ZU (SIP)
MMM... GOOD, GOOD...
NICE TO SEE EVERYONE WORKING SO HARD...
MIRROR, MIRROR, O MIRROR-SAN...
CAN YOU CONNECT ME TO AZU-NYAN, PLEASE?
KILL KILL KILL DIE DIE DIE
CLICK ...
YES?
YUMI AZUSA HERE.

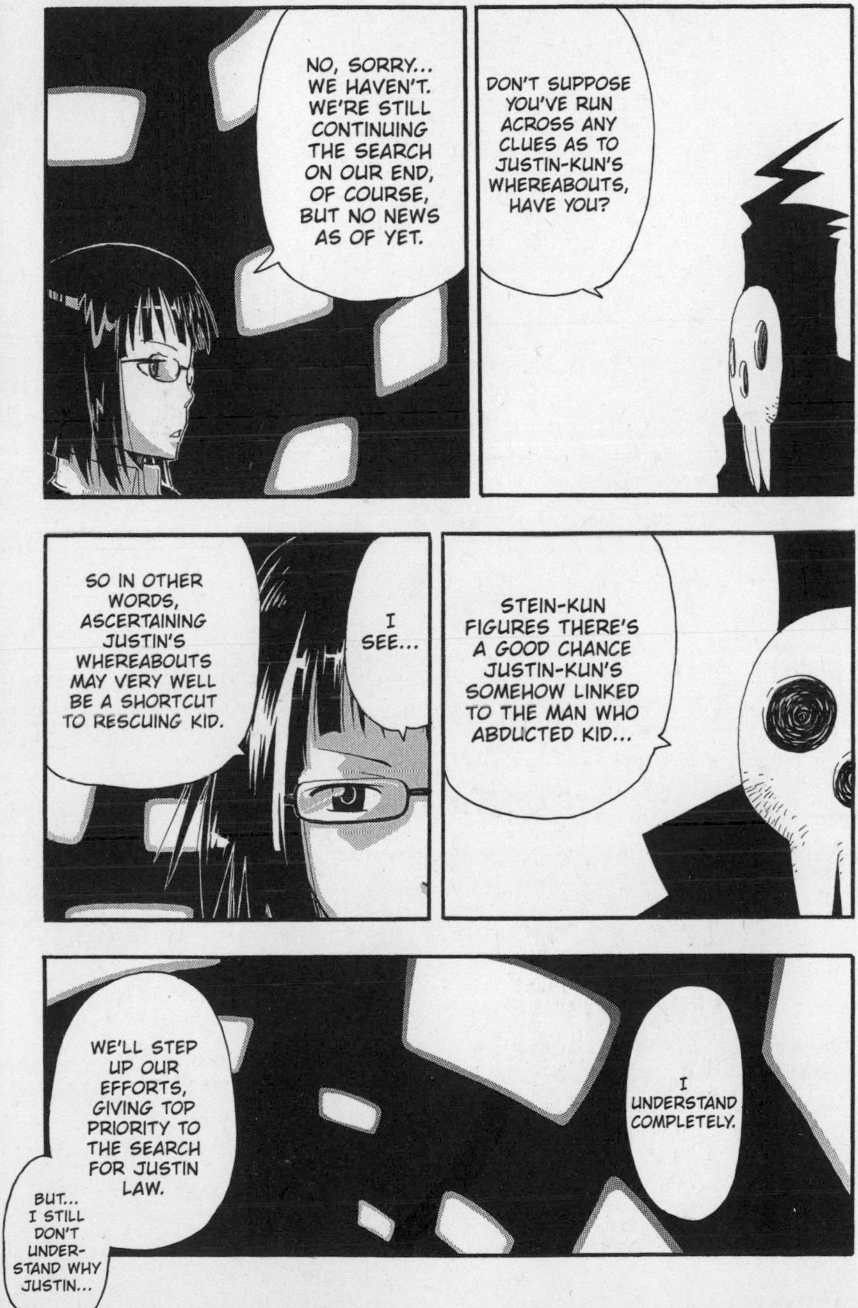
DON'T SUPPOSE YOU'VE RUN ACROSS ANY CLUES AS TO JUSTIN-KUN'S WHEREABOUTS, HAVE YOU?
NO, SORRY... WE HAVEN'T. WE'RE STILL CONTINUING THE SEARCH ON OUR END, OF COURSE, BUT NO NEWS AS OF YET.
STEIN-KUN FIGURES THERE'S A GOOD CHANCE JUSTIN-KUN'S SOMEHOW LINKED TO THE MAN WHO ABDUCTED KID...
I SEE...
SO IN OTHER WORDS, ASCERTAINING JUSTIN'S WHEREABOUTS MAY VERY WELL BE A SHORTCUT TO RESCUING KID.
I UNDERSTAND COMPLETELY.
WE'LL STEP UP OUR EFFORTS, GIVING TOP PRIORITY TO THE SEARCH FOR JUSTIN LAW.
BUT... I STILL DON'T UNDER-STAND WHY JUSTIN...

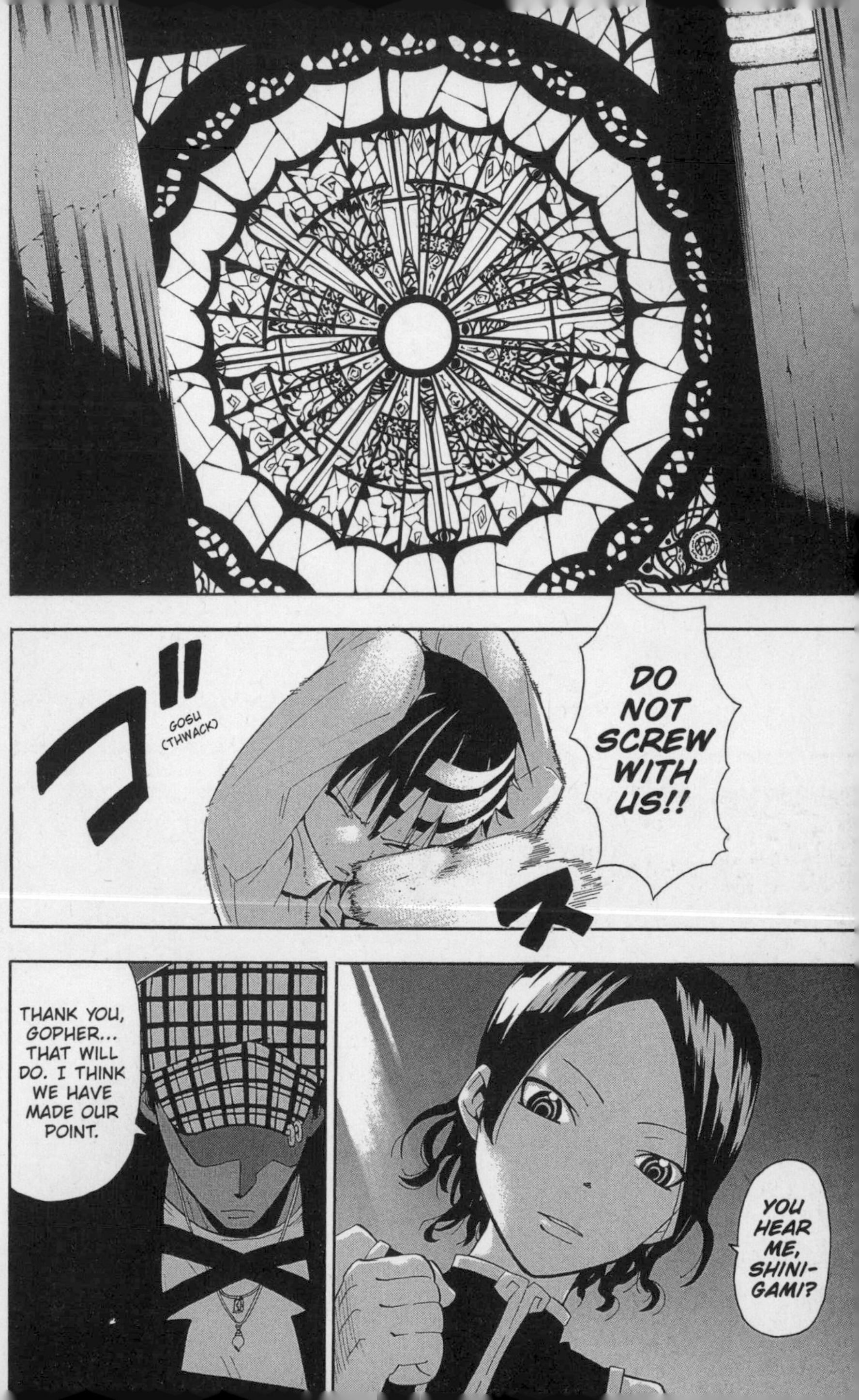
DO NOT SCREW WITH US!!
GOSU (THWACK)
YOU HEAR ME, SHINI-GAMI?
THANK YOU, GOPHER... THAT WILL DO. I THINK WE HAVE MADE OUR POINT.

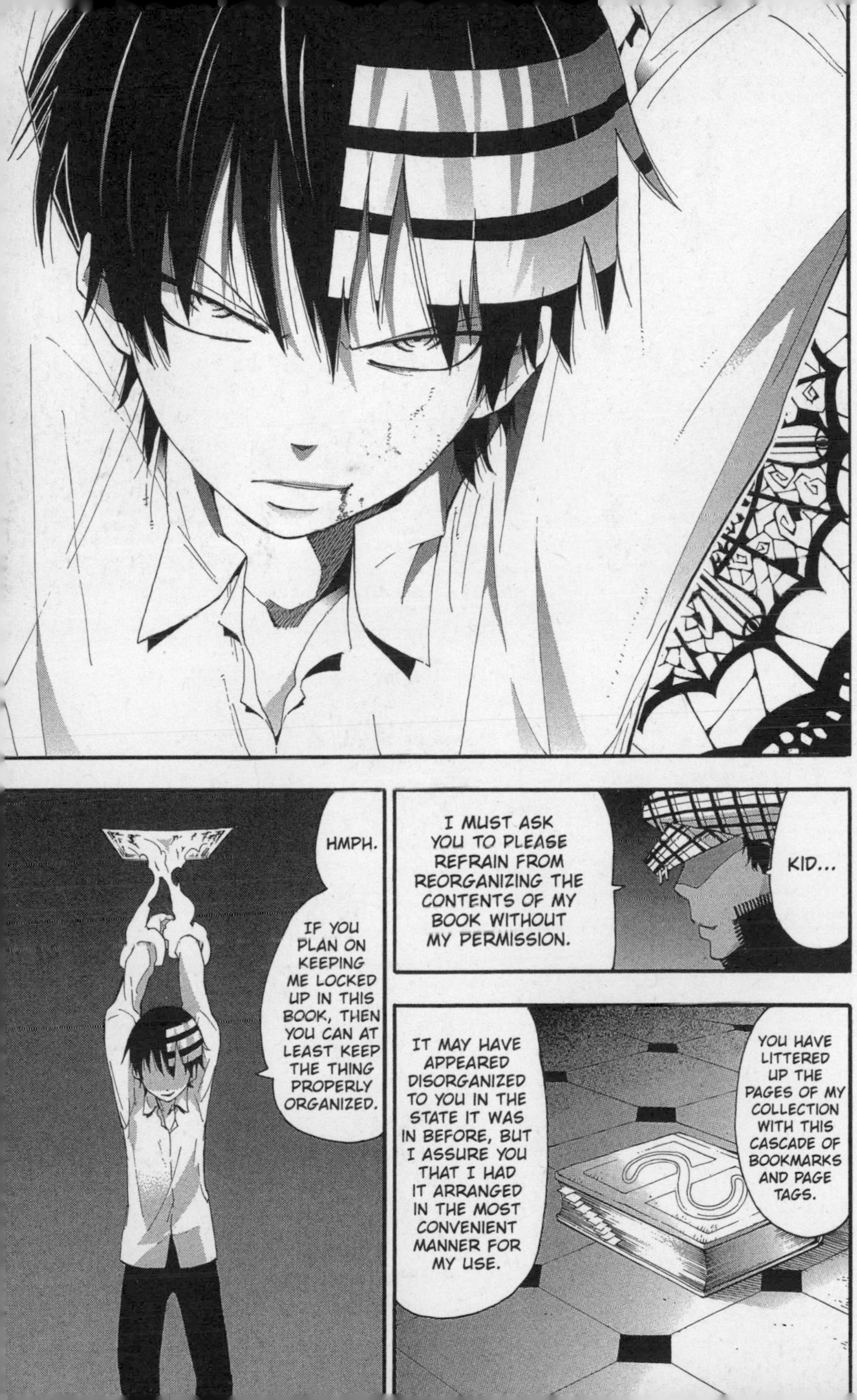
KID...
I MUST ASK YOU TO PLEASE REFRAIN FROM REORGANIZING THE CONTENTS OF MY BOOK WITHOUT MY PERMISSION.
YOU HAVE LITTERED UP THE PAGES OF MY COLLECTION WITH THIS CASCADE OF BOOKMARKS AND PAGE TAGS.
IT MAY HAVE APPEARED DISORGANIZED TO YOU IN THE STATE IT WAS IN BEFORE, BUT I ASSURE YOU THAT I HAD IT ARRANGED IN THE MOST CONVENIENT MANNER FOR MY USE.
HMPH.
IF YOU PLAN ON KEEPING ME LOCKED UP IN THIS BOOK, THEN YOU CAN AT LEAST KEEP THE THING PROPERLY ORGANIZED.

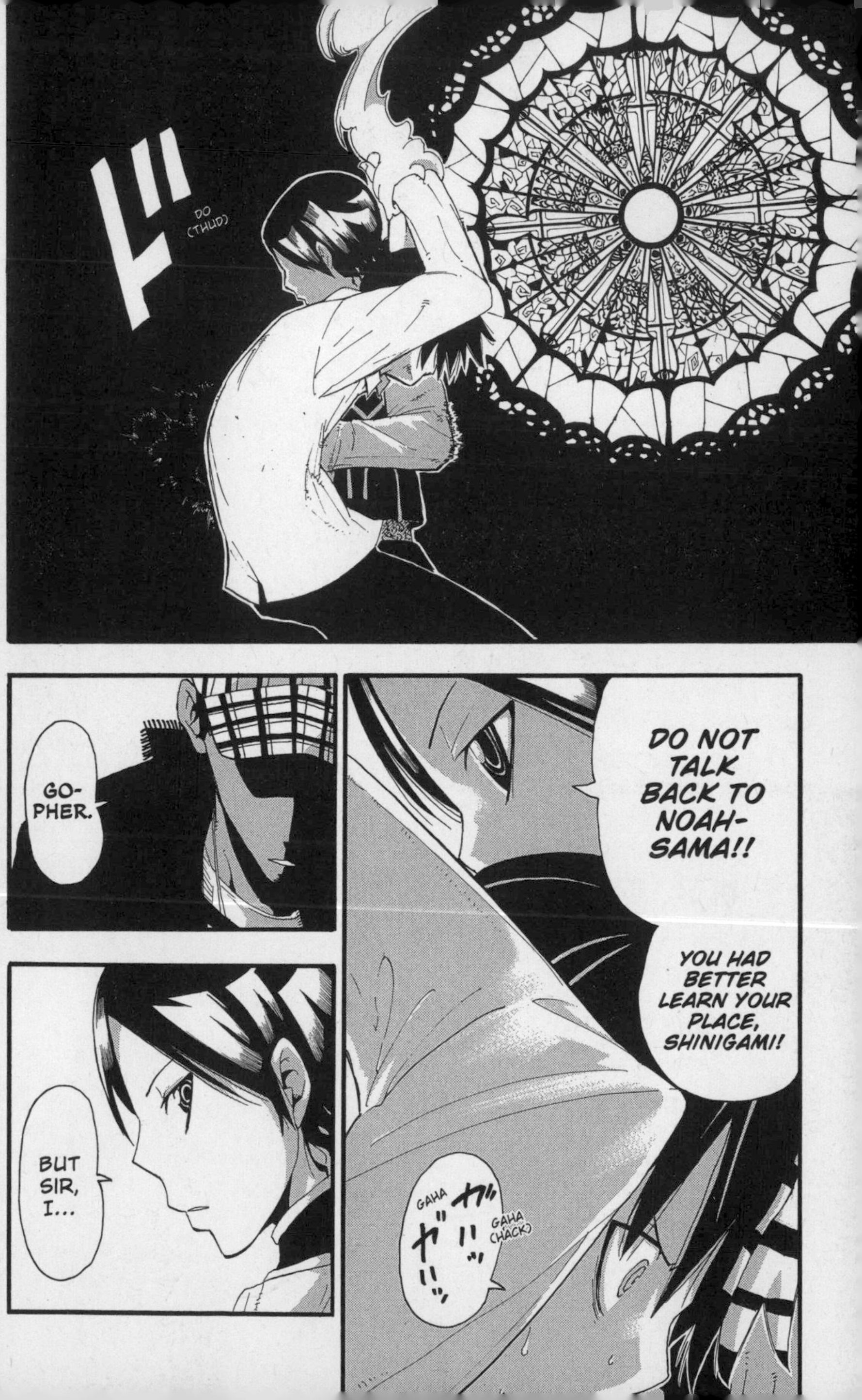
ド
DO (THUD)
DO NOT TALK BACK TO NOAH-SAMA!!
YOU HAD BETTER LEARN YOUR PLACE, SHINIGAMI!
GAHA
GAHA (HACK)
GO-PHER.
BUT SIR, I...

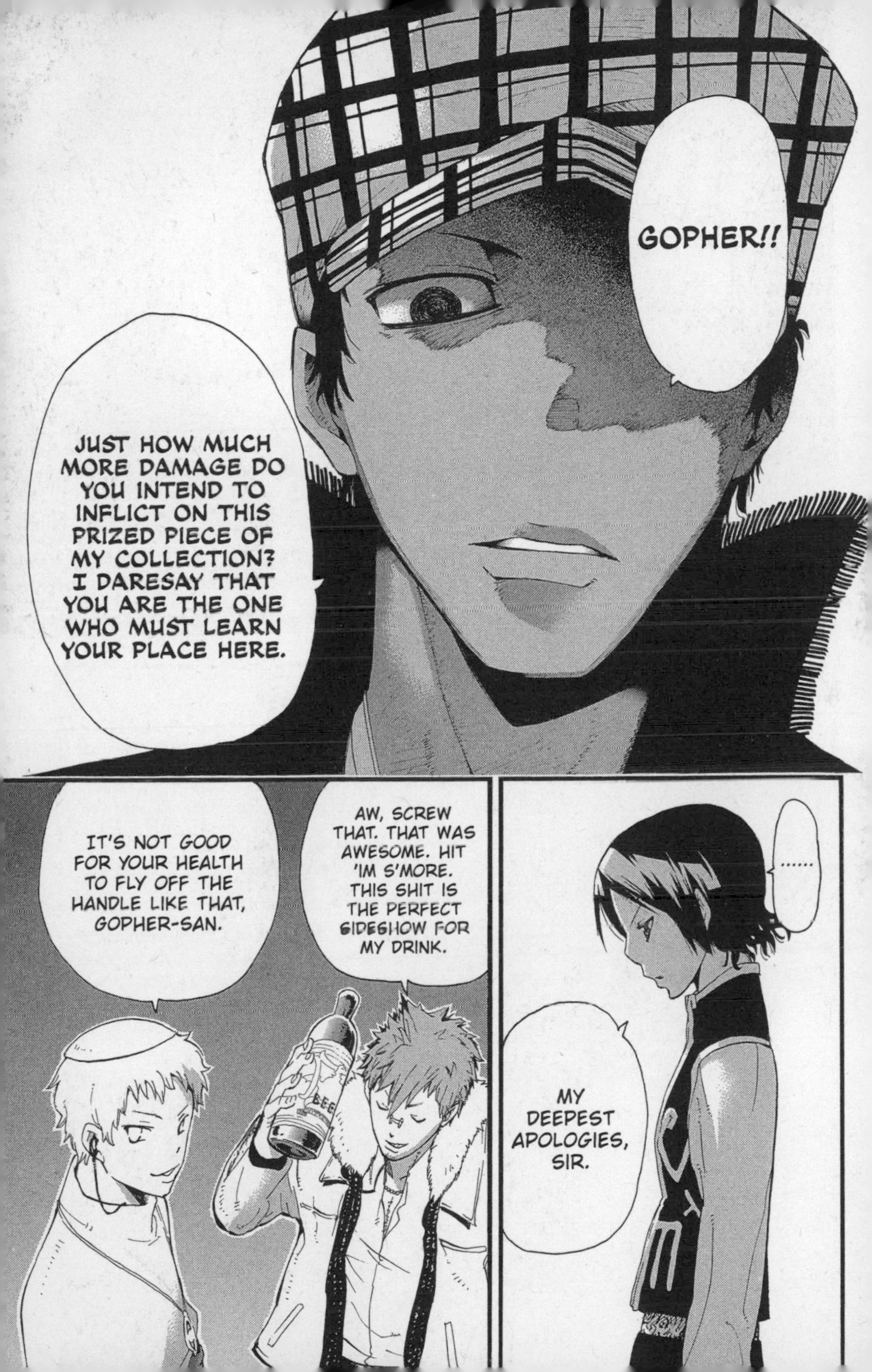
GOPHER!!
JUST HOW MUCH MORE DAMAGE DO YOU INTEND TO INFLICT ON THIS PRIZED PIECE OF MY COLLECTION? I DARESAY THAT YOU ARE THE ONE WHO MUST LEARN YOUR PLACE HERE.
......
MY DEEPEST APOLOGIES, SIR.
AW, SCREW THAT. THAT WAS AWESOME. HIT 'IM S'MORE. THIS SHIT IS THE PERFECT SIDESHOW FOR MY DRINK.
IT'S NOT GOOD FOR YOUR HEALTH TO FLY OFF THE HANDLE LIKE THAT, GOPHER-SAN.

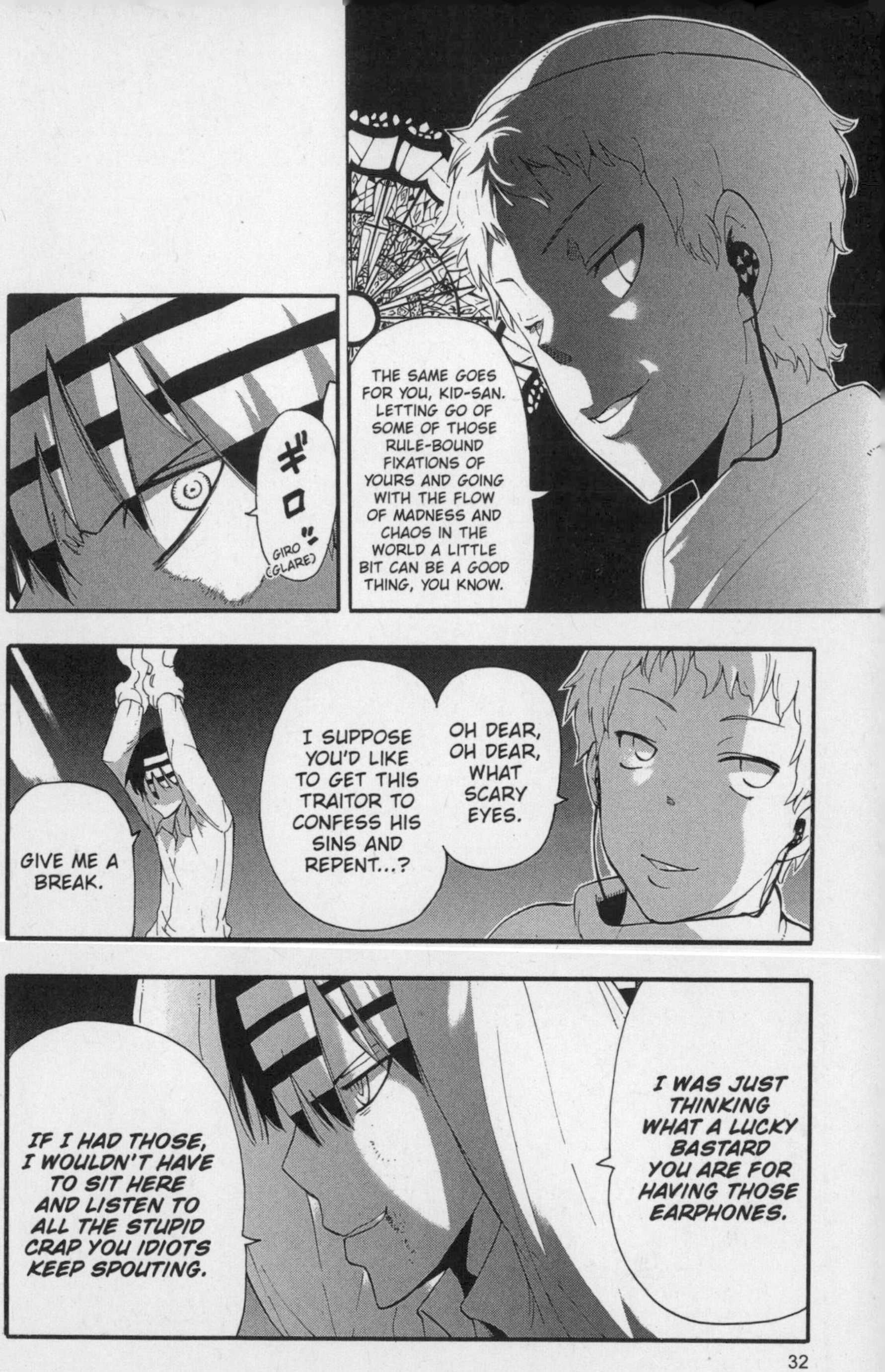
THE SAME GOES FOR YOU, KID-SAN. LETTING GO OF SOME OF THOSE RULE-BOUND FIXATIONS OF YOURS AND GOING WITH THE FLOW OF MADNESS AND CHAOS IN THE WORLD A LITTLE BIT CAN BE A GOOD THING, YOU KNOW.
ギロッ
GIRO (GLARE)
OH DEAR, OH DEAR, WHAT SCARY EYES.
I SUPPOSE YOU'D LIKE TO GET THIS TRAITOR TO CONFESS HIS SINS AND REPENT...?
GIVE ME A BREAK.
I WAS JUST THINKING WHAT A LUCKY BASTARD YOU ARE FOR HAVING THOSE EARPHONES.
IF I HAD THOSE, I WOULDN'T HAVE TO SIT HERE AND LISTEN TO ALL THE STUPID CRAP YOU IDIOTS KEEP SPOUTING.

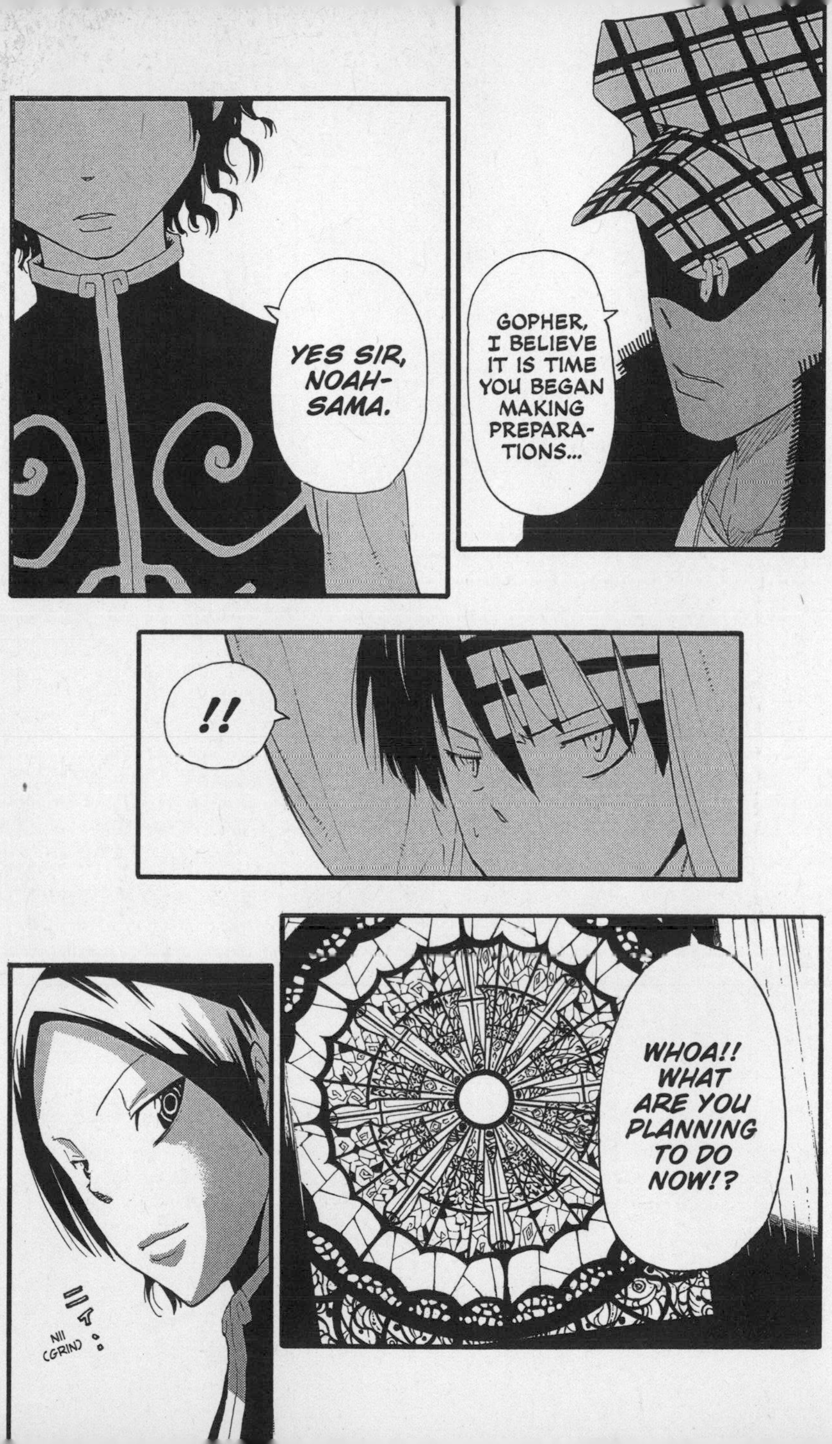
GOPHER, I BELIEVE IT IS TIME YOU BEGAN MAKING PREPARATIONS...
YES SIR, NOAH-SAMA.
!!
WHOA!! WHAT ARE YOU PLANNING TO DO NOW!?
NII (GRIN)

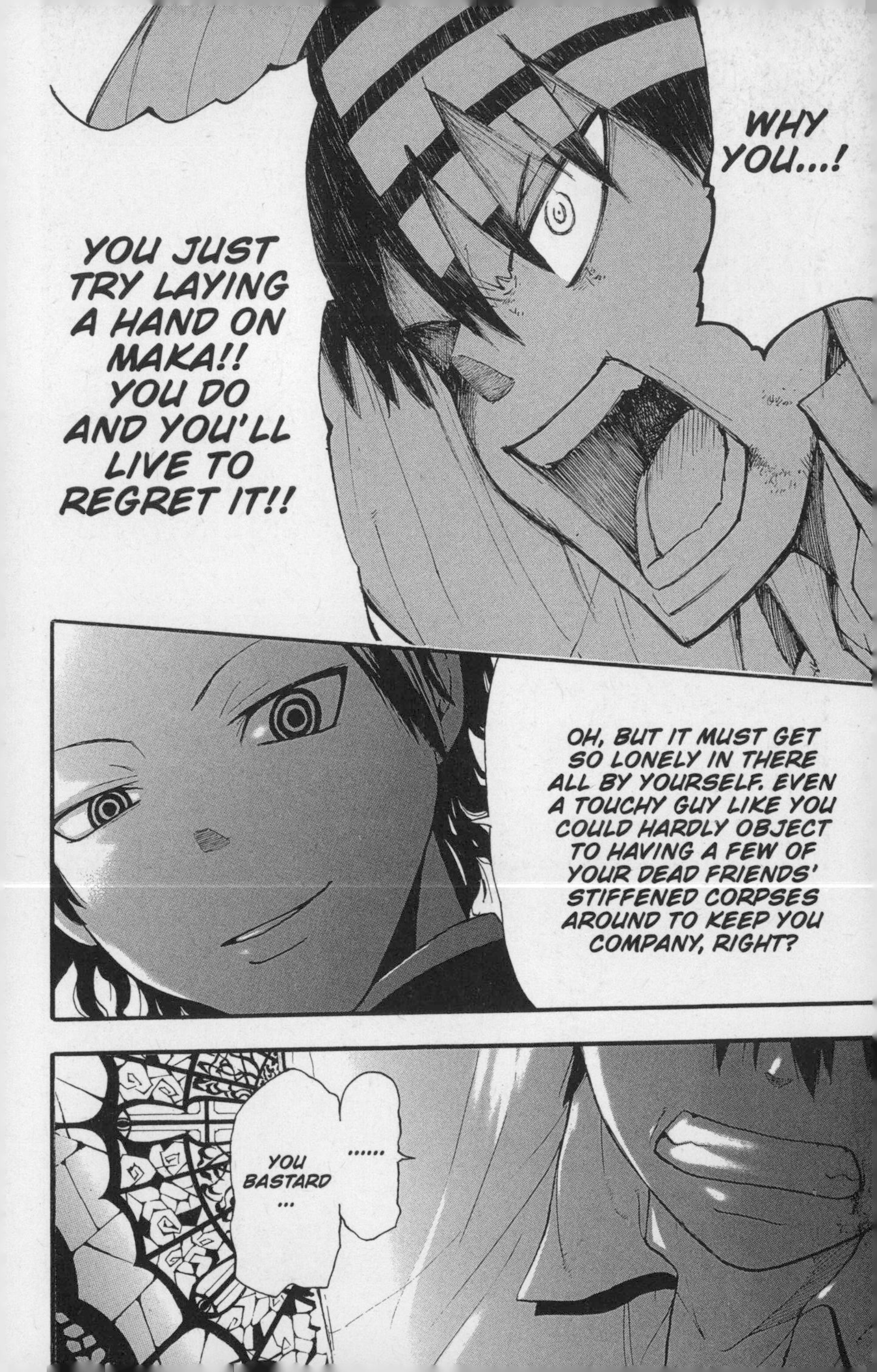
WHY YOU...!
YOU JUST TRY LAYING A HAND ON MAKA!! YOU DO AND YOU'LL LIVE TO REGRET IT!!
OH, BUT IT MUST GET SO LONELY IN THERE ALL BY YOURSELF. EVEN A TOUCHY GUY LIKE YOU COULD HARDLY OBJECT TO HAVING A FEW OF YOUR DEAD FRIENDS' STIFFENED CORPSES AROUND TO KEEP YOU COMPANY, RIGHT?
......
YOU BASTARD ...

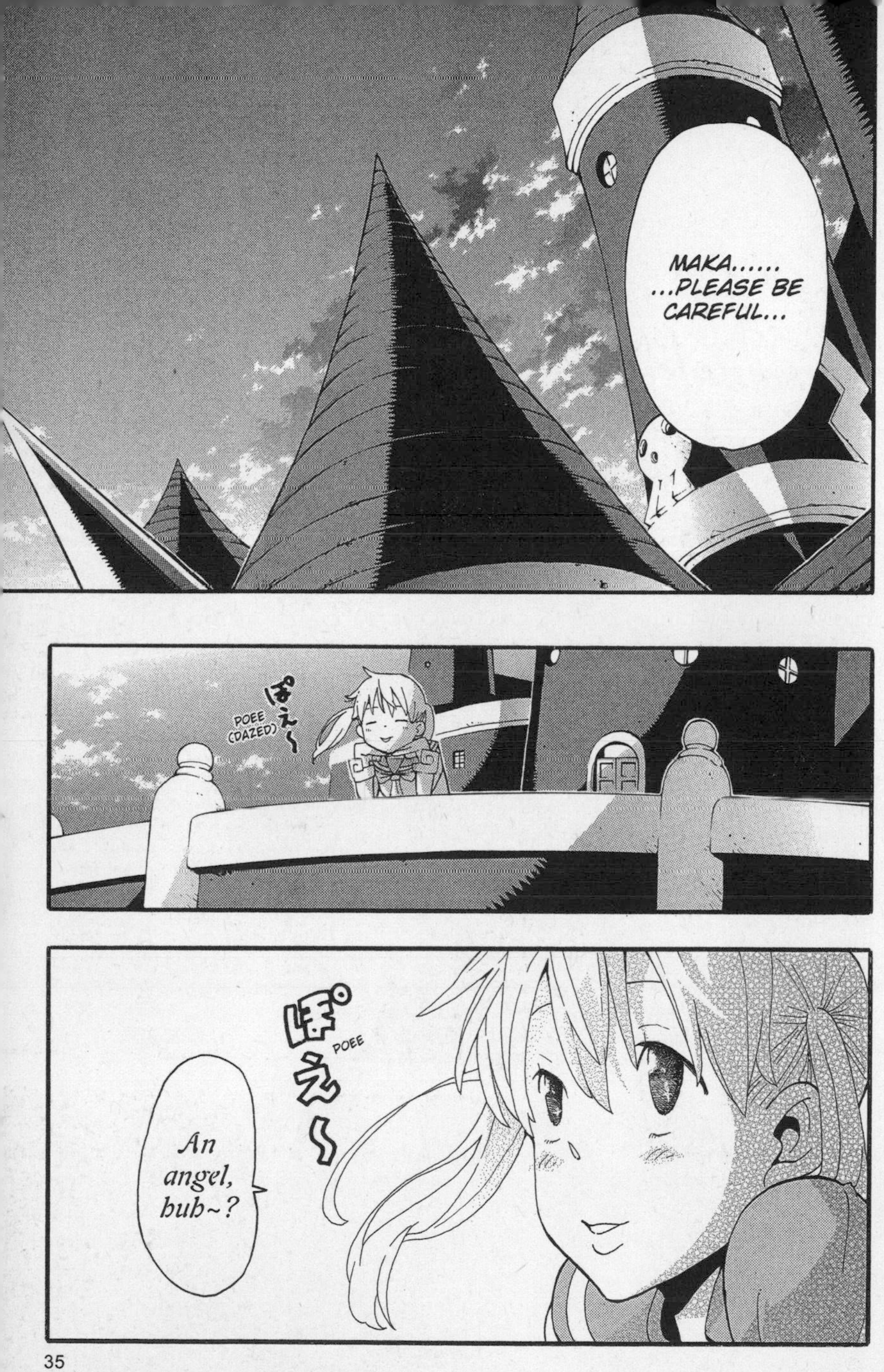
MAKA......
...PLEASE BE CAREFUL...
ぽえ~
POEE (DAZED)
ぽえ~
POEE
An angel, huh~?

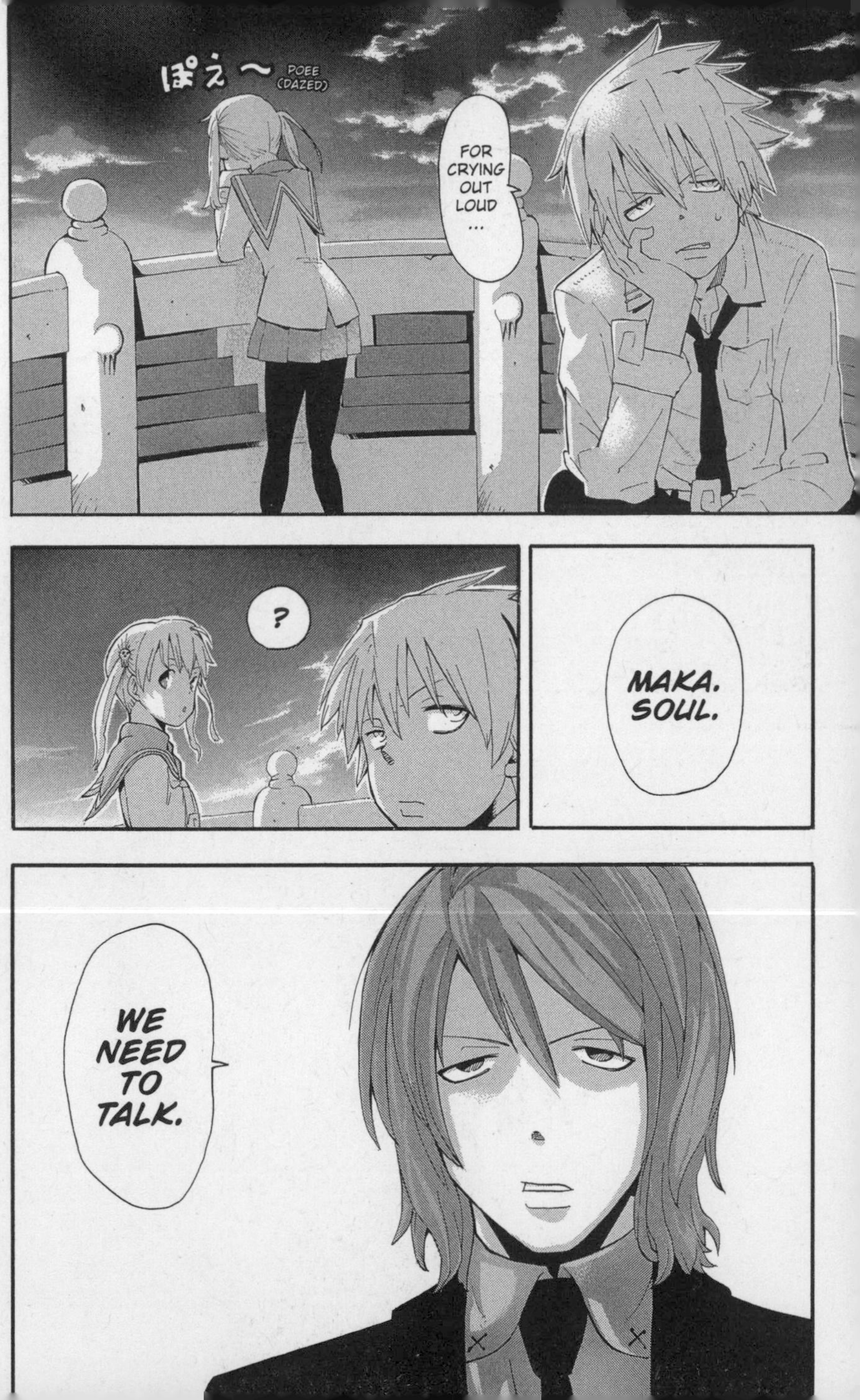
ぽえ~ POEE (DAZED)
FOR CRYING OUT LOUD ...
MAKA. SOUL.
?
WE NEED TO TALK.

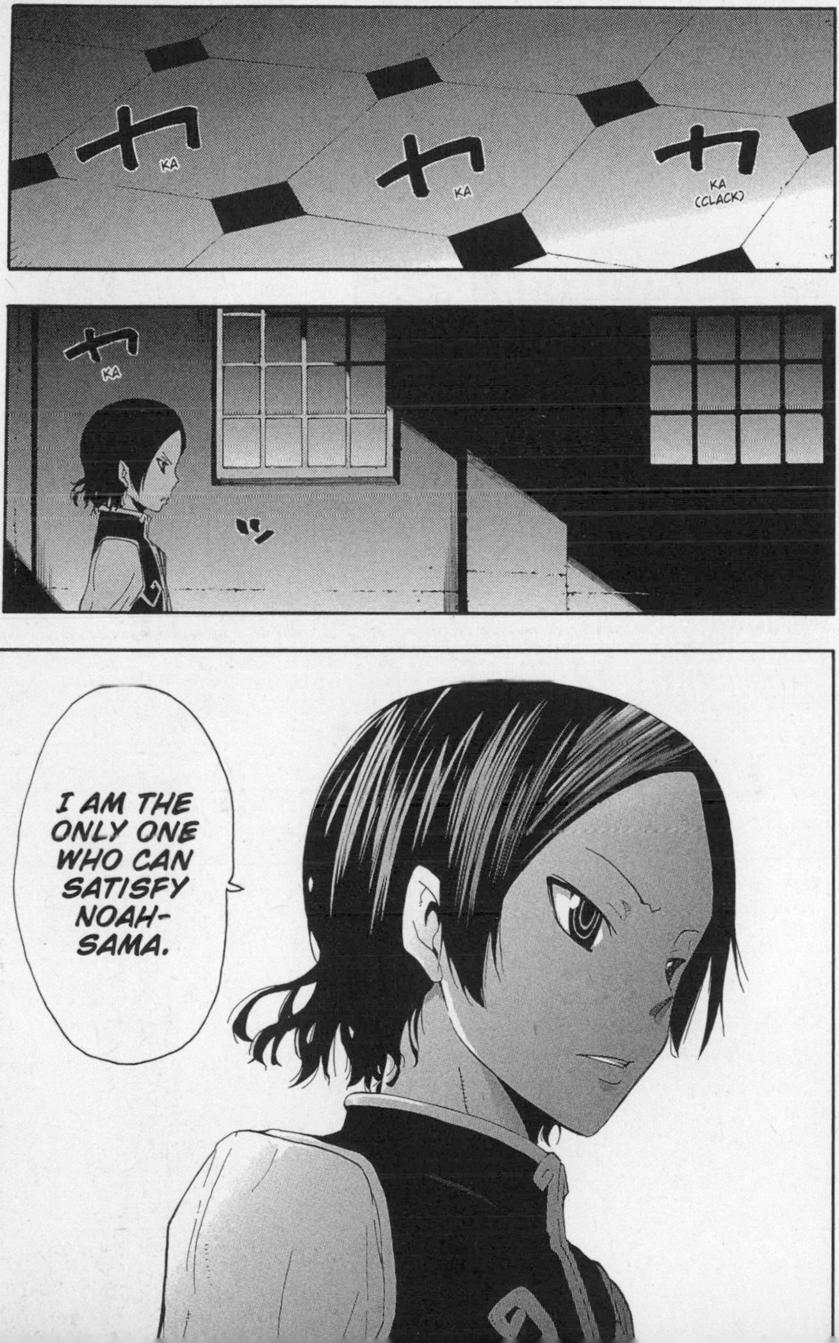
KA (CLACK)
KA
KA
KA
I AM THE ONLY ONE WHO CAN SATISFY NOAH-SAMA.

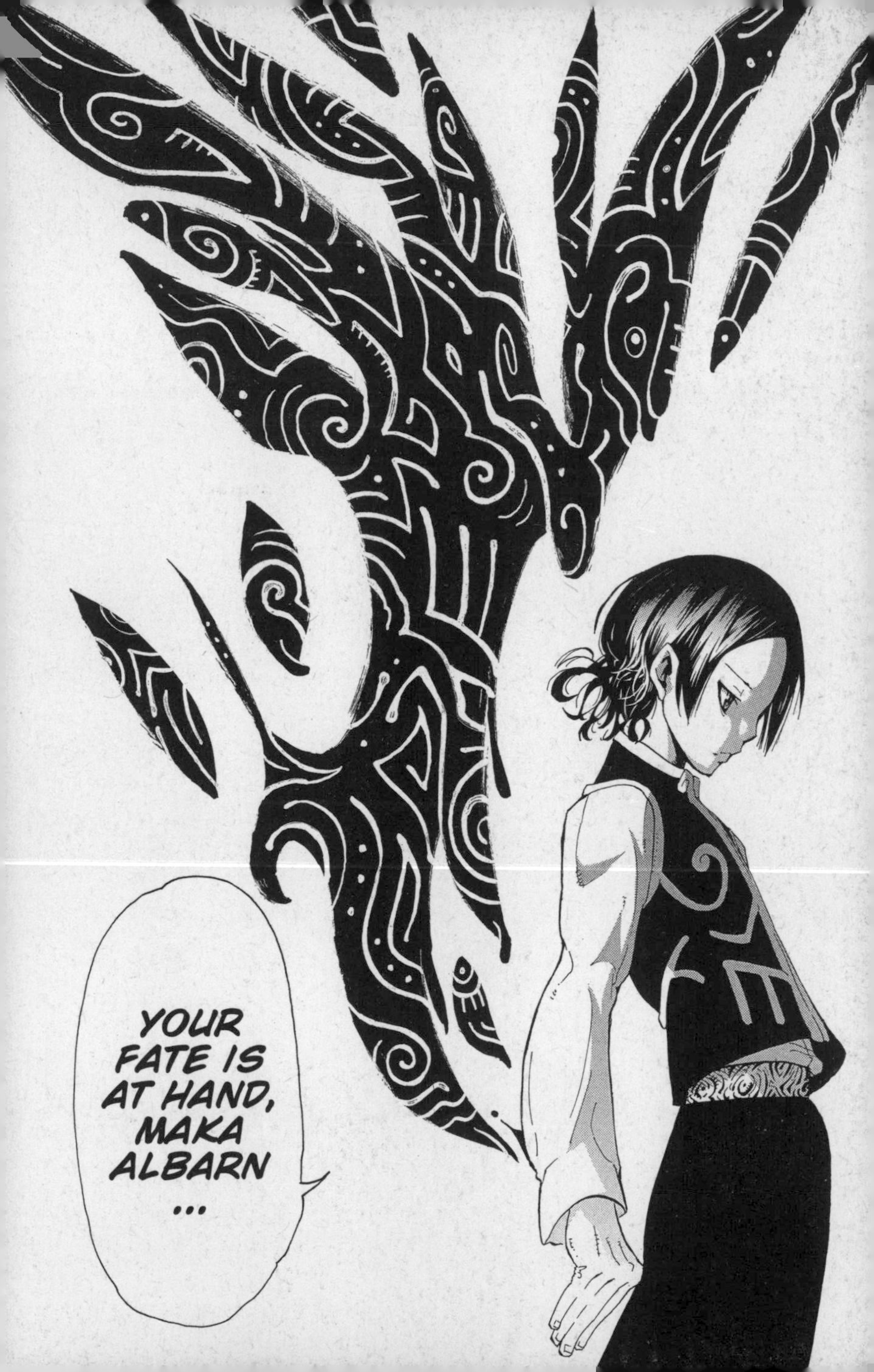
YOUR FATE IS AT HAND, MAKA ALBARN ...

SOUL EATER

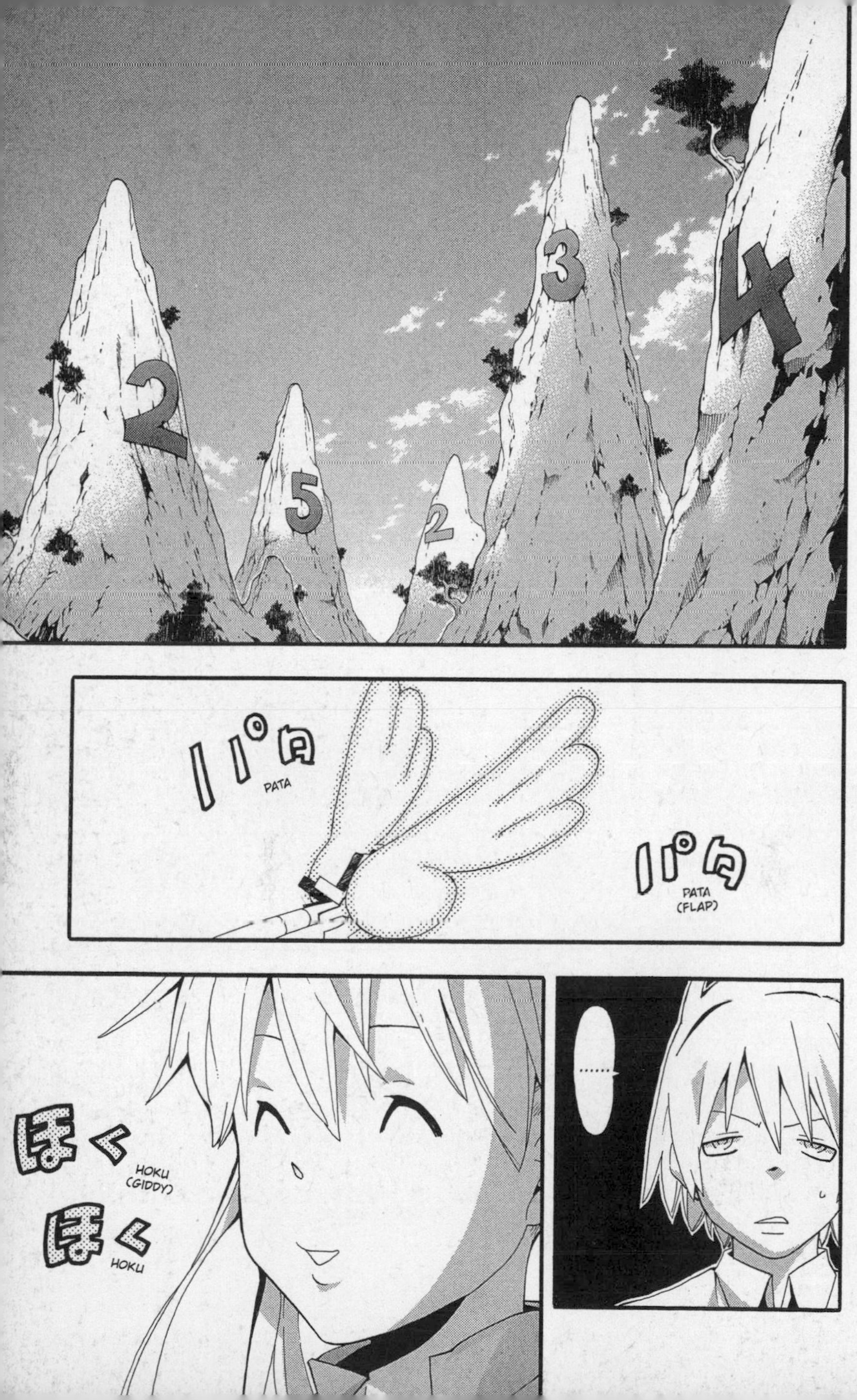

パタ
PATA (FLAP)
パタ
PATA
......
ほく
HOKU (GIDDY)
ほく
HOKU

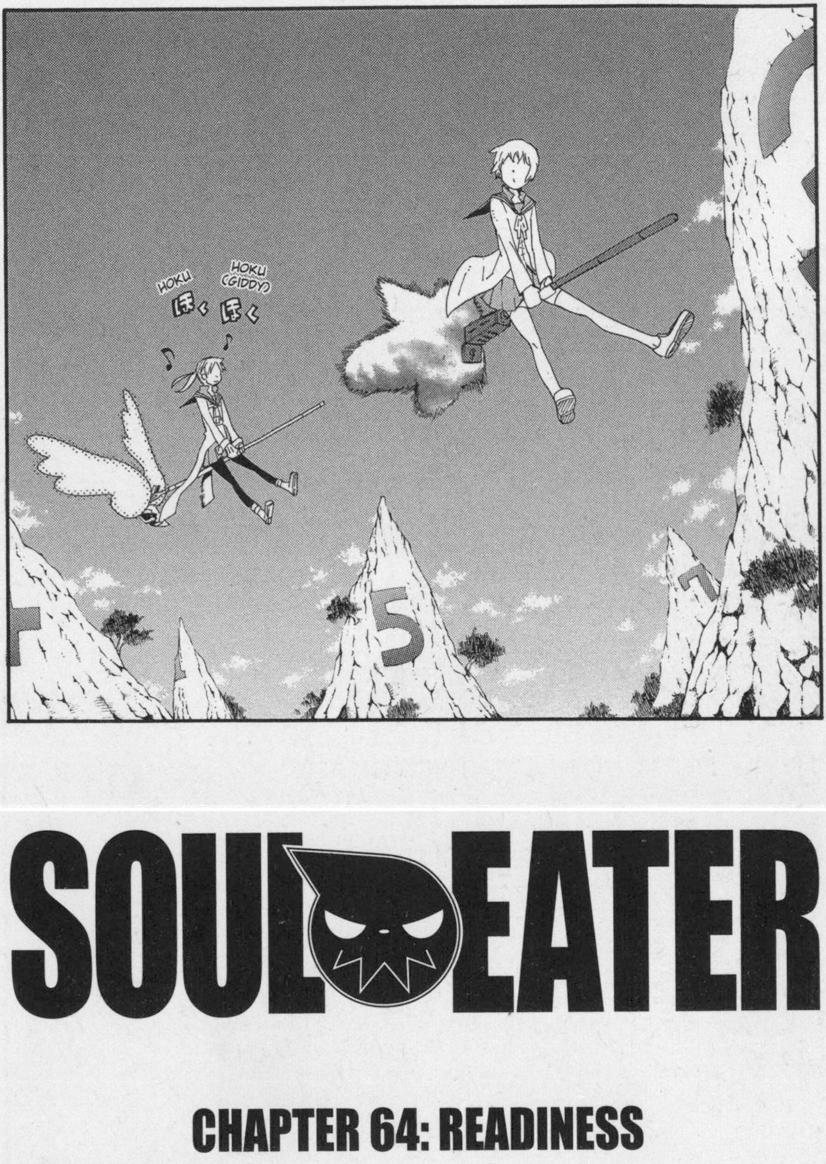
HOKU
ほく
HOKU (GIDDY)
ほく

# SOUL EATER

## CHAPTER 64: READINESS

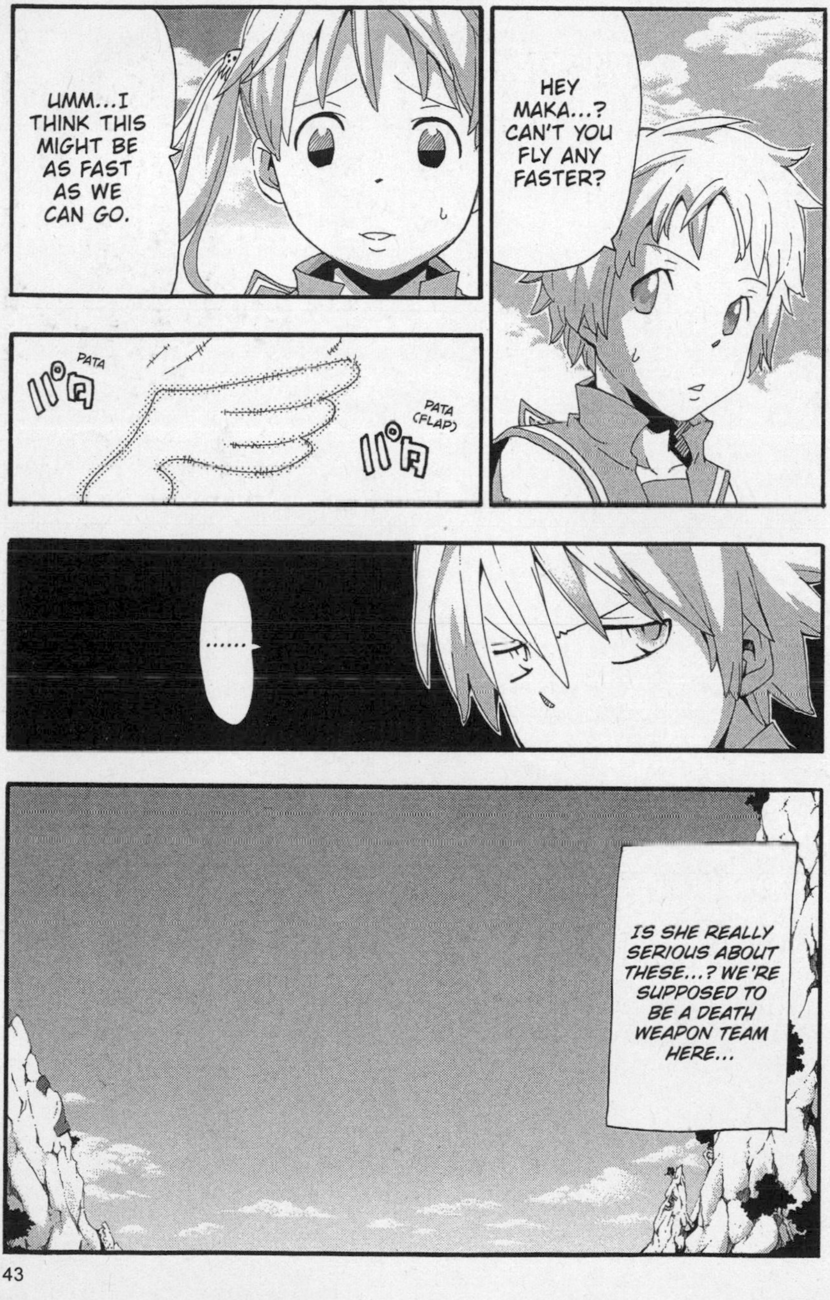
HEY MAKA...? CAN'T YOU FLY ANY FASTER?
UMM...I THINK THIS MIGHT BE AS FAST AS WE CAN GO.
PATA
PATA (FLAP)
......
IS SHE REALLY SERIOUS ABOUT THESE...? WE'RE SUPPOSED TO BE A DEATH WEAPON TEAM HERE...

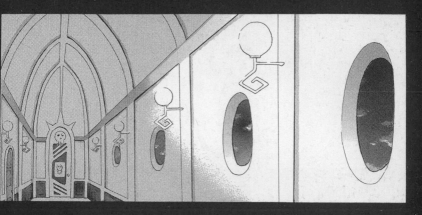

DAD?

WHAT DID YOU WANT TO TALK ABOUT?

NOW THAT SOUL IS A DEATH WEAPON AND ALL THE MEMBERS OF SPARTOI HAVE ADVANCED TO TWO-STAR STATUS...

...IT'S MY HOPE AND THE HOPE OF EVERYONE ELSE HERE AT DWMA THAT YOU WILL BE SUCCESSFUL IN PUTTING DOWN THE THREAT OF THE KISHIN AND THE WITCHES.

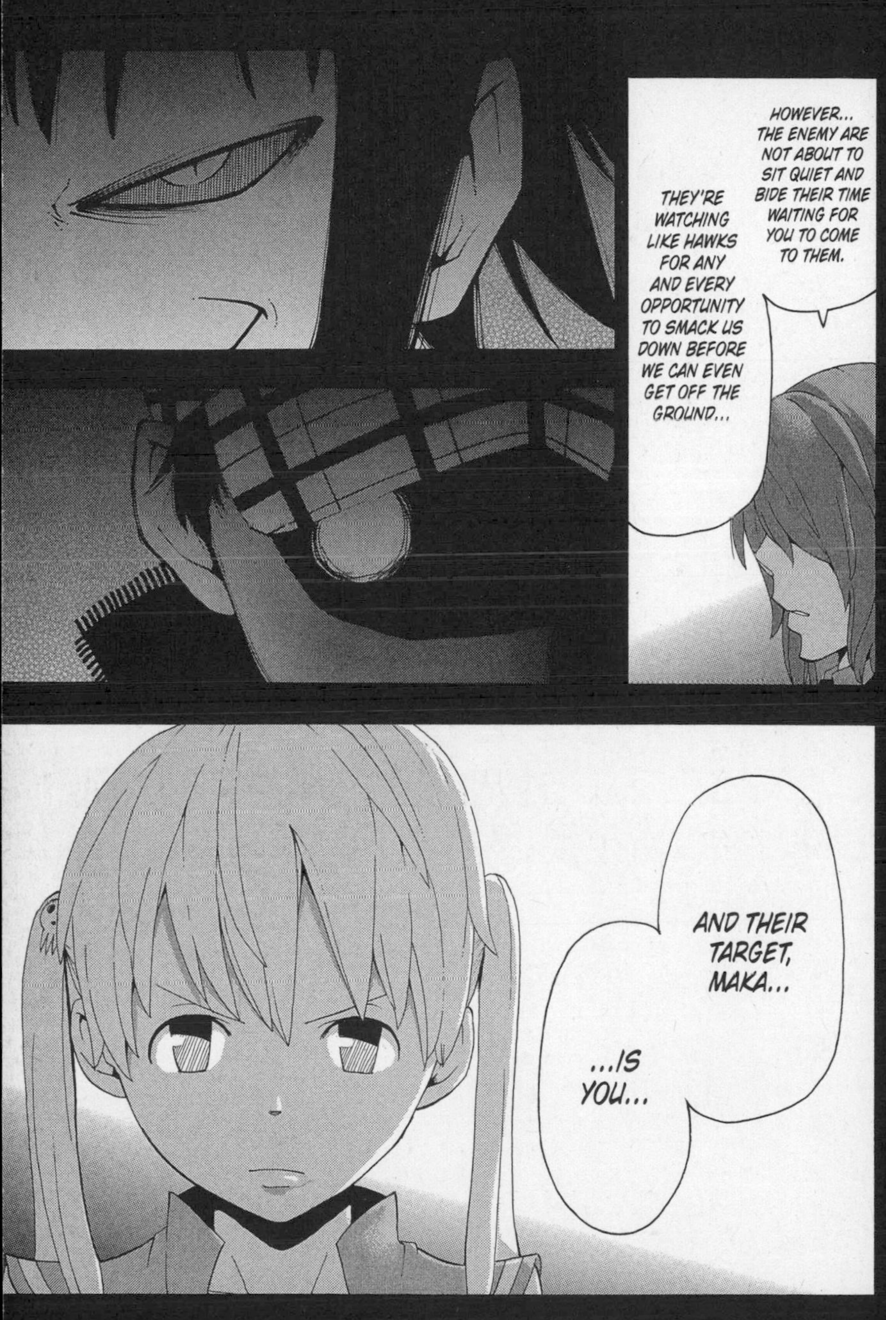
HOWEVER... THE ENEMY ARE NOT ABOUT TO SIT QUIET AND BIDE THEIR TIME WAITING FOR YOU TO COME TO THEM.
THEY'RE WATCHING LIKE HAWKS FOR ANY AND EVERY OPPORTUNITY TO SMACK US DOWN BEFORE WE CAN EVEN GET OFF THE GROUND...
AND THEIR TARGET, MAKA...
...IS YOU...

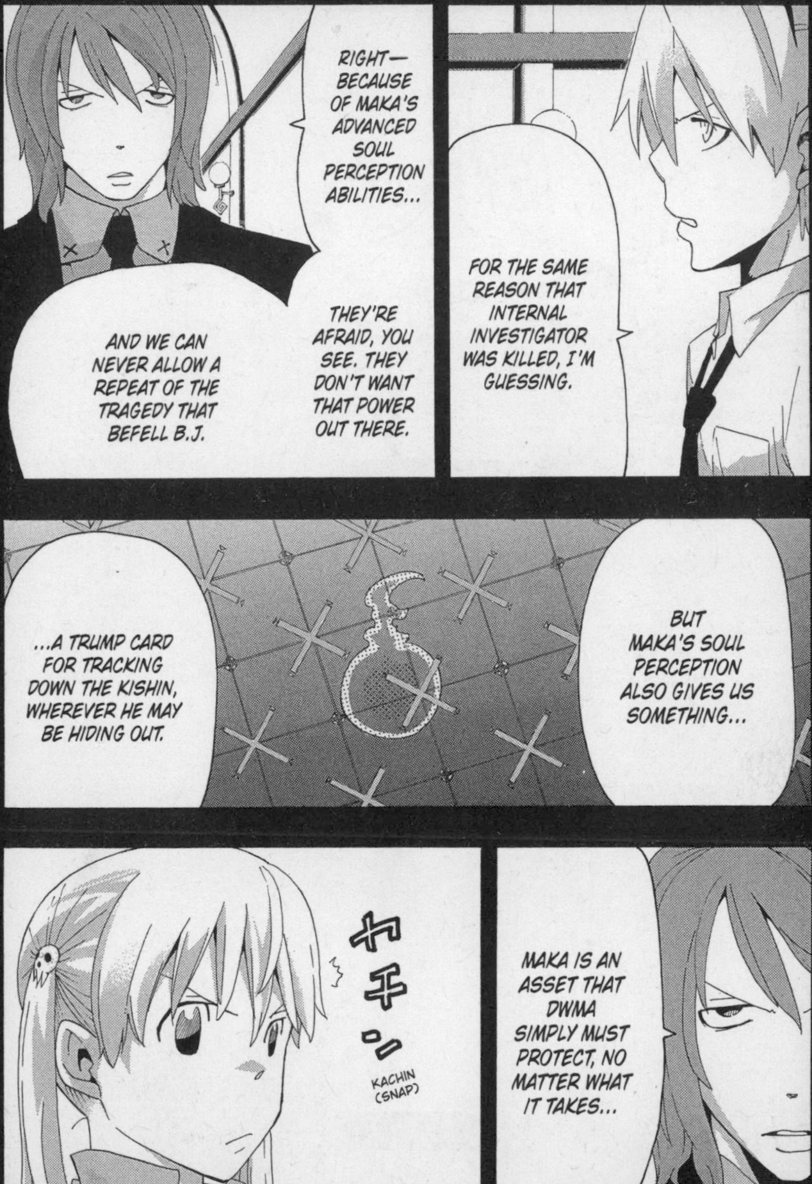
FOR THE SAME REASON THAT INTERNAL INVESTIGATOR WAS KILLED, I'M GUESSING.
RIGHT— BECAUSE OF MAKA'S ADVANCED SOUL PERCEPTION ABILITIES...
THEY'RE AFRAID, YOU SEE. THEY DON'T WANT THAT POWER OUT THERE.
AND WE CAN NEVER ALLOW A REPEAT OF THE TRAGEDY THAT BEFELL B.J.
BUT MAKA'S SOUL PERCEPTION ALSO GIVES US SOMETHING...
...A TRUMP CARD FOR TRACKING DOWN THE KISHIN, WHEREVER HE MAY BE HIDING OUT.
MAKA IS AN ASSET THAT DWMA SIMPLY MUST PROTECT, NO MATTER WHAT IT TAKES...
カチン
KACHIN (SNAP)

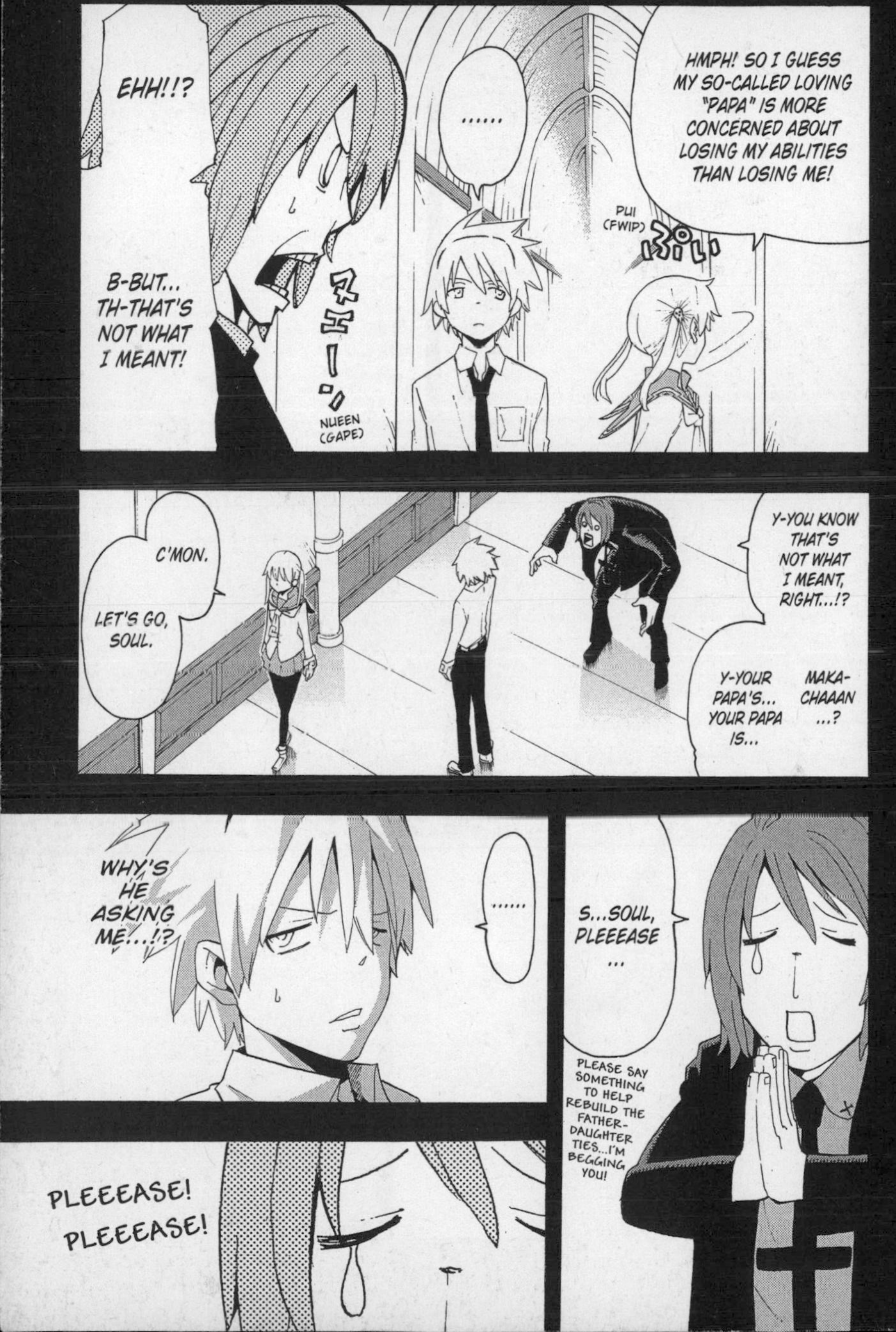
HMPH! SO I GUESS MY SO-CALLED LOVING "PAPA" IS MORE CONCERNED ABOUT LOSING MY ABILITIES THAN LOSING ME!
PUI (FWIP)
......
EHH!!?
B-BUT... TH-THAT'S NOT WHAT I MEANT!
NUEEN (GAPE)
Y-YOU KNOW THAT'S NOT WHAT I MEANT, RIGHT...!?
MAKA-CHAAAN ...?
Y-YOUR PAPA'S... YOUR PAPA IS...
C'MON.
LET'S GO, SOUL.
S...SOUL, PLEEEASE ...
PLEASE SAY SOMETHING TO HELP REBUILD THE FATHER-DAUGHTER TIES...I'M BEGGING YOU!
......
WHY'S HE ASKING ME...!?
PLEEEASE! PLEEEASE!

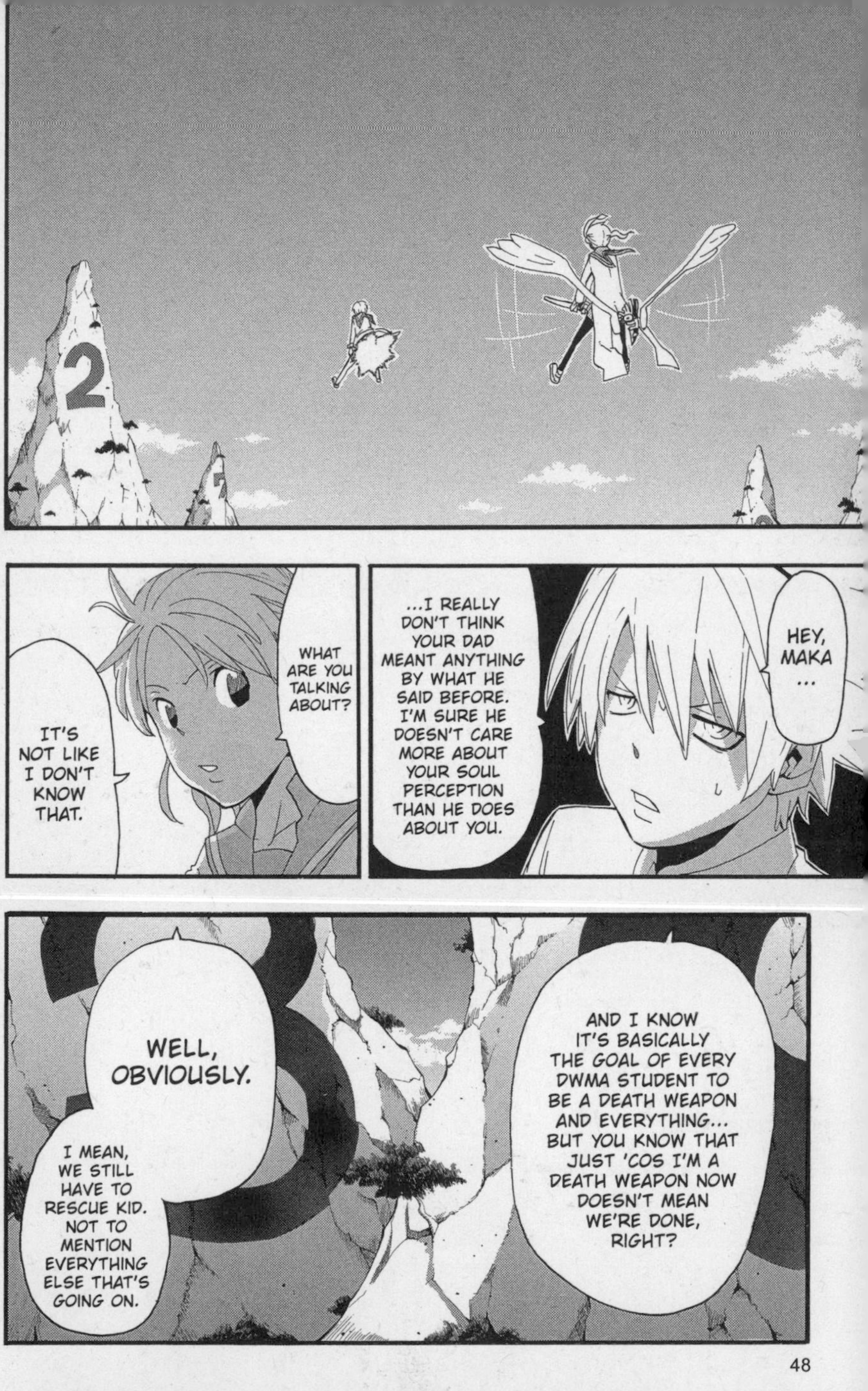
HEY, MAKA ...
...I REALLY DON'T THINK YOUR DAD MEANT ANYTHING BY WHAT HE SAID BEFORE. I'M SURE HE DOESN'T CARE MORE ABOUT YOUR SOUL PERCEPTION THAN HE DOES ABOUT YOU.
WHAT ARE YOU TALKING ABOUT?
IT'S NOT LIKE I DON'T KNOW THAT.
AND I KNOW IT'S BASICALLY THE GOAL OF EVERY DWMA STUDENT TO BE A DEATH WEAPON AND EVERYTHING... BUT YOU KNOW THAT JUST 'COS I'M A DEATH WEAPON NOW DOESN'T MEAN WE'RE DONE, RIGHT?
WELL, OBVIOUSLY.
I MEAN, WE STILL HAVE TO RESCUE KID. NOT TO MENTION EVERYTHING ELSE THAT'S GOING ON.

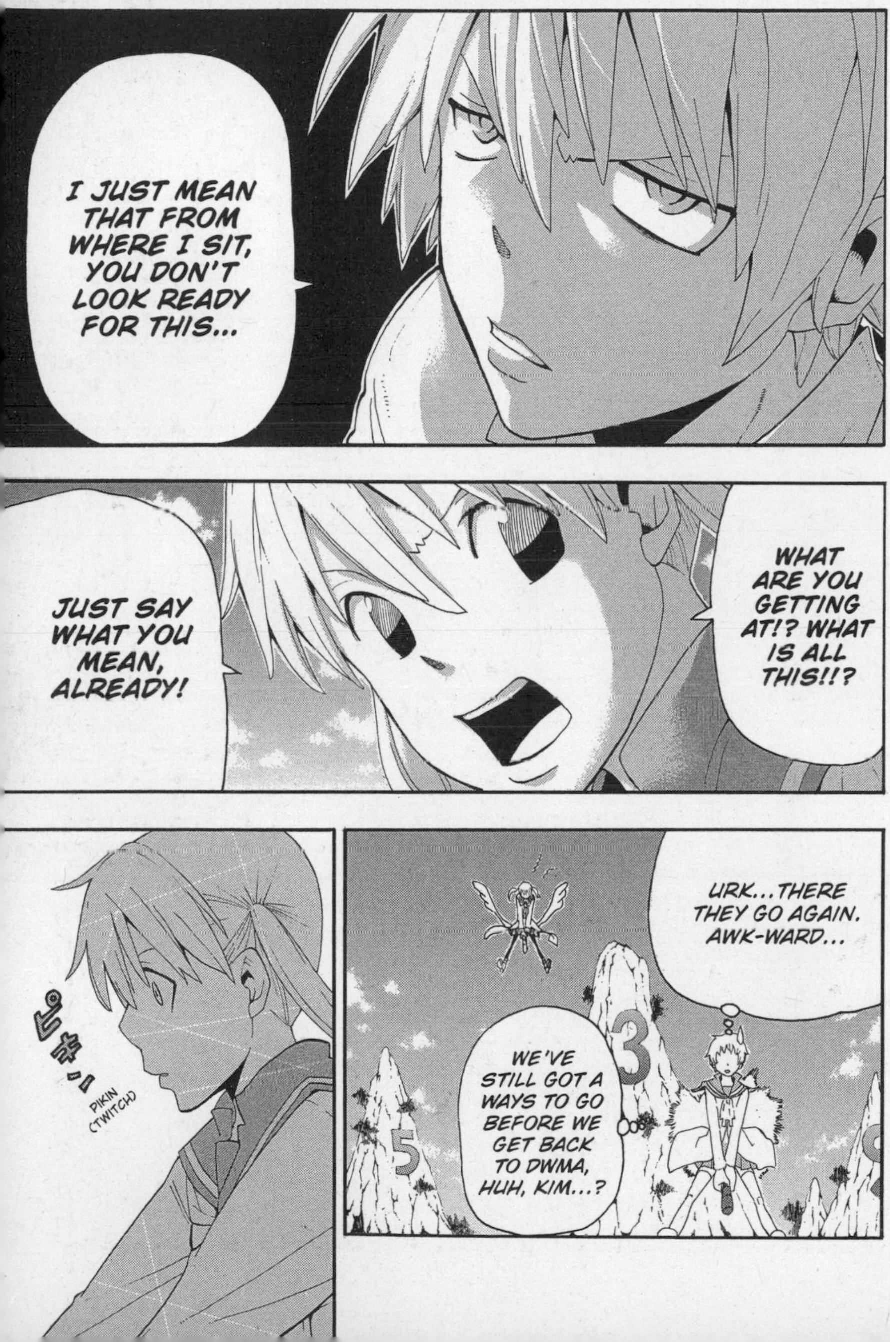
I JUST MEAN THAT FROM WHERE I SIT, YOU DON'T LOOK READY FOR THIS...
WHAT ARE YOU GETTING AT!? WHAT IS ALL THIS!!?
JUST SAY WHAT YOU MEAN, ALREADY!
URK...THERE THEY GO AGAIN. AWK-WARD...
WE'VE STILL GOT A WAYS TO GO BEFORE WE GET BACK TO DWMA, HUH, KIM...?
ピキッ
PIKIN (TWITCH)

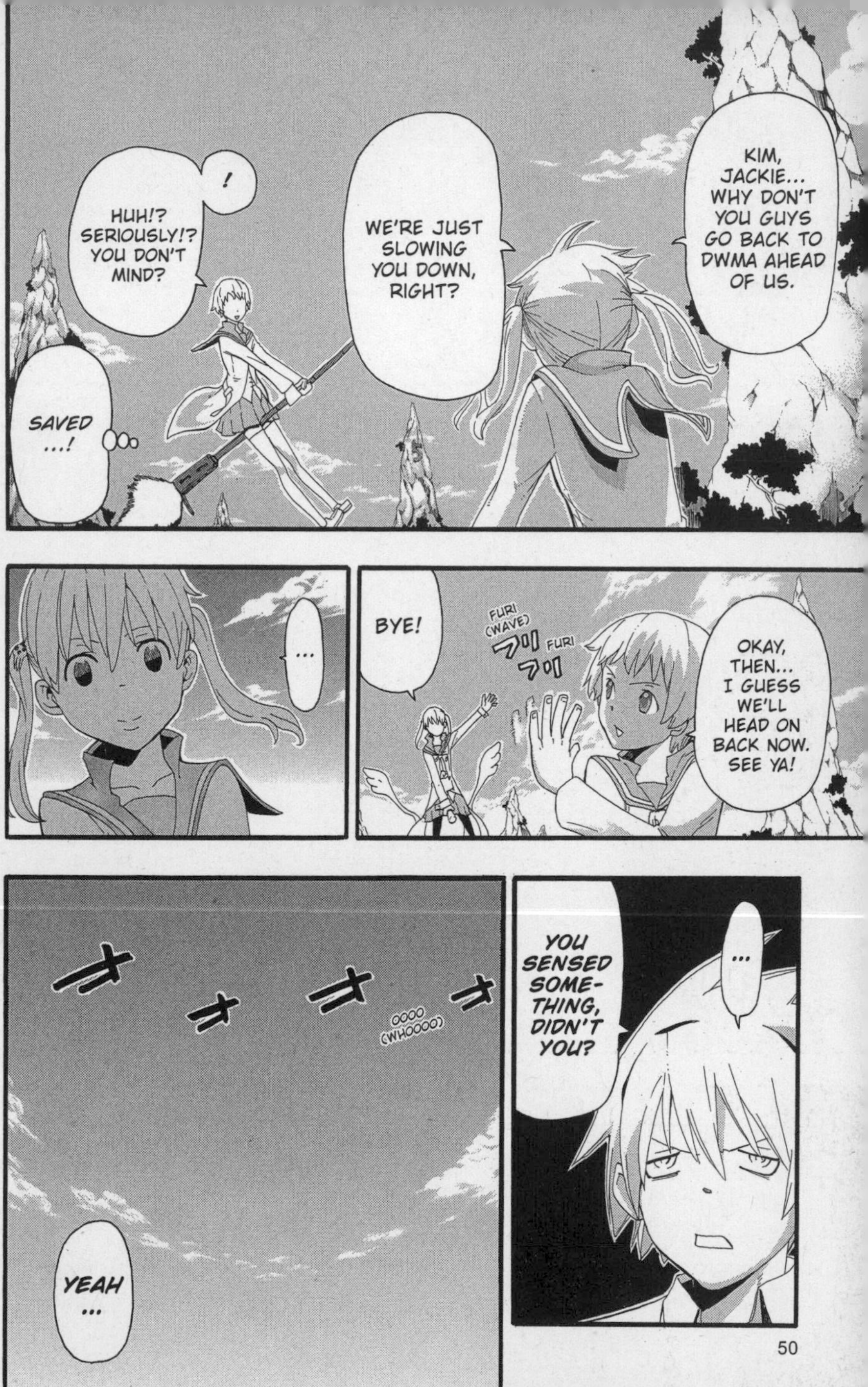
KIM, JACKIE... WHY DON'T YOU GUYS GO BACK TO DWMA AHEAD OF US.
WE'RE JUST SLOWING YOU DOWN, RIGHT?
!
HUH!? SERIOUSLY!? YOU DON'T MIND?
SAVED ...!
OKAY, THEN... I GUESS WE'LL HEAD ON BACK NOW. SEE YA!
FURI (WAVE)
FURI
BYE!
...
...
YOU SENSED SOME-THING, DIDN'T YOU?
OOOO (WHOOOO)
YEAH ...

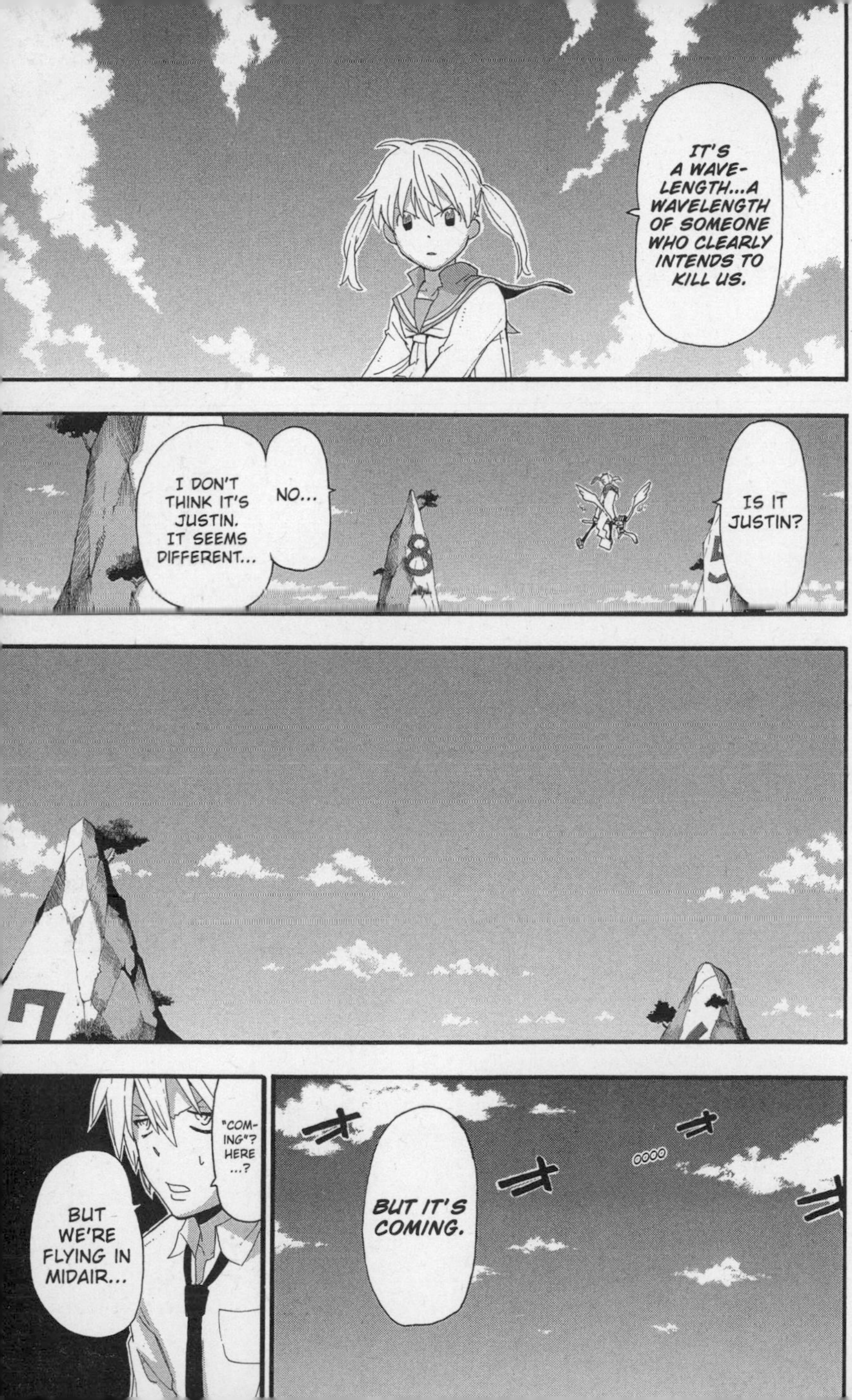
IT'S A WAVE-LENGTH...A WAVELENGTH OF SOMEONE WHO CLEARLY INTENDS TO KILL US.
IS IT JUSTIN?
NO...
I DON'T THINK IT'S JUSTIN. IT SEEMS DIFFERENT...
BUT IT'S COMING.
OOOO
"COMING"? HERE ...?
BUT WE'RE FLYING IN MIDAIR...

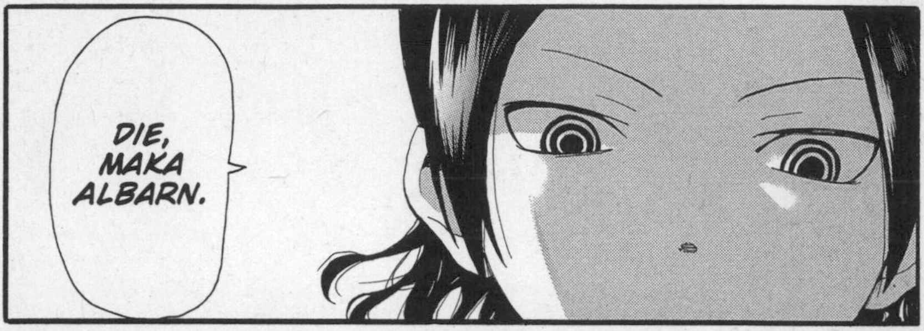
DIE, MAKA ALBARN.

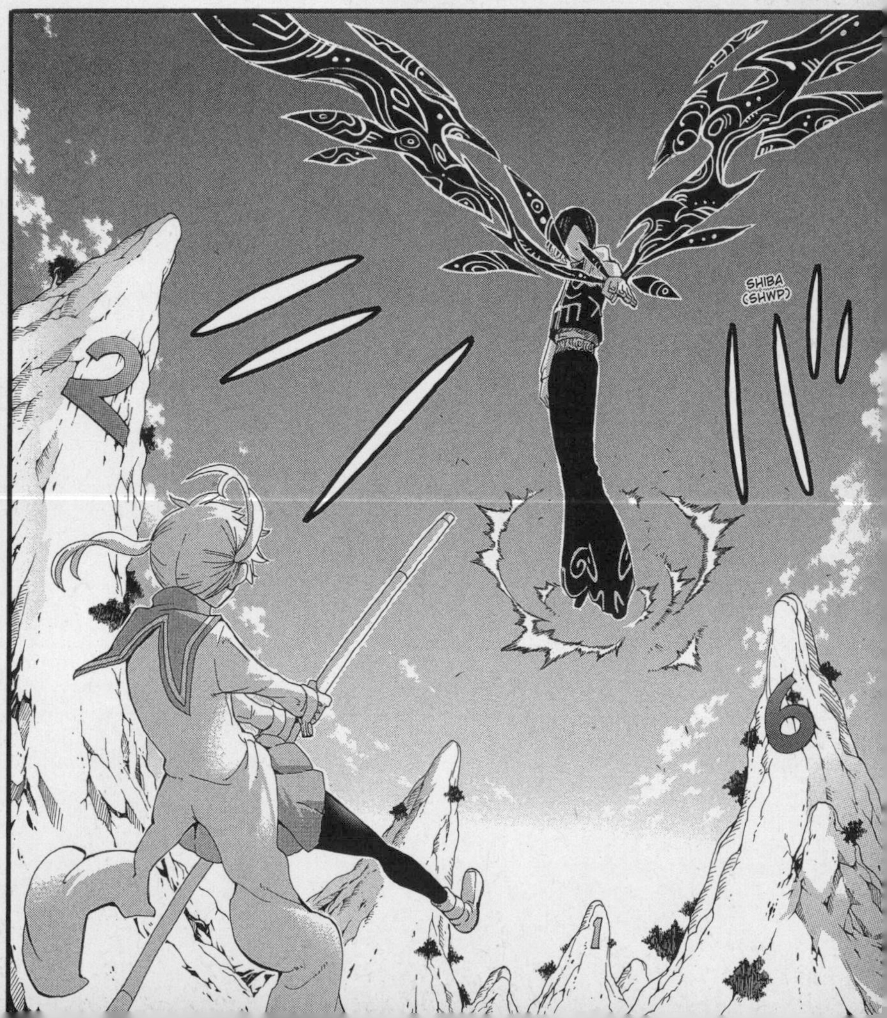
SHIBA (SHWP)

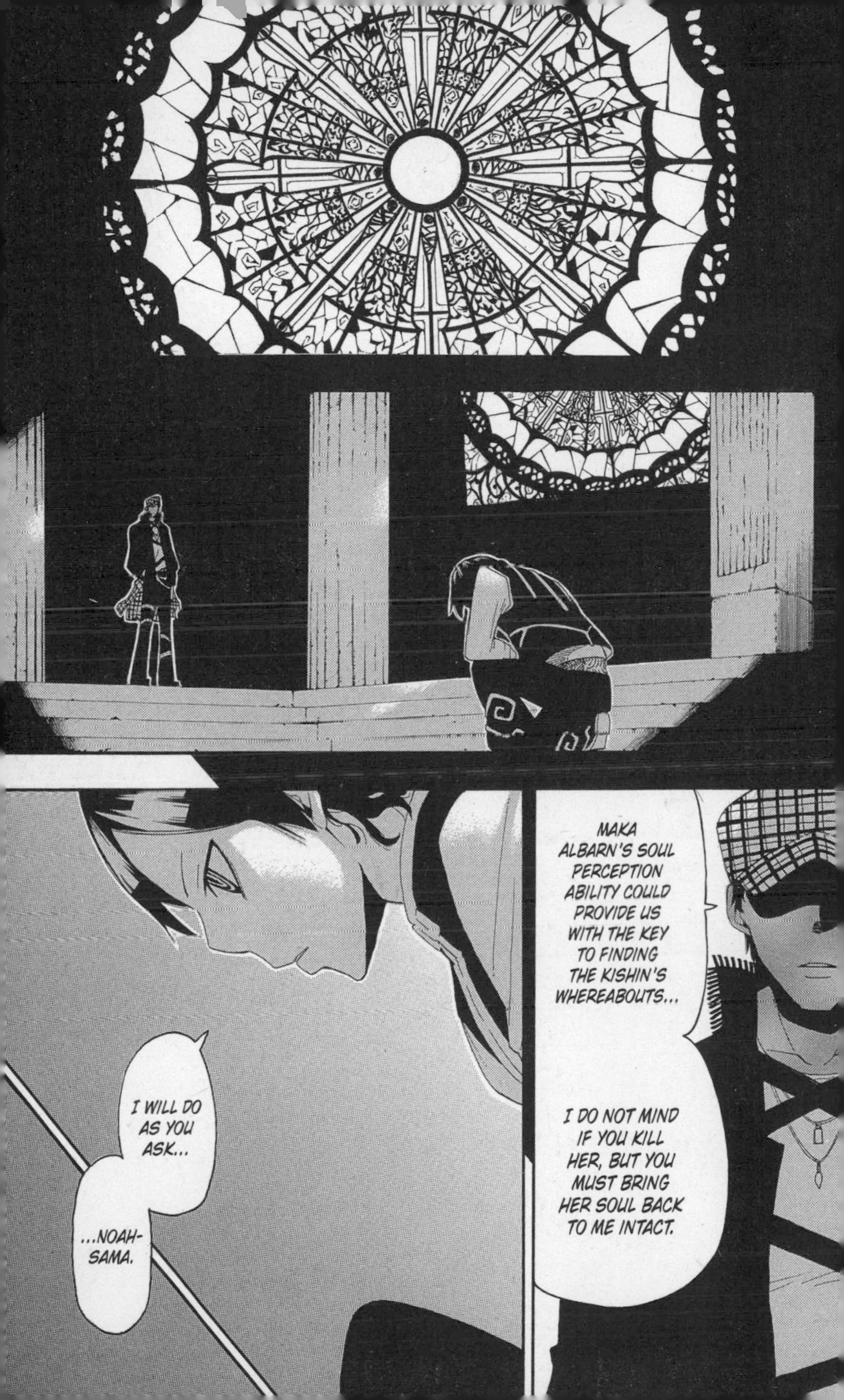
MAKA ALBARN'S SOUL PERCEPTION ABILITY COULD PROVIDE US WITH THE KEY TO FINDING THE KISHIN'S WHEREABOUTS...
I DO NOT MIND IF YOU KILL HER, BUT YOU MUST BRING HER SOUL BACK TO ME INTACT.
I WILL DO AS YOU ASK...
...NOAH-SAMA.

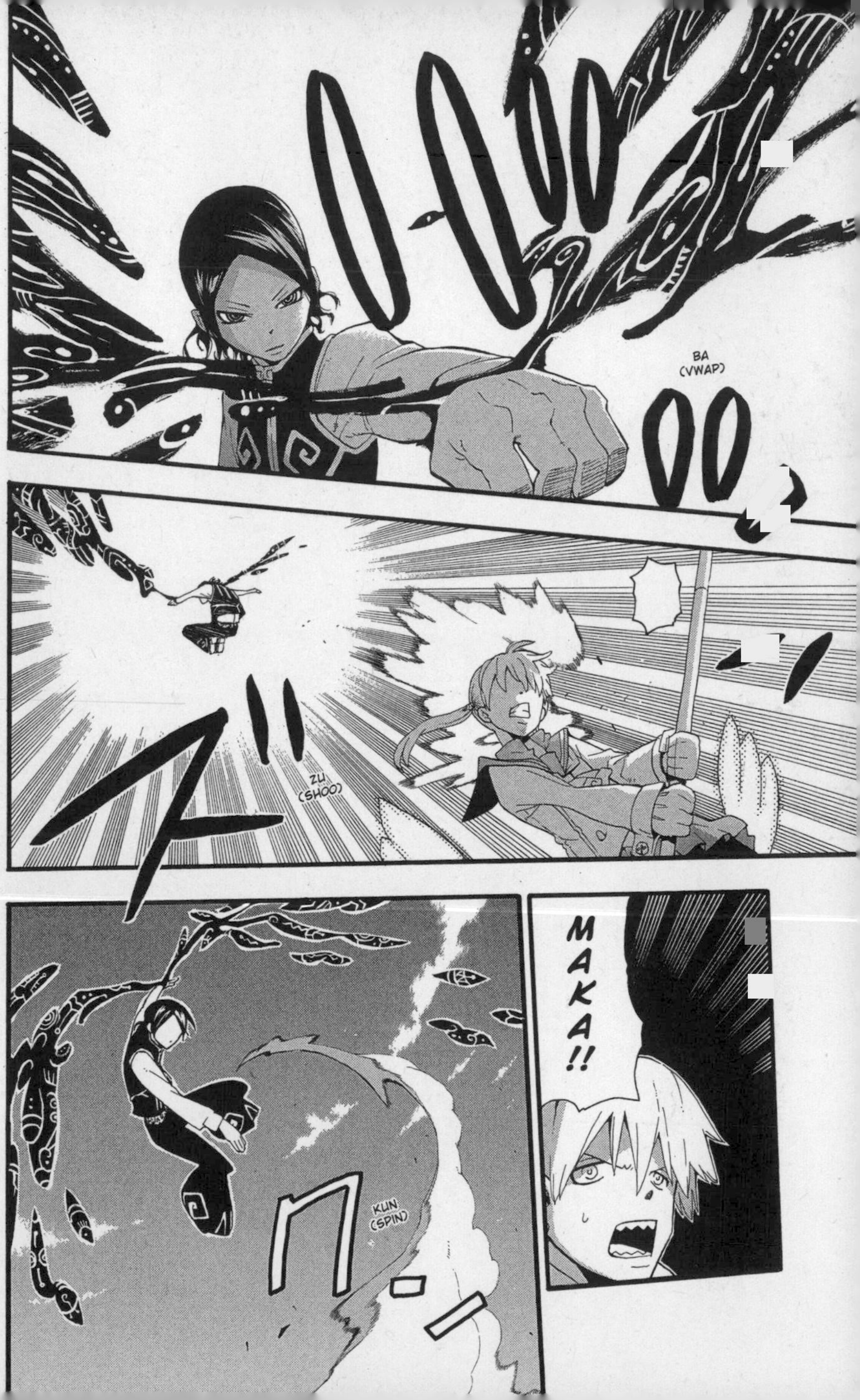
BA
(VWAP)
ZU
(SHOO)
MAKA!!
KUN
(SPIN)

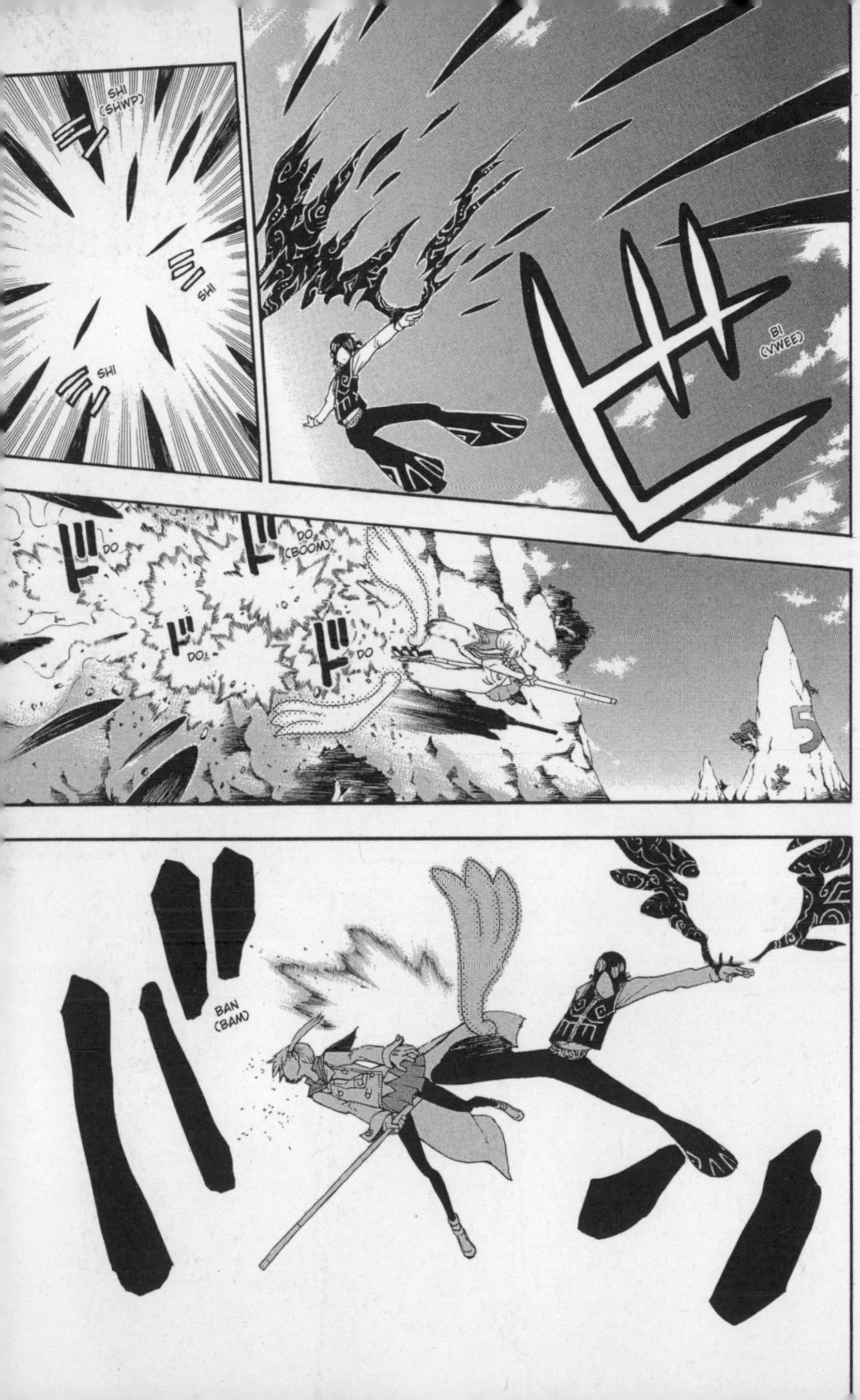
BI (VWEE)
SHI (SHWP)
SHI
SHI
DO (BOOM)
DO
DO
DO
BAN (BAM)

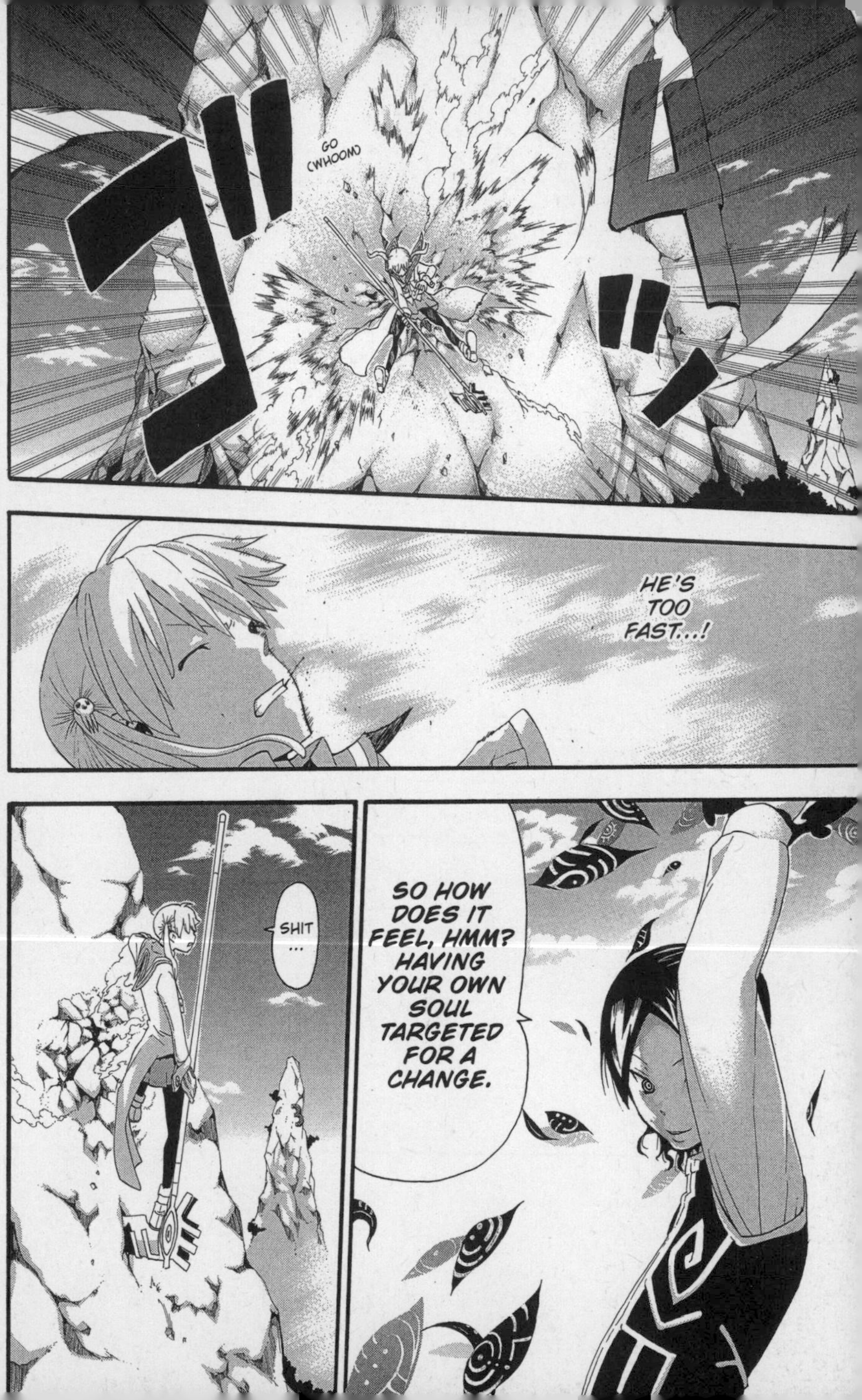
GO (WHOOM)
HE'S TOO FAST...!
SO HOW DOES IT FEEL, HMM? HAVING YOUR OWN SOUL TARGETED FOR A CHANGE.
SHIT ...

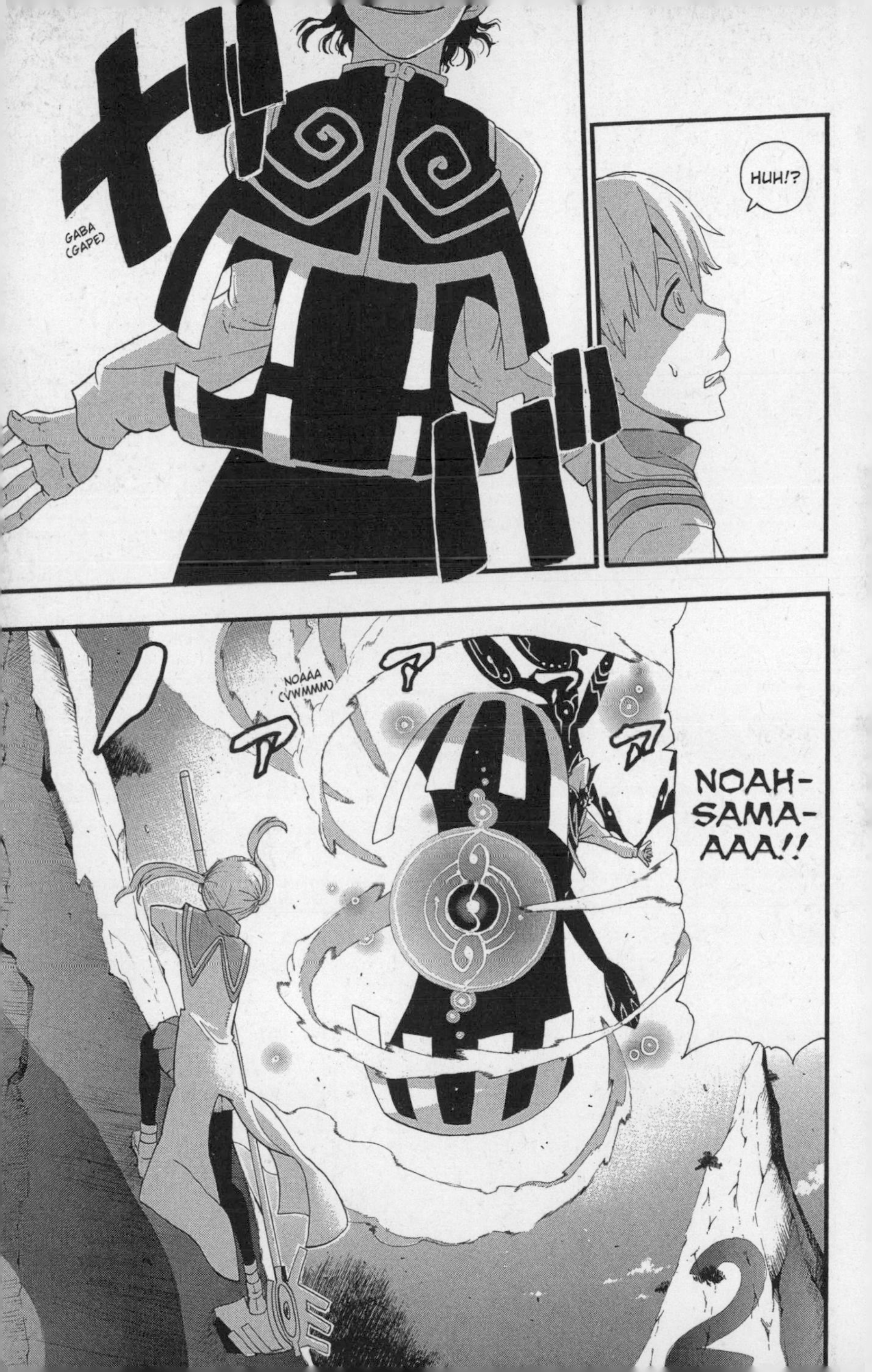
HUH!?
GABA (GAPE)
NOAH-SAMA-AAA!!
NOAAA (VWMMM)

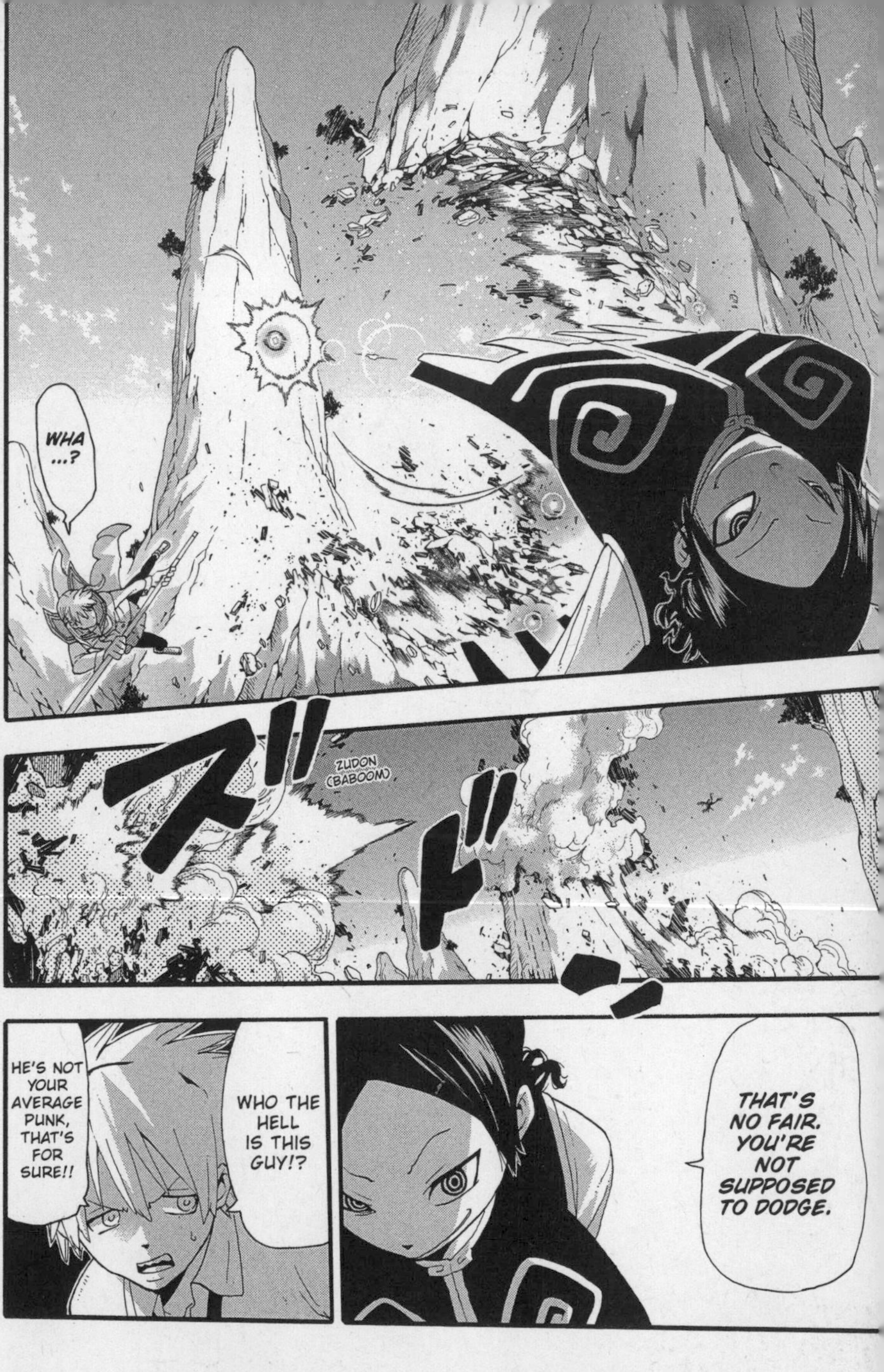
WHA ...?
ZUDON (BABOOM)
THAT'S NO FAIR. YOU'RE NOT SUPPOSED TO DODGE.
WHO THE HELL IS THIS GUY!?
HE'S NOT YOUR AVERAGE PUNK, THAT'S FOR SURE!!

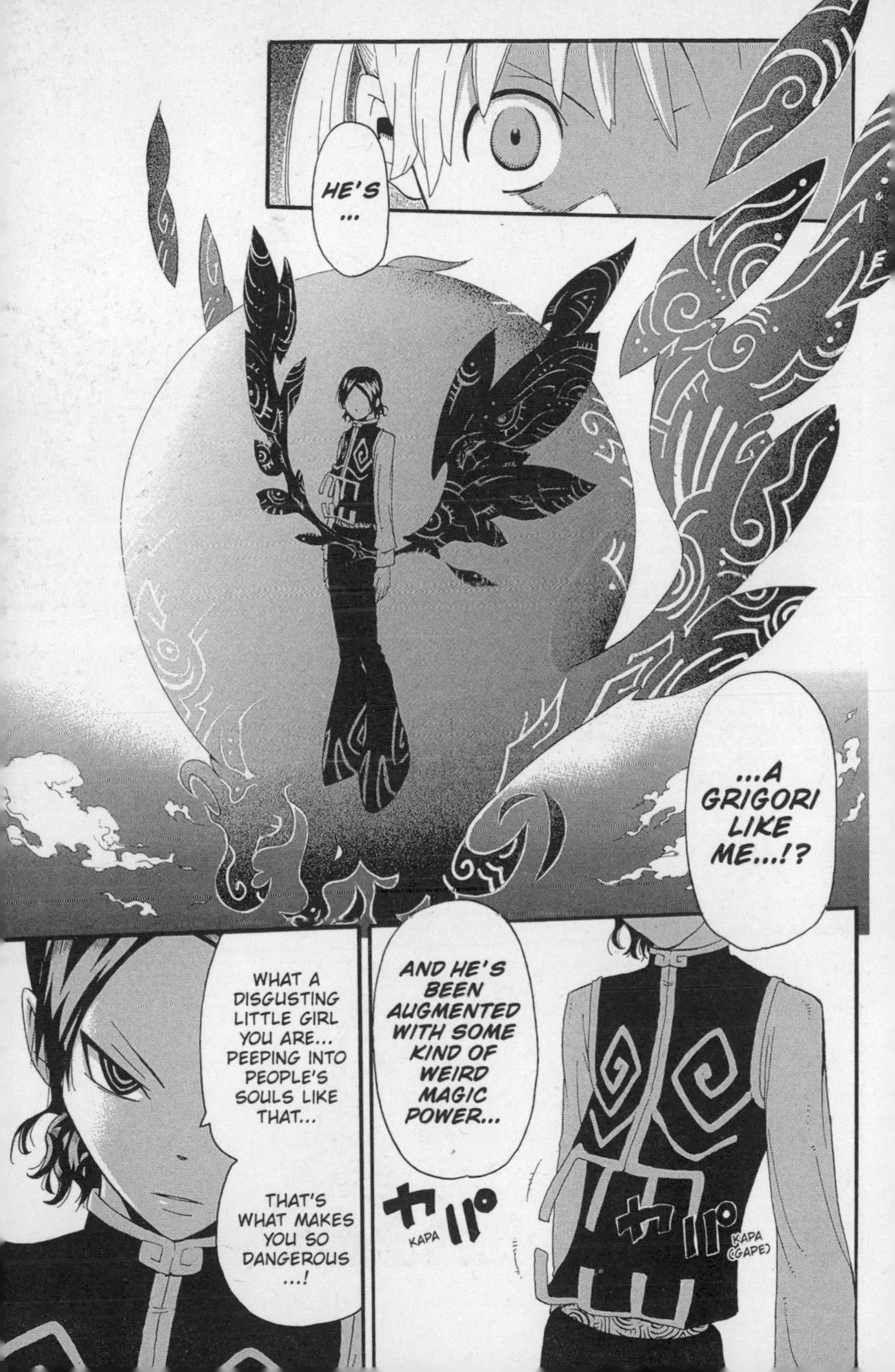
HE'S ...
...A GRIGORI LIKE ME...!?
AND HE'S BEEN AUGMENTED WITH SOME KIND OF WEIRD MAGIC POWER...
カパ
KAPA (GAPE)
カパ
KAPA
WHAT A DISGUSTING LITTLE GIRL YOU ARE... PEEPING INTO PEOPLE'S SOULS LIKE THAT...
THAT'S WHAT MAKES YOU SO DANGEROUS ...!

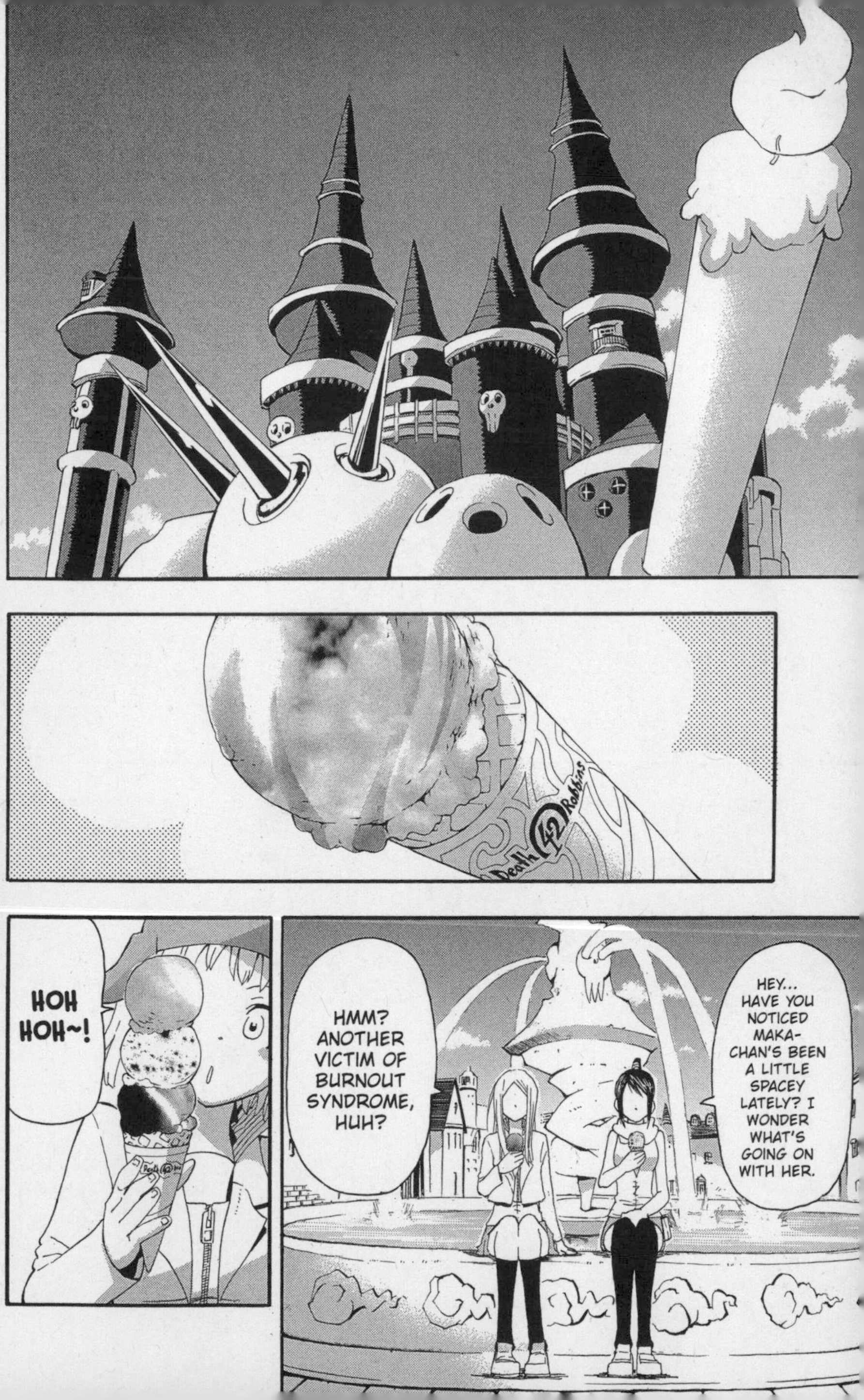
Death 42 Robbins
HEY... HAVE YOU NOTICED MAKA-CHAN'S BEEN A LITTLE SPACEY LATELY? I WONDER WHAT'S GOING ON WITH HER.
HMM? ANOTHER VICTIM OF BURNOUT SYNDROME, HUH?
HOH HOH~!

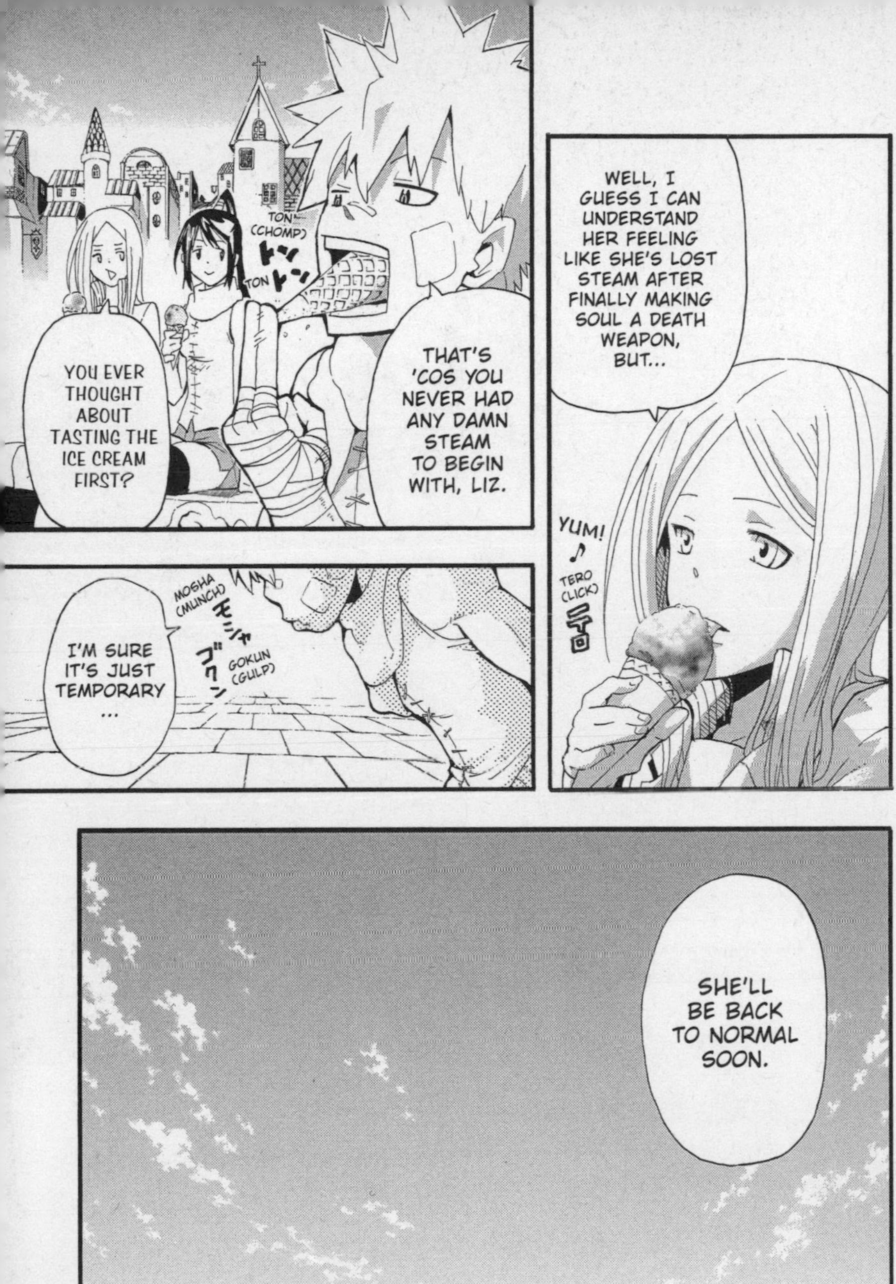
WELL, I GUESS I CAN UNDERSTAND HER FEELING LIKE SHE'S LOST STEAM AFTER FINALLY MAKING SOUL A DEATH WEAPON, BUT...
YUM! ♪
TERO (LICK)
テロ
TON (CHOMP)
トン
TON
トン
THAT'S 'COS YOU NEVER HAD ANY DAMN STEAM TO BEGIN WITH, LIZ.
YOU EVER THOUGHT ABOUT TASTING THE ICE CREAM FIRST?
MOSHA (MUNCH)
モシャ
GOKUN (GULP)
ゴクン
I'M SURE IT'S JUST TEMPORARY ...
SHE'LL BE BACK TO NORMAL SOON.

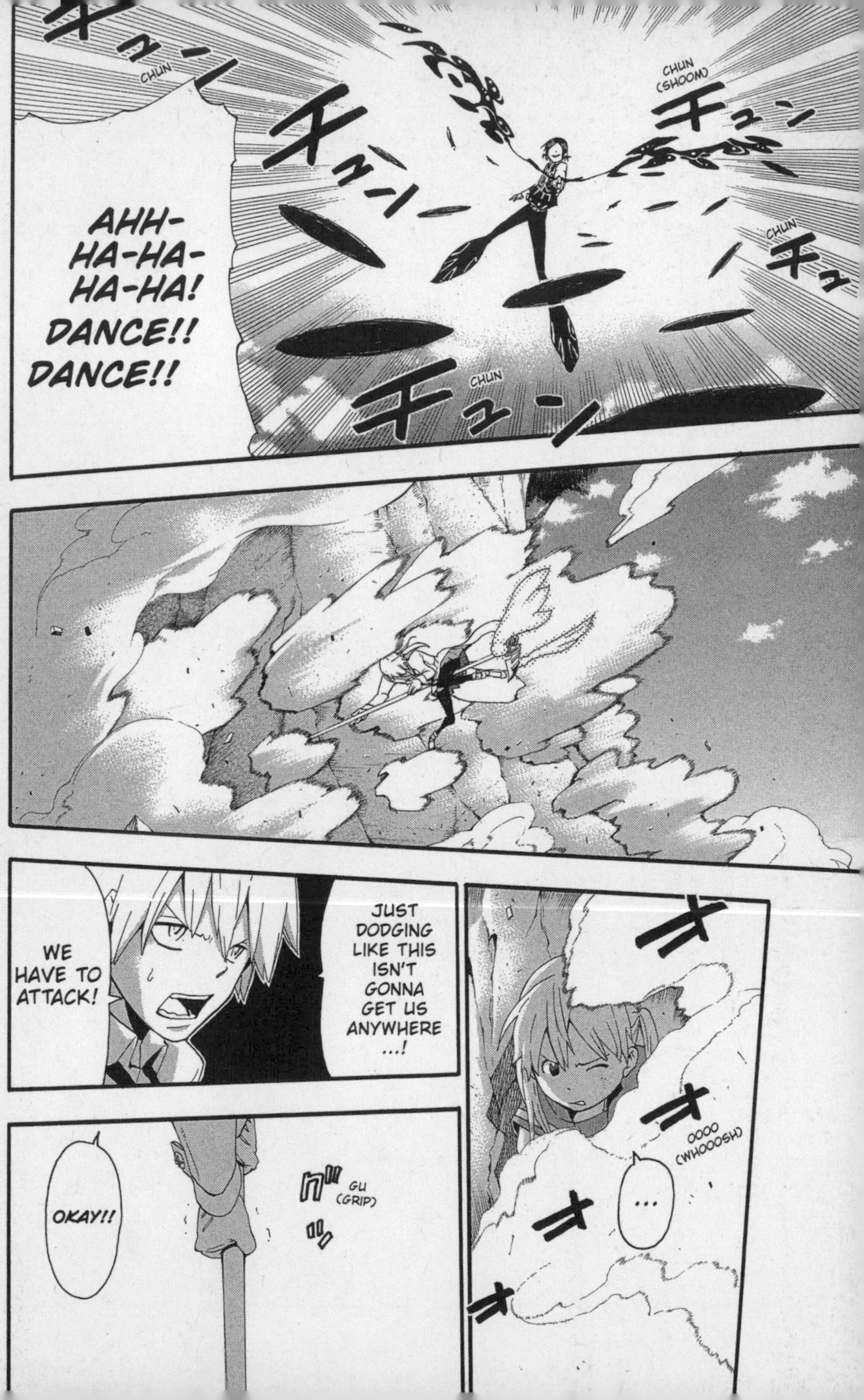
CHUN (SHOOM)
CHUN
CHUN
AHH-HA-HA-HA-HA! DANCE!! DANCE!!
CHUN
OOOO (WHOOOSH)
...
JUST DODGING LIKE THIS ISN'T GONNA GET US ANYWHERE ...!
WE HAVE TO ATTACK!
GU (GRIP)
OKAY!!

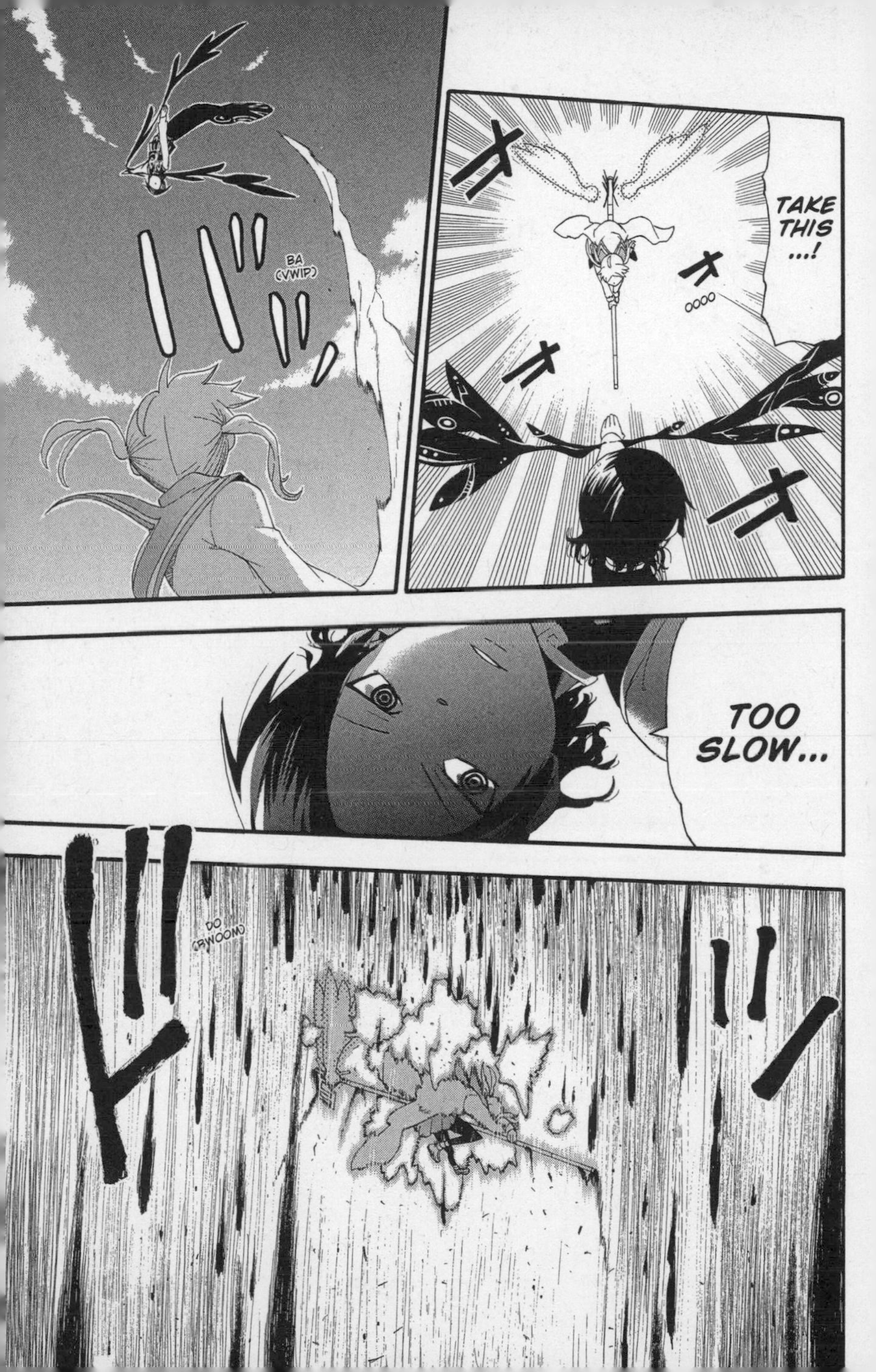

TAKE THIS ...!
OOOO
BA (VWIP)
TOO SLOW...
DO (BWOOM)

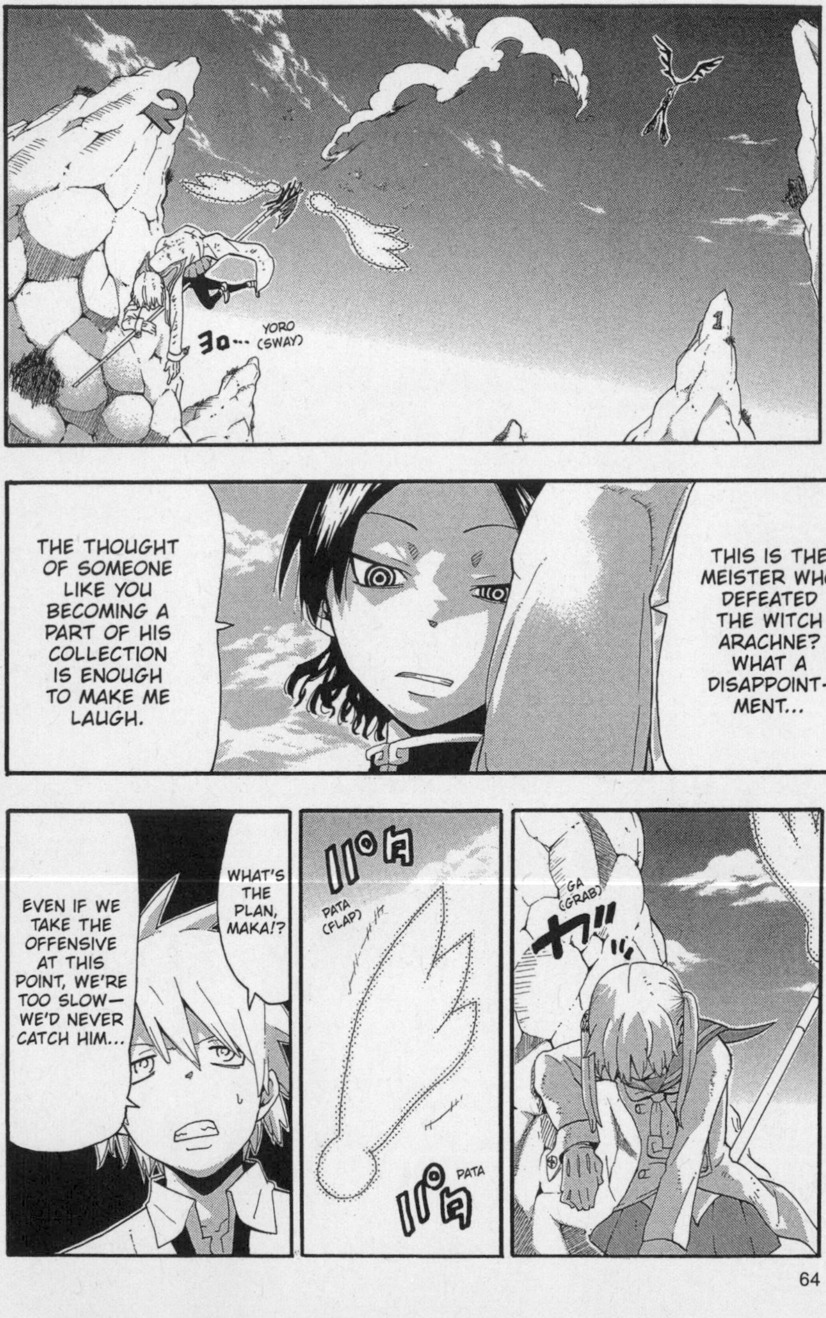
YORO (SWAY)
THIS IS THE MEISTER WHO DEFEATED THE WITCH ARACHNE? WHAT A DISAPPOINTMENT...
THE THOUGHT OF SOMEONE LIKE YOU BECOMING A PART OF HIS COLLECTION IS ENOUGH TO MAKE ME LAUGH.
GA (GRAB)
PATA (FLAP)
PATA
WHAT'S THE PLAN, MAKA!?
EVEN IF WE TAKE THE OFFENSIVE AT THIS POINT, WE'RE TOO SLOW—WE'D NEVER CATCH HIM...

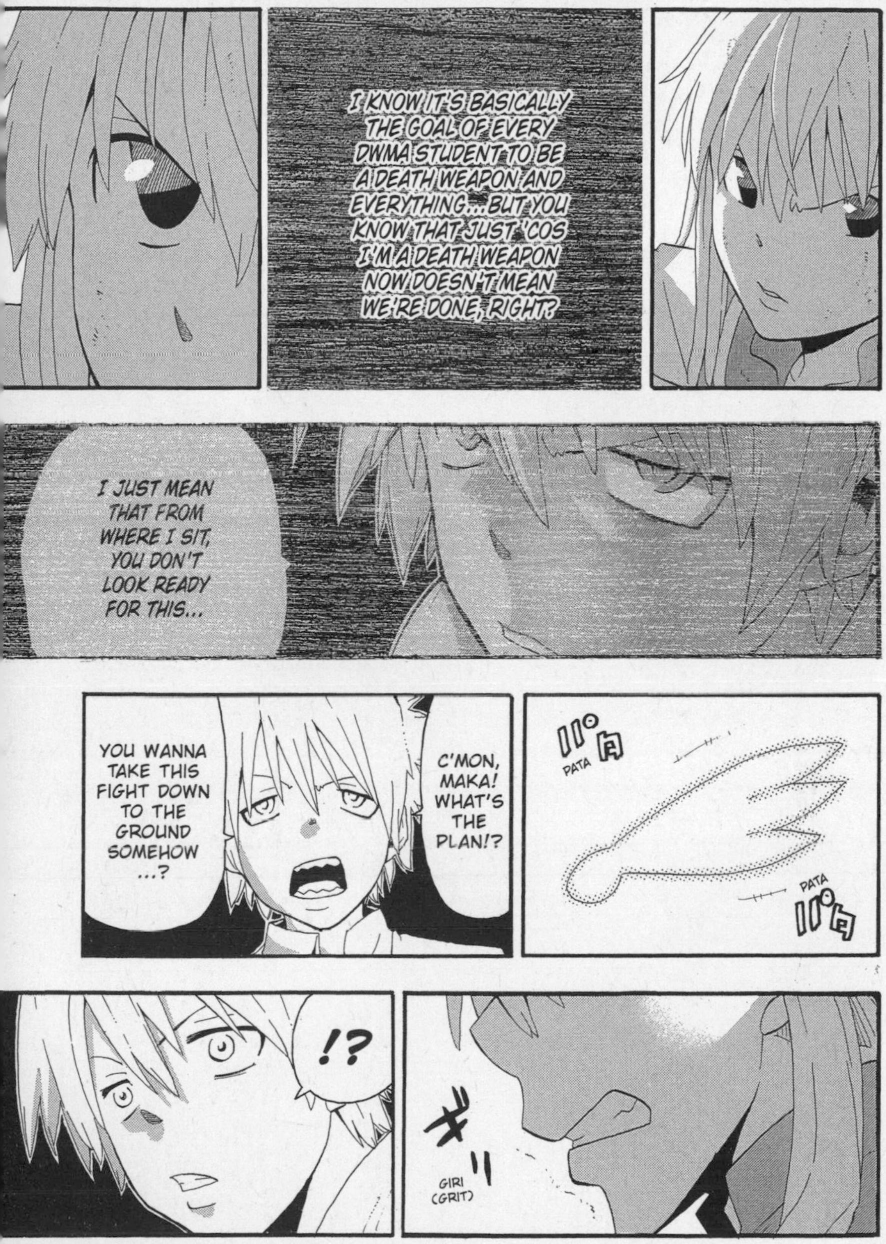
I KNOW IT'S BASICALLY THE GOAL OF EVERY DWMA STUDENT TO BE A DEATH WEAPON AND EVERYTHING... BUT YOU KNOW THAT JUST 'COS I'M A DEATH WEAPON NOW DOESN'T MEAN WE'RE DONE, RIGHT?
I JUST MEAN THAT FROM WHERE I SIT, YOU DON'T LOOK READY FOR THIS...
PATA
PATA
C'MON, MAKA! WHAT'S THE PLAN!?
YOU WANNA TAKE THIS FIGHT DOWN TO THE GROUND SOMEHOW ...?
GIRI (GRIT)
!?

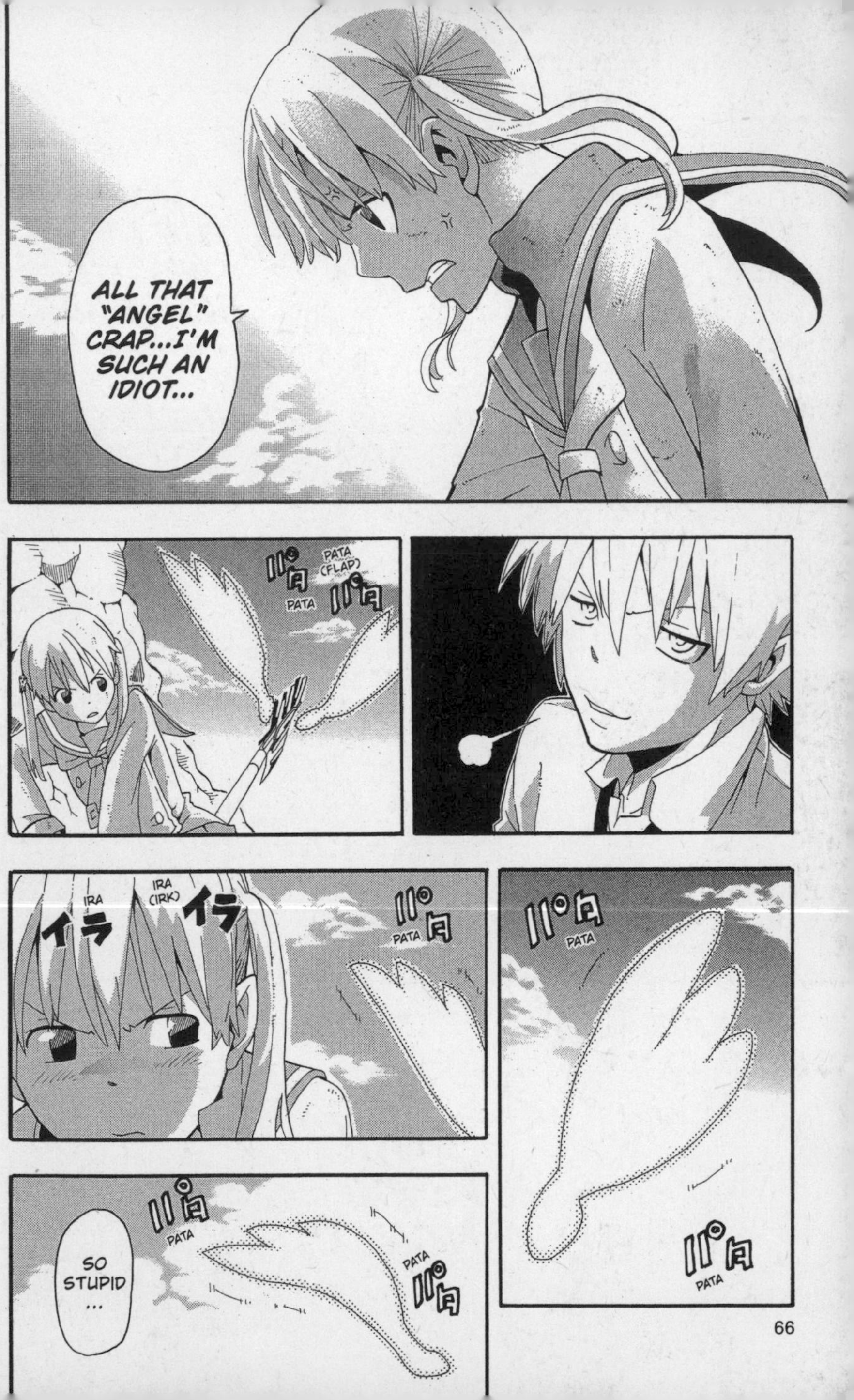
ALL THAT "ANGEL" CRAP...I'M SUCH AN IDIOT...
パタ
PATA (FLAP)
パタ
PATA
パタ
PATA
パタ
PATA
イラ
IRA (IRK)
イラ
IRA
パタ
PATA
パタ
PATA
SO STUPID...
PATA
パタ

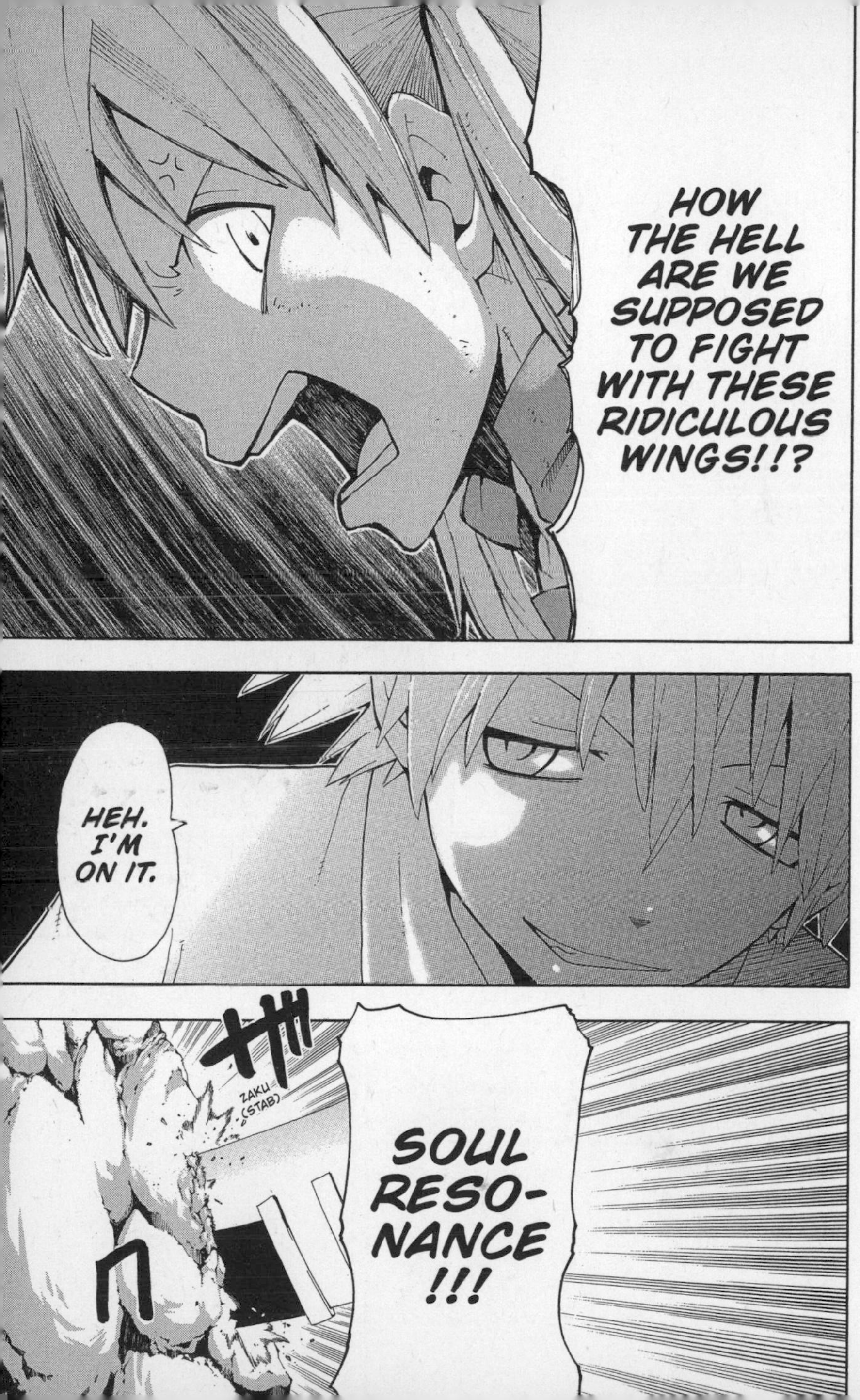
HOW THE HELL ARE WE SUPPOSED TO FIGHT WITH THESE RIDICULOUS WINGS!!?
HEH. I'M ON IT.
SOUL RESO-NANCE !!!
ZAKU (STAB)

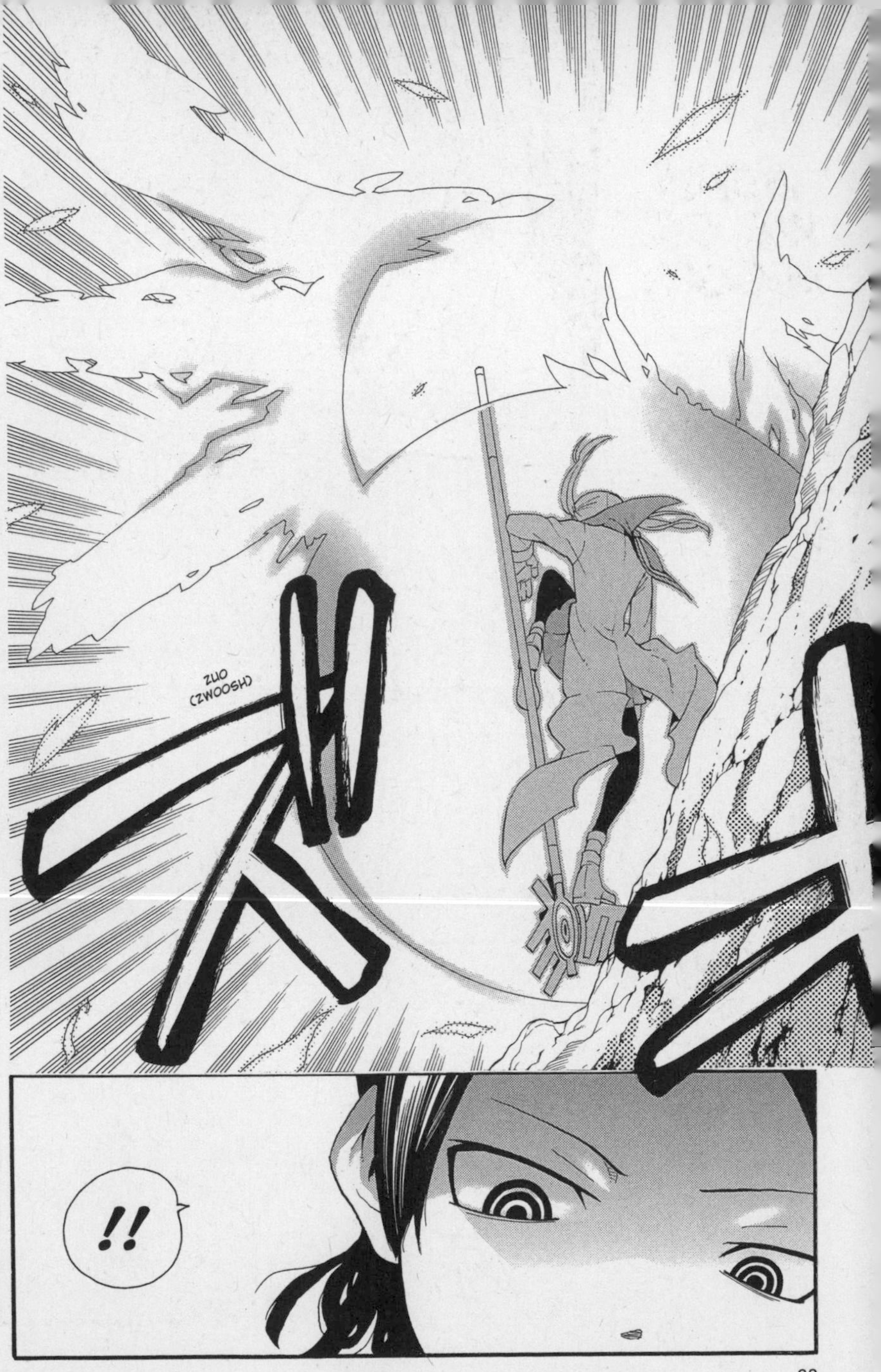
ZUO
(ZWOOSH)
!!

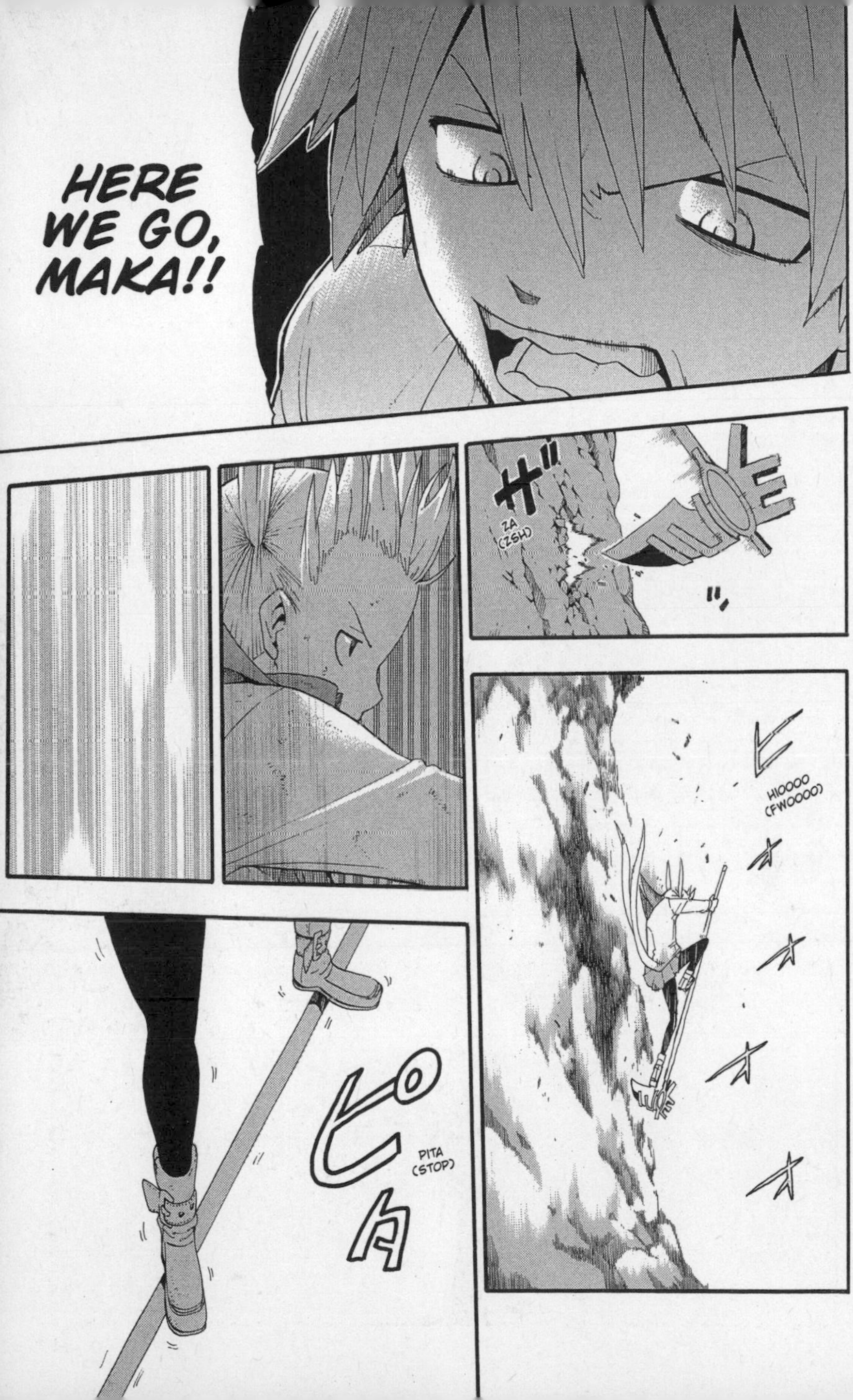
HERE WE GO, MAKA!!
ZA (ZSH)
HIOOOO (FWOOOO)
PITA (STOP)

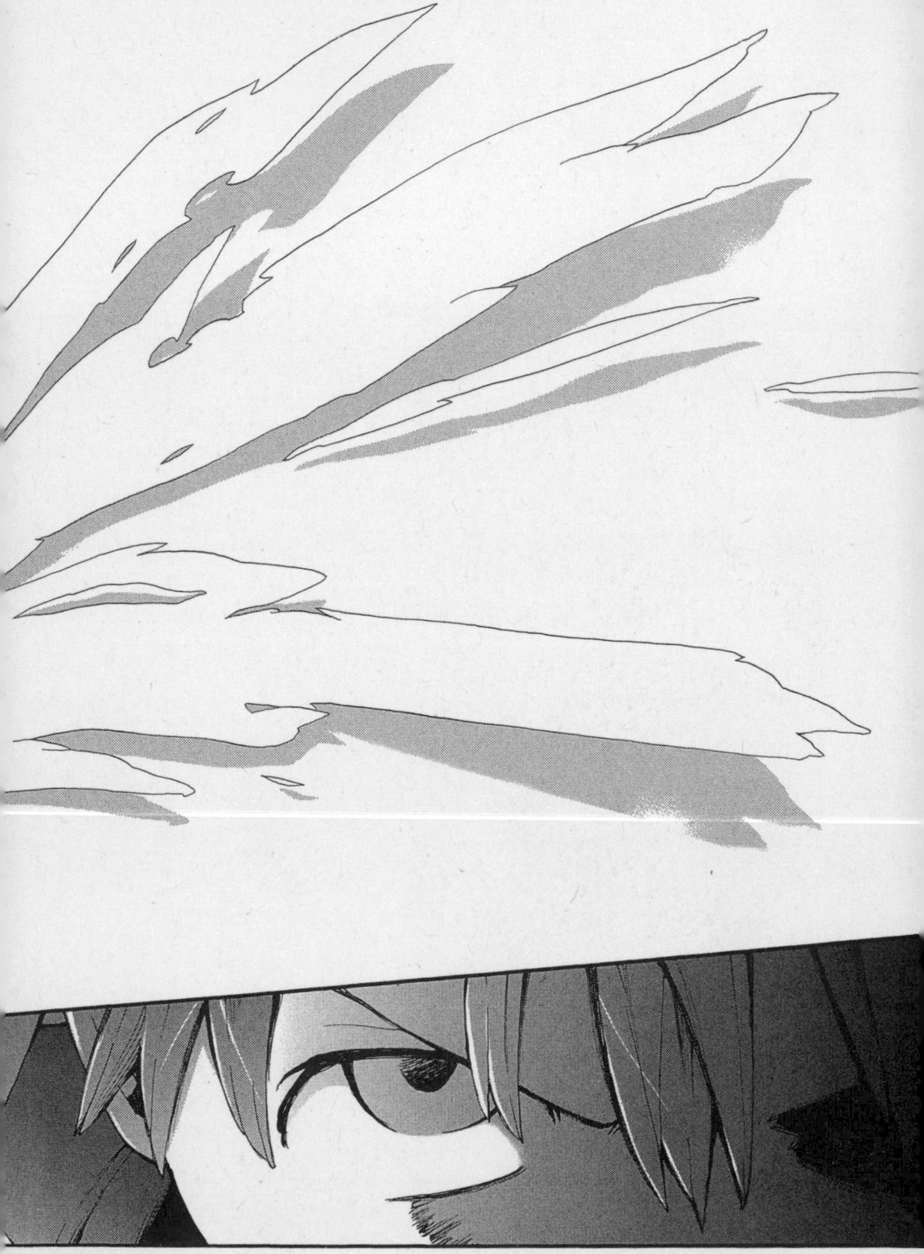

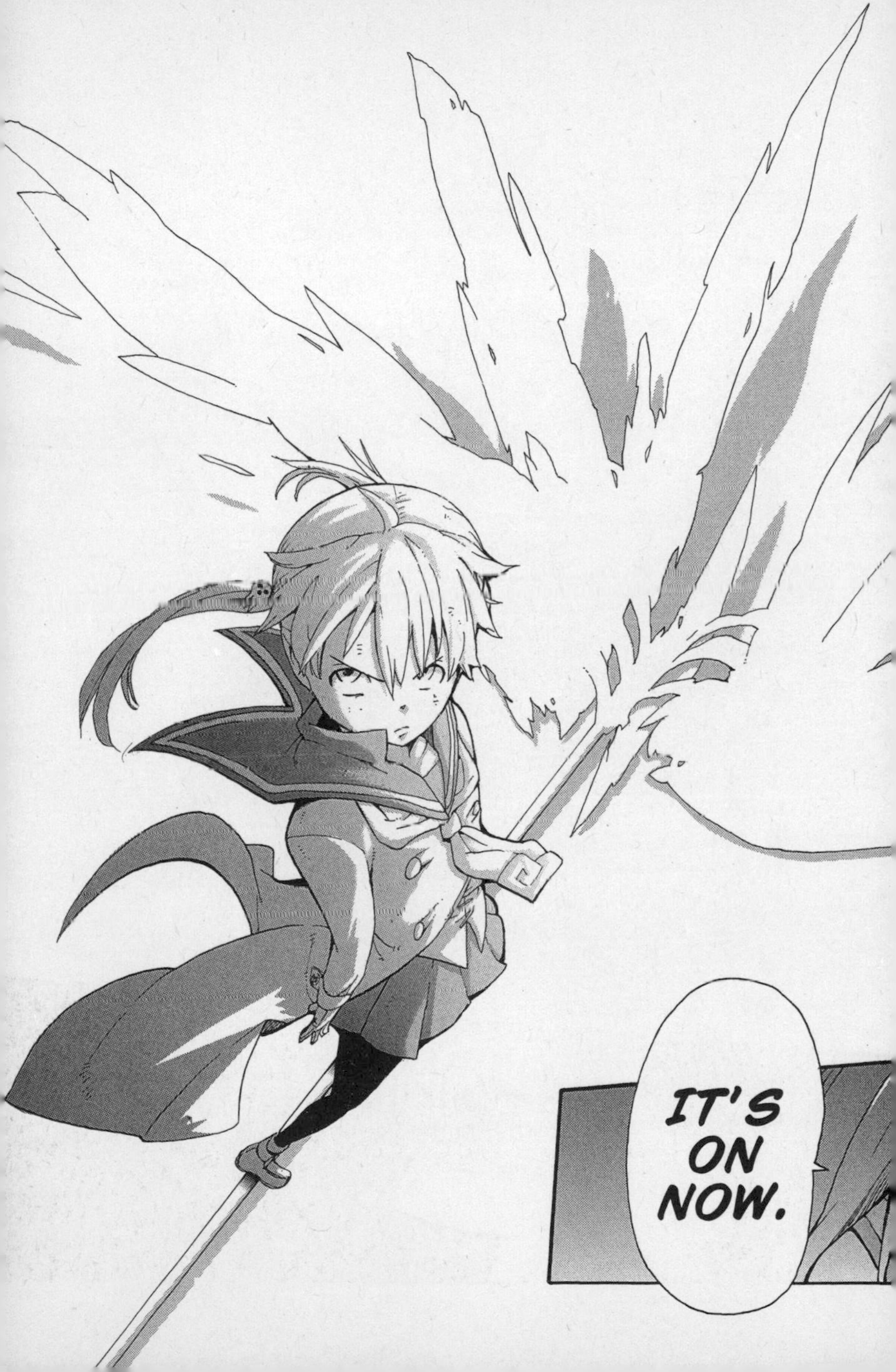
IT'S ON NOW.

SOUL EATER

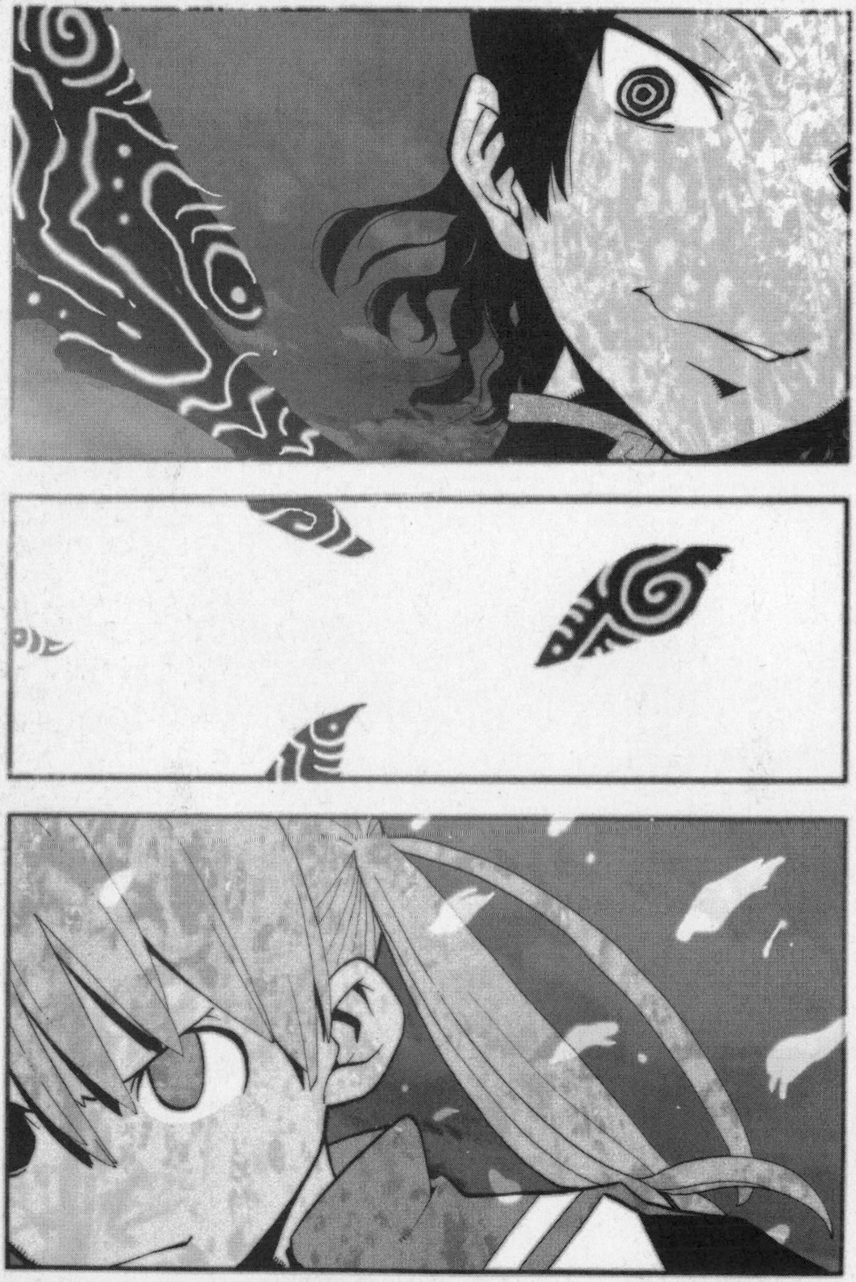

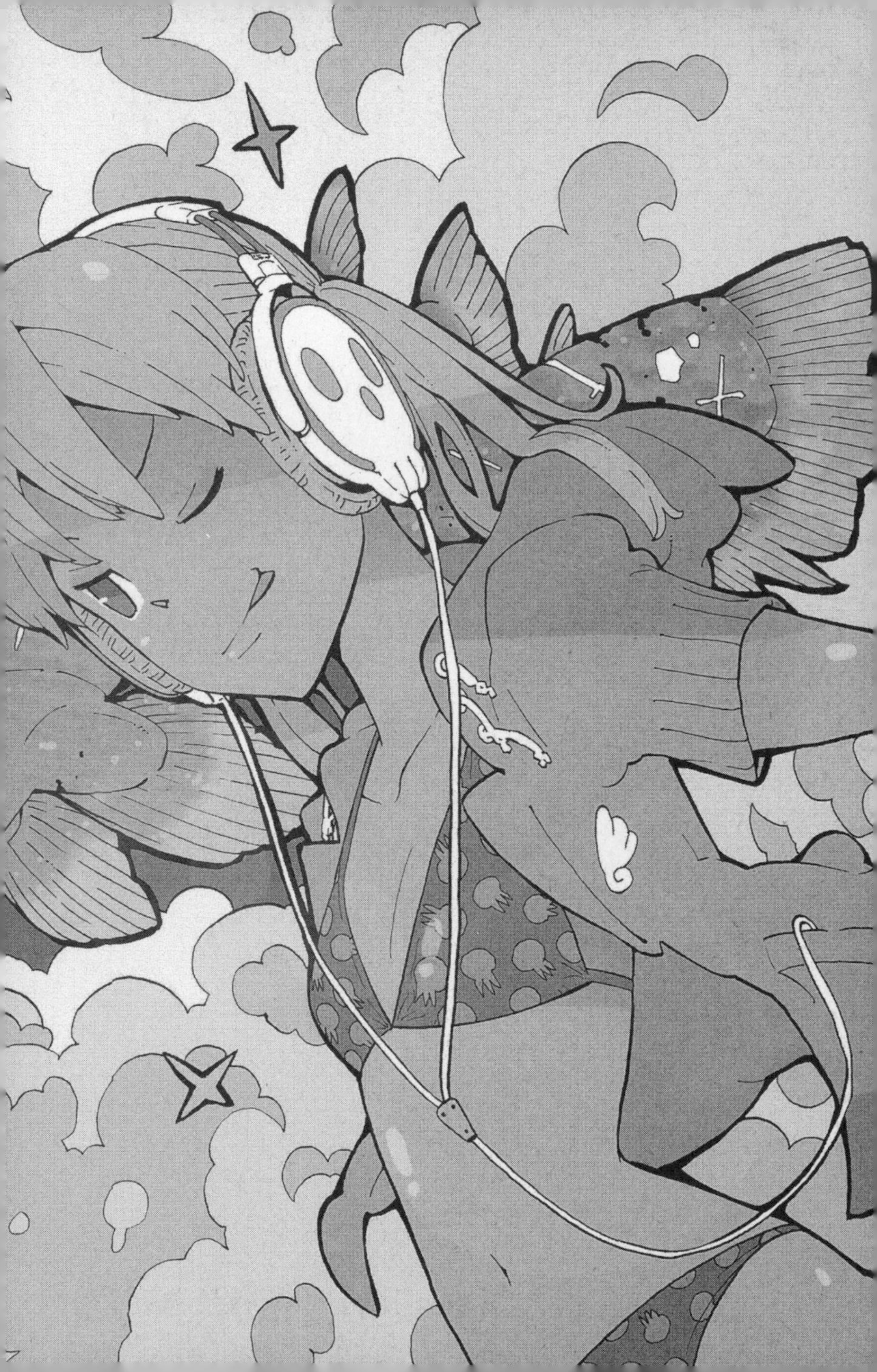

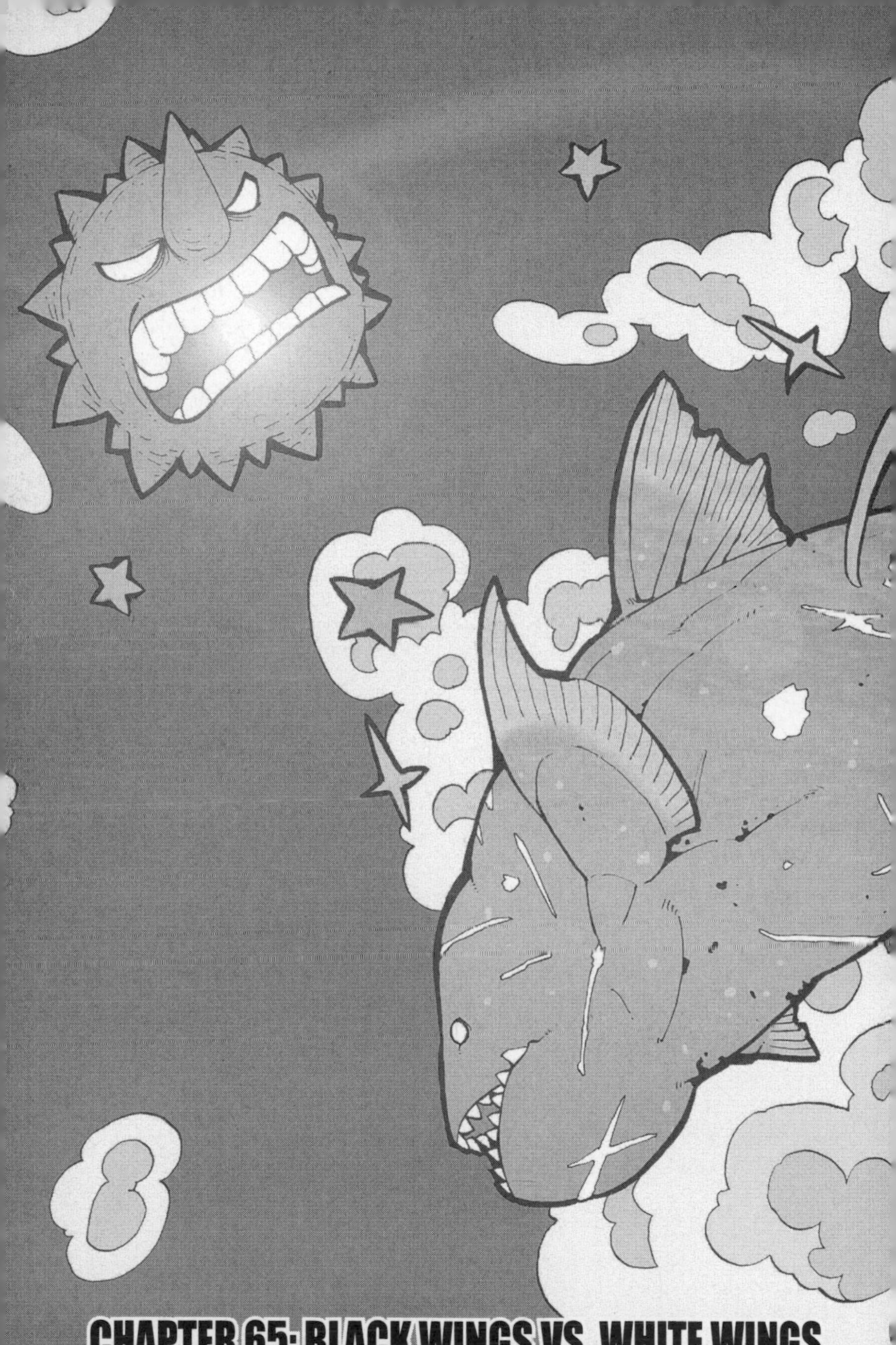

# CHAPTER 65: BLACK WINGS VS. WHITE WINGS

SOUL EATER

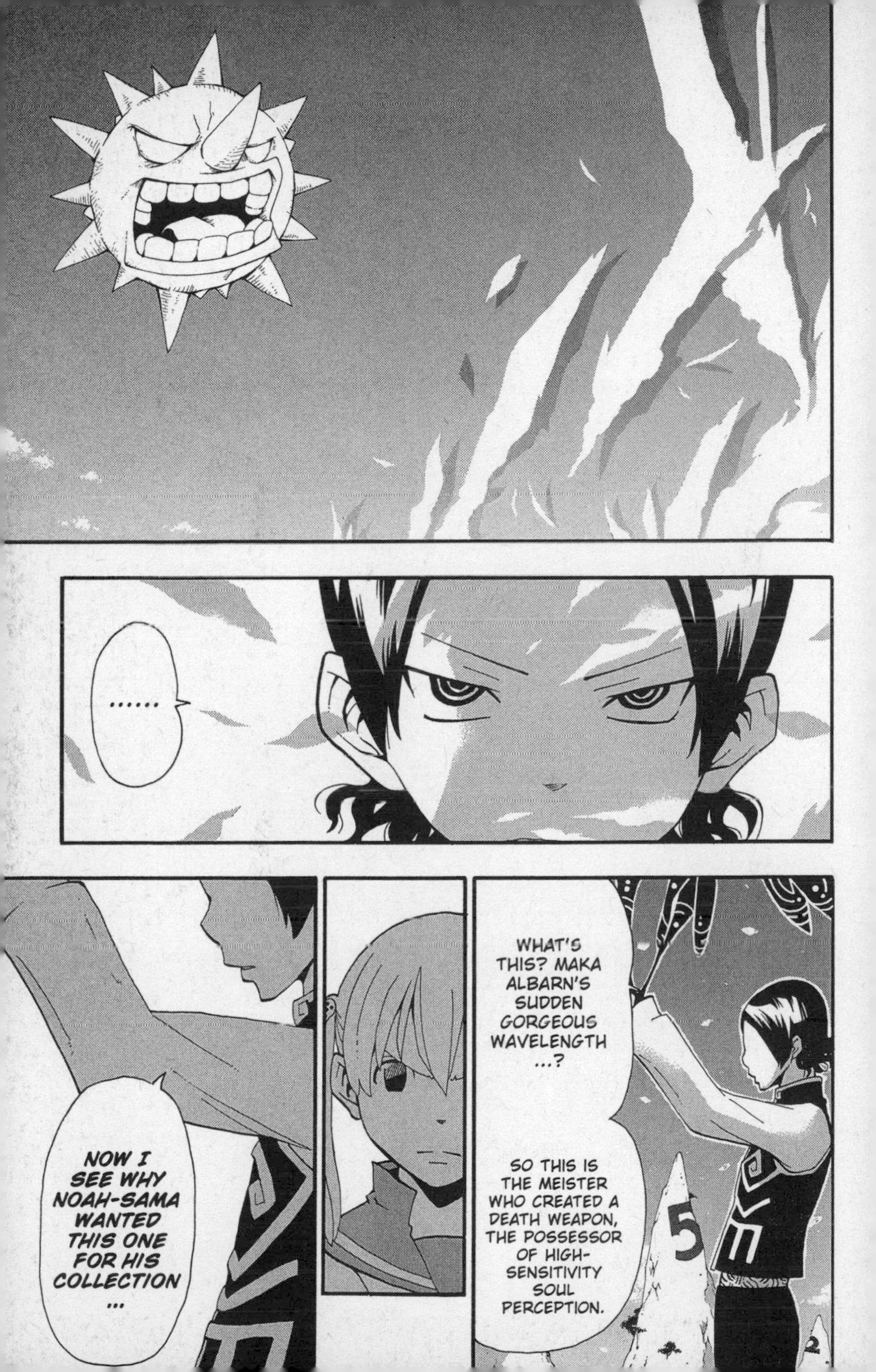
......
WHAT'S THIS? MAKA ALBARN'S SUDDEN GORGEOUS WAVELENGTH ...?
SO THIS IS THE MEISTER WHO CREATED A DEATH WEAPON, THE POSSESSOR OF HIGH-SENSITIVITY SOUL PERCEPTION.
NOW I SEE WHY NOAH-SAMA WANTED THIS ONE FOR HIS COLLECTION ...

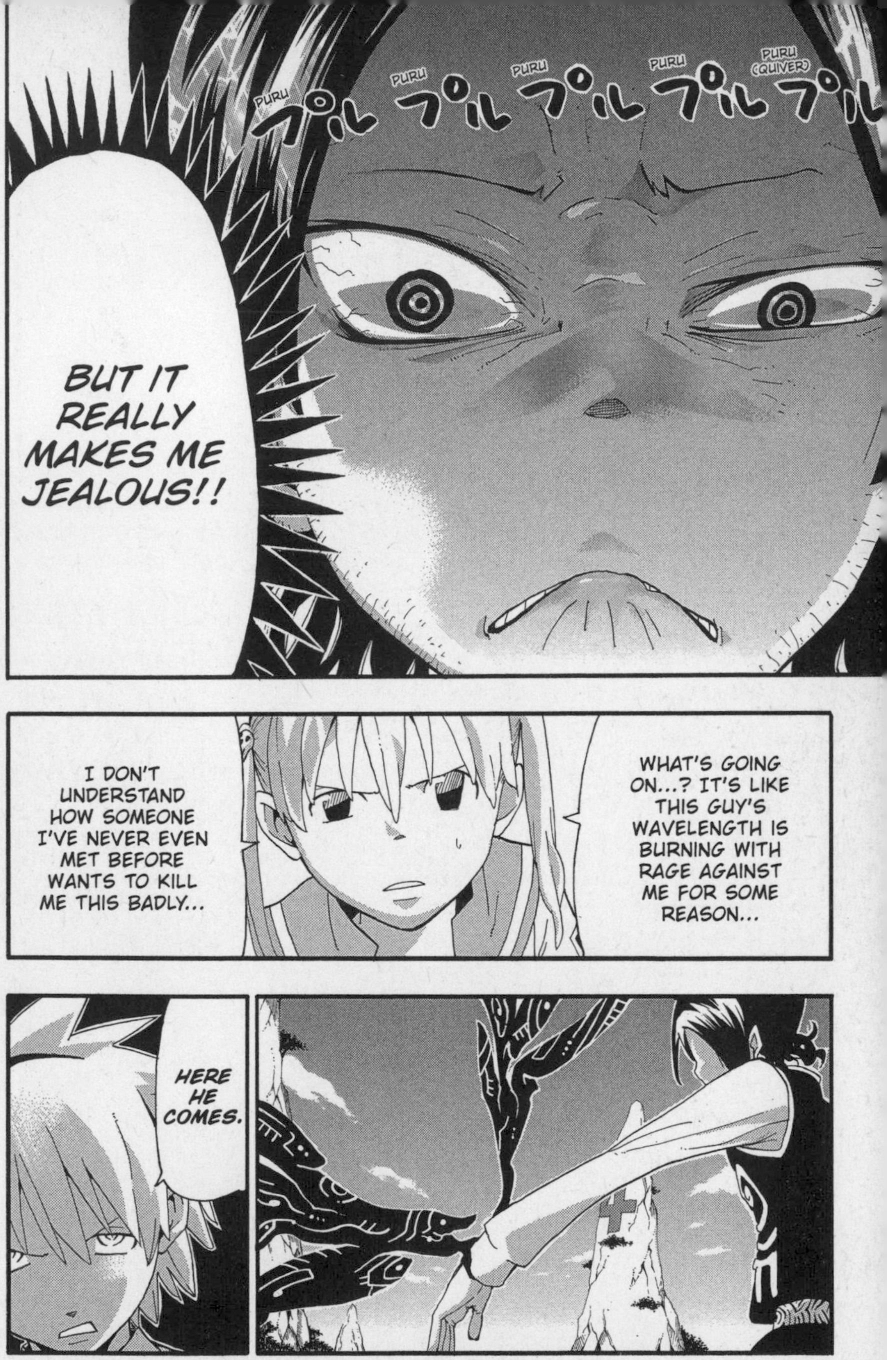

PURU PURU PURU PURU PURU (QUIVER)
BUT IT REALLY MAKES ME JEALOUS!!
WHAT'S GOING ON...? IT'S LIKE THIS GUY'S WAVELENGTH IS BURNING WITH RAGE AGAINST ME FOR SOME REASON...
I DON'T UNDERSTAND HOW SOMEONE I'VE NEVER EVEN MET BEFORE WANTS TO KILL ME THIS BADLY...
HERE HE COMES.

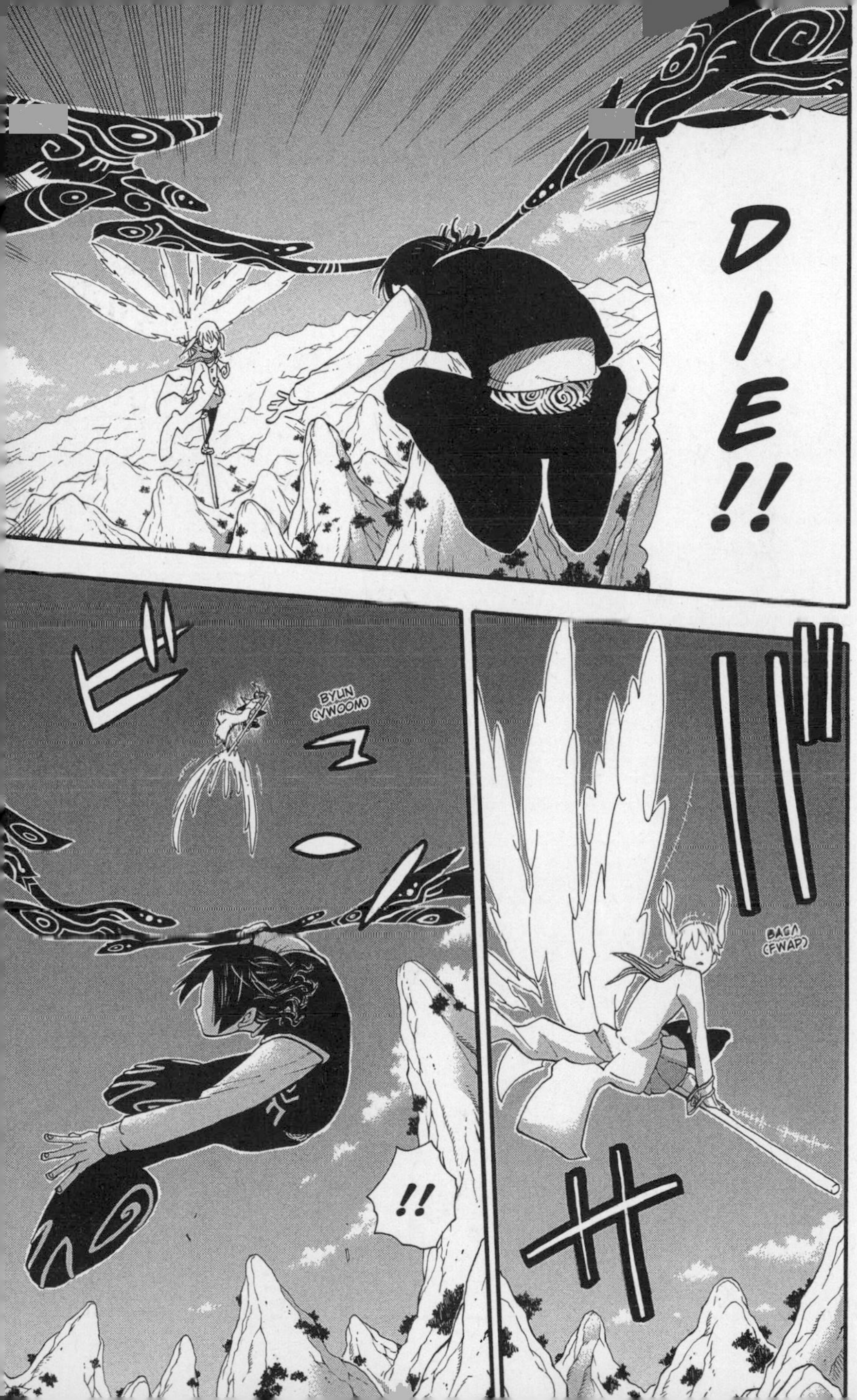
DIE!!
BASA
(FWAP)
BYUN
(VWOOM)
!!

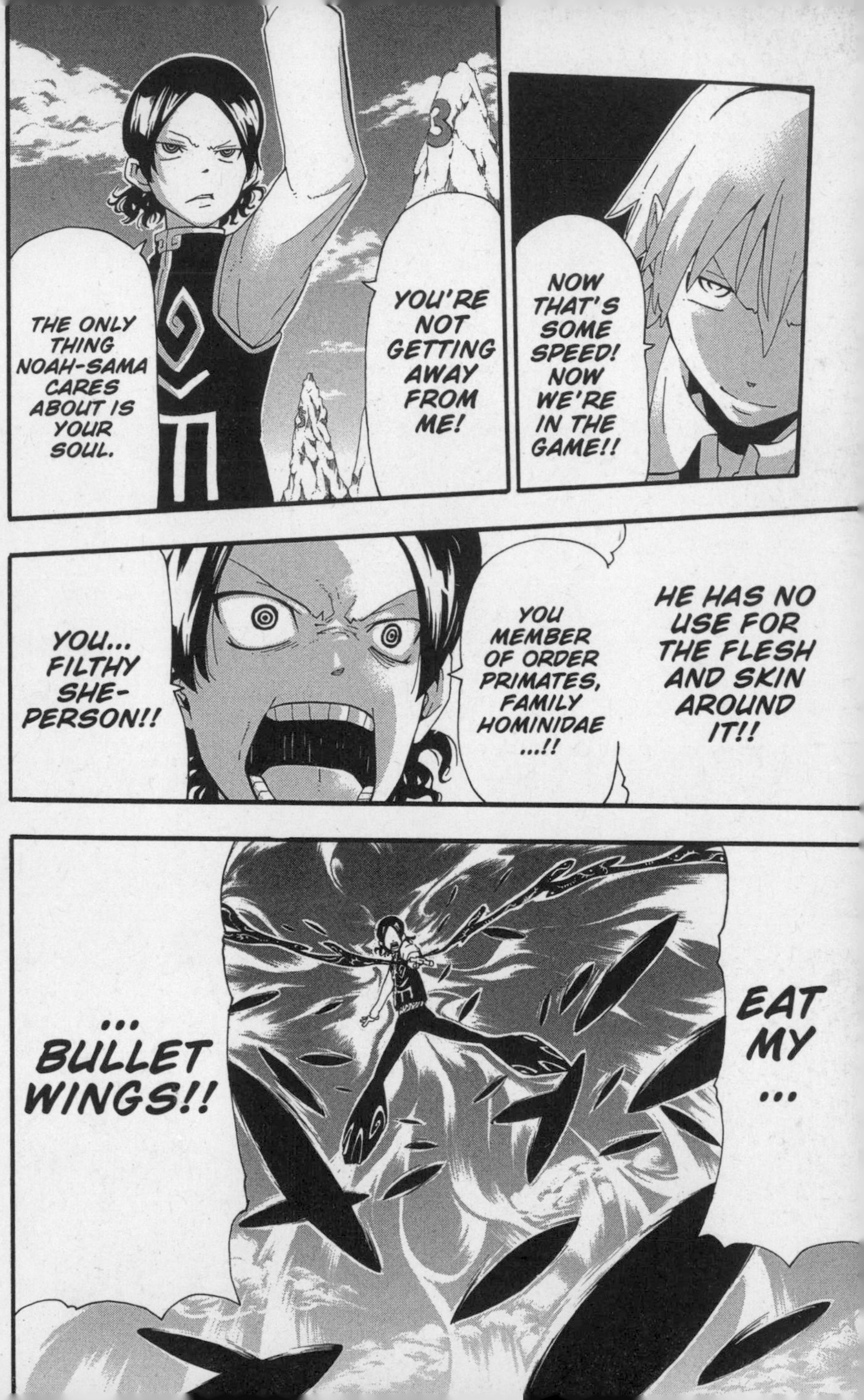
NOW THAT'S SOME SPEED! NOW WE'RE IN THE GAME!!
YOU'RE NOT GETTING AWAY FROM ME!
THE ONLY THING NOAH-SAMA CARES ABOUT IS YOUR SOUL.
HE HAS NO USE FOR THE FLESH AND SKIN AROUND IT!!
YOU MEMBER OF ORDER PRIMATES, FAMILY HOMINIDAE ...!!
YOU... FILTHY SHE-PERSON!!
EAT MY ...
... BULLET WINGS!!

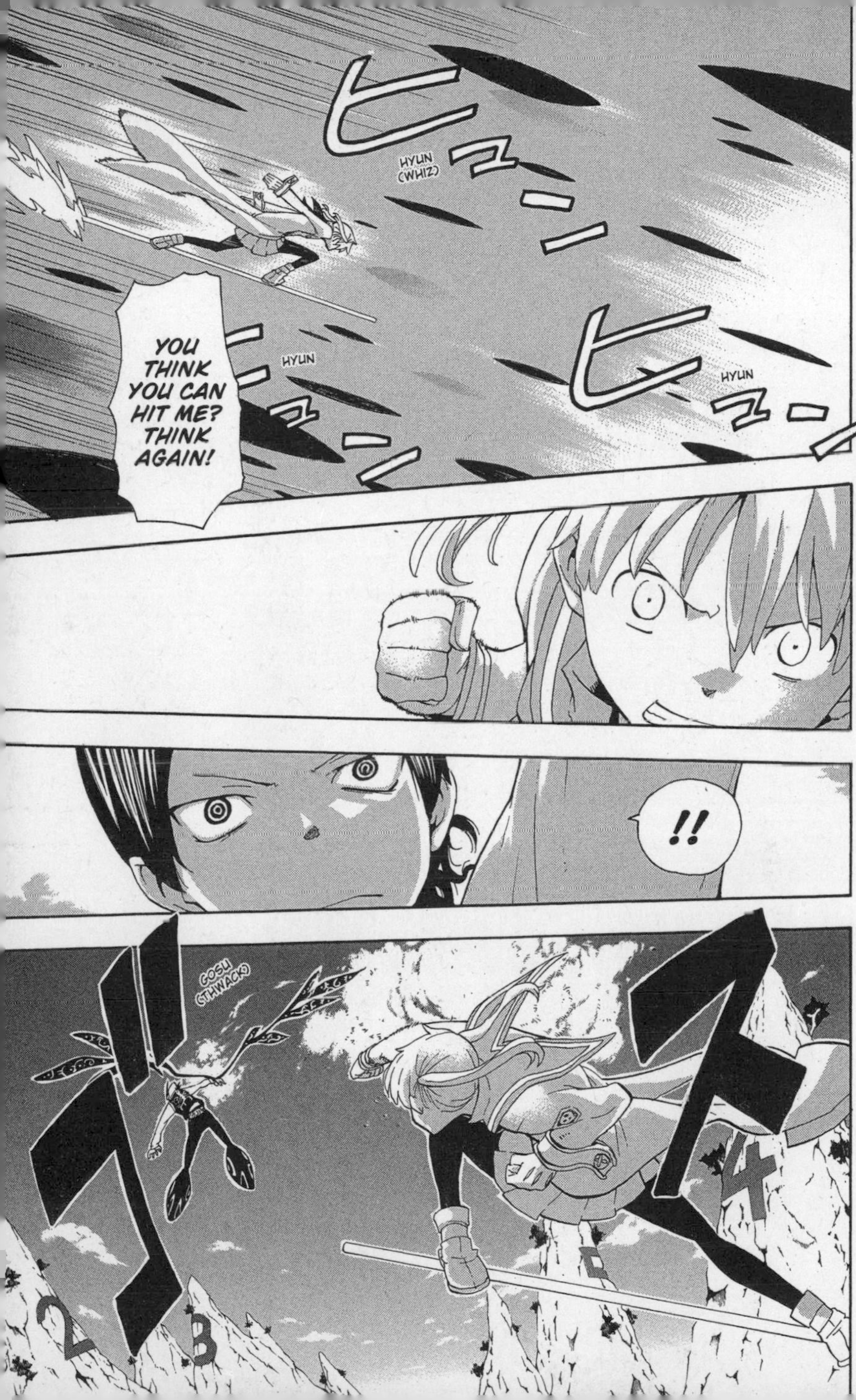
HYUN (WHIZ)
HYUN
HYUN
YOU THINK YOU CAN HIT ME? THINK AGAIN!
!!
GOSU (THWACK)

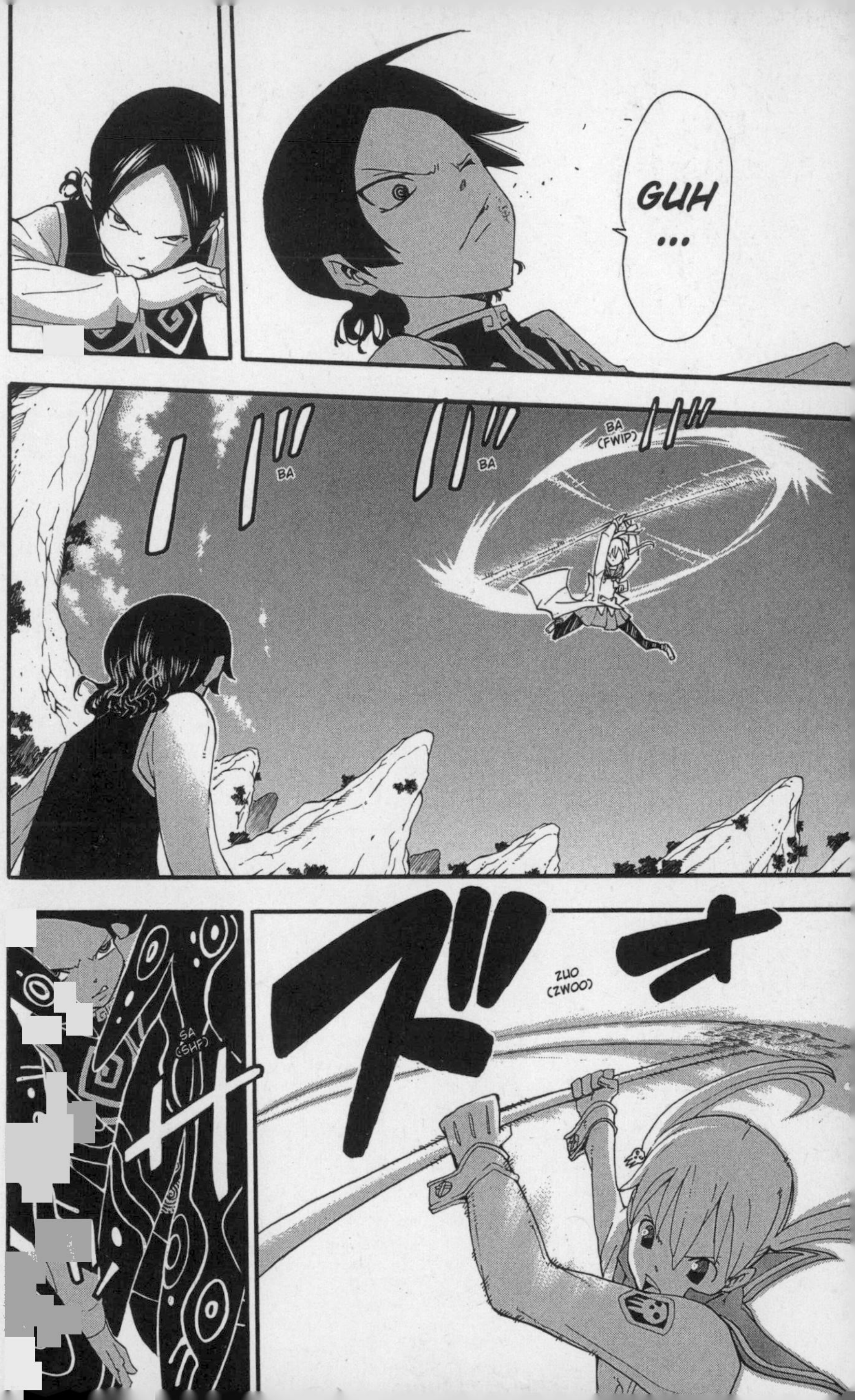
GUH ...
BA (FWIP)
BA
BA
ZUO (ZWOO)
SA (SHF)

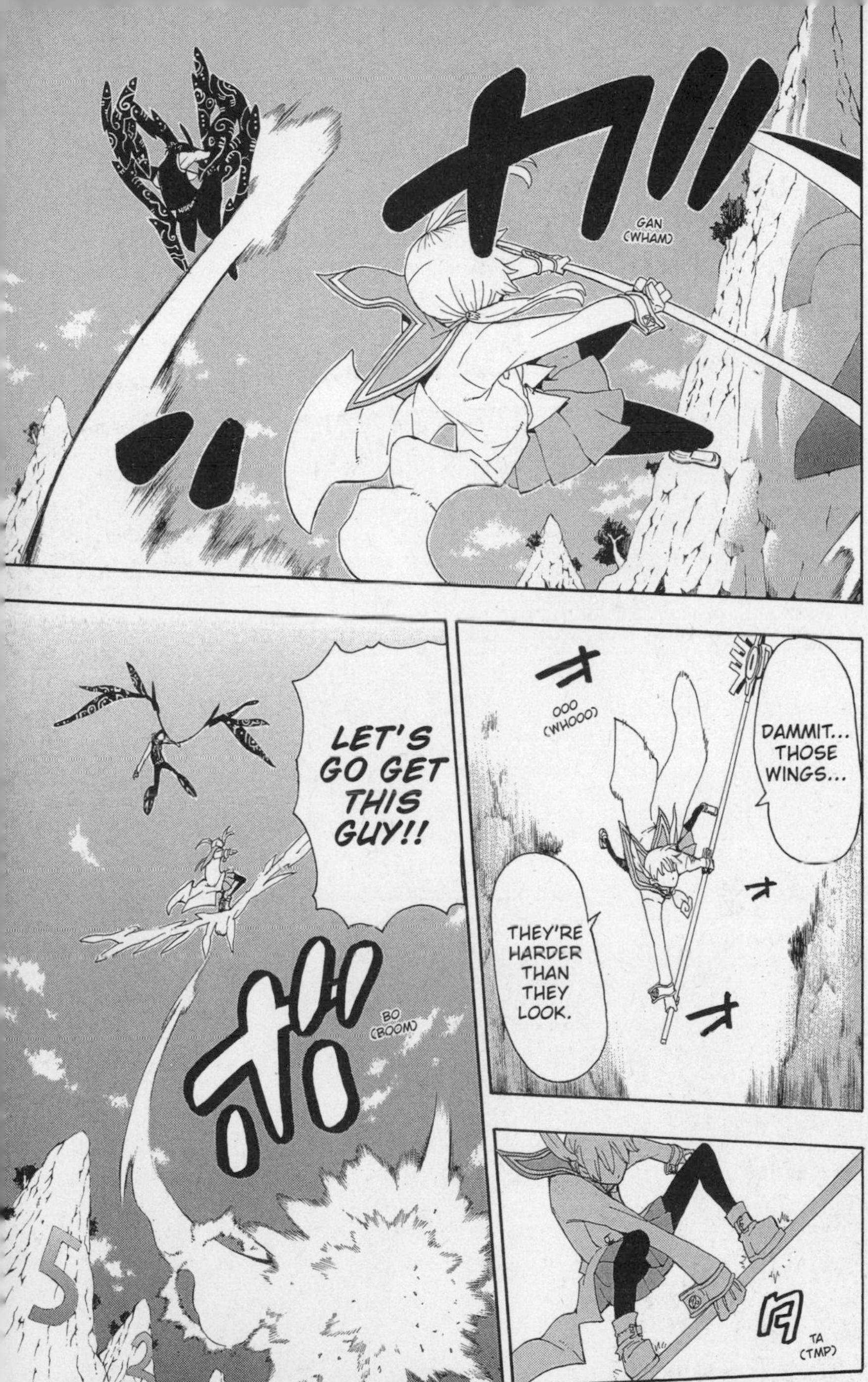
GAN (WHAM)
DAMMIT... THOSE WINGS...
OOO (WHOOO)
THEY'RE HARDER THAN THEY LOOK.
TA (TMP)
LET'S GO GET THIS GUY!!
BO (BOOM)

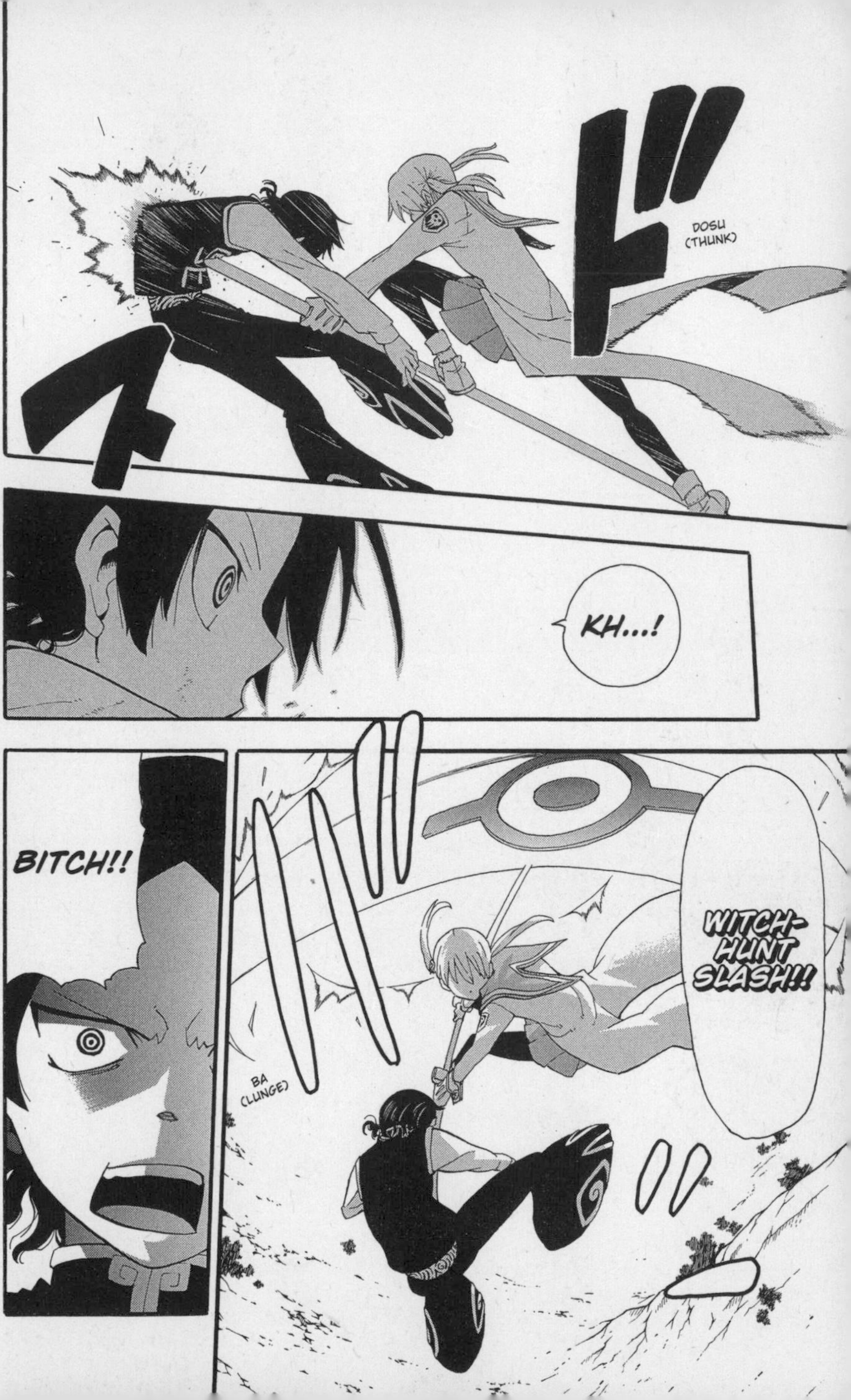
DOSU
(THUNK)
KH...!
WITCH-HUNT SLASH!!
BA
(LUNGE)
BITCH!!

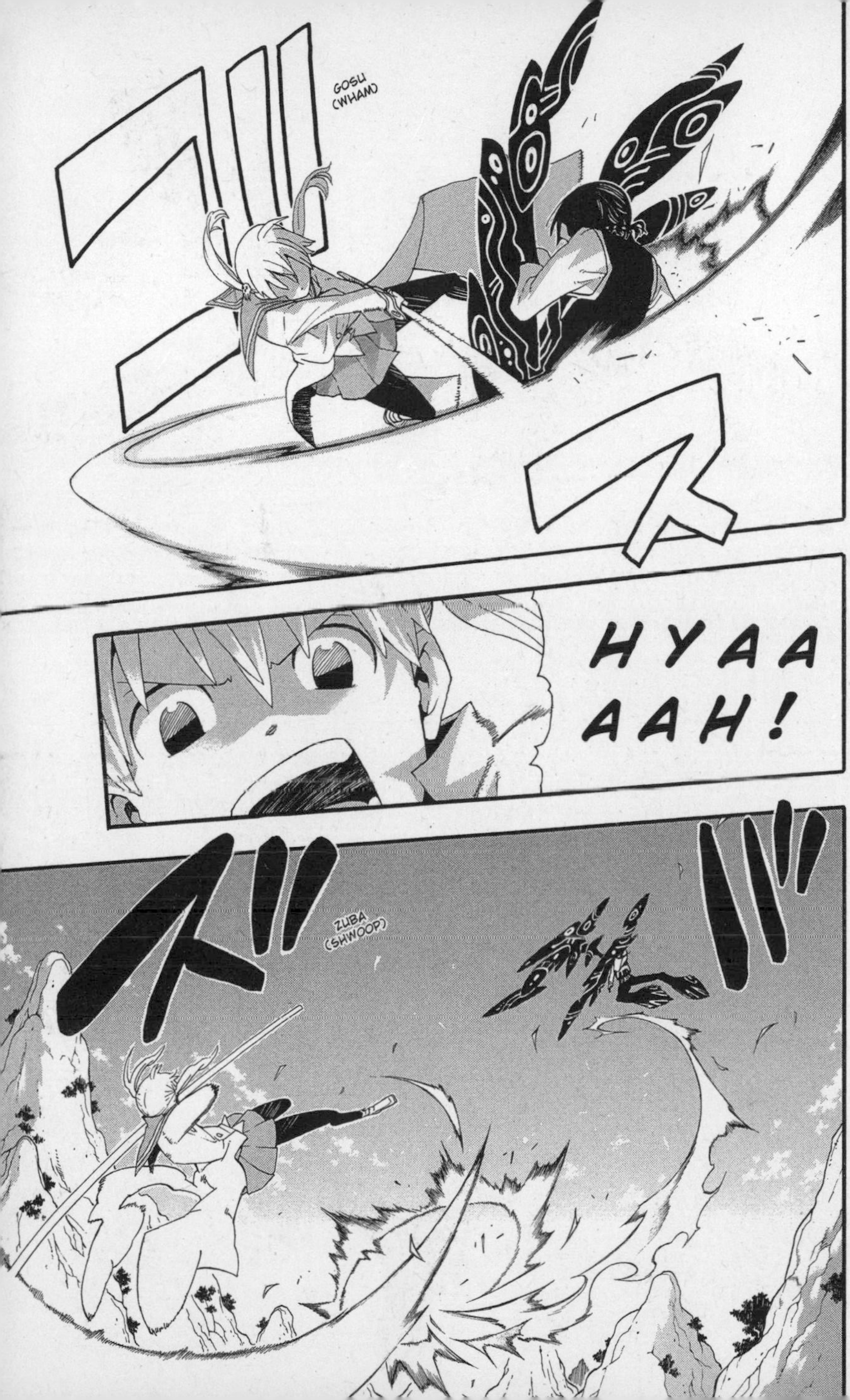
GOSU
(WHAM)
HYAA AAH!
ZUBA
(SHWOOP)

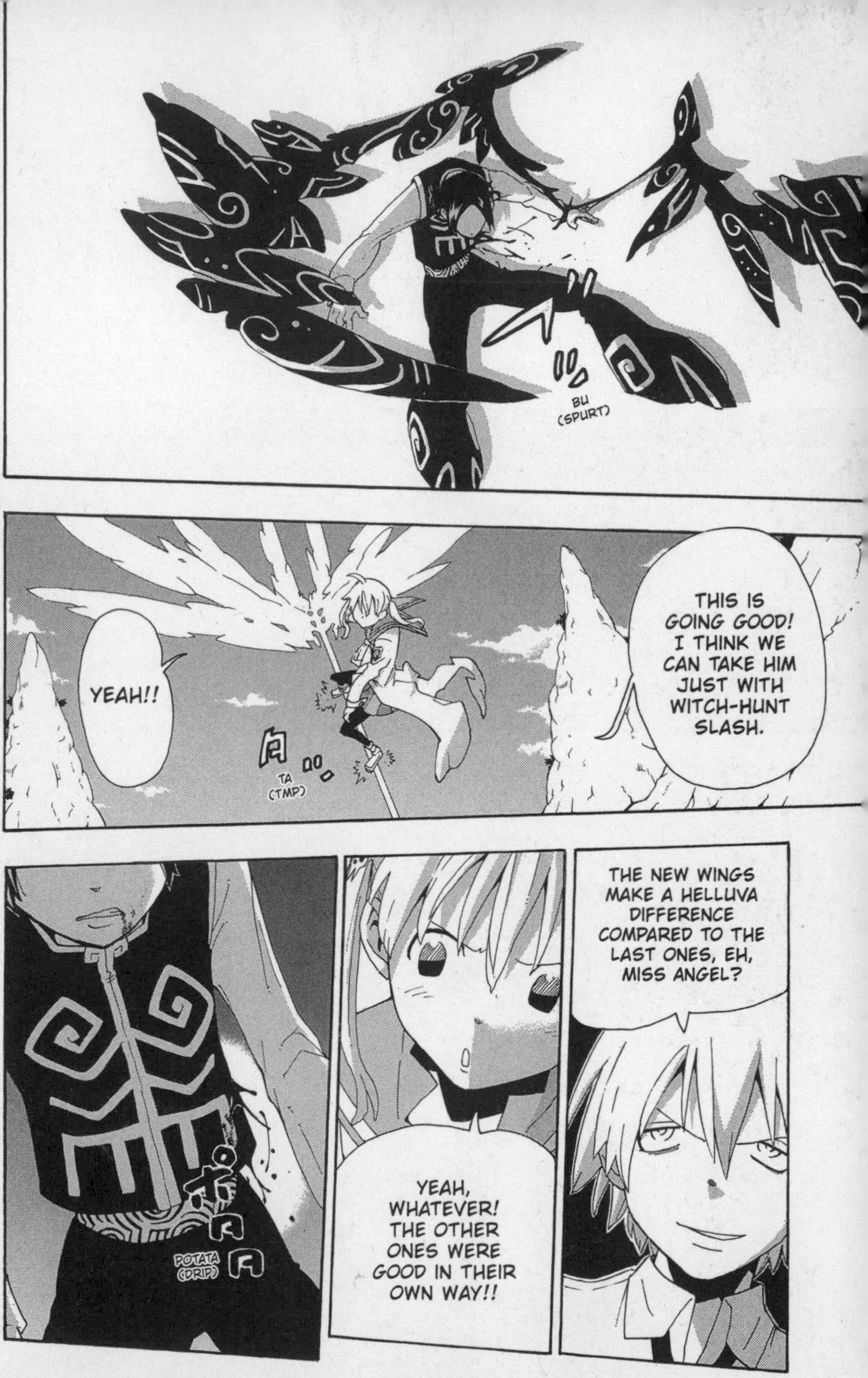
BU (SPURT)
THIS IS GOING GOOD! I THINK WE CAN TAKE HIM JUST WITH WITCH-HUNT SLASH.
YEAH!!
TA (TMP)
THE NEW WINGS MAKE A HELLUVA DIFFERENCE COMPARED TO THE LAST ONES, EH, MISS ANGEL?
YEAH, WHATEVER! THE OTHER ONES WERE GOOD IN THEIR OWN WAY!!
POTATA (DRIP)

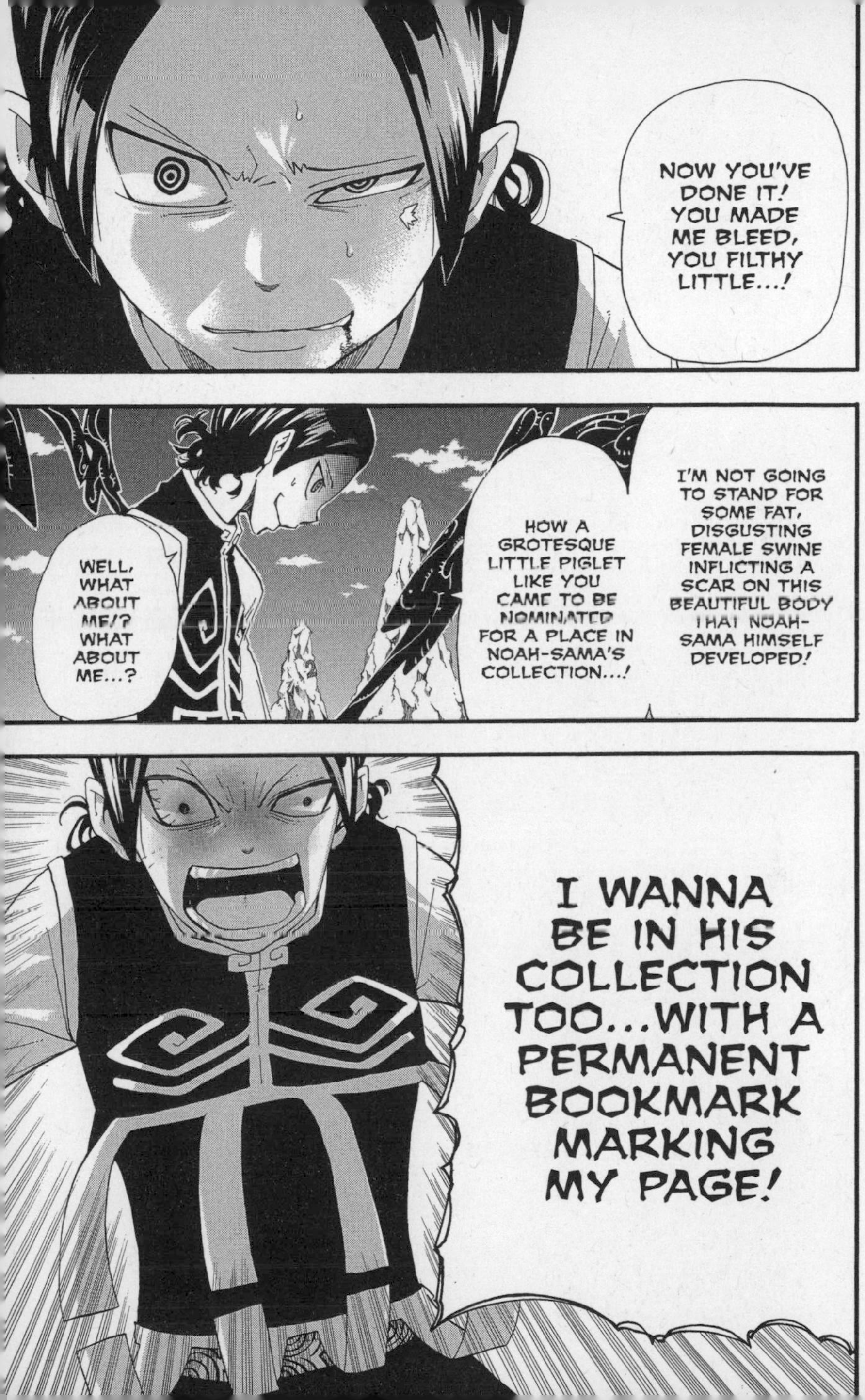
NOW YOU'VE DONE IT! YOU MADE ME BLEED, YOU FILTHY LITTLE...!
I'M NOT GOING TO STAND FOR SOME FAT, DISGUSTING FEMALE SWINE INFLICTING A SCAR ON THIS BEAUTIFUL BODY THAT NOAH-SAMA HIMSELF DEVELOPED!
HOW A GROTESQUE LITTLE PIGLET LIKE YOU CAME TO BE NOMINATED FOR A PLACE IN NOAH-SAMA'S COLLECTION...!
WELL, WHAT ABOUT ME!? WHAT ABOUT ME...?
I WANNA BE IN HIS COLLECTION TOO...WITH A PERMANENT BOOKMARK MARKING MY PAGE!

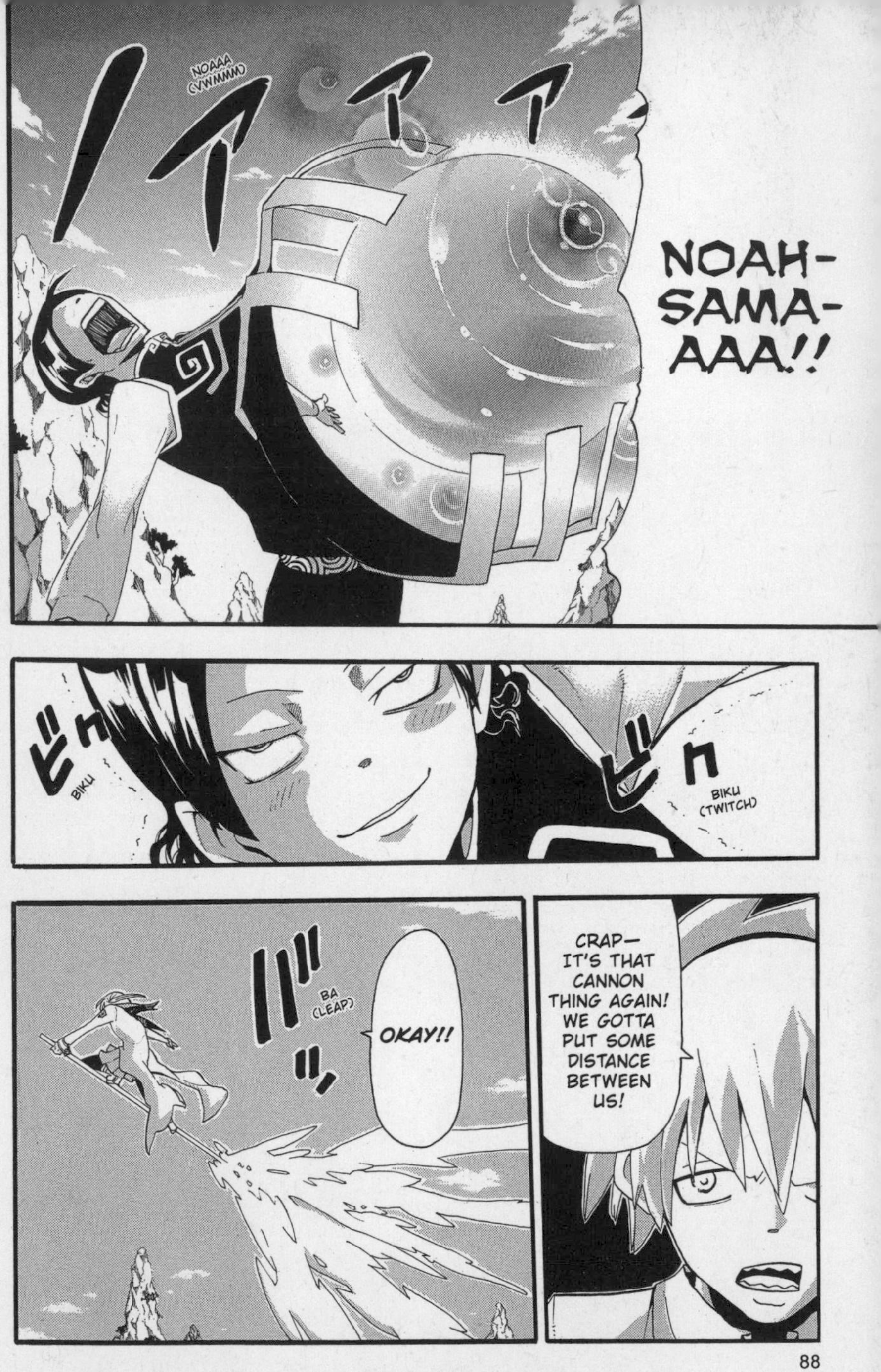
NOAAA (VWMMM)
NOAH-SAMA-AAA!!
BIKU (TWITCH)
BIKU
CRAP— IT'S THAT CANNON THING AGAIN! WE GOTTA PUT SOME DISTANCE BETWEEN US!
OKAY!!
BA (LEAP)

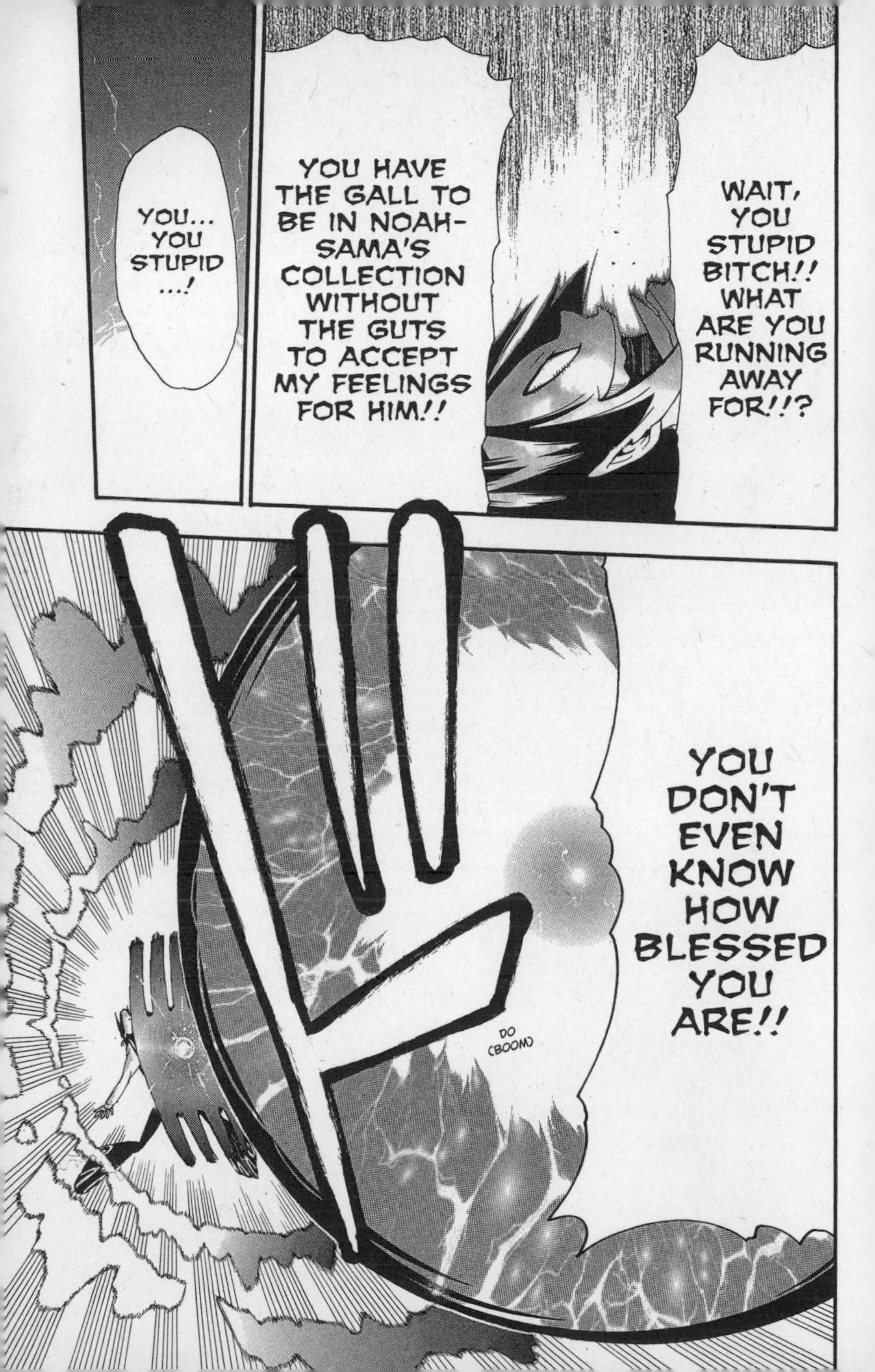
WAIT, YOU STUPID BITCH!! WHAT ARE YOU RUNNING AWAY FOR!!?
YOU HAVE THE GALL TO BE IN NOAH-SAMA'S COLLECTION WITHOUT THE GUTS TO ACCEPT MY FEELINGS FOR HIM!!
YOU... YOU STUPID ...!
YOU DON'T EVEN KNOW HOW BLESSED YOU ARE!!
DO (BOOM)

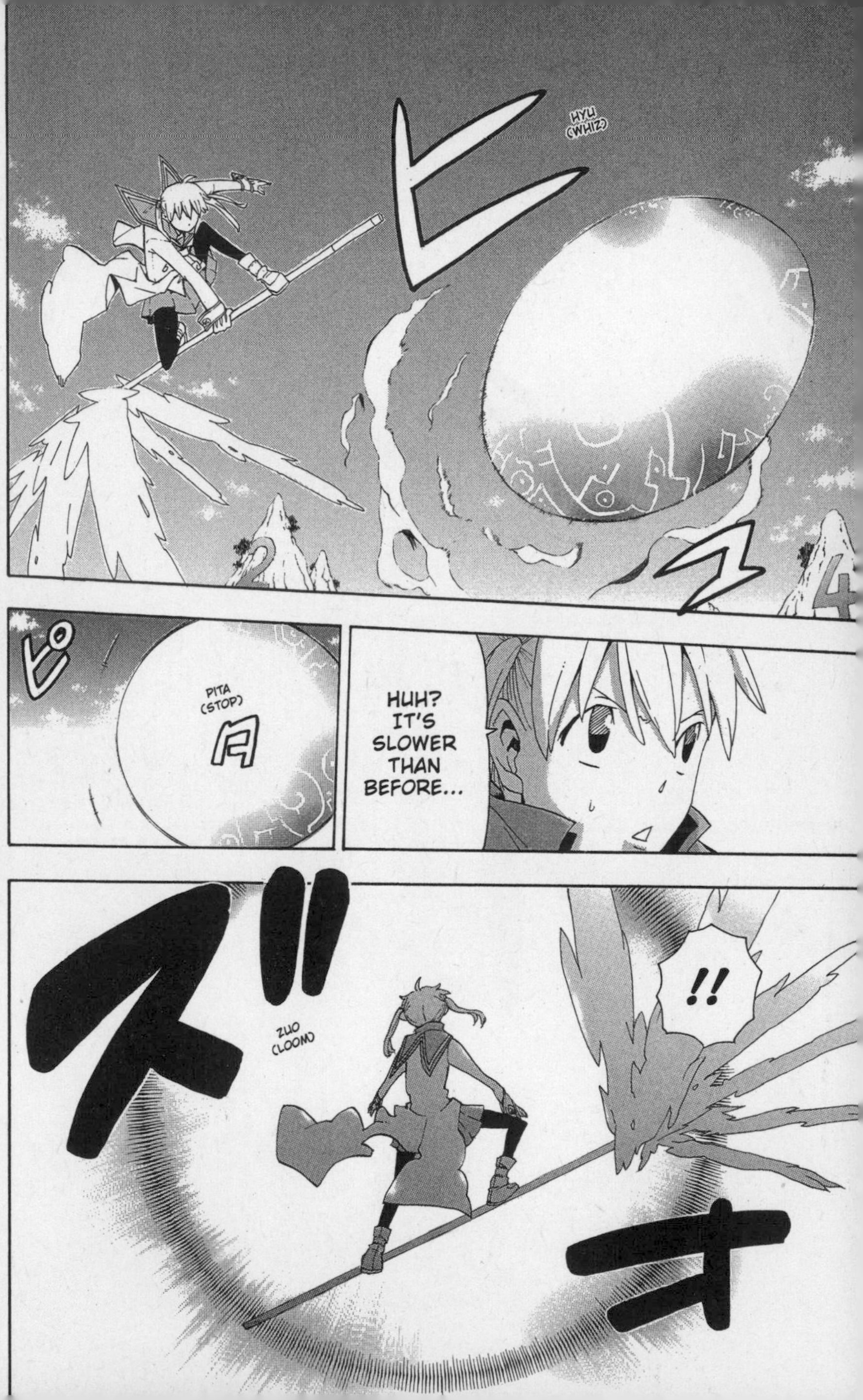
ヒ
HYU (WHIZ)
ュ
HUH? IT'S SLOWER THAN BEFORE...
ピ
PITA (STOP)
タ
!!
ズ
ZUO (LOOM)
オ

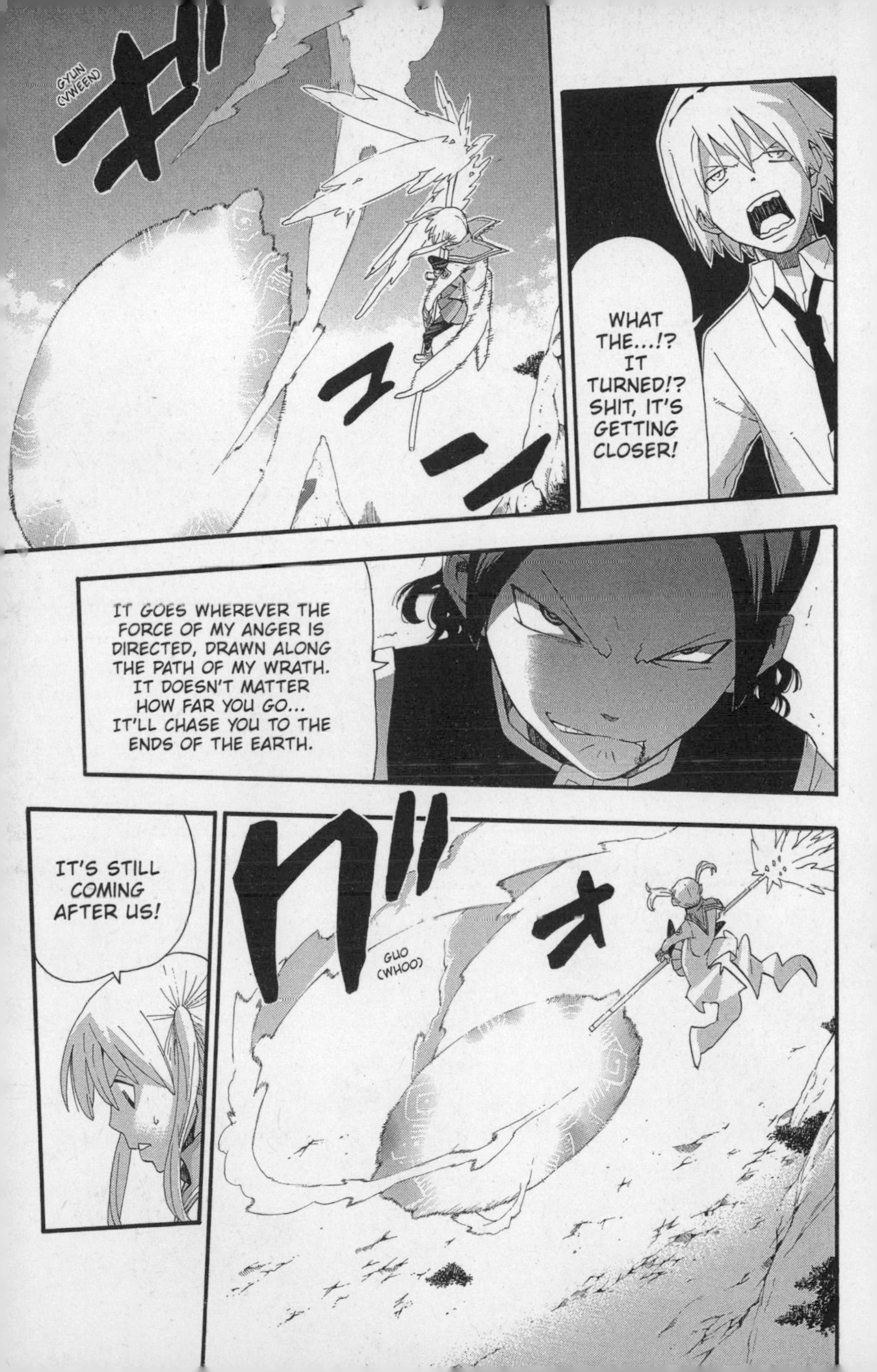
WHAT THE...!? IT TURNED!? SHIT, IT'S GETTING CLOSER!
GYLIN (VWEEN)
IT GOES WHEREVER THE FORCE OF MY ANGER IS DIRECTED, DRAWN ALONG THE PATH OF MY WRATH. IT DOESN'T MATTER HOW FAR YOU GO... IT'LL CHASE YOU TO THE ENDS OF THE EARTH.
GUO (WHOO)
IT'S STILL COMING AFTER US!

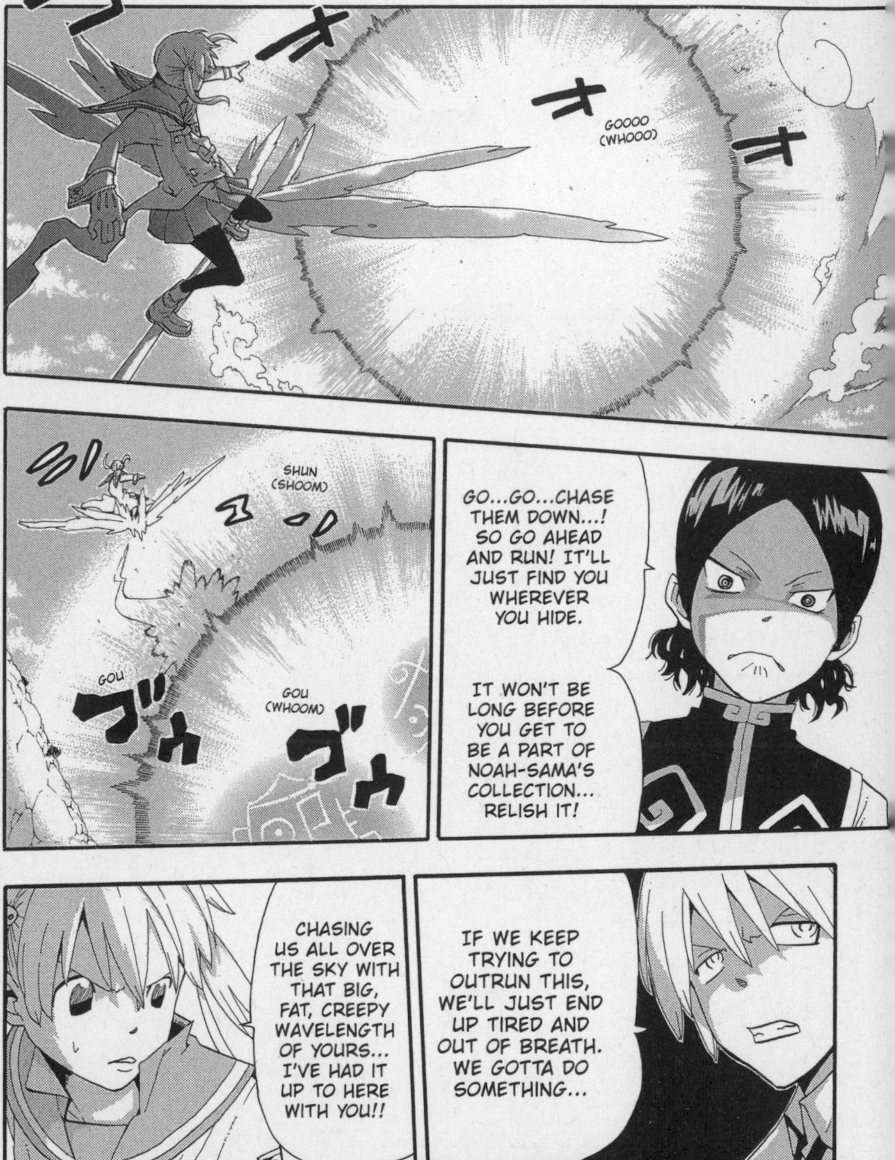
GOOOO (WHOOO)
GO...GO...CHASE THEM DOWN...! SO GO AHEAD AND RUN! IT'LL JUST FIND YOU WHEREVER YOU HIDE.
IT WON'T BE LONG BEFORE YOU GET TO BE A PART OF NOAH-SAMA'S COLLECTION... RELISH IT!
SHUN (SHOOM)
GOU (WHOOM)
GOU
IF WE KEEP TRYING TO OUTRUN THIS, WE'LL JUST END UP TIRED AND OUT OF BREATH. WE GOTTA DO SOMETHING...
CHASING US ALL OVER THE SKY WITH THAT BIG, FAT, CREEPY WAVELENGTH OF YOURS... I'VE HAD IT UP TO HERE WITH YOU!!

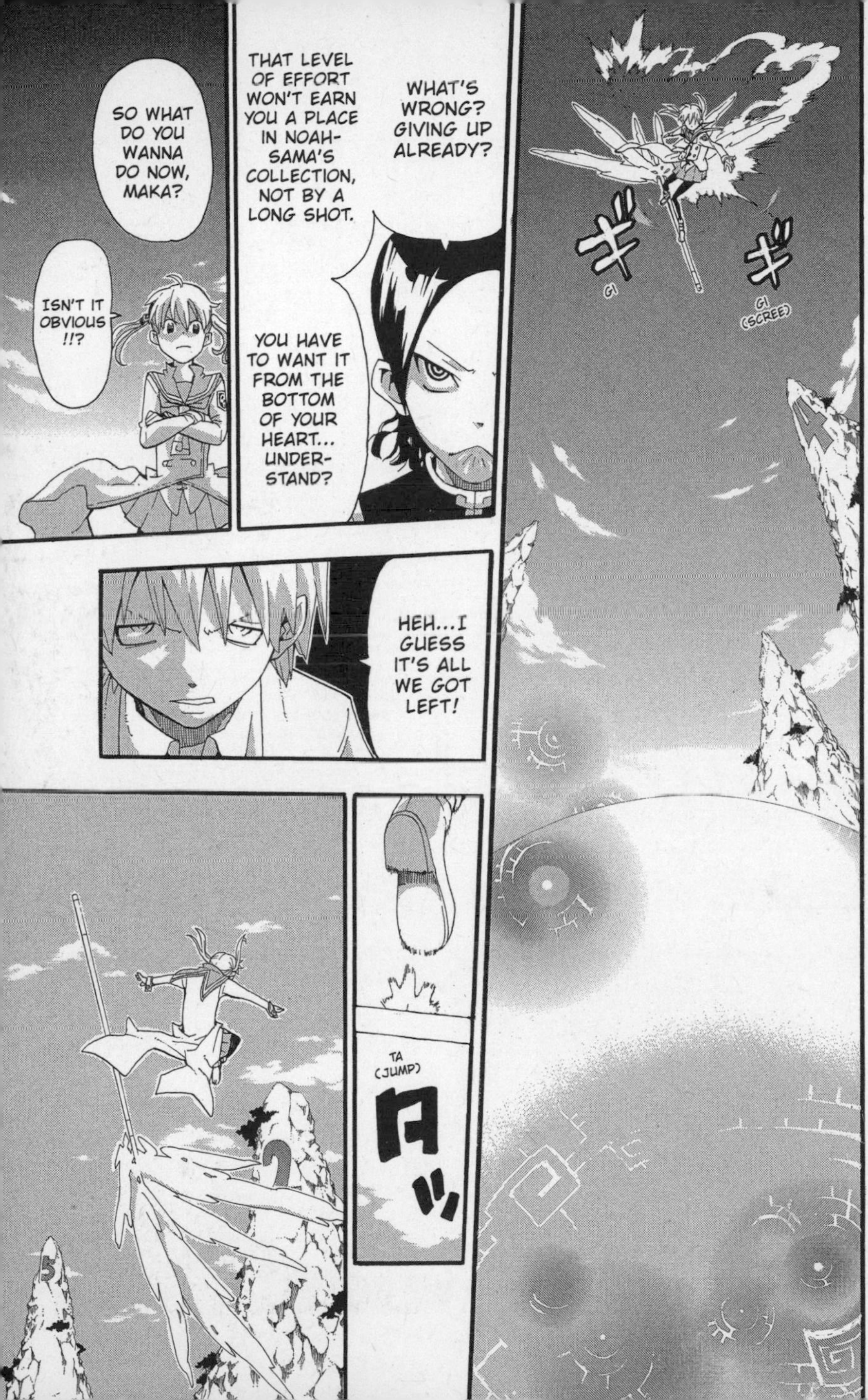
GI
GI (SCREE)
WHAT'S WRONG? GIVING UP ALREADY?
THAT LEVEL OF EFFORT WON'T EARN YOU A PLACE IN NOAH-SAMA'S COLLECTION, NOT BY A LONG SHOT.
YOU HAVE TO WANT IT FROM THE BOTTOM OF YOUR HEART... UNDER-STAND?
SO WHAT DO YOU WANNA DO NOW, MAKA?
ISN'T IT OBVIOUS !!?
HEH...I GUESS IT'S ALL WE GOT LEFT!
TA (JUMP)

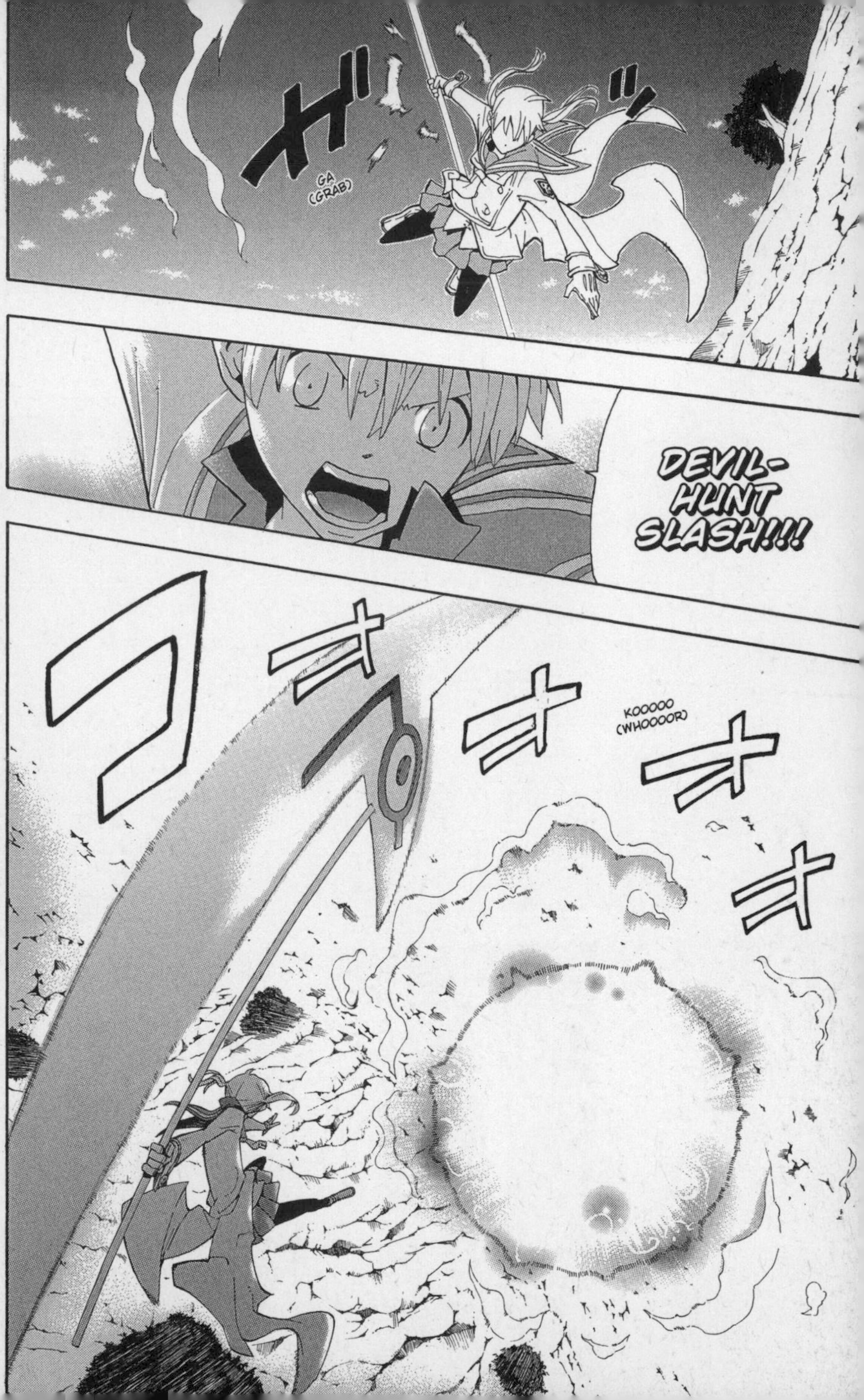
GA
(GRAB)
DEVIL-HUNT SLASH!!!
KOOOOO
(WHOOOOR)

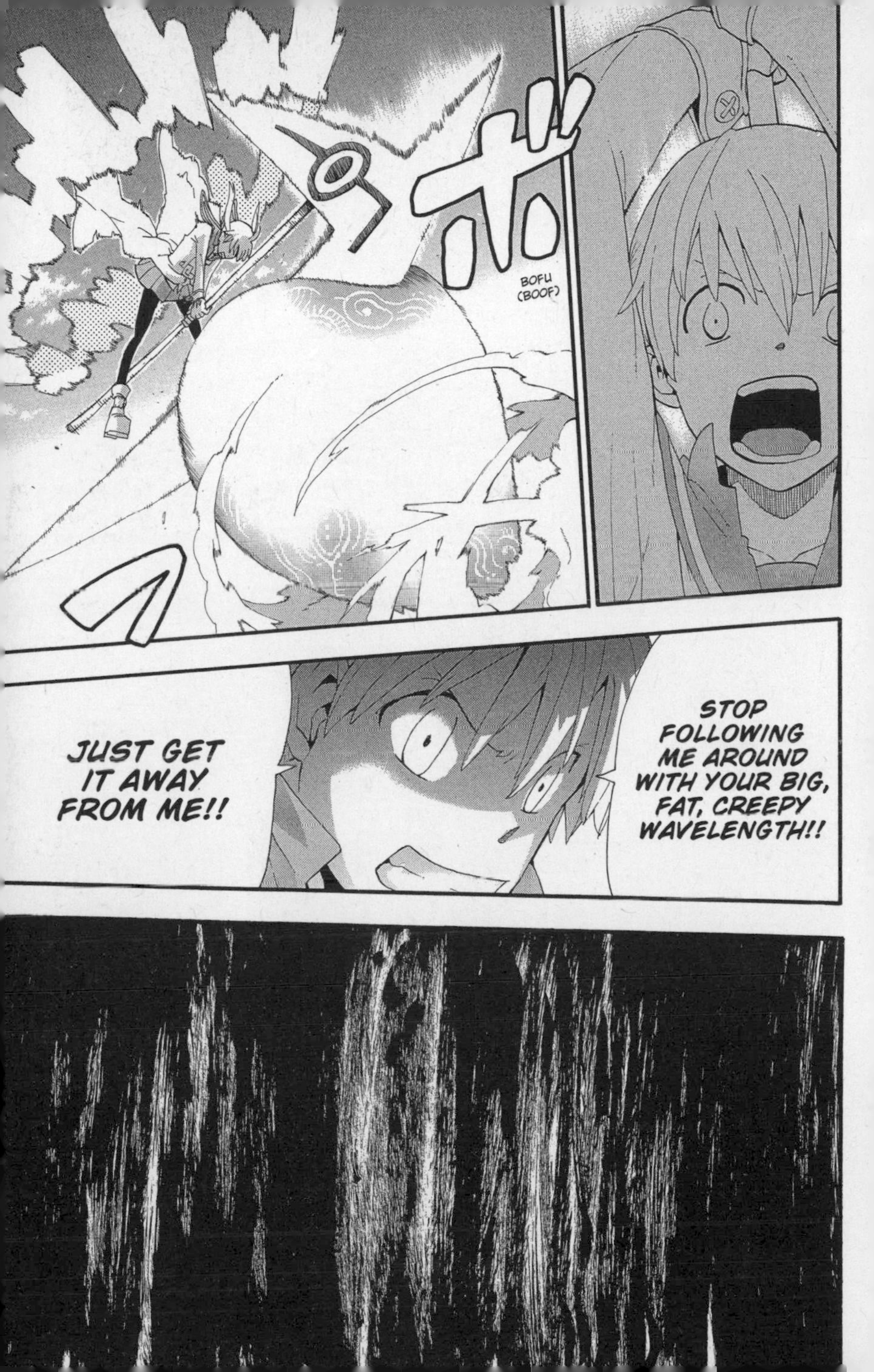
BOFU (BOOF)
STOP FOLLOWING ME AROUND WITH YOUR BIG, FAT, CREEPY WAVELENGTH!!
JUST GET IT AWAY FROM ME!!

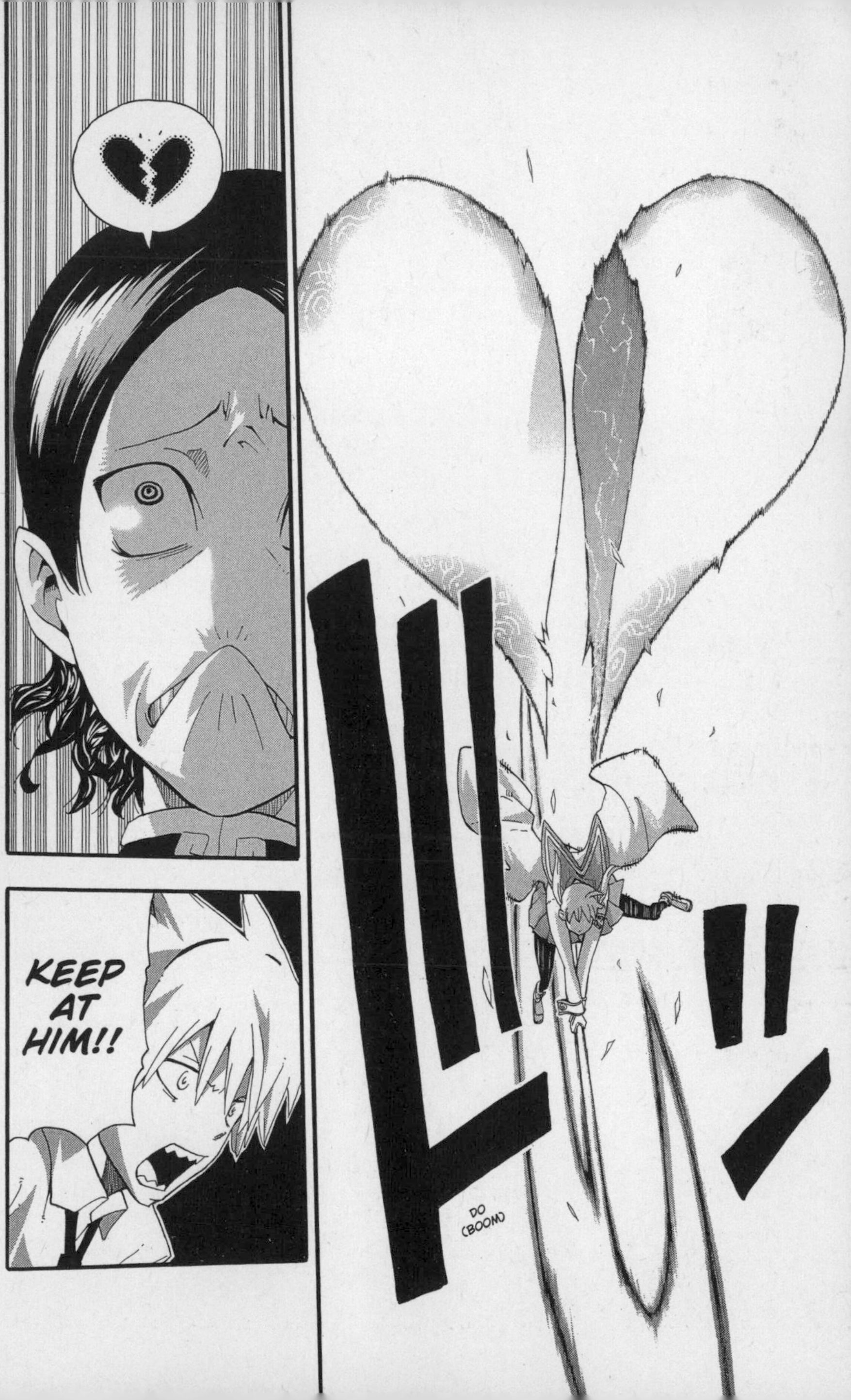
DO
(BOOM)
KEEP AT HIM!!

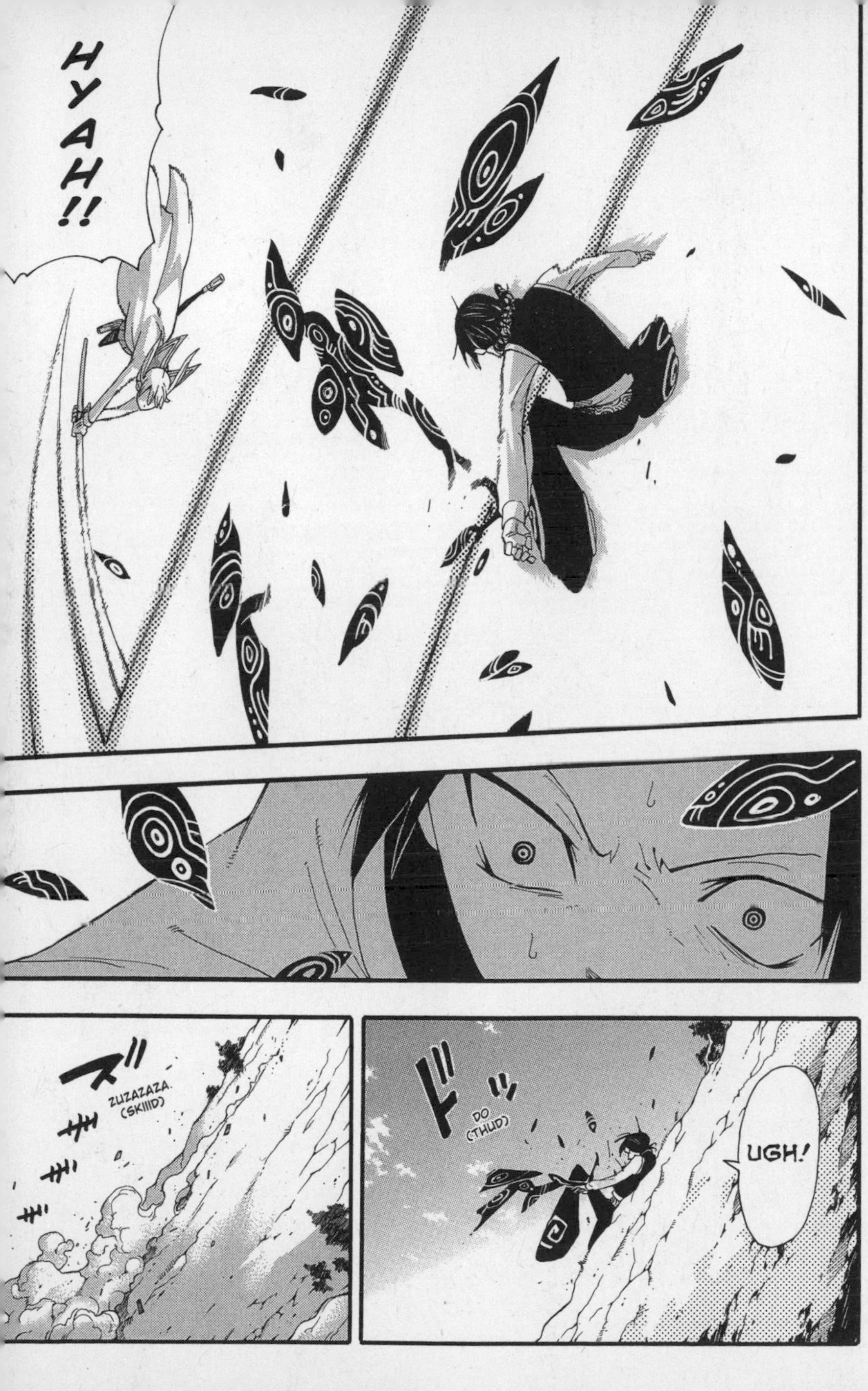
HYAH!!
DO
(THUD)
UGH!
ZUZAZAZA
(SKIIID)

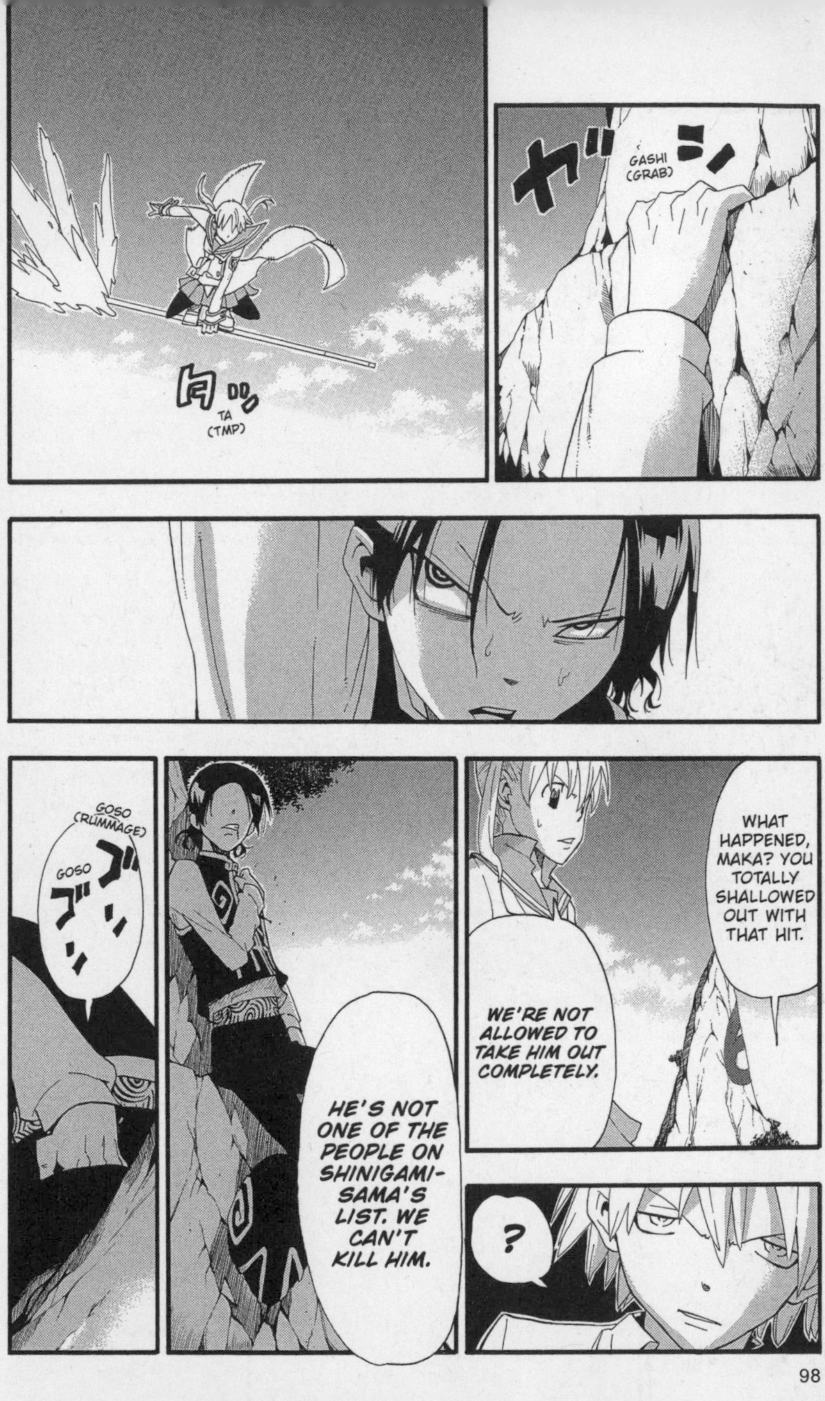
GASHI (GRAB)
TA (TMP)
WHAT HAPPENED, MAKA? YOU TOTALLY SHALLOWED OUT WITH THAT HIT.
WE'RE NOT ALLOWED TO TAKE HIM OUT COMPLETELY.
?
HE'S NOT ONE OF THE PEOPLE ON SHINIGAMI-SAMA'S LIST. WE CAN'T KILL HIM.
GOSO (RUMMAGE)
GOSO

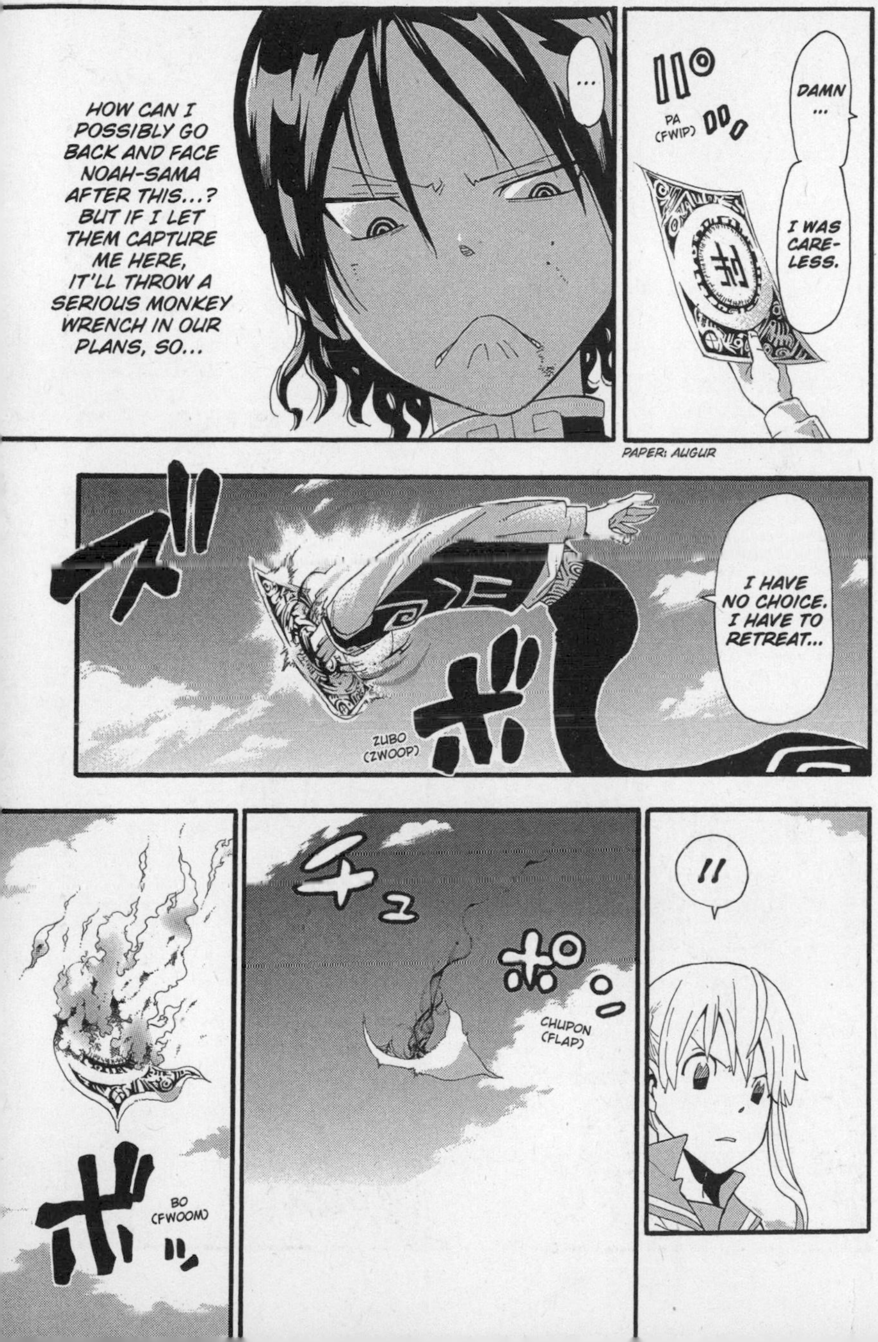
DAMN...
PA (FWIP)
I WAS CARELESS.
PAPER: AUGUR
...
HOW CAN I POSSIBLY GO BACK AND FACE NOAH-SAMA AFTER THIS...? BUT IF I LET THEM CAPTURE ME HERE, IT'LL THROW A SERIOUS MONKEY WRENCH IN OUR PLANS, SO...
I HAVE NO CHOICE. I HAVE TO RETREAT...
ZUBO (ZWOOP)
!!
CHUPON (FLAP)
BO (FWOOM)

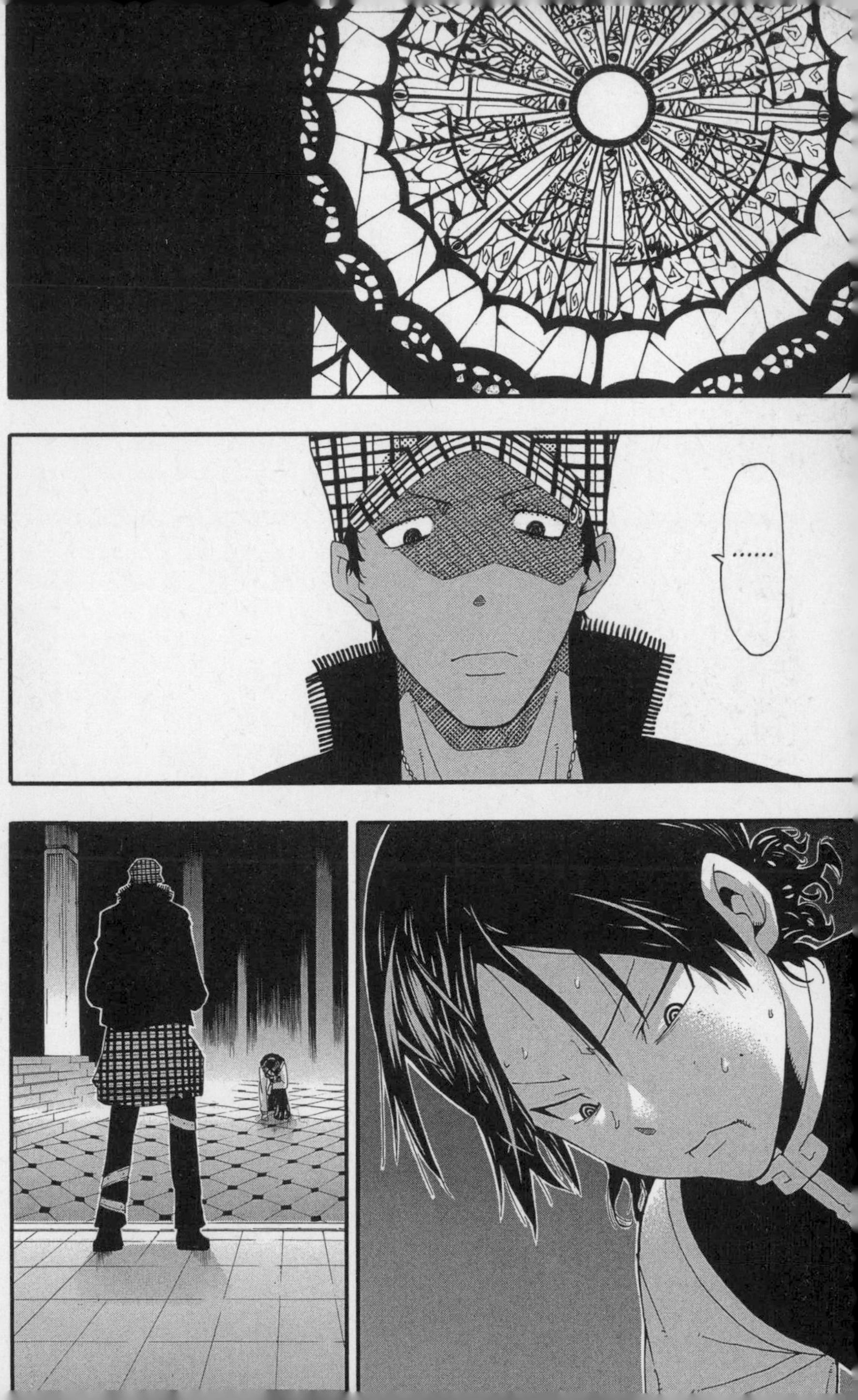
......

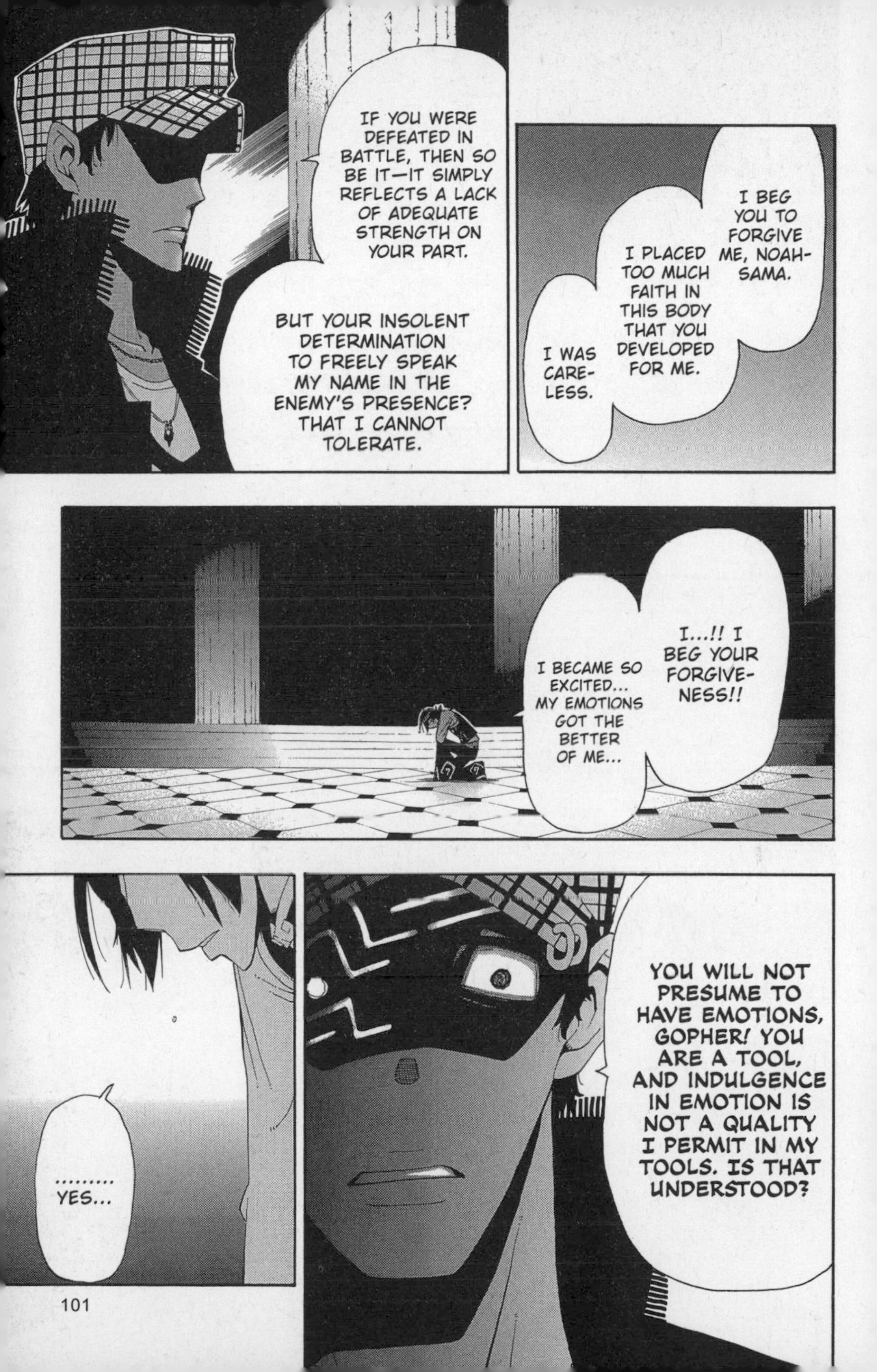
I BEG YOU TO FORGIVE ME, NOAH-SAMA.
I PLACED TOO MUCH FAITH IN THIS BODY THAT YOU DEVELOPED FOR ME.
I WAS CARE-LESS.
IF YOU WERE DEFEATED IN BATTLE, THEN SO BE IT—IT SIMPLY REFLECTS A LACK OF ADEQUATE STRENGTH ON YOUR PART.
BUT YOUR INSOLENT DETERMINATION TO FREELY SPEAK MY NAME IN THE ENEMY'S PRESENCE? THAT I CANNOT TOLERATE.
I...!! I BEG YOUR FORGIVE-NESS!!
I BECAME SO EXCITED... MY EMOTIONS GOT THE BETTER OF ME...
YOU WILL NOT PRESUME TO HAVE EMOTIONS, GOPHER! YOU ARE A TOOL, AND INDULGENCE IN EMOTION IS NOT A QUALITY I PERMIT IN MY TOOLS. IS THAT UNDERSTOOD?
......... YES...

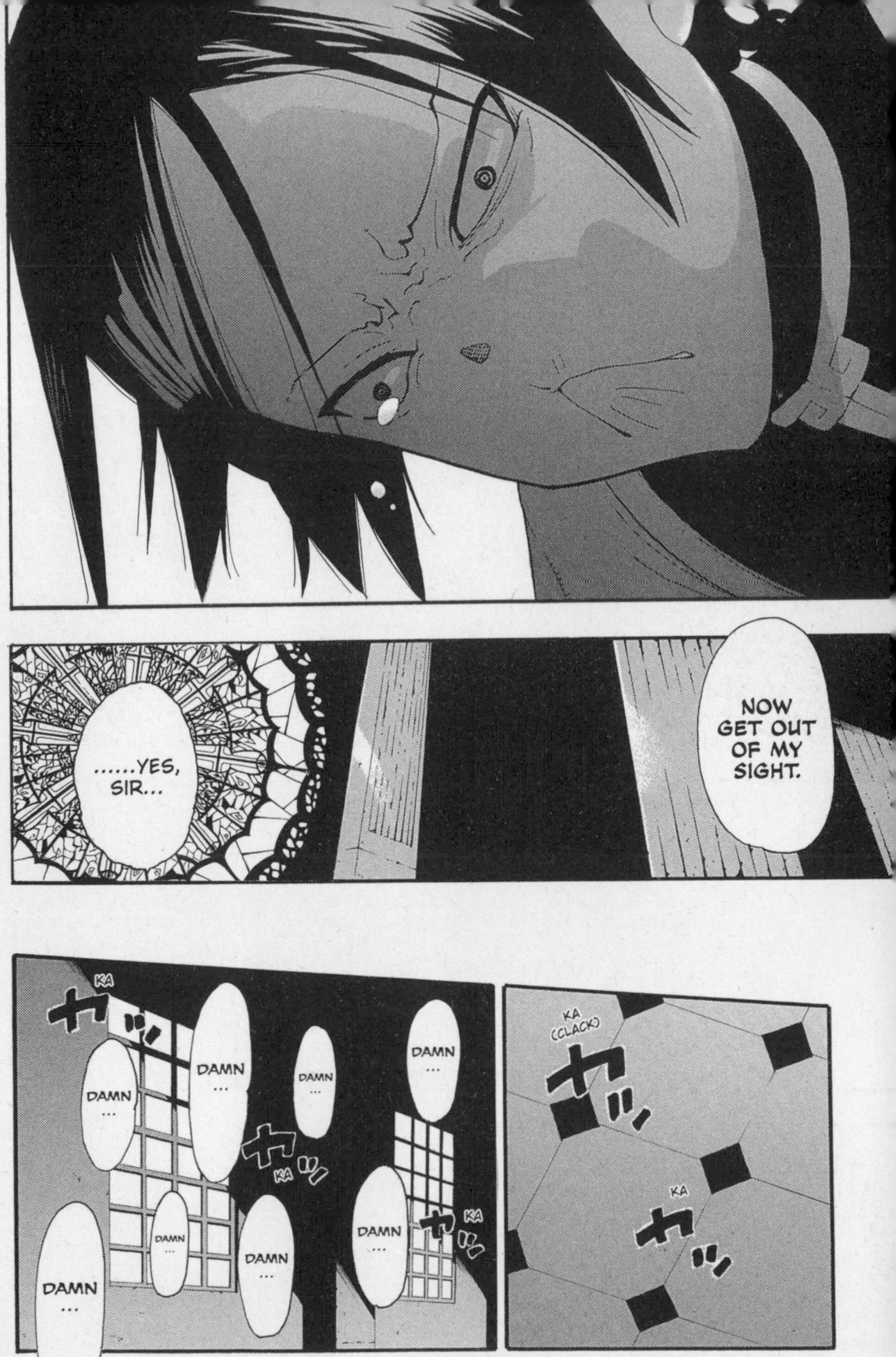
NOW GET OUT OF MY SIGHT.
......YES, SIR...
KA (CLACK)
KA
DAMN...
KA
DAMN...
DAMN...
KA
DAMN...
KA
DAMN...
DAMN...
DAMN...
DAMN...

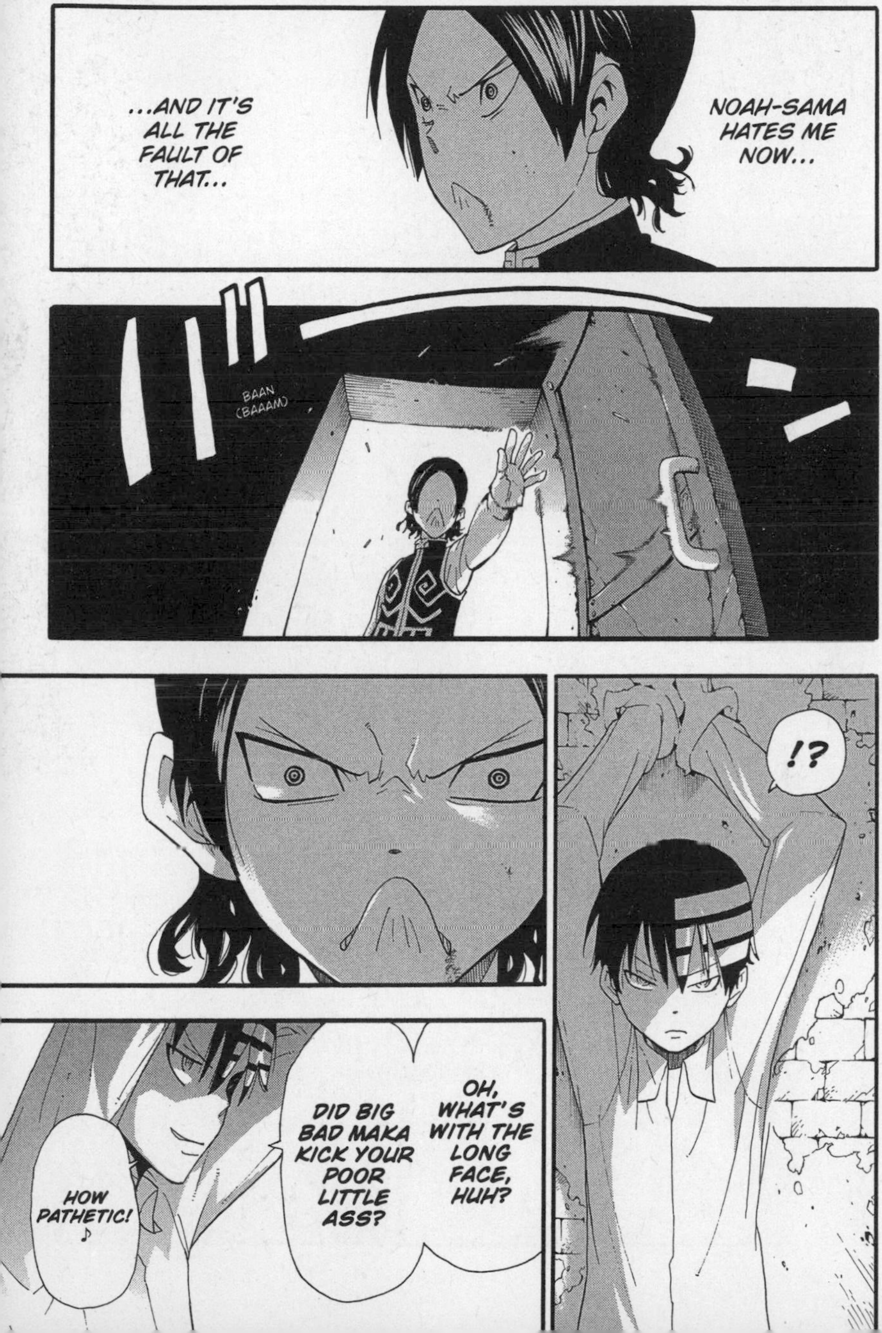
NOAH-SAMA HATES ME NOW...
...AND IT'S ALL THE FAULT OF THAT...
BAAN (BAAAM)
!?
OH, WHAT'S WITH THE LONG FACE, HUH?
DID BIG BAD MAKA KICK YOUR POOR LITTLE ASS?
HOW PATHETIC! ♪

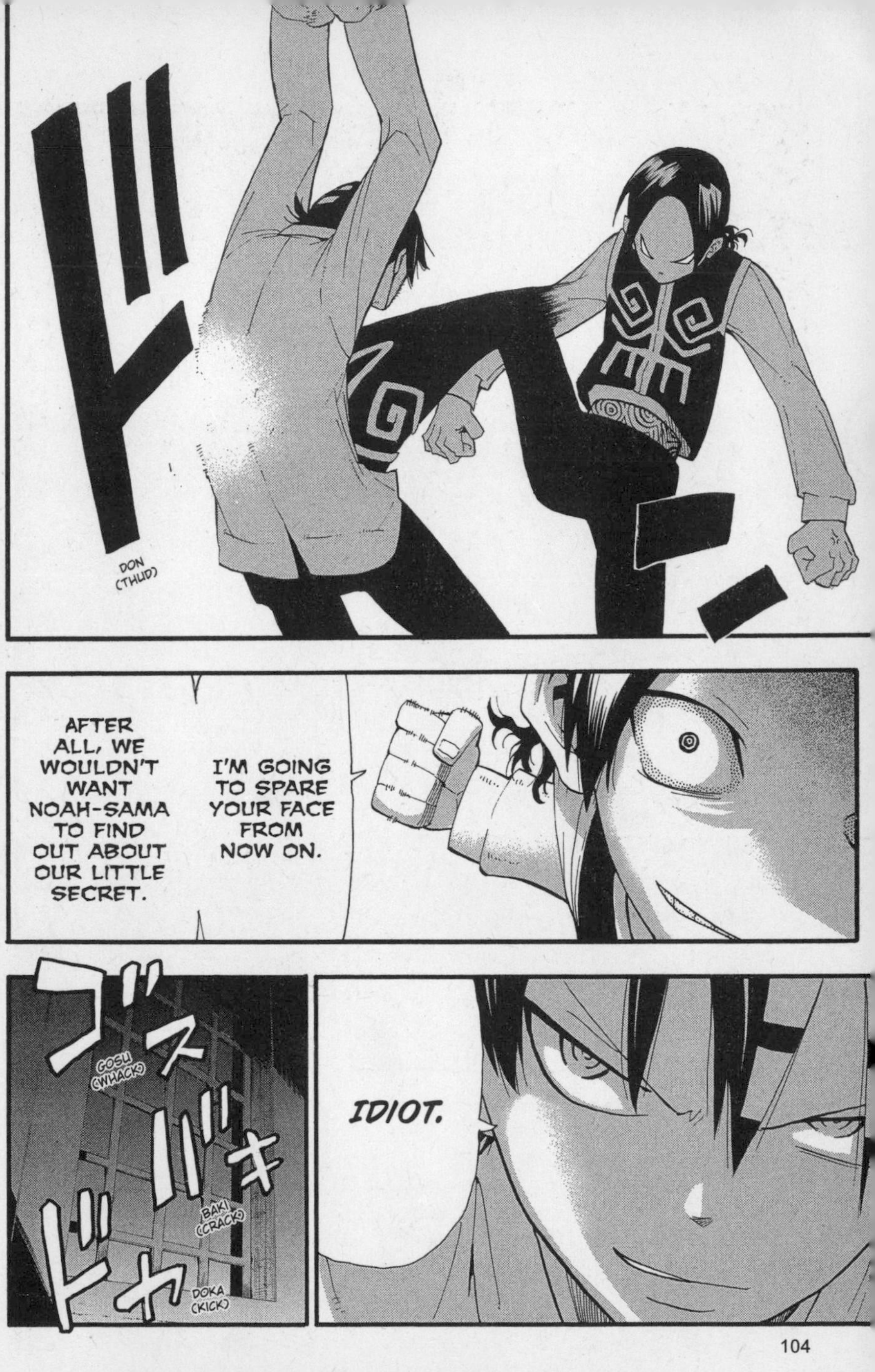
DON
(THUD)
I'M GOING TO SPARE YOUR FACE FROM NOW ON.
AFTER ALL, WE WOULDN'T WANT NOAH-SAMA TO FIND OUT ABOUT OUR LITTLE SECRET.
IDIOT.
GOSU
(WHACK)
BAKI
(CRACK)
DOKA
(KICK)

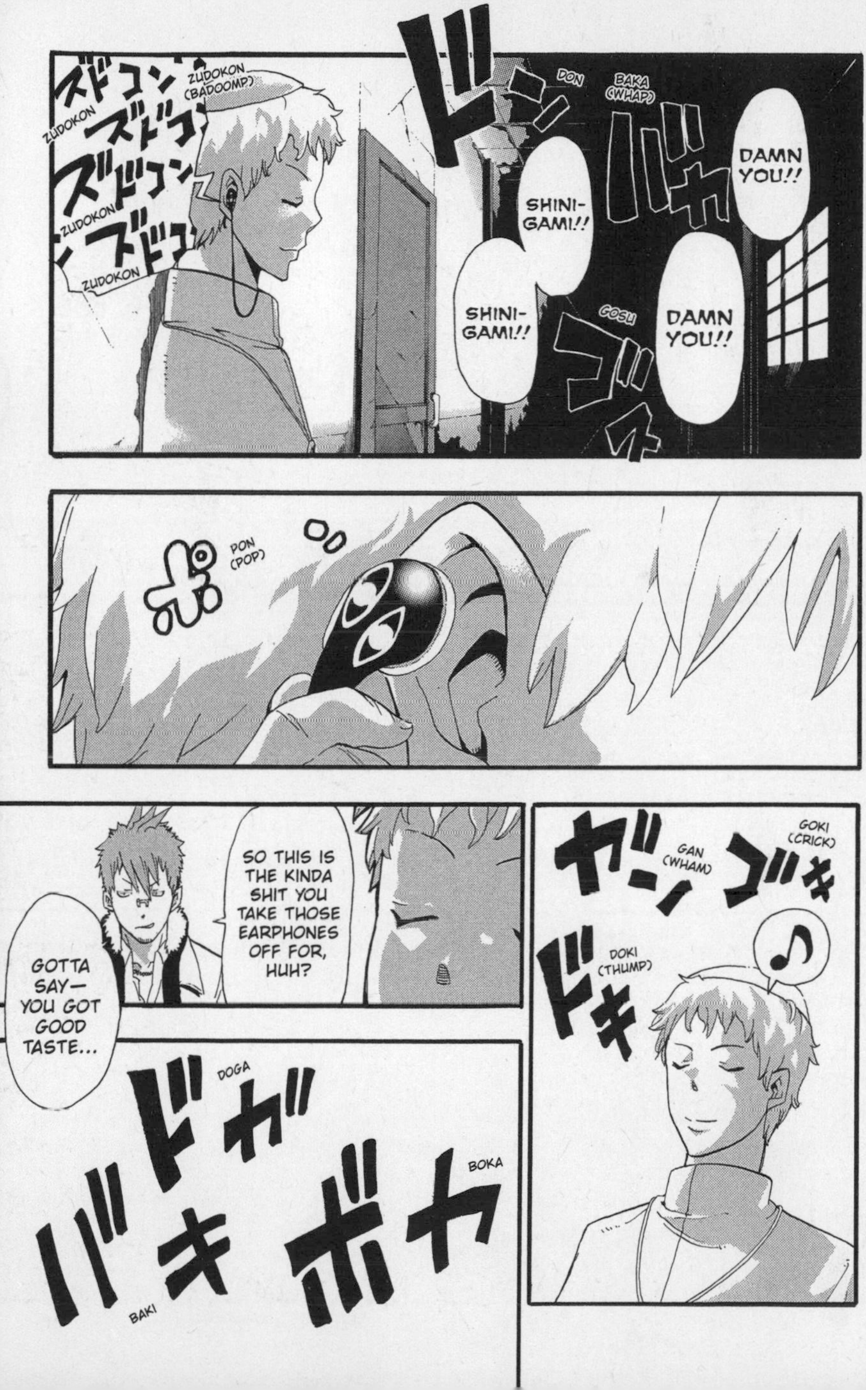
DAMN YOU!!
BAKA (WHAP)
DON
SHINI-GAMI!!
DAMN YOU!!
GOSU
SHINI-GAMI!!
ZUDOKON (BADOOMP)
ZUDOKON
ZUDOKON
ZUDOKON
PON (POP)
GOKI (CRICK)
GAN (WHAM)
DOKI (THUMP)
♪
SO THIS IS THE KINDA SHIT YOU TAKE THOSE EARPHONES OFF FOR, HUH?
GOTTA SAY— YOU GOT GOOD TASTE...
BOKA
DOGA
BAKI

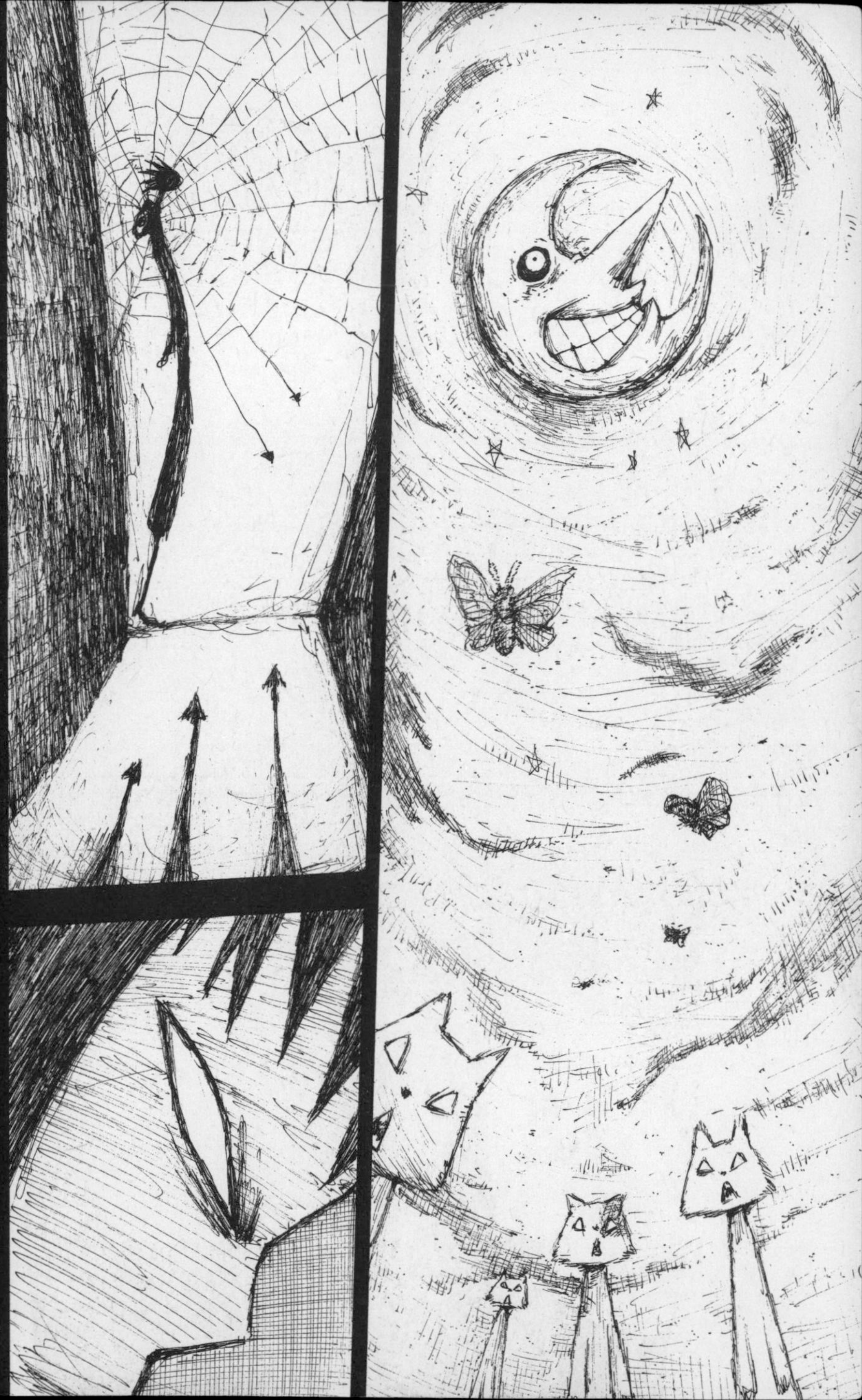

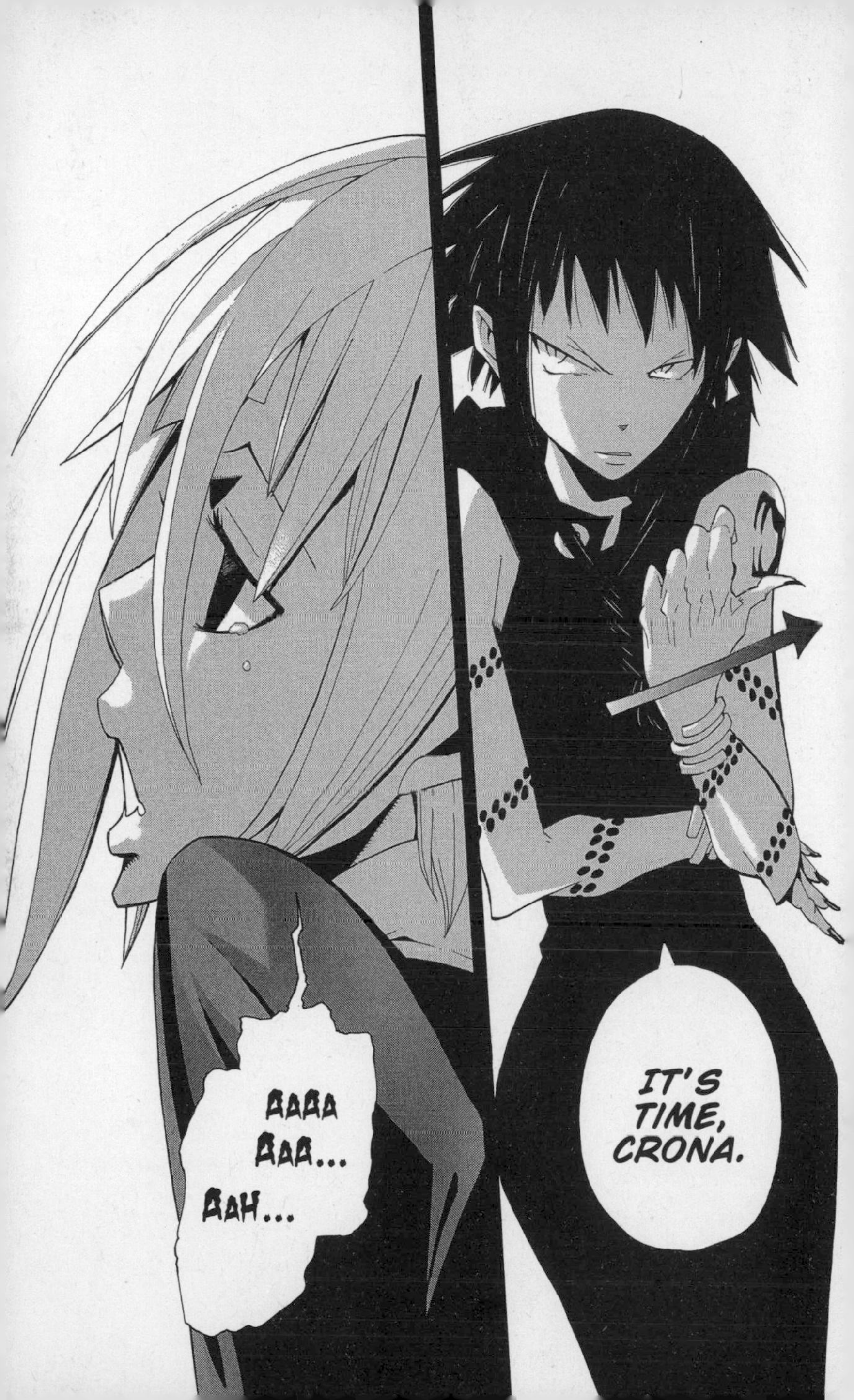
IT'S TIME, CRONA.
AAAA AAA... AAH...

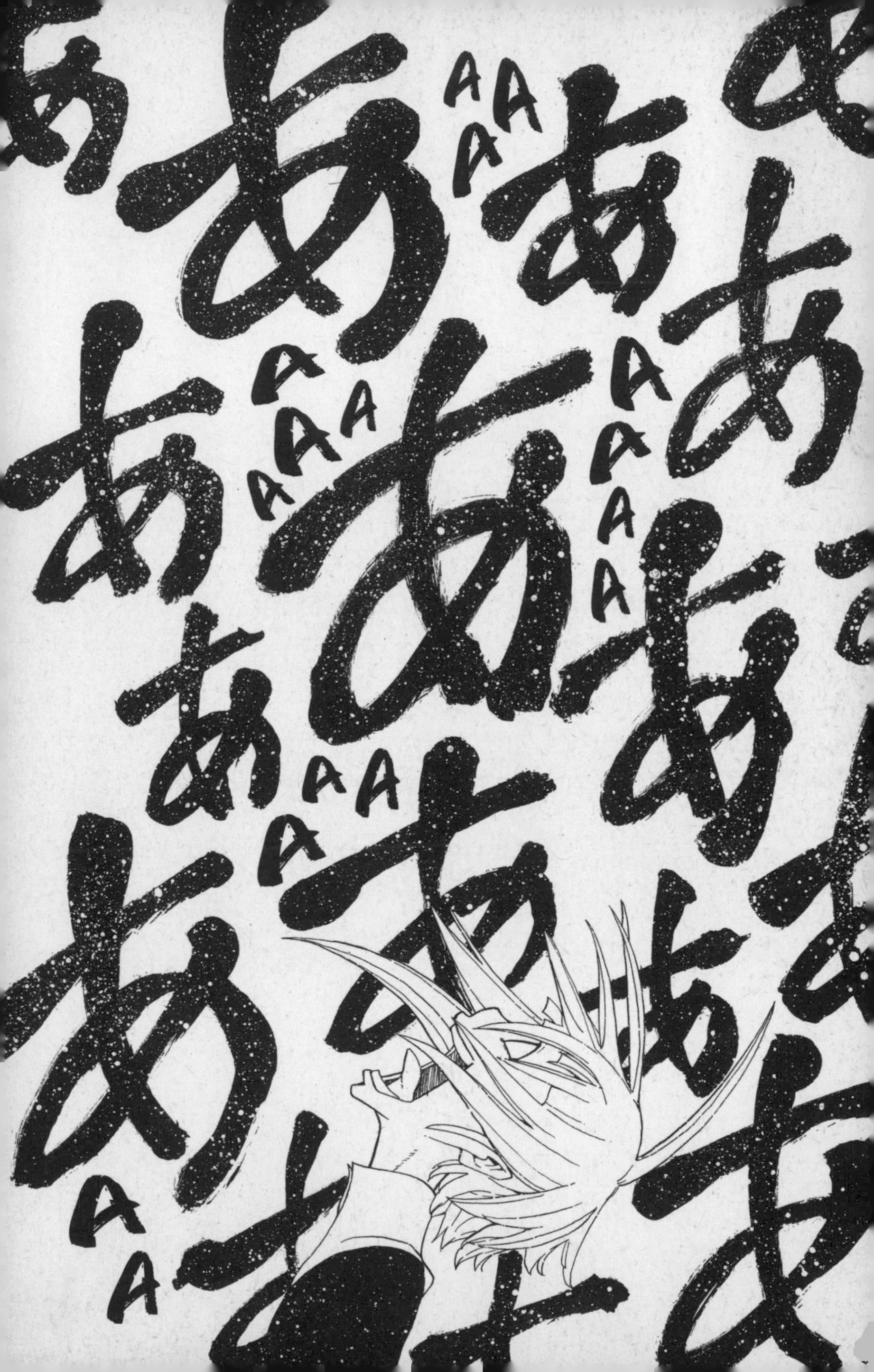

あああああ
AAA
AAAAA
AAAAAA
AAA
AA

SOUL EATER

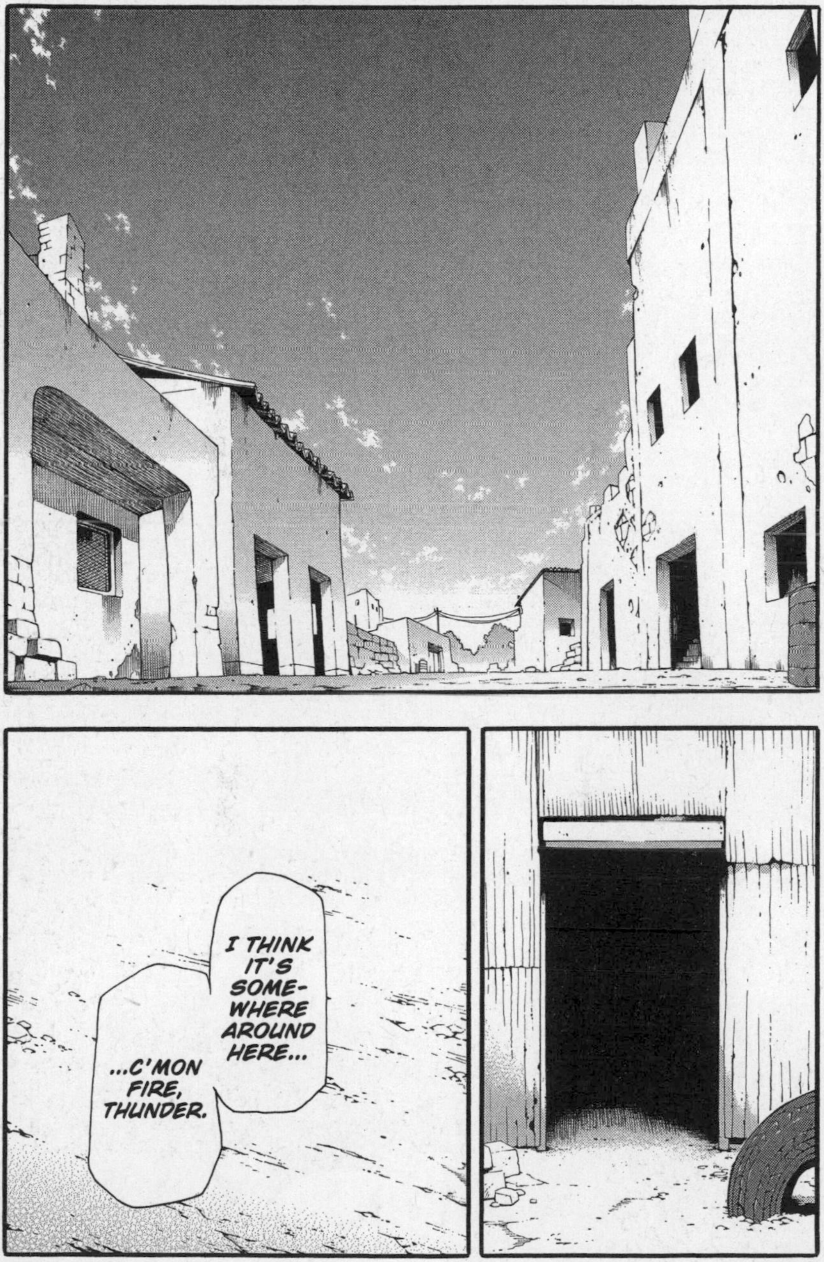
I THINK IT'S SOME-WHERE AROUND HERE...
...C'MON FIRE, THUNDER.

CENTRAL AFRICA

# SOUL EATER

## CHAPTER 66: THE WITCH'S RESEARCH (PART 1)

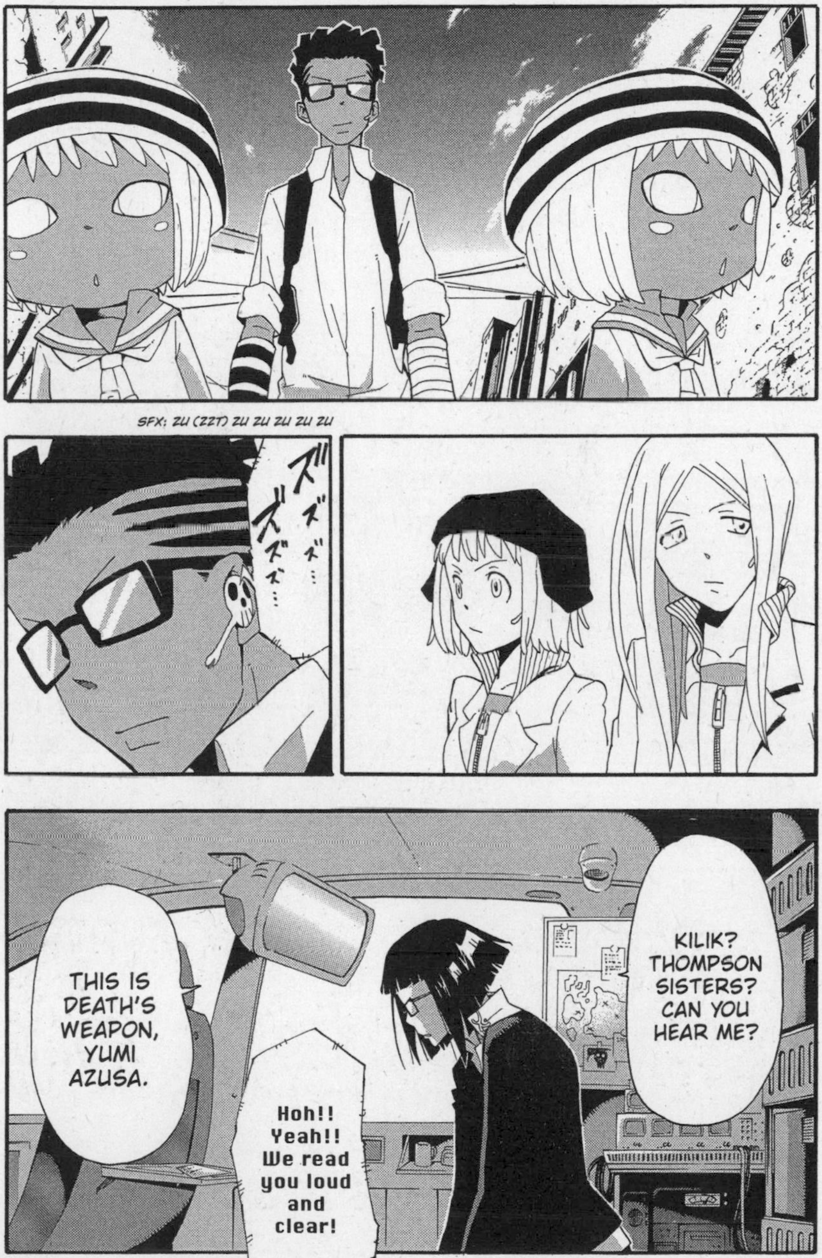
SFX: ZU (ZZT) ZU ZU ZU ZU ZU
ズズズ… ズズズ…
KILIK? THOMPSON SISTERS? CAN YOU HEAR ME?
THIS IS DEATH'S WEAPON, YUMI AZUSA.
Hoh!! Yeah!! We read you loud and clear!

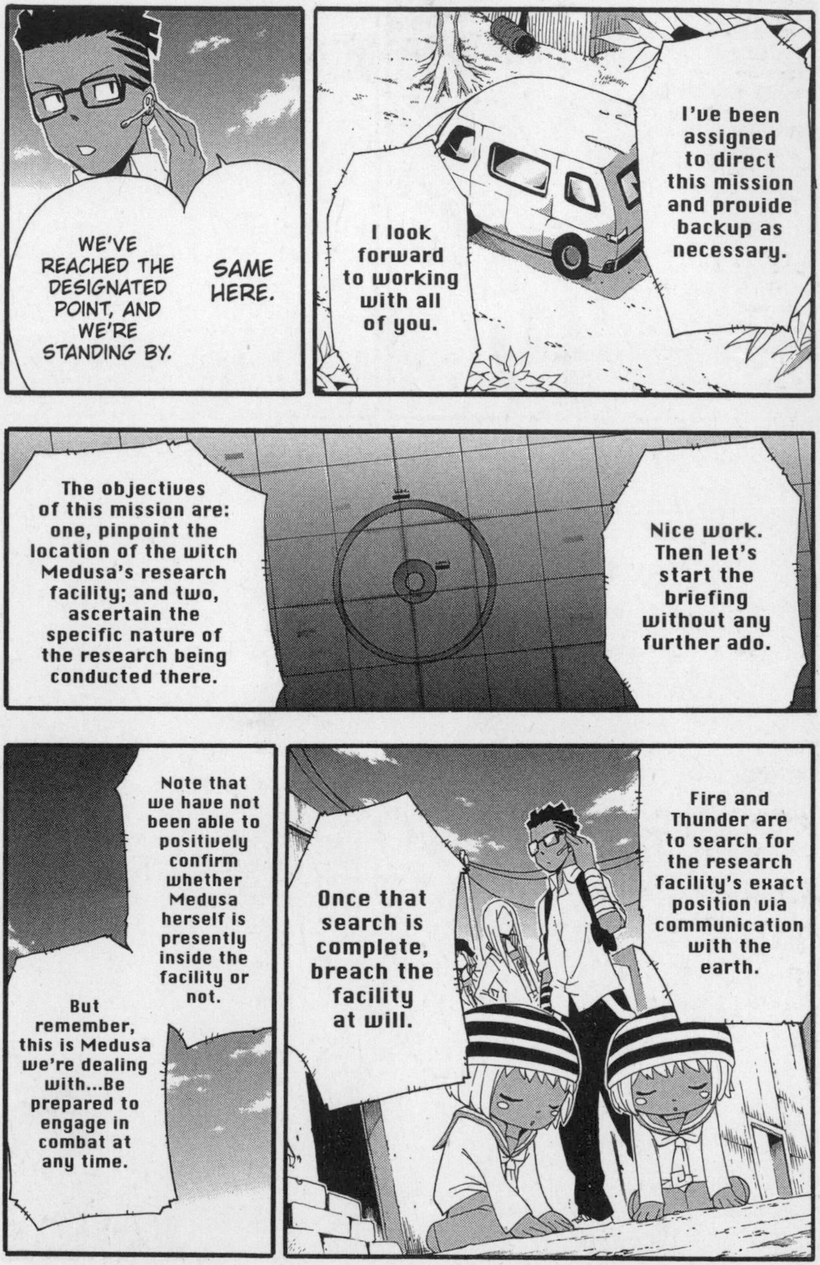
I've been assigned to direct this mission and provide backup as necessary.
I look forward to working with all of you.
WE'VE REACHED THE DESIGNATED POINT, AND WE'RE STANDING BY.
SAME HERE.
Nice work. Then let's start the briefing without any further ado.
The objectives of this mission are: one, pinpoint the location of the witch Medusa's research facility; and two, ascertain the specific nature of the research being conducted there.
Fire and Thunder are to search for the research facility's exact position via communication with the earth.
Once that search is complete, breach the facility at will.
Note that we have not been able to positively confirm whether Medusa herself is presently inside the facility or not.
But remember, this is Medusa we're dealing with...Be prepared to engage in combat at any time.

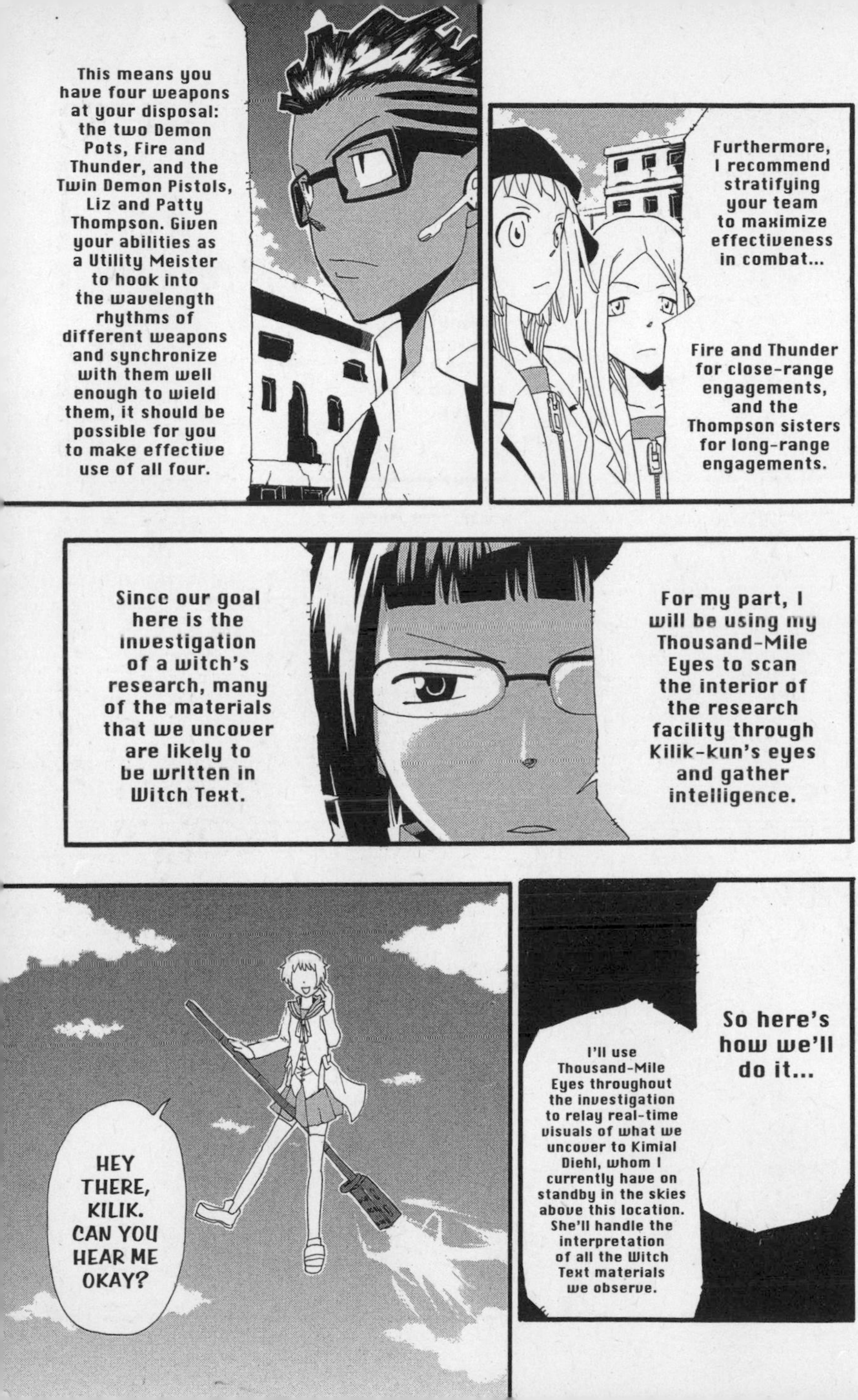
Furthermore, I recommend stratifying your team to maximize effectiveness in combat...
Fire and Thunder for close-range engagements, and the Thompson sisters for long-range engagements.
This means you have four weapons at your disposal: the two Demon Pots, Fire and Thunder, and the Twin Demon Pistols, Liz and Patty Thompson. Given your abilities as a Utility Meister to hook into the wavelength rhythms of different weapons and synchronize with them well enough to wield them, it should be possible for you to make effective use of all four.
For my part, I will be using my Thousand-Mile Eyes to scan the interior of the research facility through Kilik-kun's eyes and gather intelligence.
Since our goal here is the investigation of a witch's research, many of the materials that we uncover are likely to be written in Witch Text.
So here's how we'll do it...
I'll use Thousand-Mile Eyes throughout the investigation to relay real-time visuals of what we uncover to Kimial Diehl, whom I currently have on standby in the skies above this location. She'll handle the interpretation of all the Witch Text materials we observe.
HEY THERE, KILIK. CAN YOU HEAR ME OKAY?

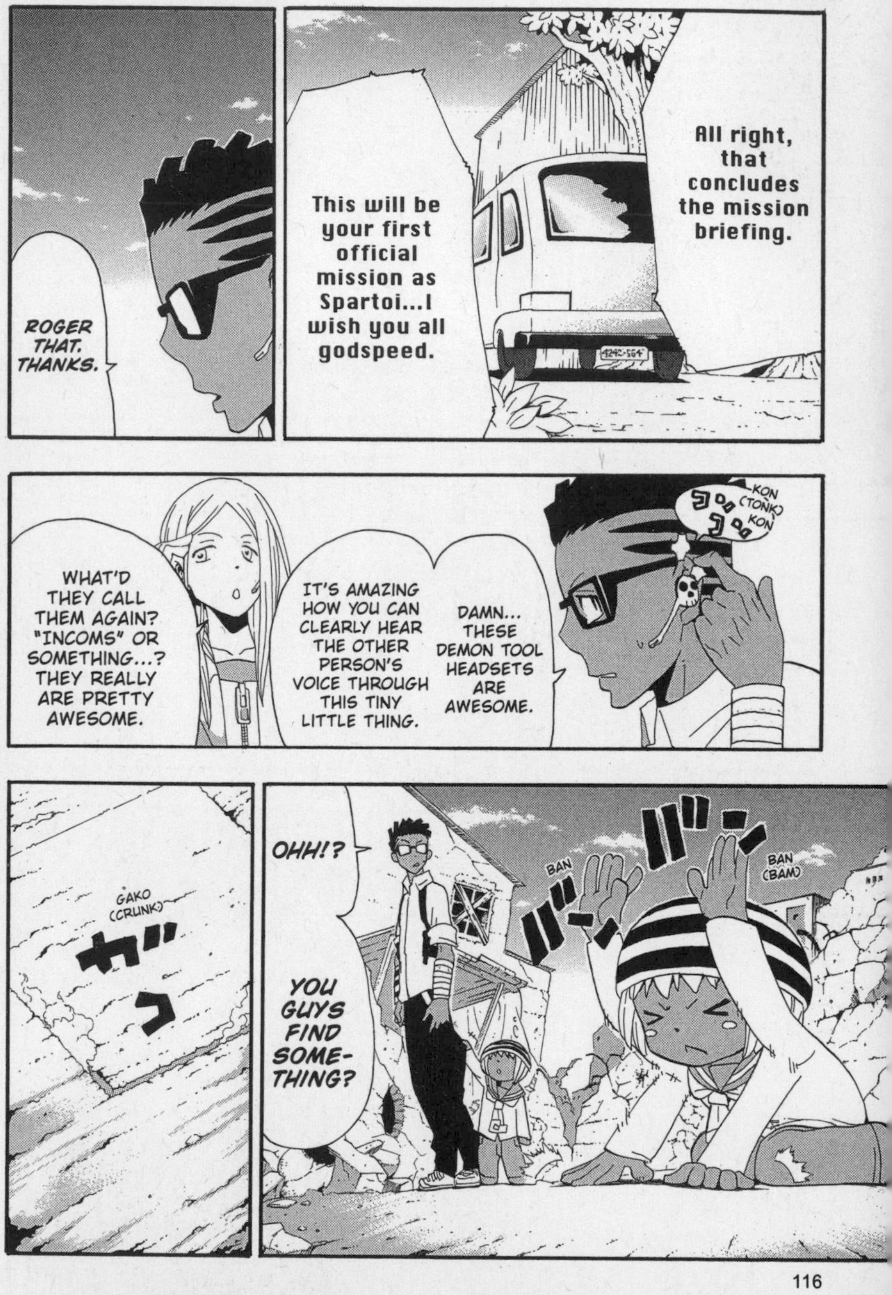
All right, that concludes the mission briefing.
This will be your first official mission as Spartoi...I wish you all godspeed.
ROGER THAT. THANKS.
KON (TONK) KON
DAMN... THESE DEMON TOOL HEADSETS ARE AWESOME.
IT'S AMAZING HOW YOU CAN CLEARLY HEAR THE OTHER PERSON'S VOICE THROUGH THIS TINY LITTLE THING.
WHAT'D THEY CALL THEM AGAIN? "INCOMS" OR SOMETHING...? THEY REALLY ARE PRETTY AWESOME.
BAN (BAM)
BAN
OHH!?
YOU GUYS FIND SOMETHING?
GAKO (CRUNK)

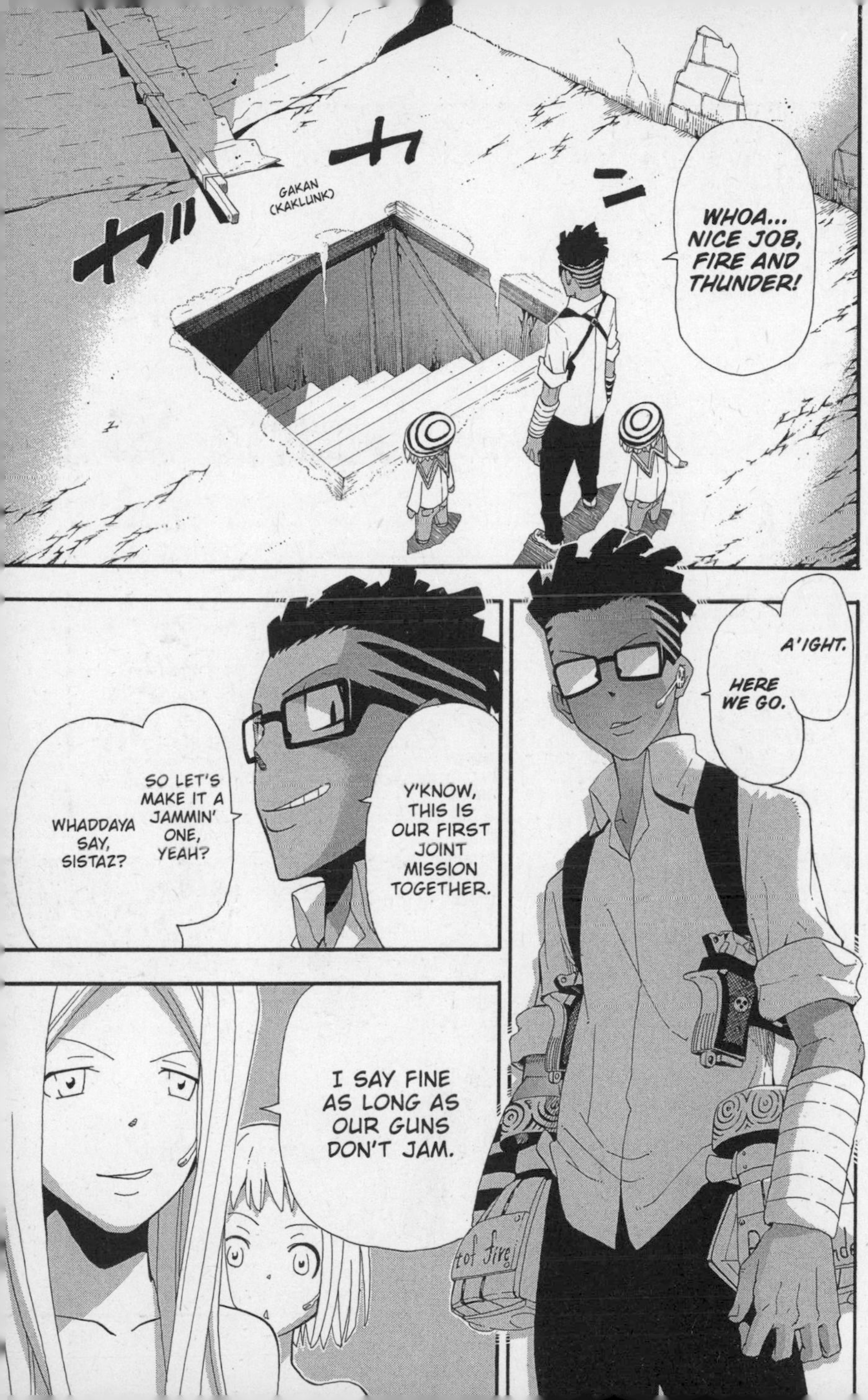
GAKAN (KAKLUNK)
WHOA... NICE JOB, FIRE AND THUNDER!
A'IGHT.
HERE WE GO.
Y'KNOW, THIS IS OUR FIRST JOINT MISSION TOGETHER.
SO LET'S MAKE IT A JAMMIN' ONE, YEAH?
WHADDAYA SAY, SISTAZ?
I SAY FINE AS LONG AS OUR GUNS DON'T JAM.

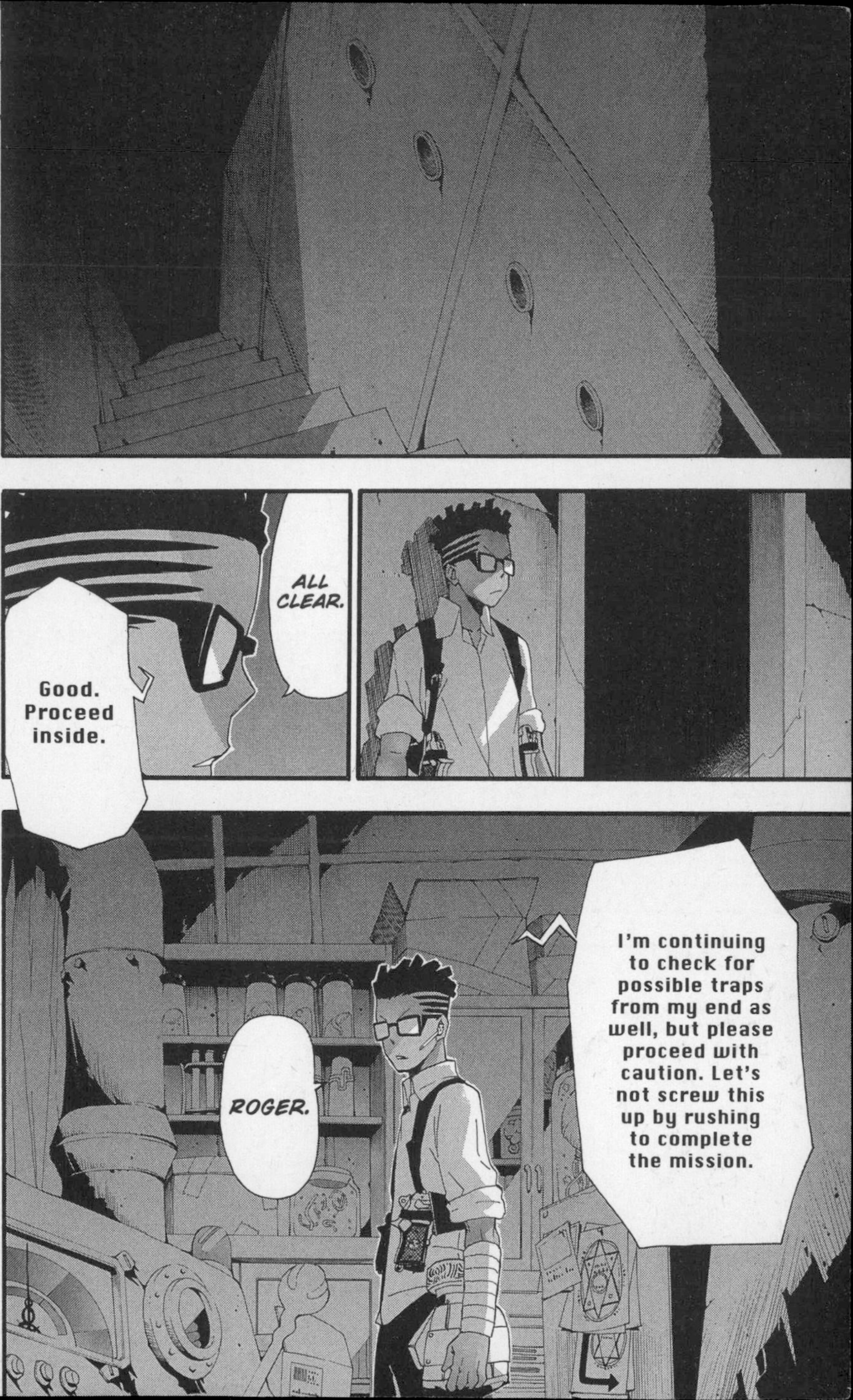
ALL CLEAR.
Good. Proceed inside.
I'm continuing to check for possible traps from my end as well, but please proceed with caution. Let's not screw this up by rushing to complete the mission.
ROGER.

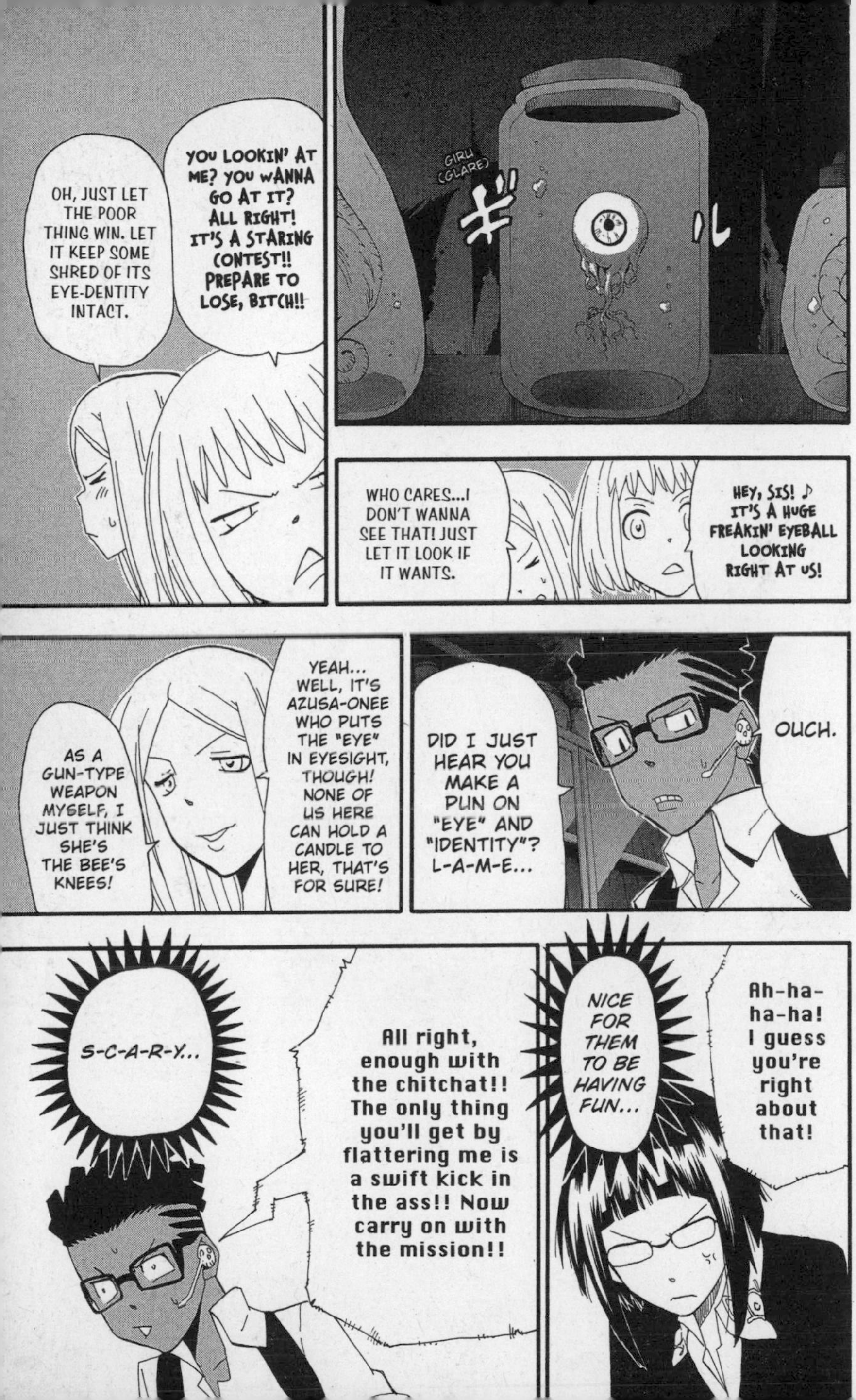
GIRU (GLARE)
ギ
ル
HEY, SIS! ♪ IT'S A HUGE FREAKIN' EYEBALL LOOKING RIGHT AT US!
WHO CARES...I DON'T WANNA SEE THAT! JUST LET IT LOOK IF IT WANTS.
YOU LOOKIN' AT ME? YOU WANNA GO AT IT? ALL RIGHT! IT'S A STARING CONTEST!! PREPARE TO LOSE, BITCH!!
OH, JUST LET THE POOR THING WIN. LET IT KEEP SOME SHRED OF ITS EYE-DENTITY INTACT.
OUCH.
DID I JUST HEAR YOU MAKE A PUN ON "EYE" AND "IDENTITY"? L-A-M-E...
YEAH... WELL, IT'S AZUSA-ONEE WHO PUTS THE "EYE" IN EYESIGHT, THOUGH! NONE OF US HERE CAN HOLD A CANDLE TO HER, THAT'S FOR SURE!
AS A GUN-TYPE WEAPON MYSELF, I JUST THINK SHE'S THE BEE'S KNEES!
Ah-ha-ha-ha! I guess you're right about that!
NICE FOR THEM TO BE HAVING FUN...
All right, enough with the chitchat!! The only thing you'll get by flattering me is a swift kick in the ass!! Now carry on with the mission!!
S-C-A-R-Y...

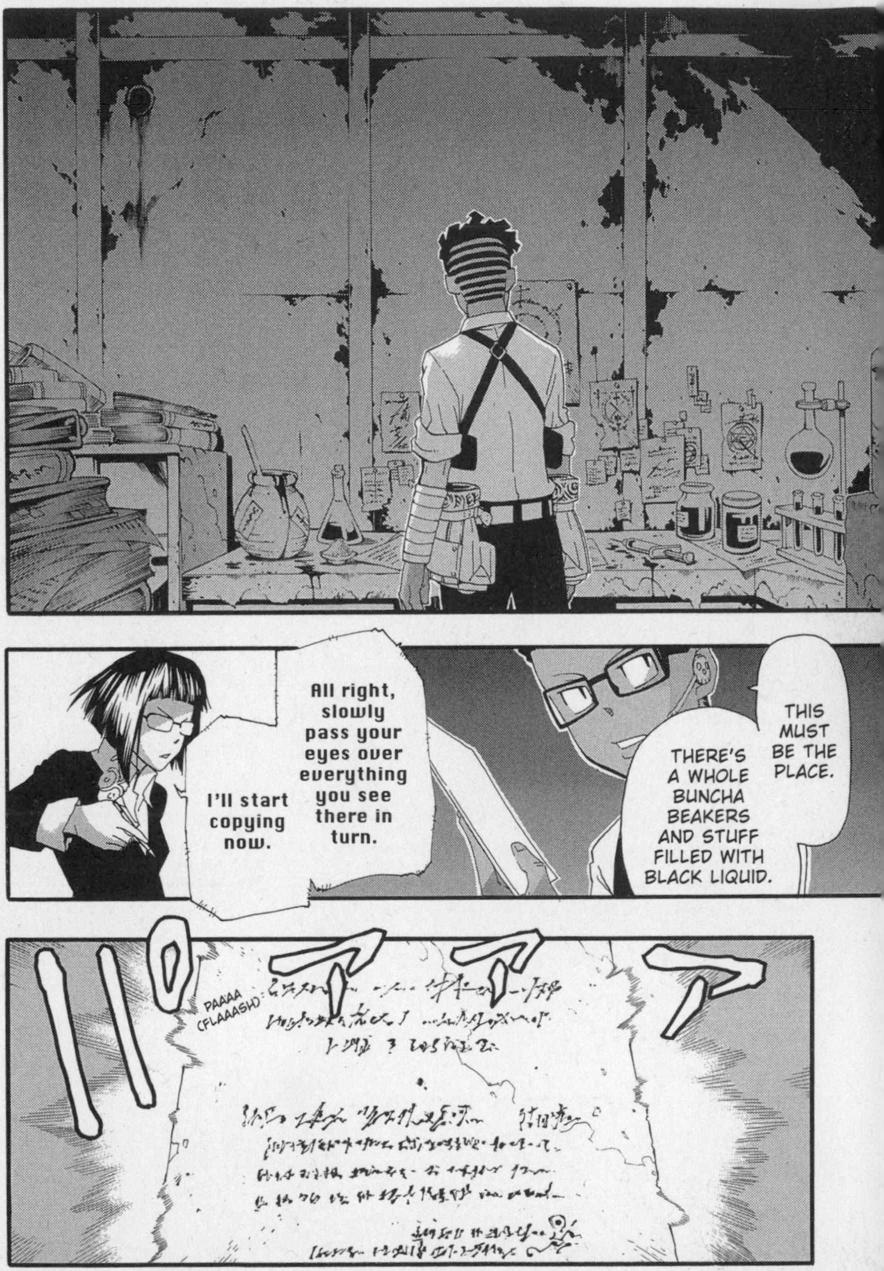
THIS MUST BE THE PLACE.
THERE'S A WHOLE BUNCHA BEAKERS AND STUFF FILLED WITH BLACK LIQUID.
All right, slowly pass your eyes over everything you see there in turn.
I'll start copying now.
PAAAA (FLAAASH)

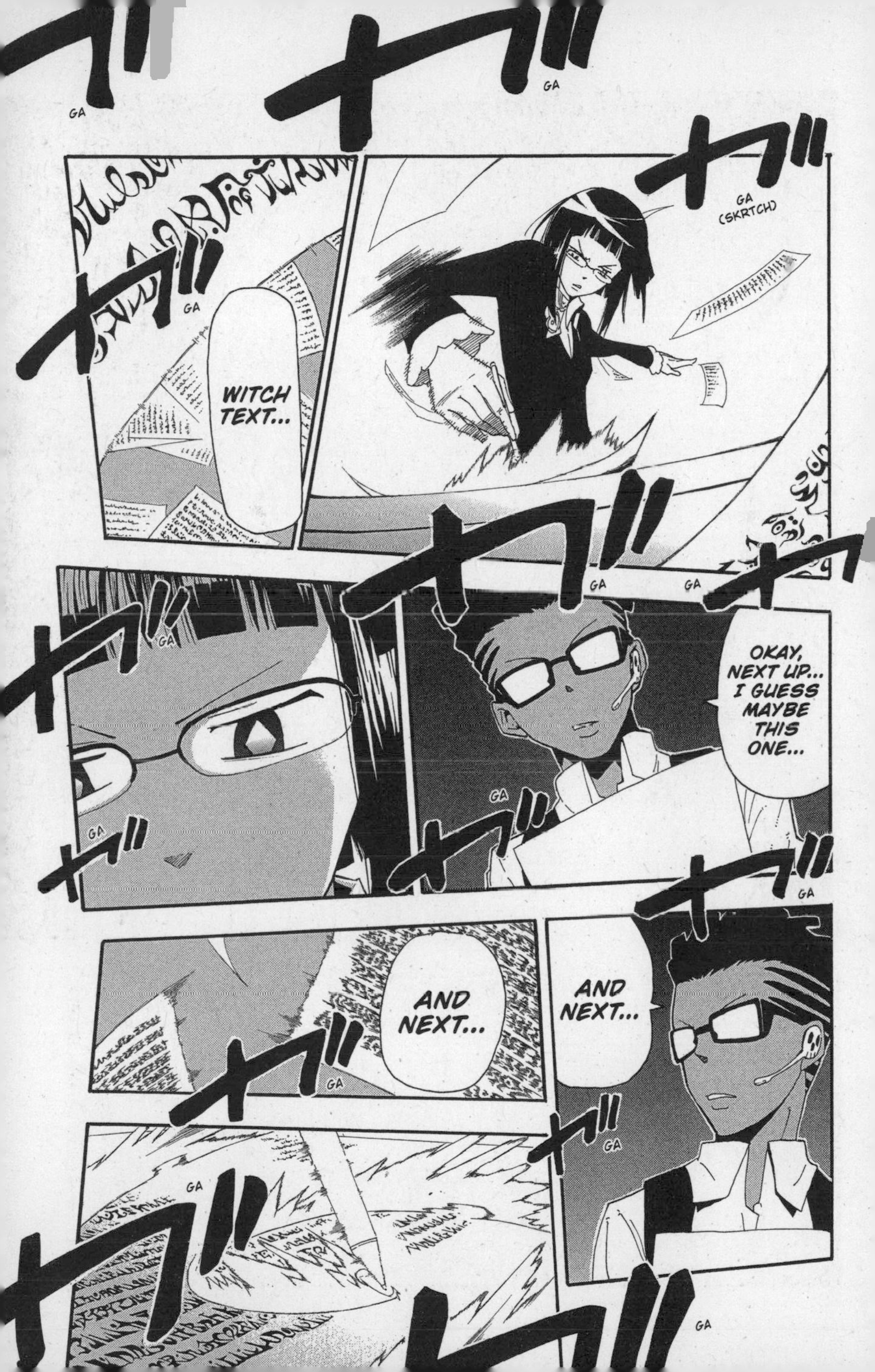
GA
GA
GA
(SKRTCH)
GA
WITCH TEXT...
GA
GA
OKAY, NEXT UP... I GUESS MAYBE THIS ONE...
GA
GA
GA
GA
AND NEXT...
GA
AND NEXT...
GA
GA
GA

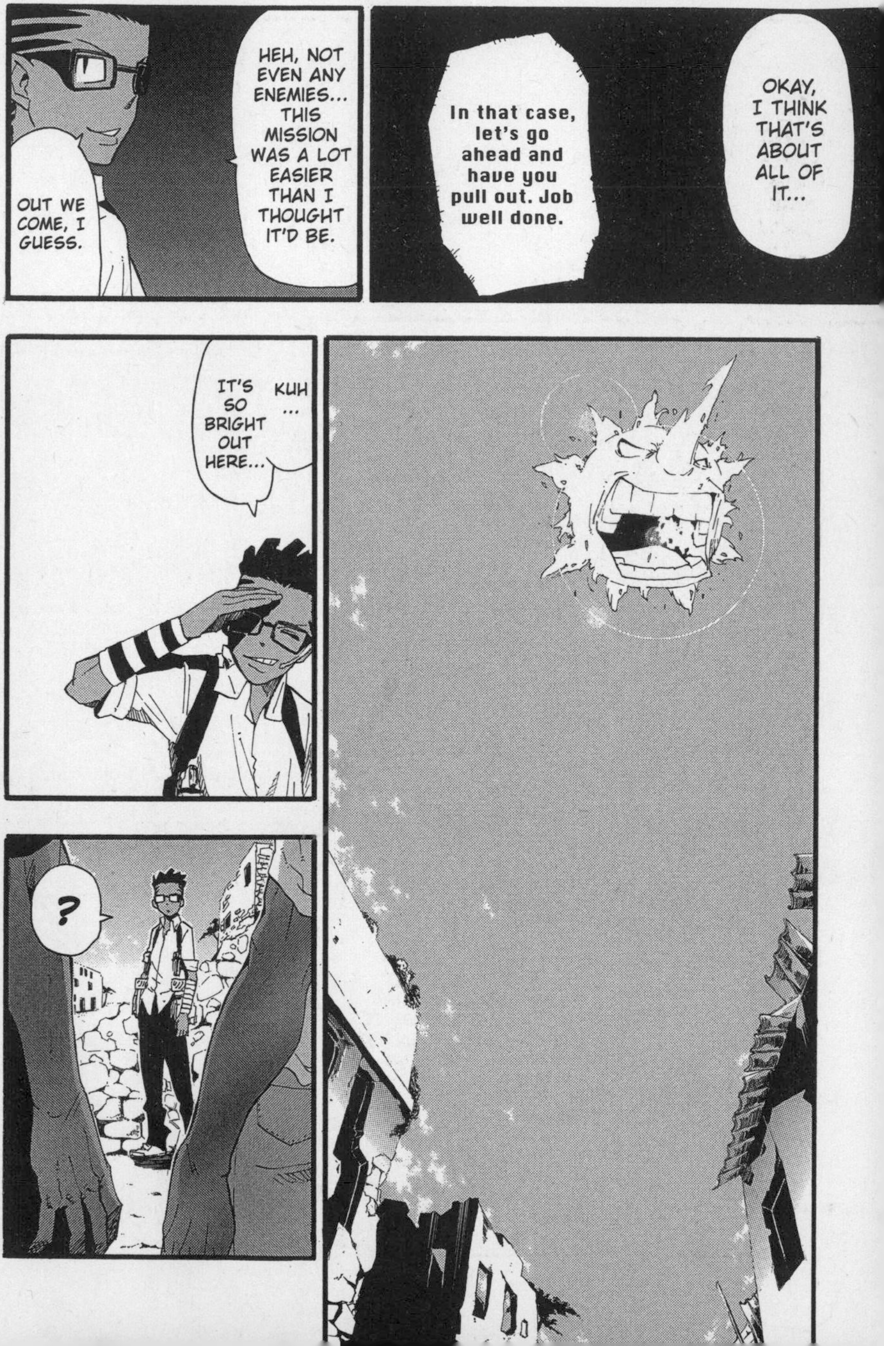
OKAY, I THINK THAT'S ABOUT ALL OF IT...
In that case, let's go ahead and have you pull out. Job well done.
HEH, NOT EVEN ANY ENEMIES... THIS MISSION WAS A LOT EASIER THAN I THOUGHT IT'D BE.
OUT WE COME, I GUESS.
KUH...
IT'S SO BRIGHT OUT HERE...
?

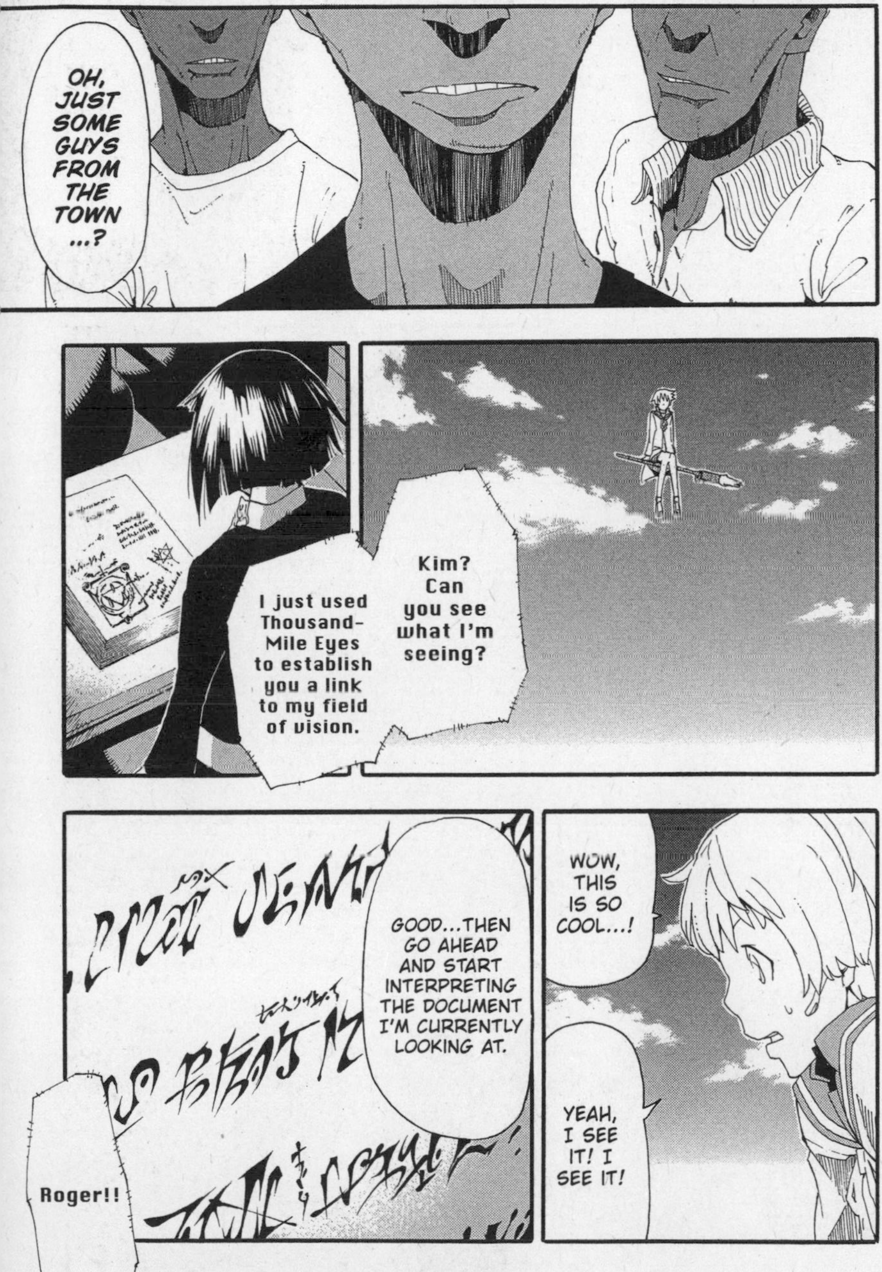
OH, JUST SOME GUYS FROM THE TOWN ...?
Kim? Can you see what I'm seeing?
I just used Thousand-Mile Eyes to establish you a link to my field of vision.
WOW, THIS IS SO COOL...!
YEAH, I SEE IT! I SEE IT!
GOOD...THEN GO AHEAD AND START INTERPRETING THE DOCUMENT I'M CURRENTLY LOOKING AT.
Roger!!

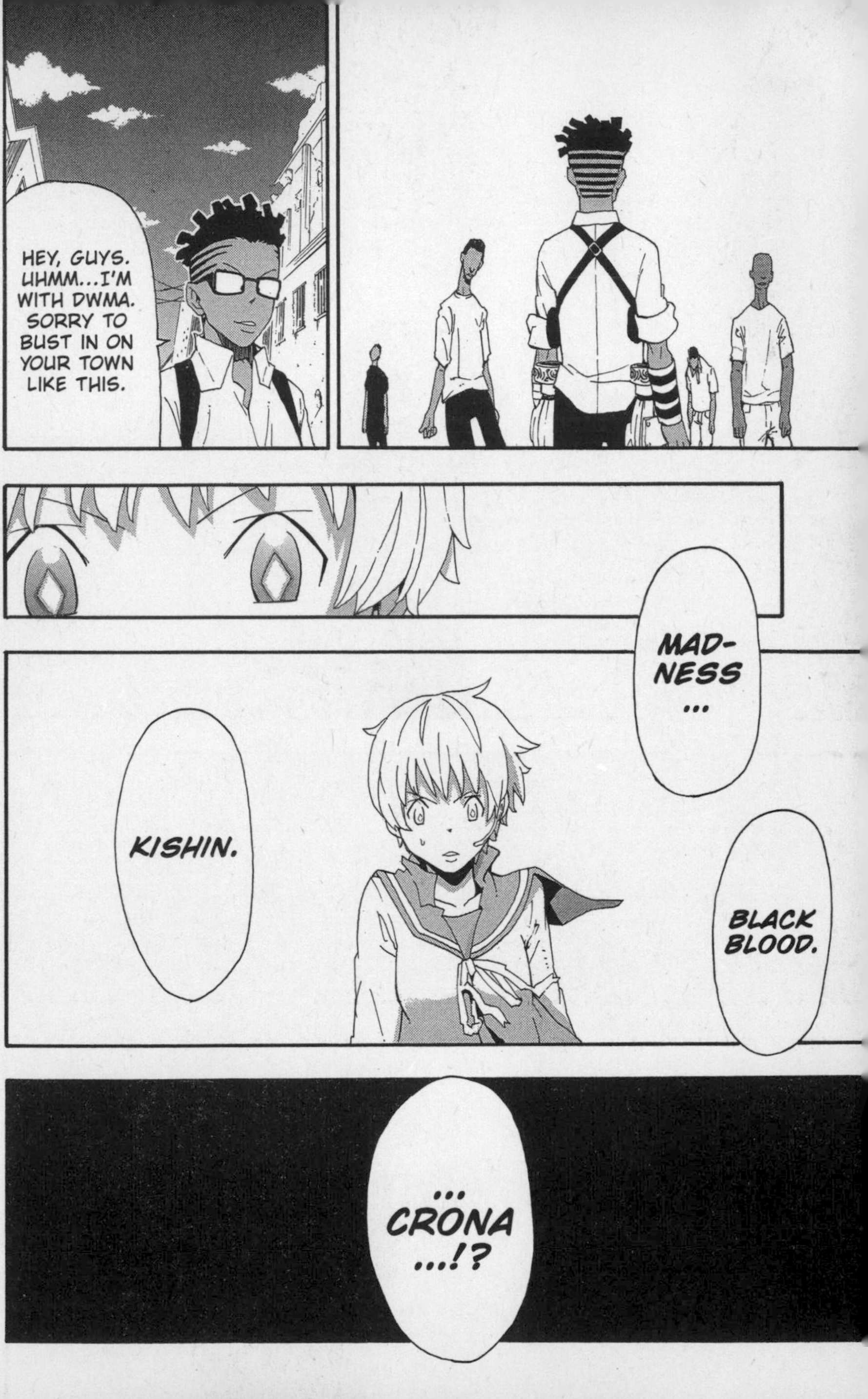
HEY, GUYS. UHMM...I'M WITH DWMA. SORRY TO BUST IN ON YOUR TOWN LIKE THIS.
MAD-NESS...
BLACK BLOOD.
KISHIN.
...CRONA...!?

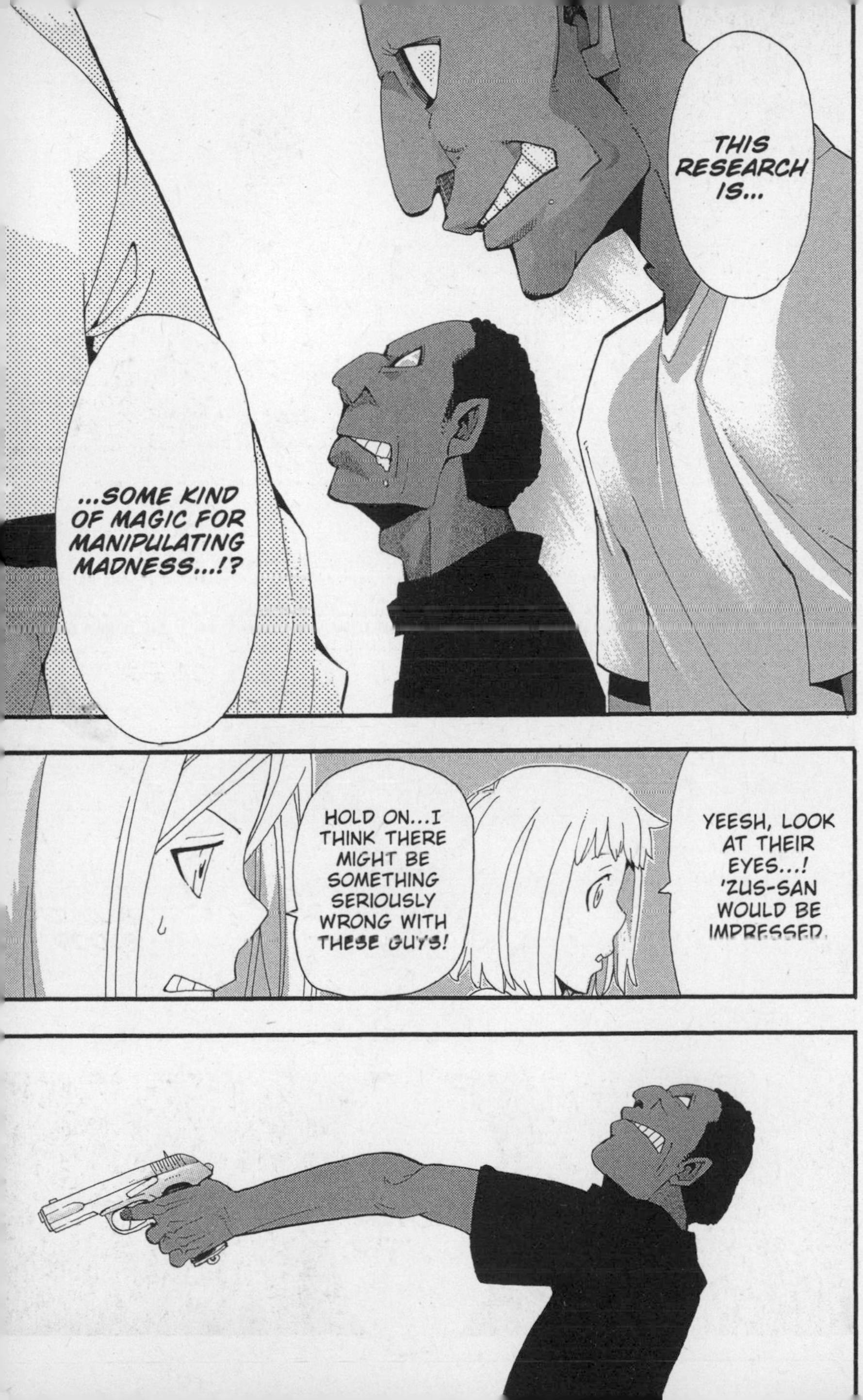
THIS RESEARCH IS...
...SOME KIND OF MAGIC FOR MANIPULATING MADNESS...!?
YEESH, LOOK AT THEIR EYES...! 'ZUS-SAN WOULD BE IMPRESSED.
HOLD ON...I THINK THERE MIGHT BE SOMETHING SERIOUSLY WRONG WITH THESE GUYS!

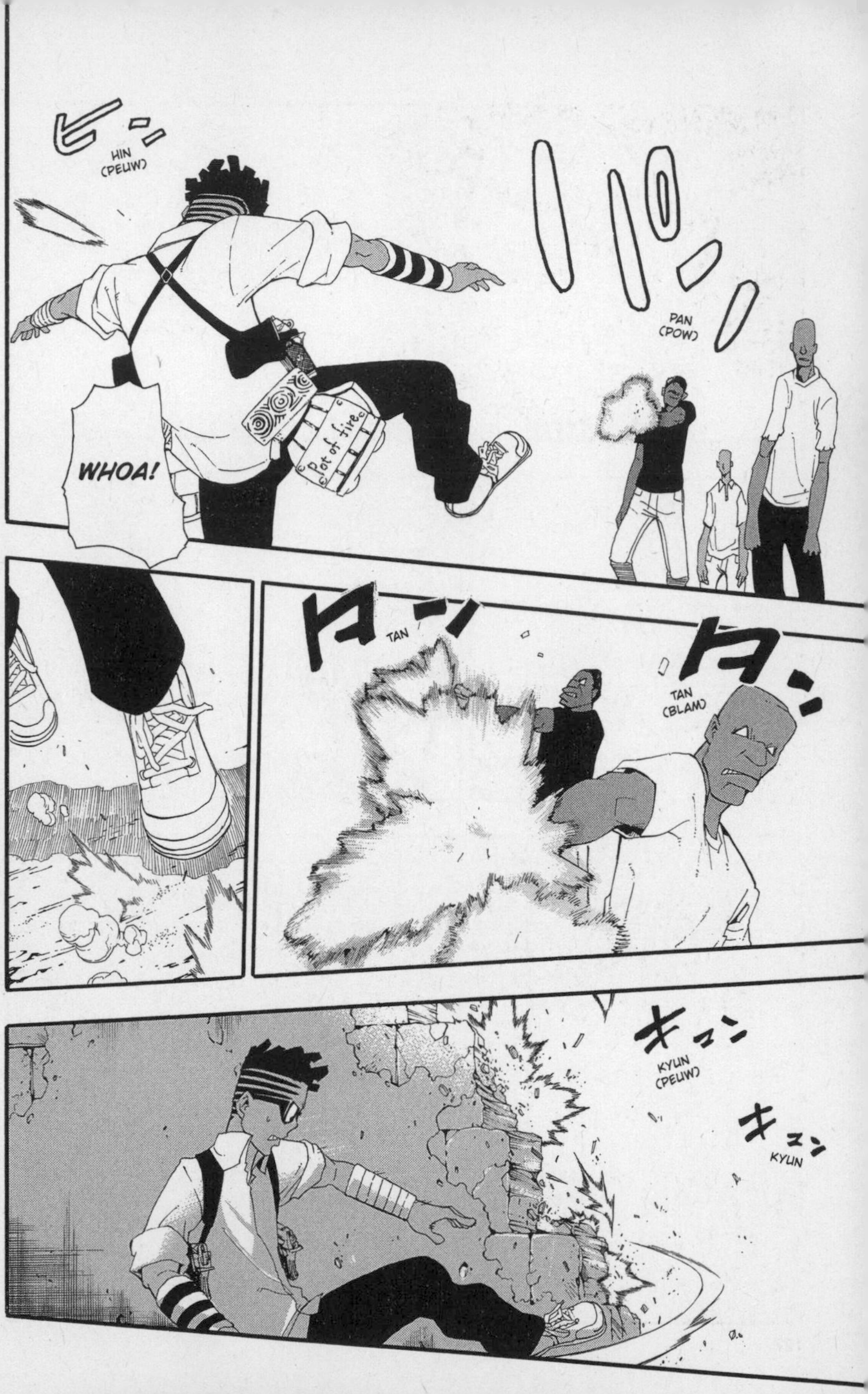
PAN
(POW)
HIN
(PEUW)
WHOA!
TAN
(BLAM)
TAN
KYUN
(PEUW)
KYUN

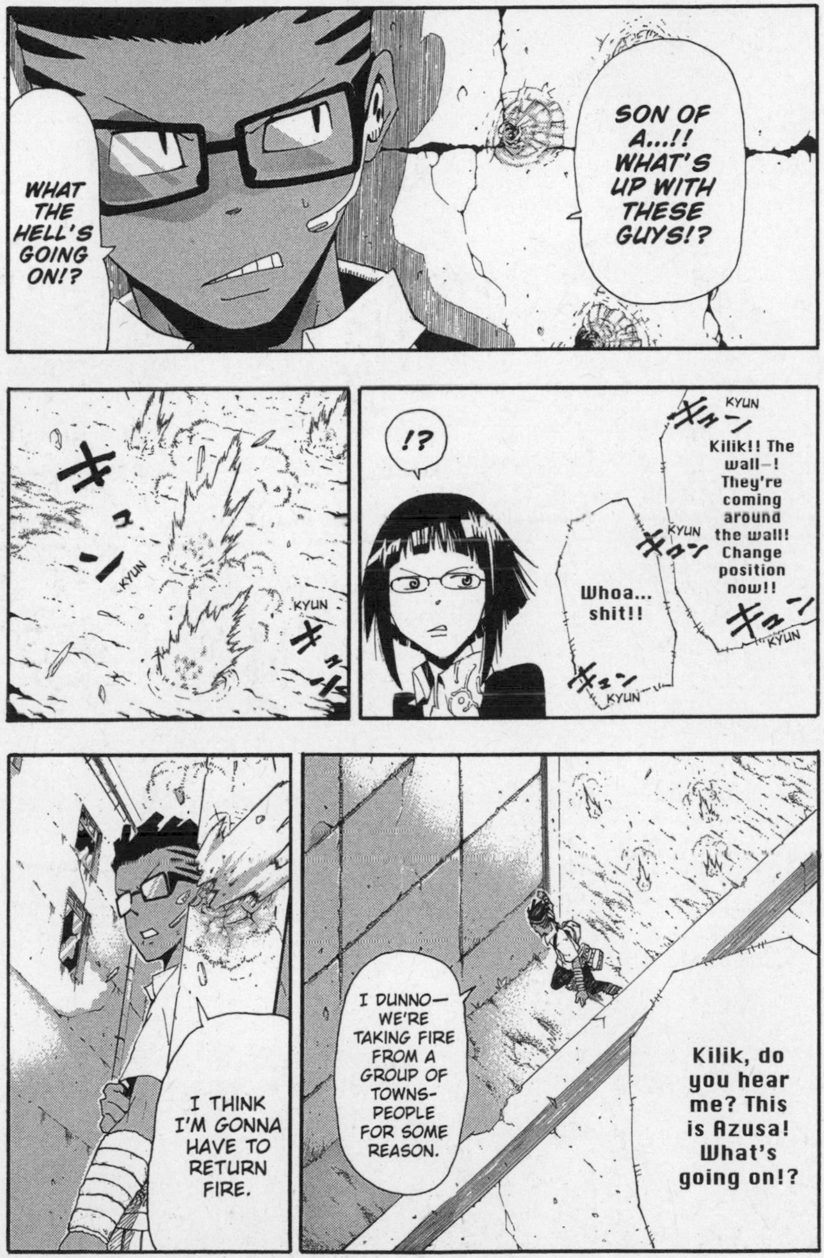
SON OF A...!! WHAT'S UP WITH THESE GUYS!?
WHAT THE HELL'S GOING ON!?
KYUN
Kilik!! The wall—! They're coming around the wall! Change position now!!
!?
KYUN
KYUN
Whoa... shit!!
KYUN
KYUN
KYUN
Kilik, do you hear me? This is Azusa! What's going on!?
I DUNNO— WE'RE TAKING FIRE FROM A GROUP OF TOWNS-PEOPLE FOR SOME REASON.
I THINK I'M GONNA HAVE TO RETURN FIRE.

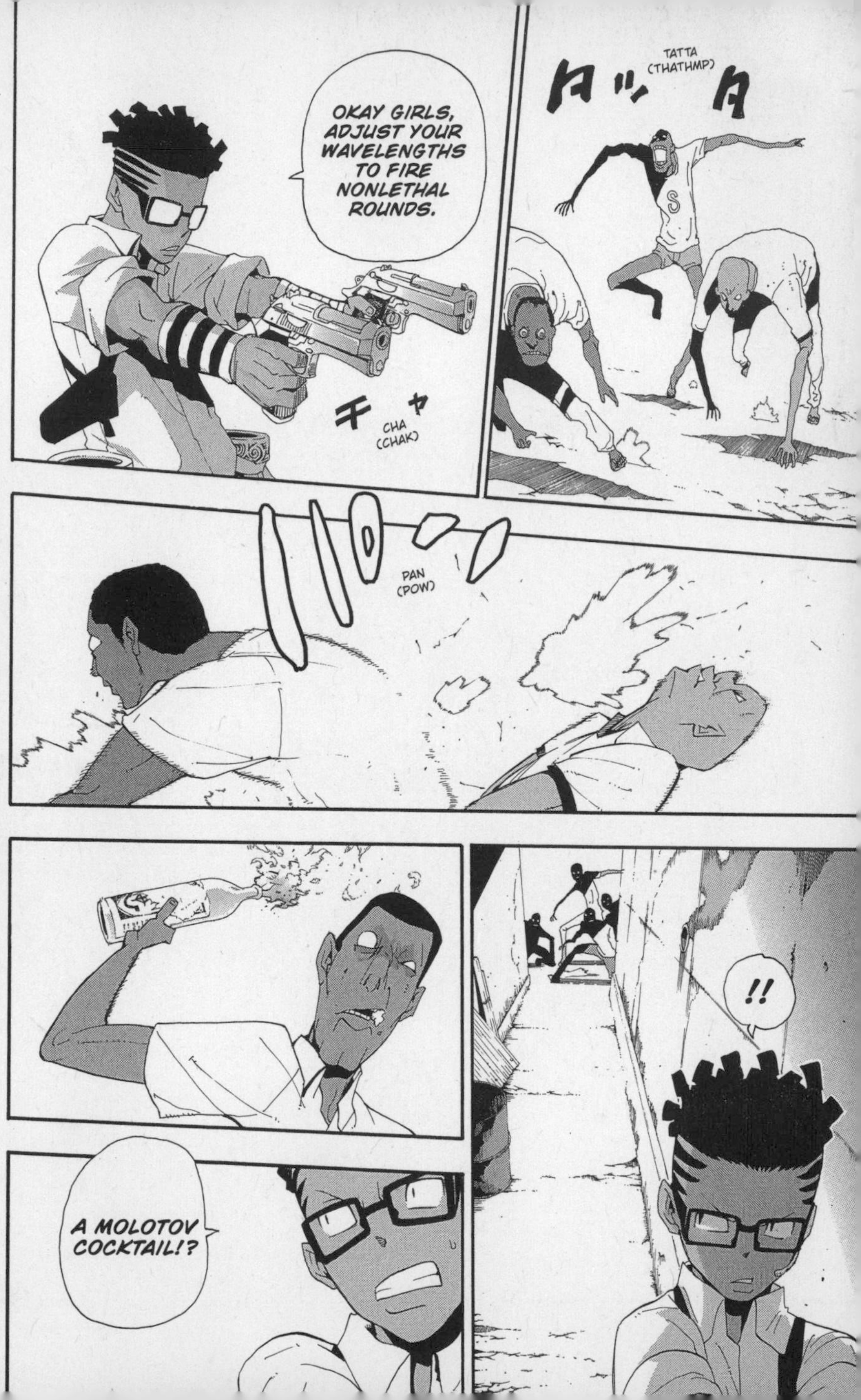
TATTA (THATHMP)
OKAY GIRLS, ADJUST YOUR WAVELENGTHS TO FIRE NONLETHAL ROUNDS.
CHA (CHAK)
PAN (POW)
!!
A MOLOTOV COCKTAIL!?

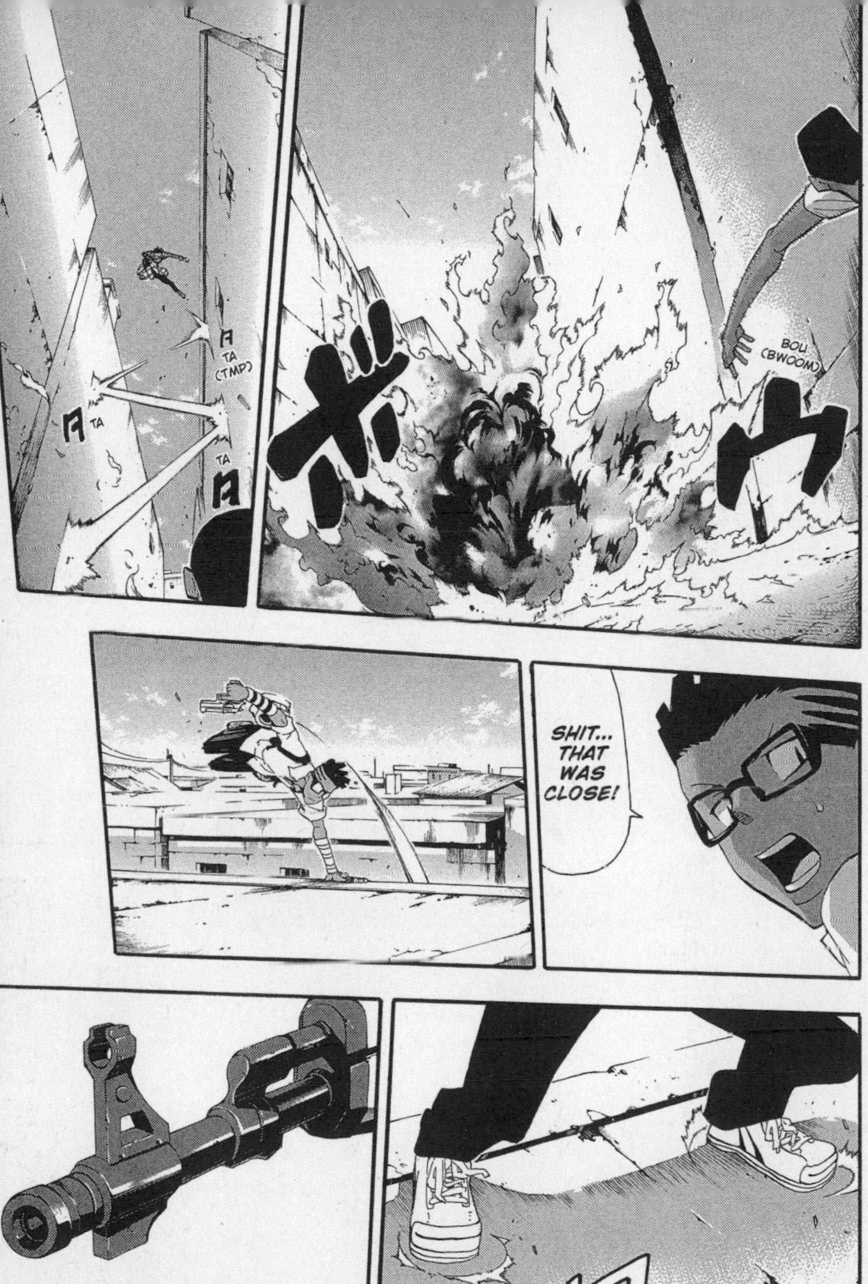
BOU (BWOOM)
TA (TMP)
TA
TA
SHIT... THAT WAS CLOSE!
TA

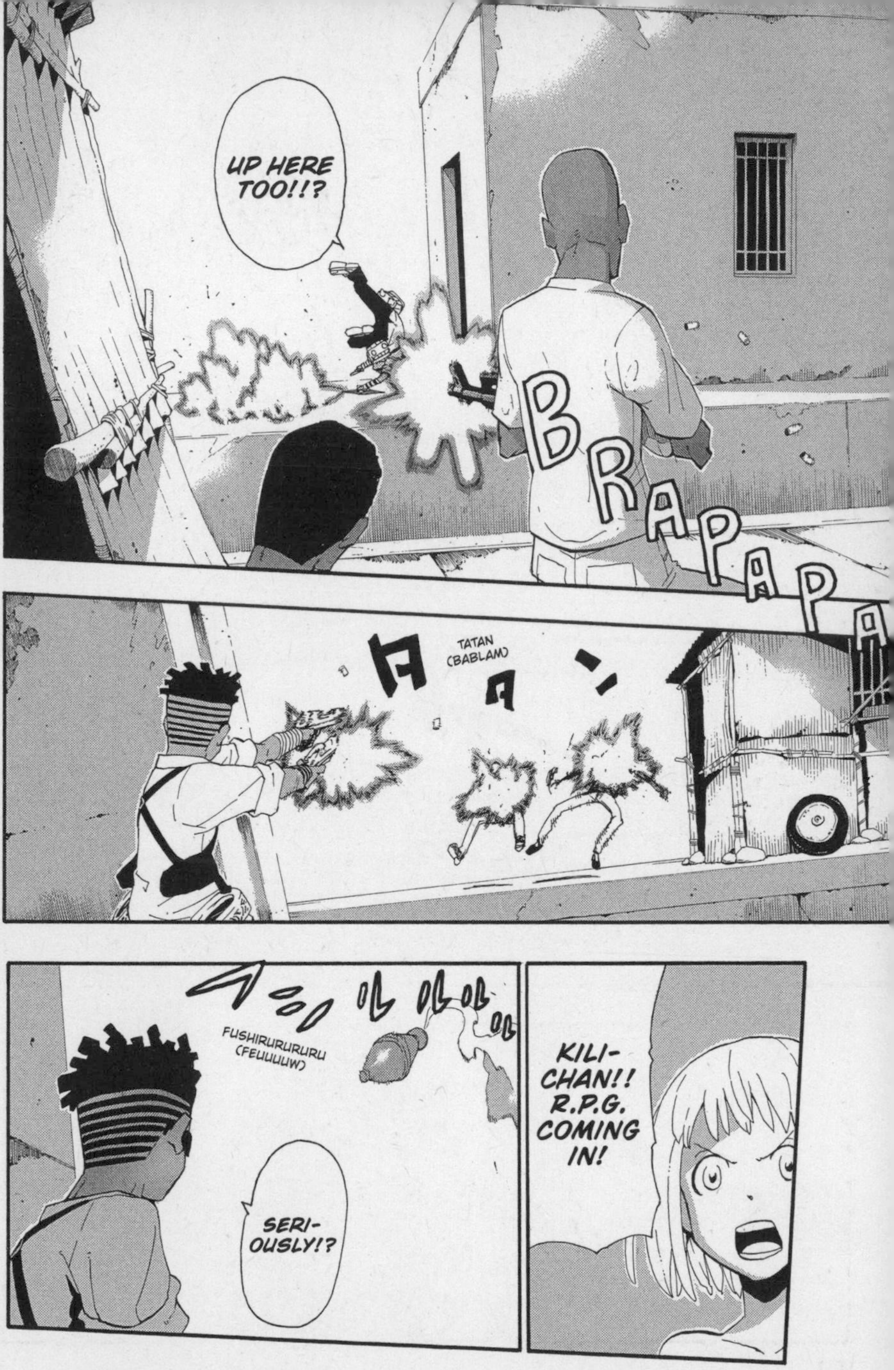
UP HERE TOO!!?
BRAPAPAPA
TATAN (BABLAM)
KILI-CHAN!! R.P.G. COMING IN!
FUSHIRURURURU (FEUUUUW)
SERI-OUSLY!?

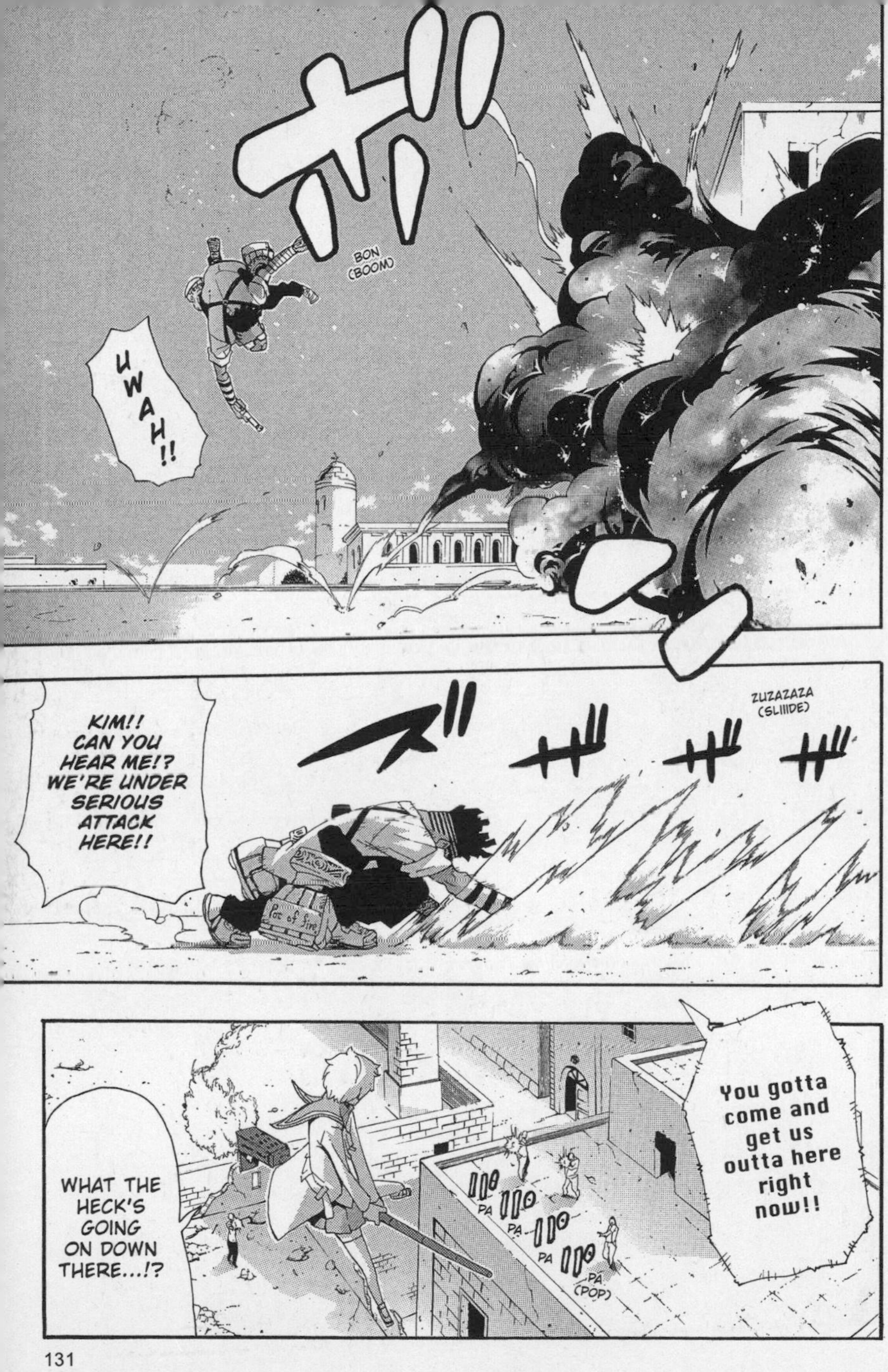
BON (BOOM)
UWAH!!
ZUZAZAZA (SLIIIDE)
KIM!! CAN YOU HEAR ME!? WE'RE UNDER SERIOUS ATTACK HERE!!
You gotta come and get us outta here right now!!
PA
PA
PA
PA (POP)
WHAT THE HECK'S GOING ON DOWN THERE...!?

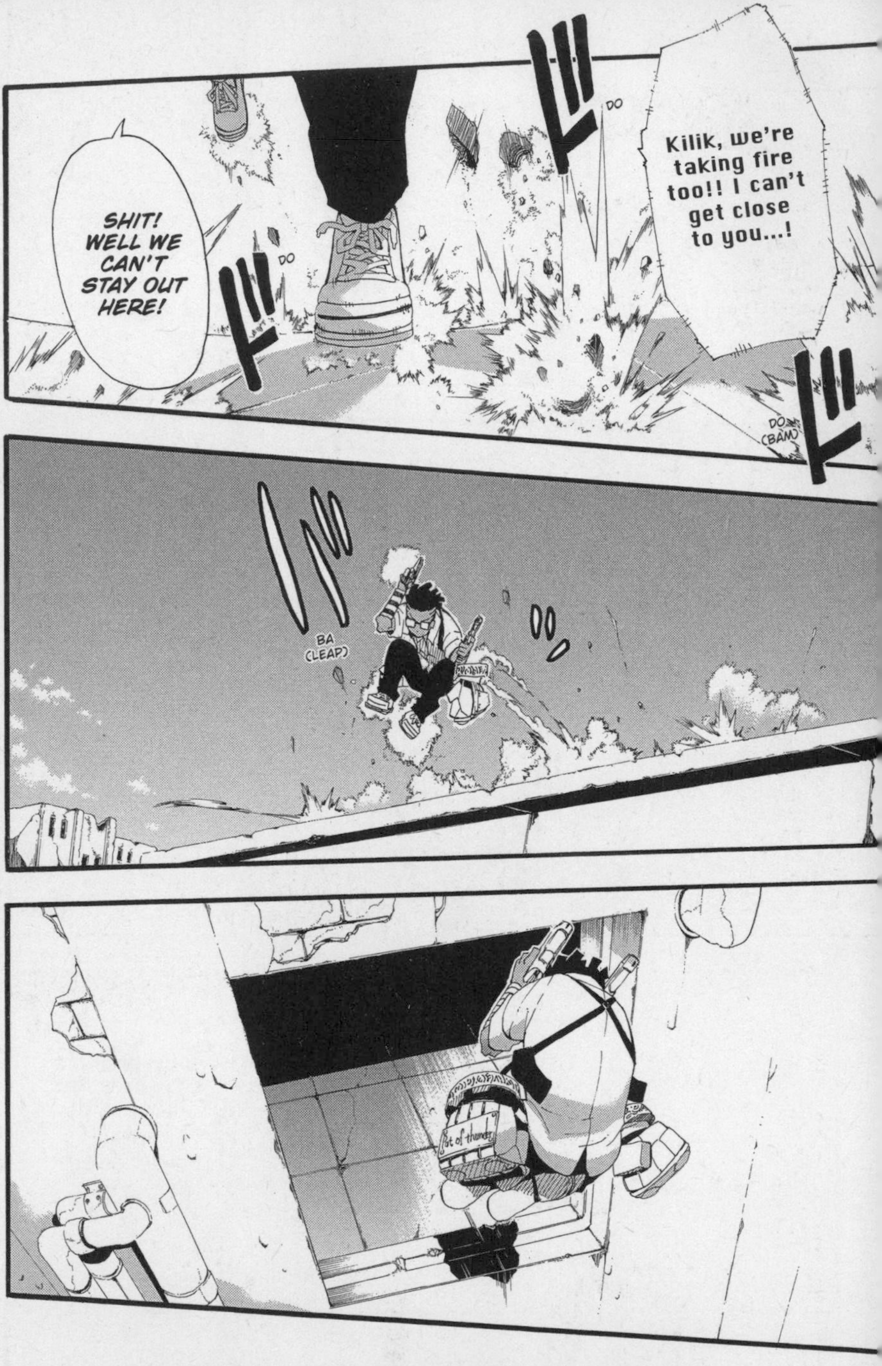
DO (BAM)
Kilik, we're taking fire too!! I can't get close to you...!
DO
DO
SHIT! WELL WE CAN'T STAY OUT HERE!
BA (LEAP)

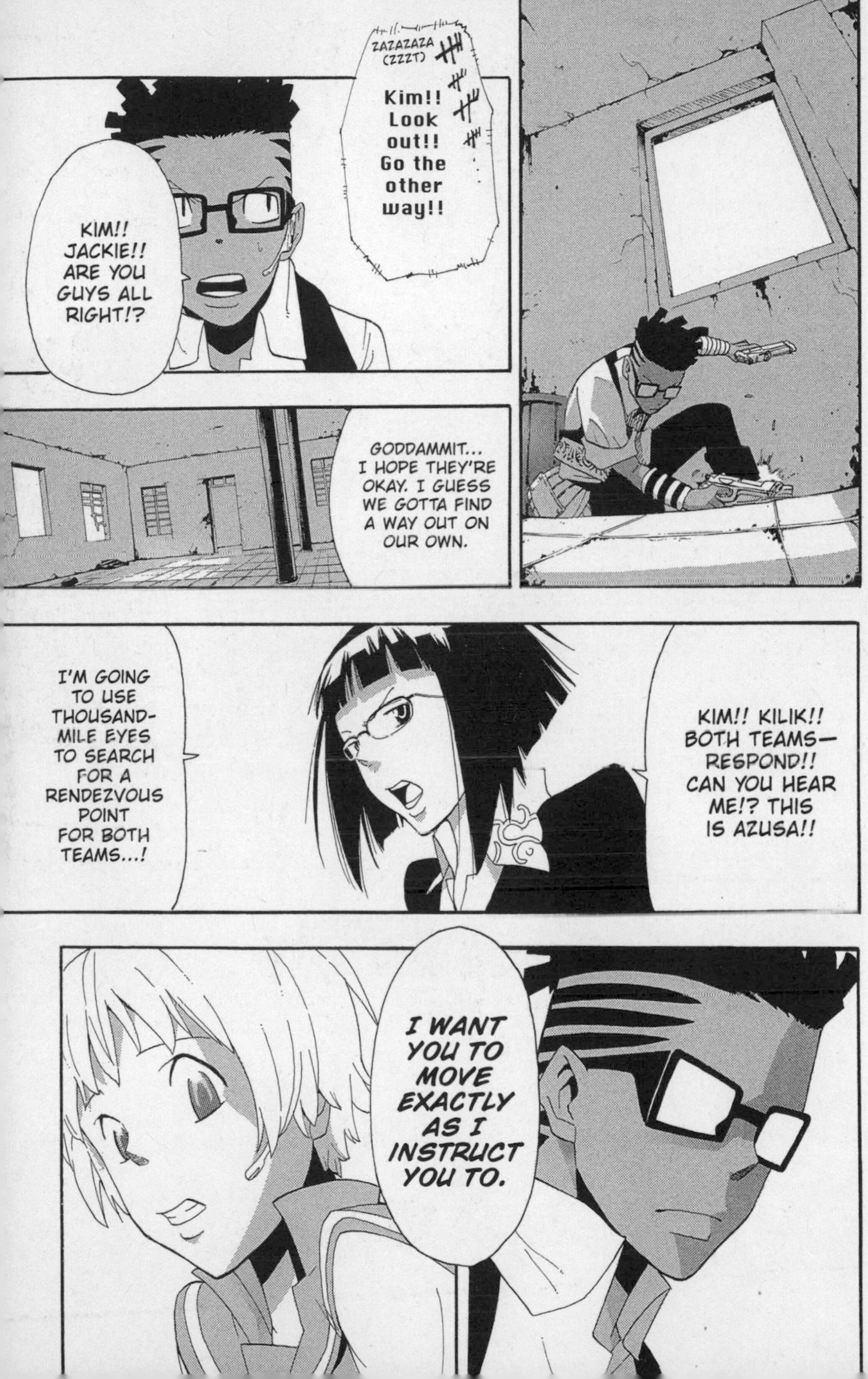
ZAZAZAZA (ZZZT)
Kim!! Look out!! Go the other way!!
KIM!! JACKIE!! ARE YOU GUYS ALL RIGHT!?
GODDAMMIT... I HOPE THEY'RE OKAY. I GUESS WE GOTTA FIND A WAY OUT ON OUR OWN.
KIM!! KILIK!! BOTH TEAMS—RESPOND!! CAN YOU HEAR ME!? THIS IS AZUSA!!
I'M GOING TO USE THOUSAND-MILE EYES TO SEARCH FOR A RENDEZVOUS POINT FOR BOTH TEAMS...!
I WANT YOU TO MOVE EXACTLY AS I INSTRUCT YOU TO.

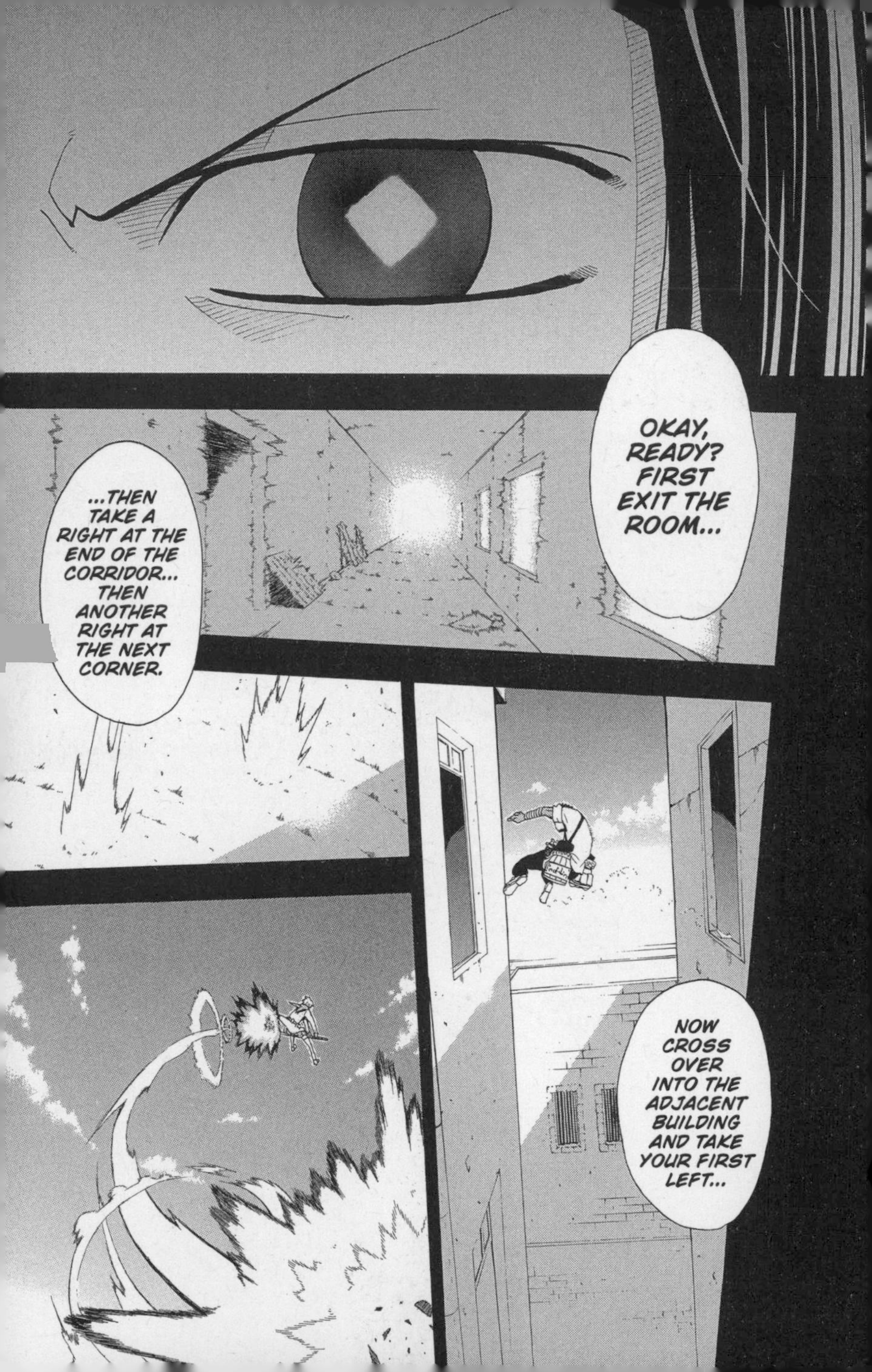
OKAY, READY? FIRST EXIT THE ROOM...
...THEN TAKE A RIGHT AT THE END OF THE CORRIDOR... THEN ANOTHER RIGHT AT THE NEXT CORNER.
NOW CROSS OVER INTO THE ADJACENT BUILDING AND TAKE YOUR FIRST LEFT...

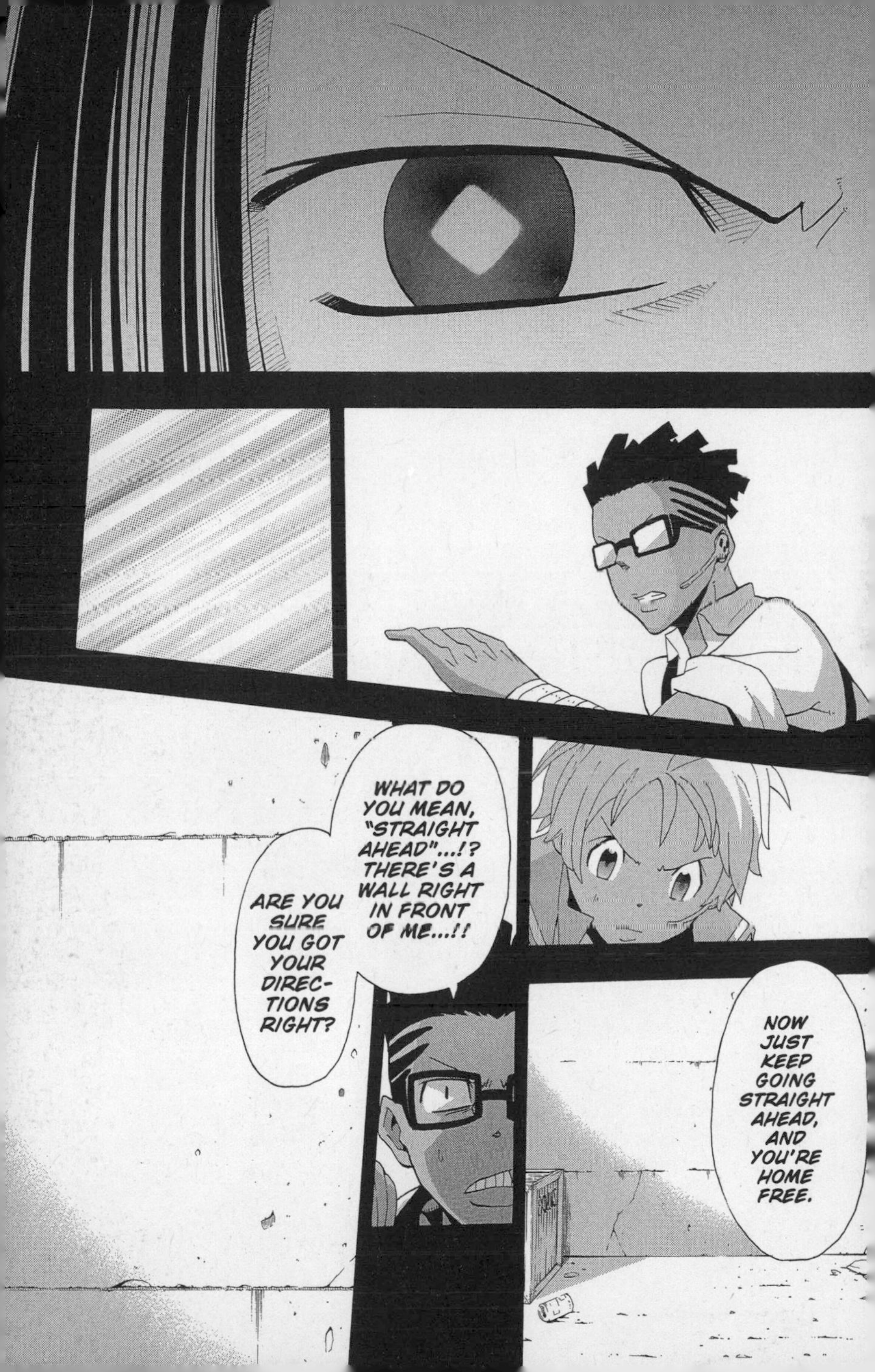
NOW JUST KEEP GOING STRAIGHT AHEAD, AND YOU'RE HOME FREE.
WHAT DO YOU MEAN, "STRAIGHT AHEAD"...!? THERE'S A WALL RIGHT IN FRONT OF ME...!!
ARE YOU SURE YOU GOT YOUR DIREC-TIONS RIGHT?

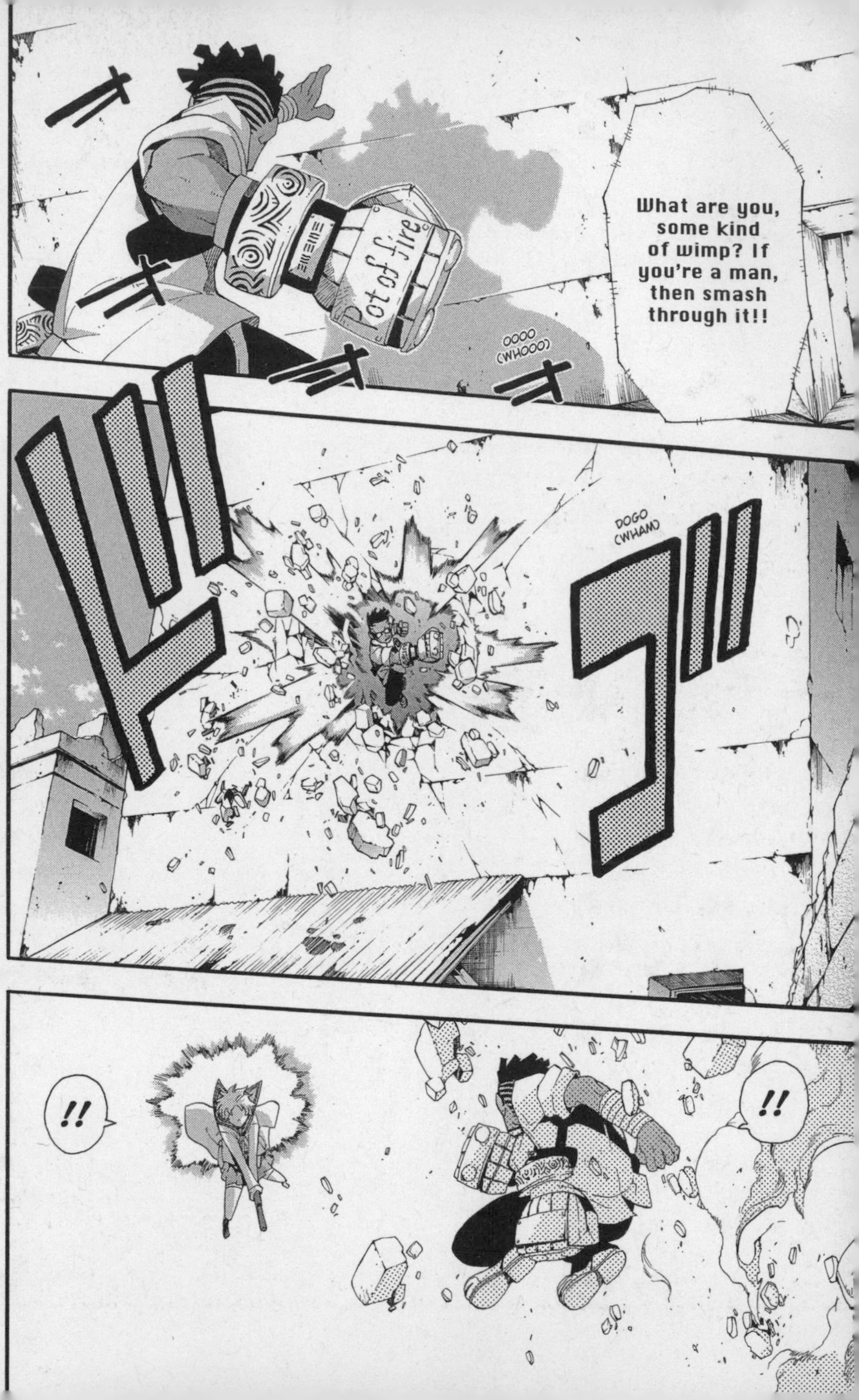
What are you, some kind of wimp? If you're a man, then smash through it!!
OOOO (WHOOO)
DOGO (WHAM)
!!
!!

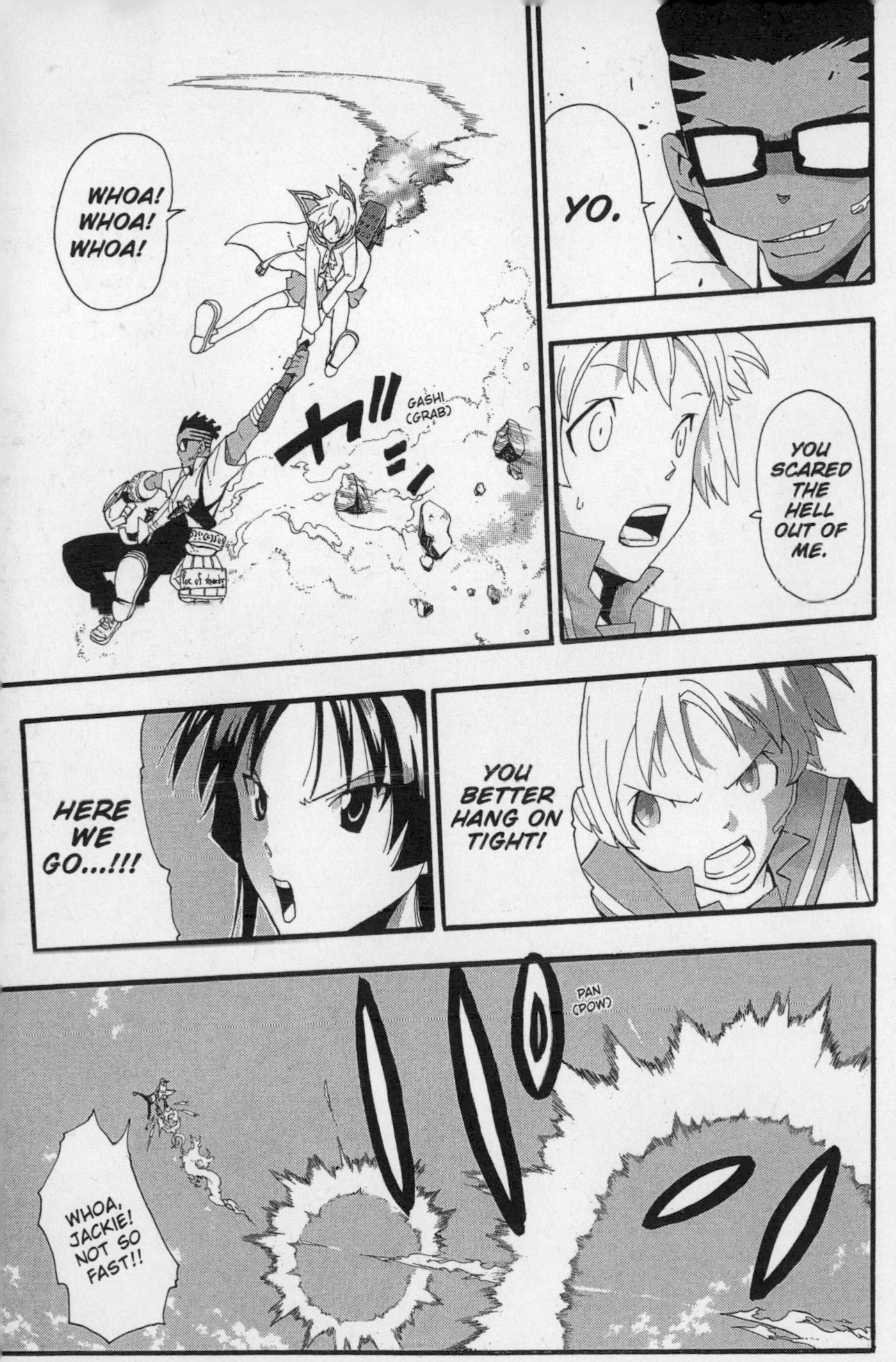
YO.
YOU SCARED THE HELL OUT OF ME.
WHOA! WHOA! WHOA!
GASHI (GRAB)
YOU BETTER HANG ON TIGHT!
HERE WE GO...!!!
PAN (POW)
WHOA, JACKIE! NOT SO FAST!!

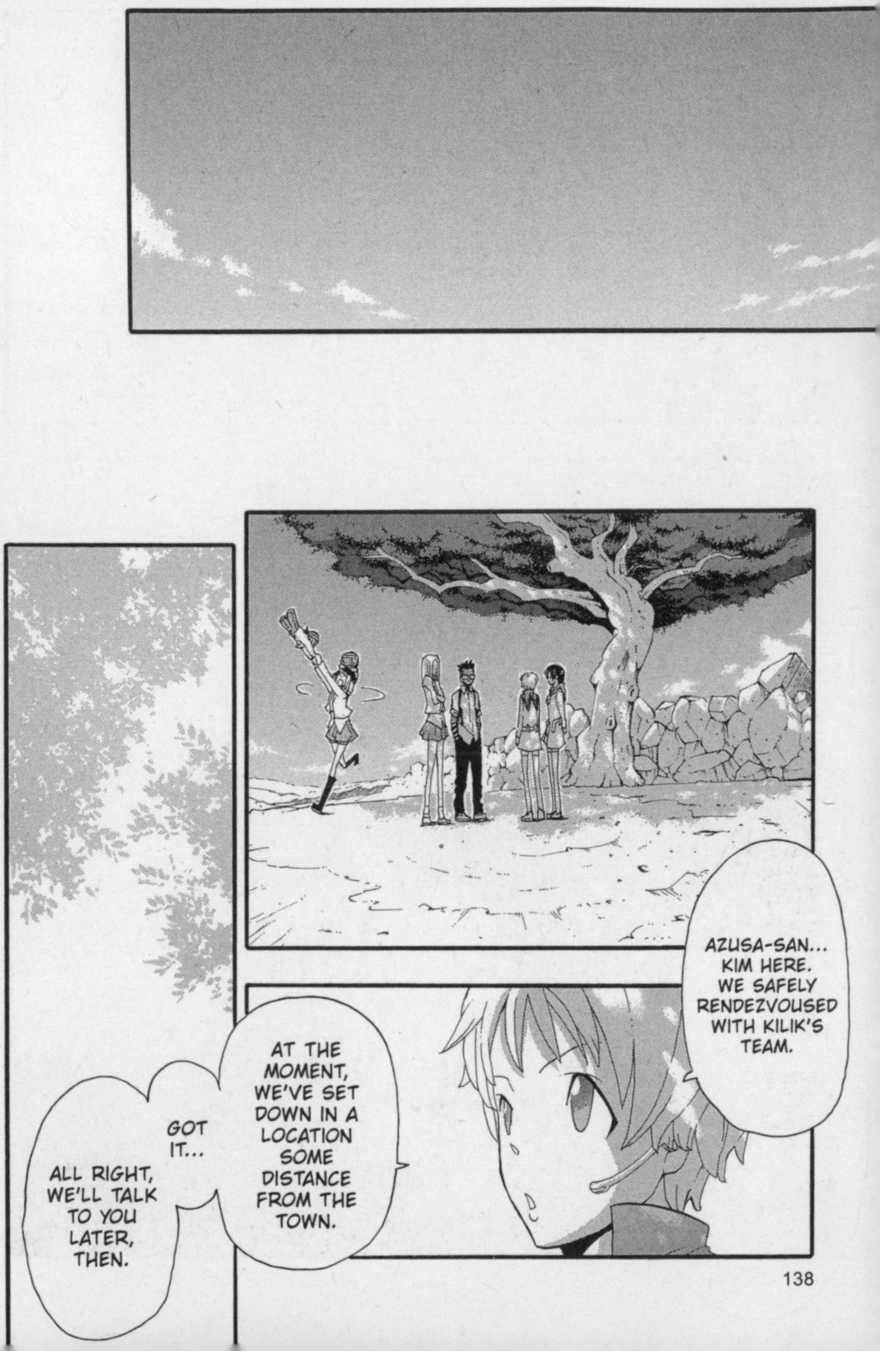
AZUSA-SAN... KIM HERE. WE SAFELY RENDEZVOUSED WITH KILIK'S TEAM.
AT THE MOMENT, WE'VE SET DOWN IN A LOCATION SOME DISTANCE FROM THE TOWN.
GOT IT...
ALL RIGHT, WE'LL TALK TO YOU LATER, THEN.

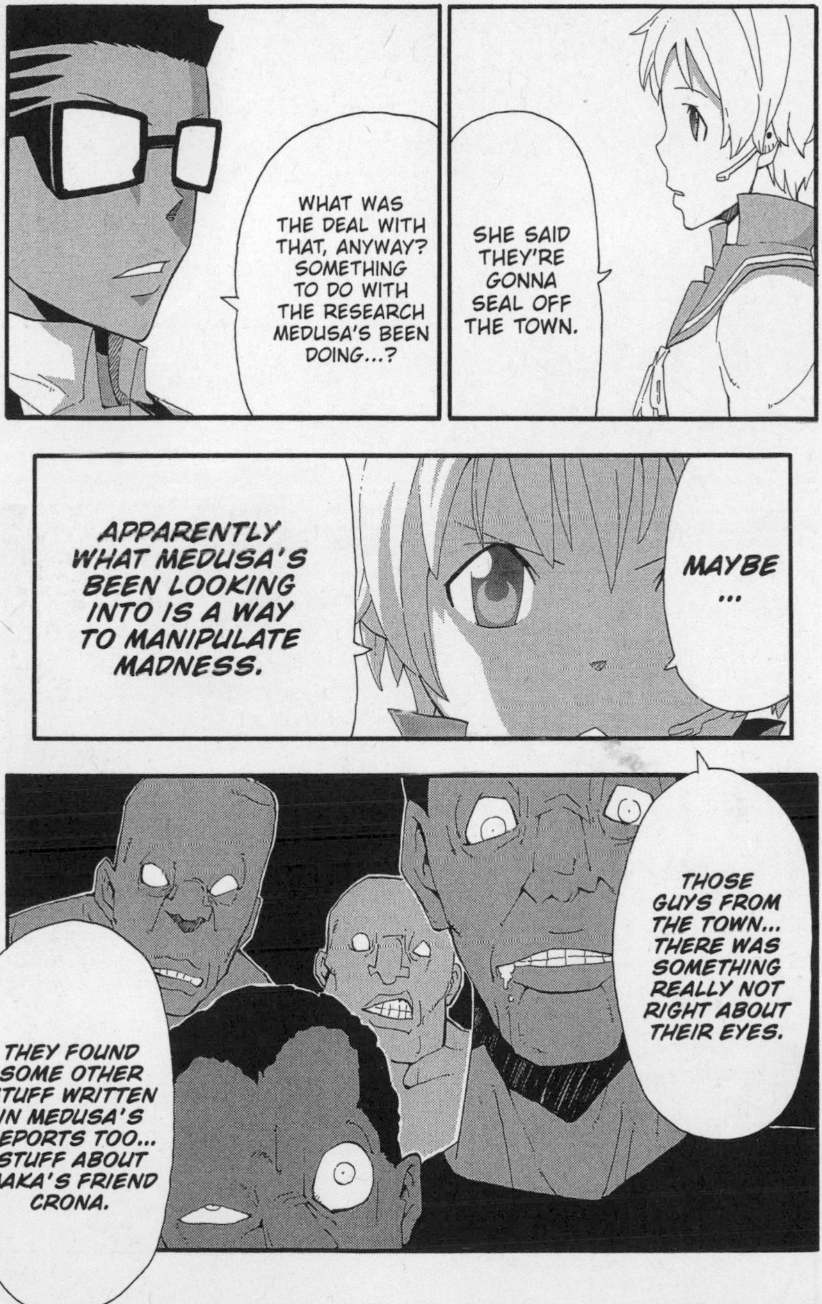
SHE SAID THEY'RE GONNA SEAL OFF THE TOWN.
WHAT WAS THE DEAL WITH THAT, ANYWAY? SOMETHING TO DO WITH THE RESEARCH MEDUSA'S BEEN DOING...?
MAYBE ...
APPARENTLY WHAT MEDUSA'S BEEN LOOKING INTO IS A WAY TO MANIPULATE MADNESS.
THOSE GUYS FROM THE TOWN... THERE WAS SOMETHING REALLY NOT RIGHT ABOUT THEIR EYES.
THEY FOUND SOME OTHER STUFF WRITTEN IN MEDUSA'S REPORTS TOO... STUFF ABOUT MAKA'S FRIEND CRONA.

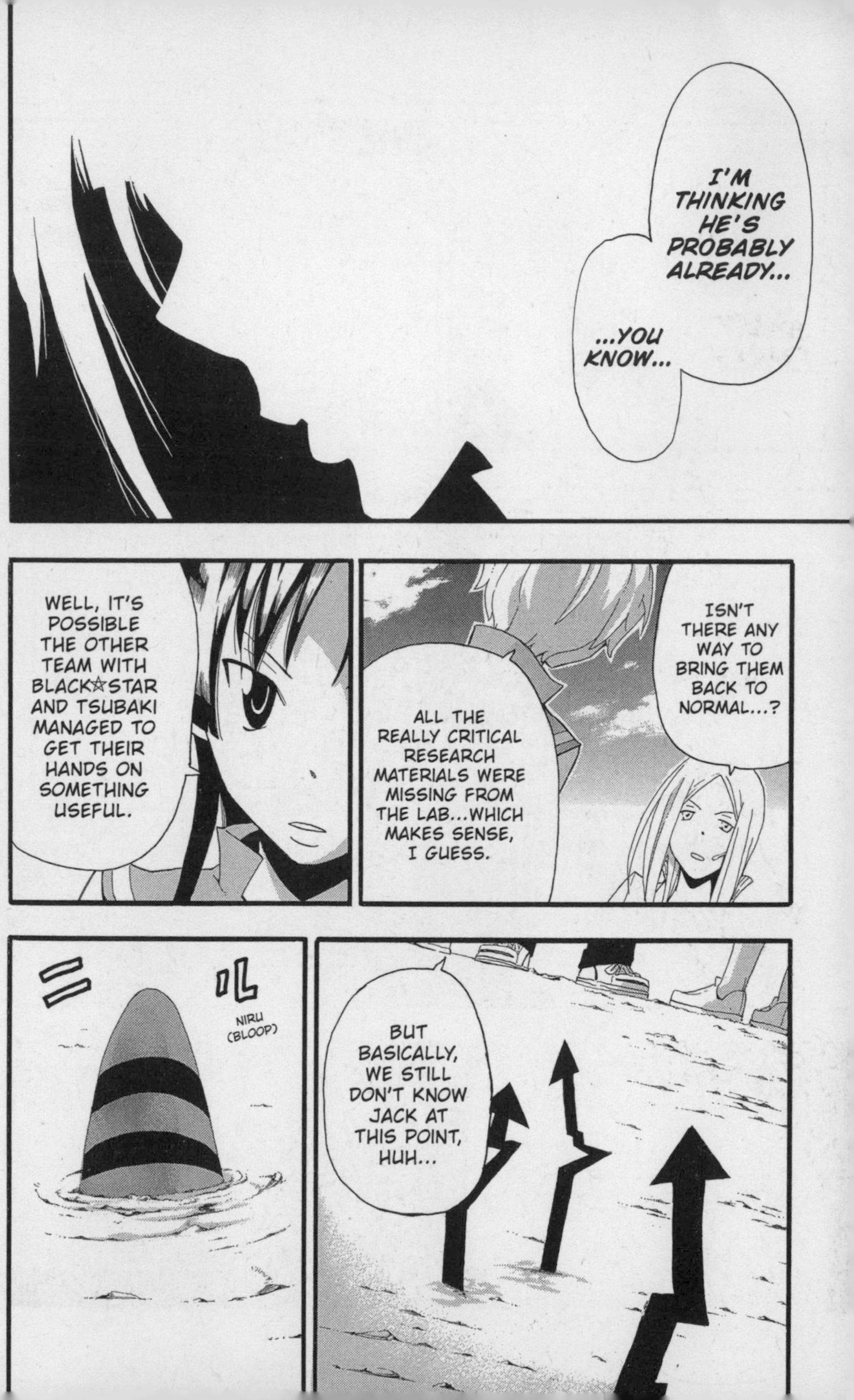
I'M THINKING HE'S PROBABLY ALREADY...
...YOU KNOW...
ISN'T THERE ANY WAY TO BRING THEM BACK TO NORMAL...?
ALL THE REALLY CRITICAL RESEARCH MATERIALS WERE MISSING FROM THE LAB...WHICH MAKES SENSE, I GUESS.
WELL, IT'S POSSIBLE THE OTHER TEAM WITH BLACK☆STAR AND TSUBAKI MANAGED TO GET THEIR HANDS ON SOMETHING USEFUL.
BUT BASICALLY, WE STILL DON'T KNOW JACK AT THIS POINT, HUH...
NIRU (BLOOP)

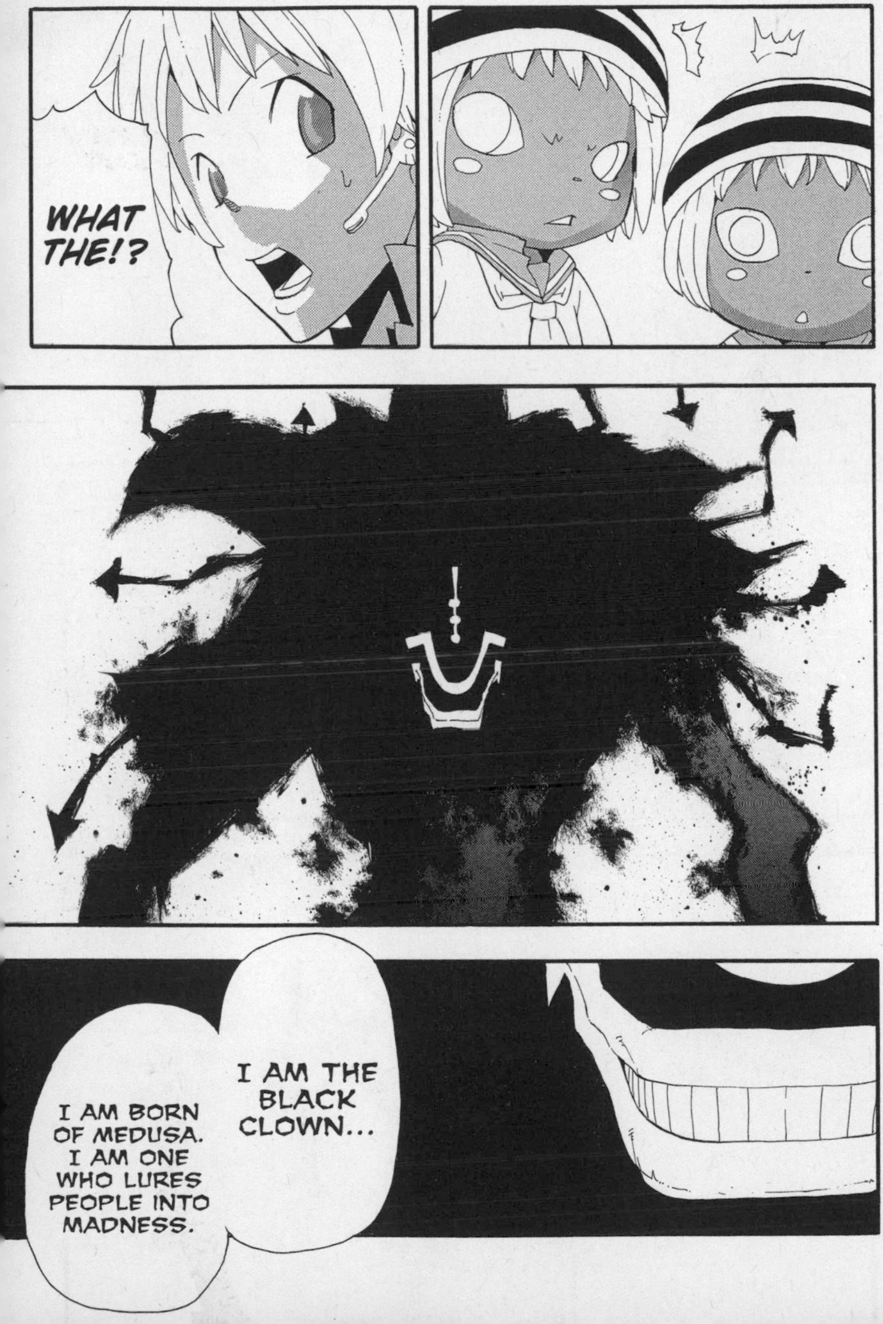
WHAT THE!?
I AM THE BLACK CLOWN...
I AM BORN OF MEDUSA. I AM ONE WHO LURES PEOPLE INTO MADNESS.

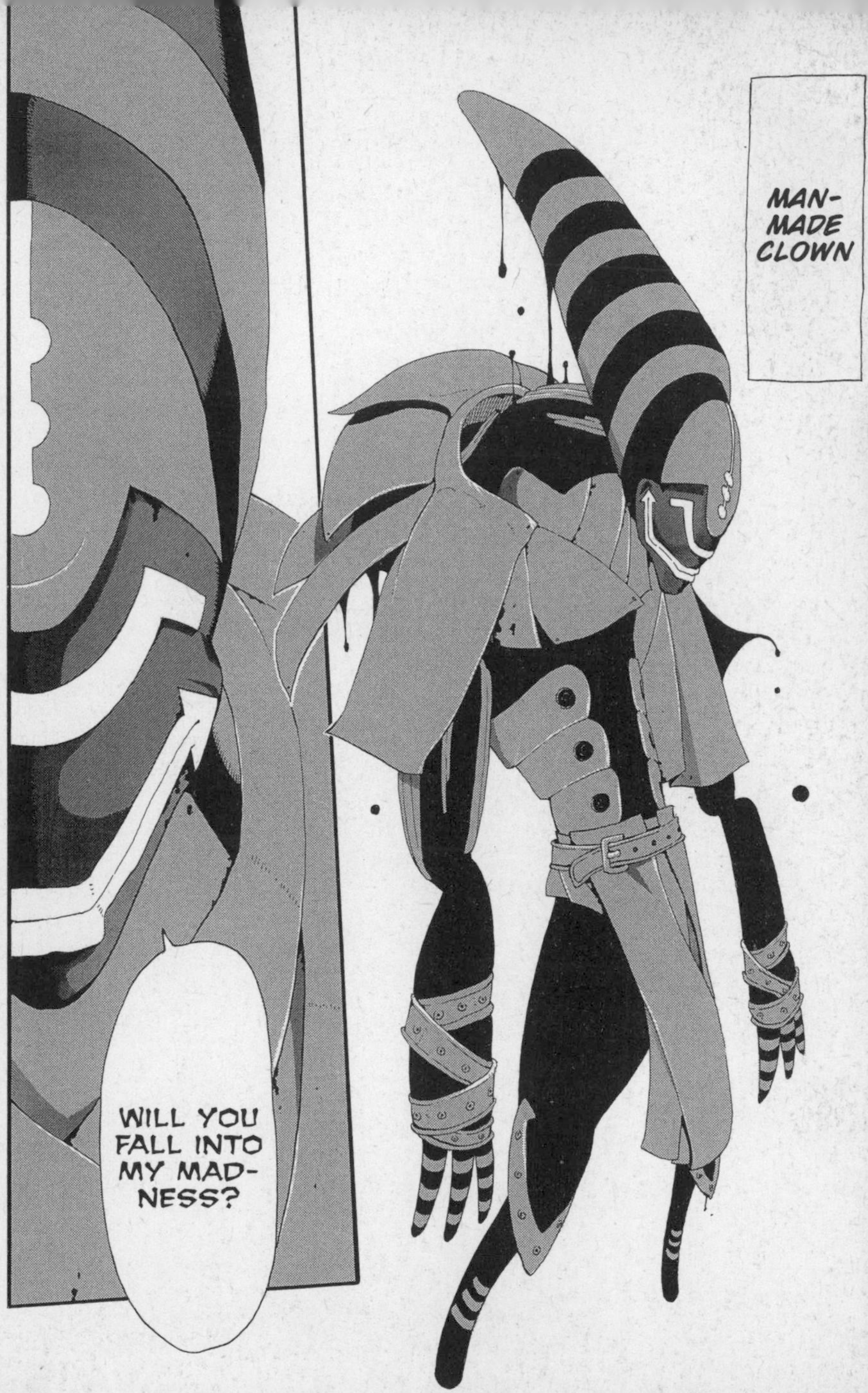
MAN-MADE CLOWN
WILL YOU FALL INTO MY MADNESS?

SOUL EATER

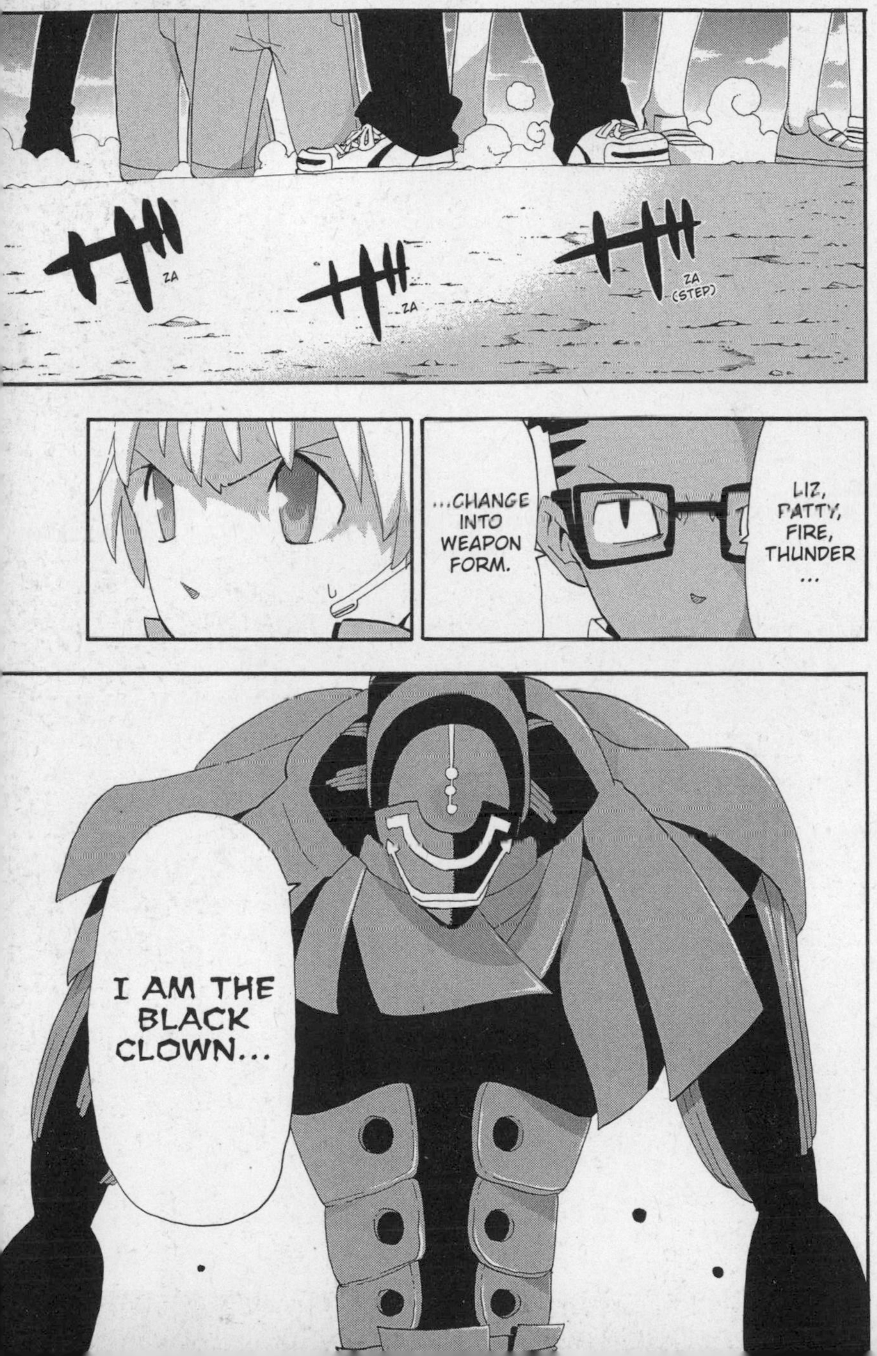
ZA (STEP)
ZA
ZA
LIZ, PATTY, FIRE, THUNDER...
...CHANGE INTO WEAPON FORM.
I AM THE BLACK CLOWN...

...WILL YOU FALL INTO MY MADNESS?

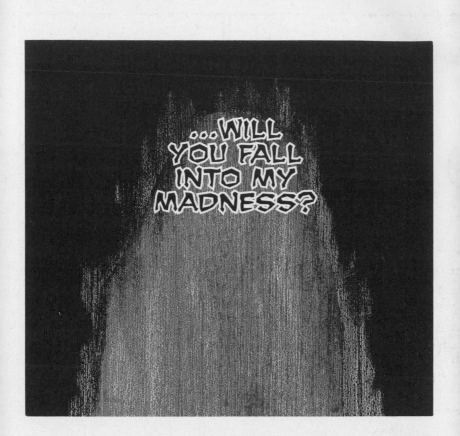

# SOUL EATER

## CHAPTER 67: THE WITCH'S RESEARCH (PART 2)

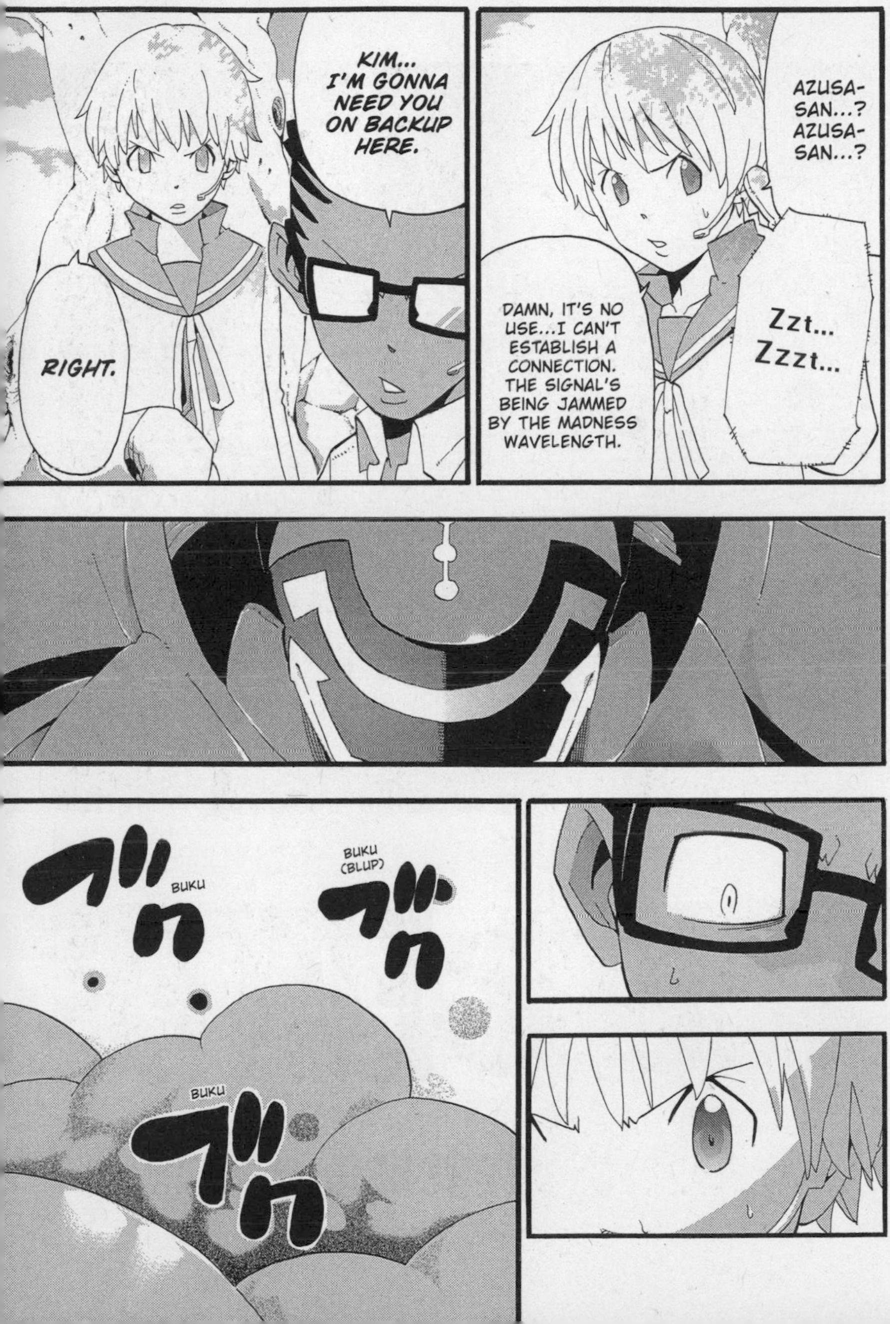
AZUSA-SAN...? AZUSA-SAN...?
Zzt... Zzzt...
DAMN, IT'S NO USE...I CAN'T ESTABLISH A CONNECTION. THE SIGNAL'S BEING JAMMED BY THE MADNESS WAVELENGTH.
KIM... I'M GONNA NEED YOU ON BACKUP HERE.
RIGHT.
ブク
BUKU (BLUP)
ブク
BUKU
ブク
BUKU

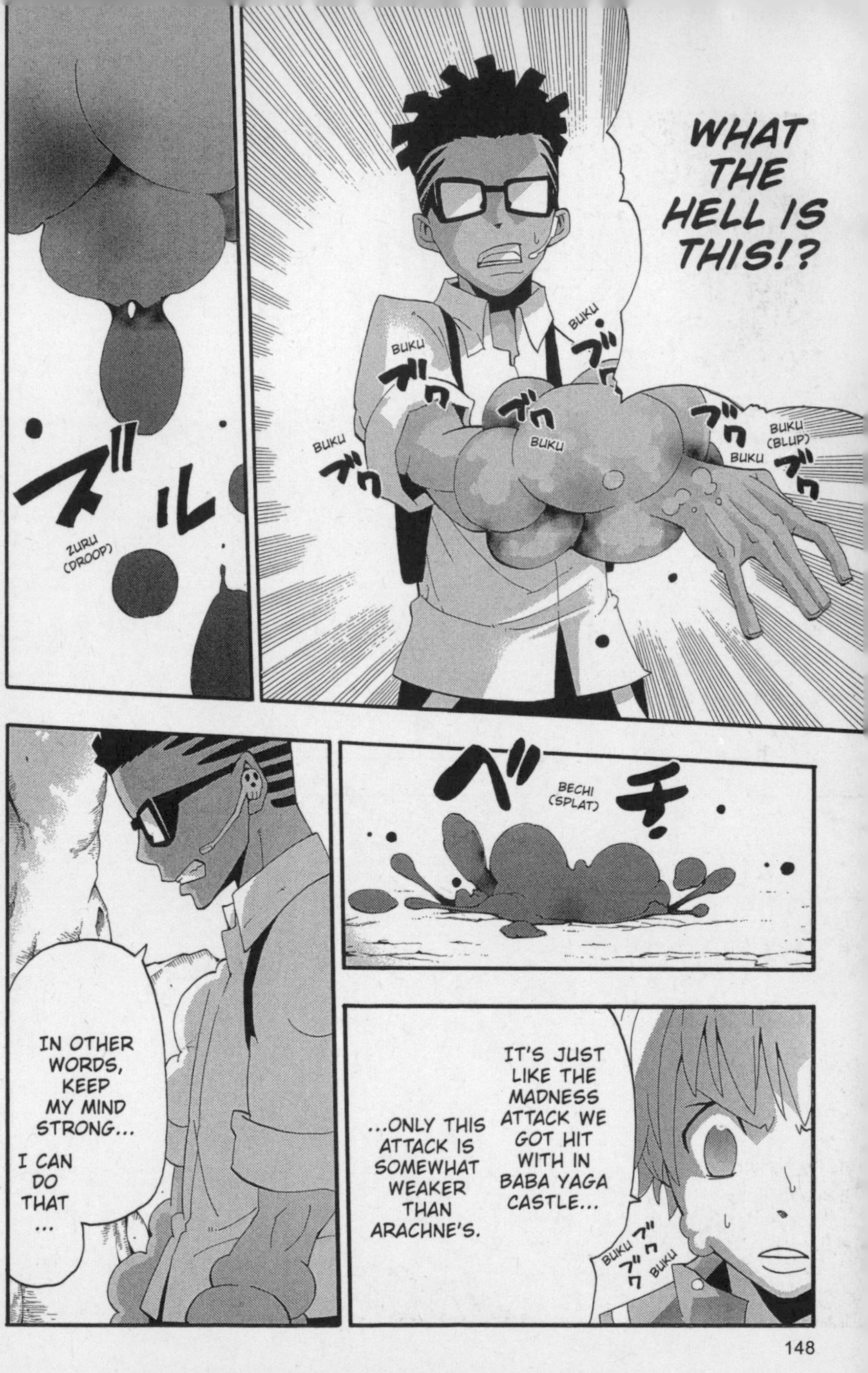
WHAT THE HELL IS THIS!?
ブク
BUKU
ブク
BUKU
ブク
BUKU
ブク
BUKU
ブク
BUKU (BLUP)
ブク
BUKU
ズル
ZURU (DROOP)
ベチ
BECHI (SPLAT)
IT'S JUST LIKE THE MADNESS ATTACK WE GOT HIT WITH IN BABA YAGA CASTLE...
...ONLY THIS ATTACK IS SOMEWHAT WEAKER THAN ARACHNE'S.
ブク
BUKU
ブク
BUKU
IN OTHER WORDS, KEEP MY MIND STRONG...
I CAN DO THAT...

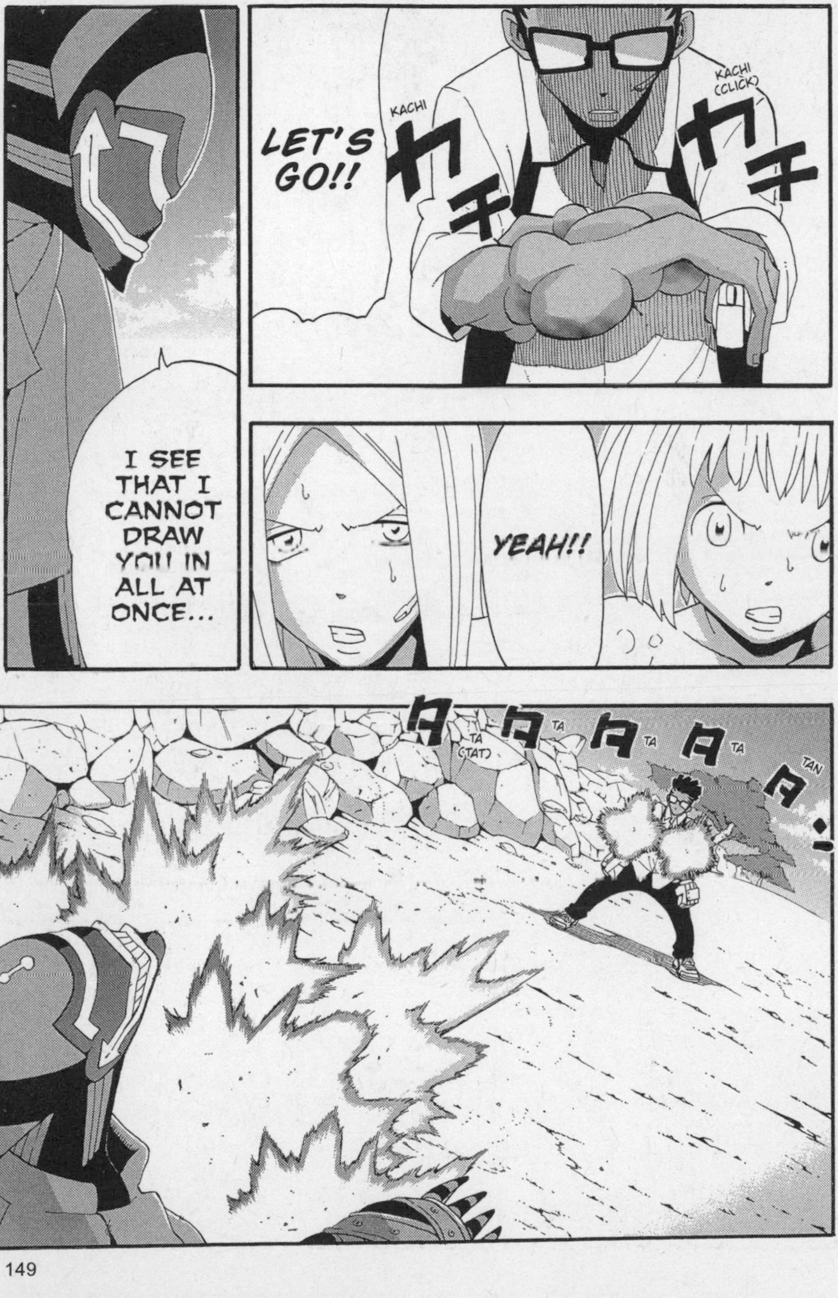
KACHI (CLICK)
KACHI
LET'S GO!!
YEAH!!
I SEE THAT I CANNOT DRAW YOU IN ALL AT ONCE...
TA (TAT) TA TA TA TAN

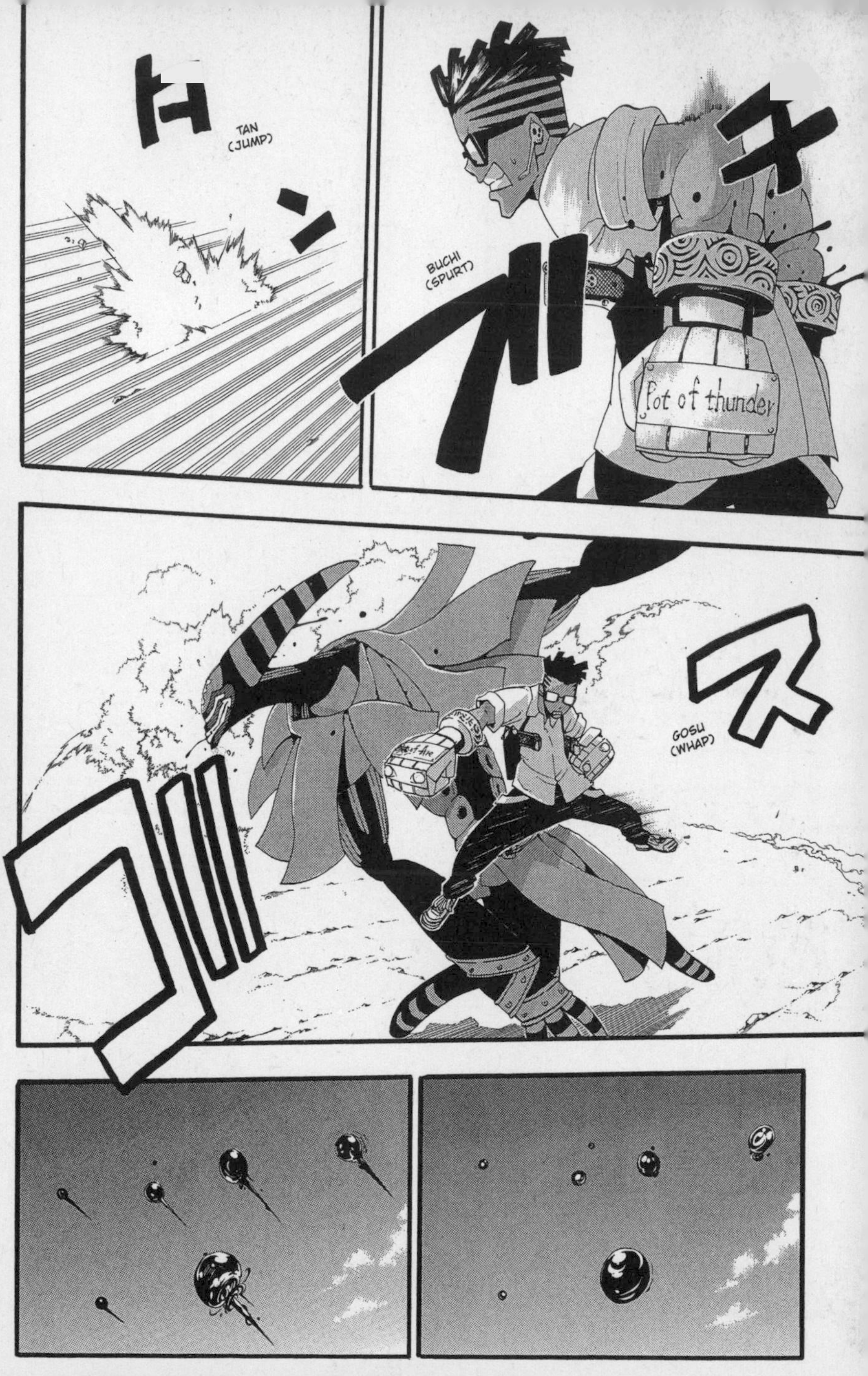
BUCHI
(SPURT)
TAN
(JUMP)
GOSU
(WHAP)

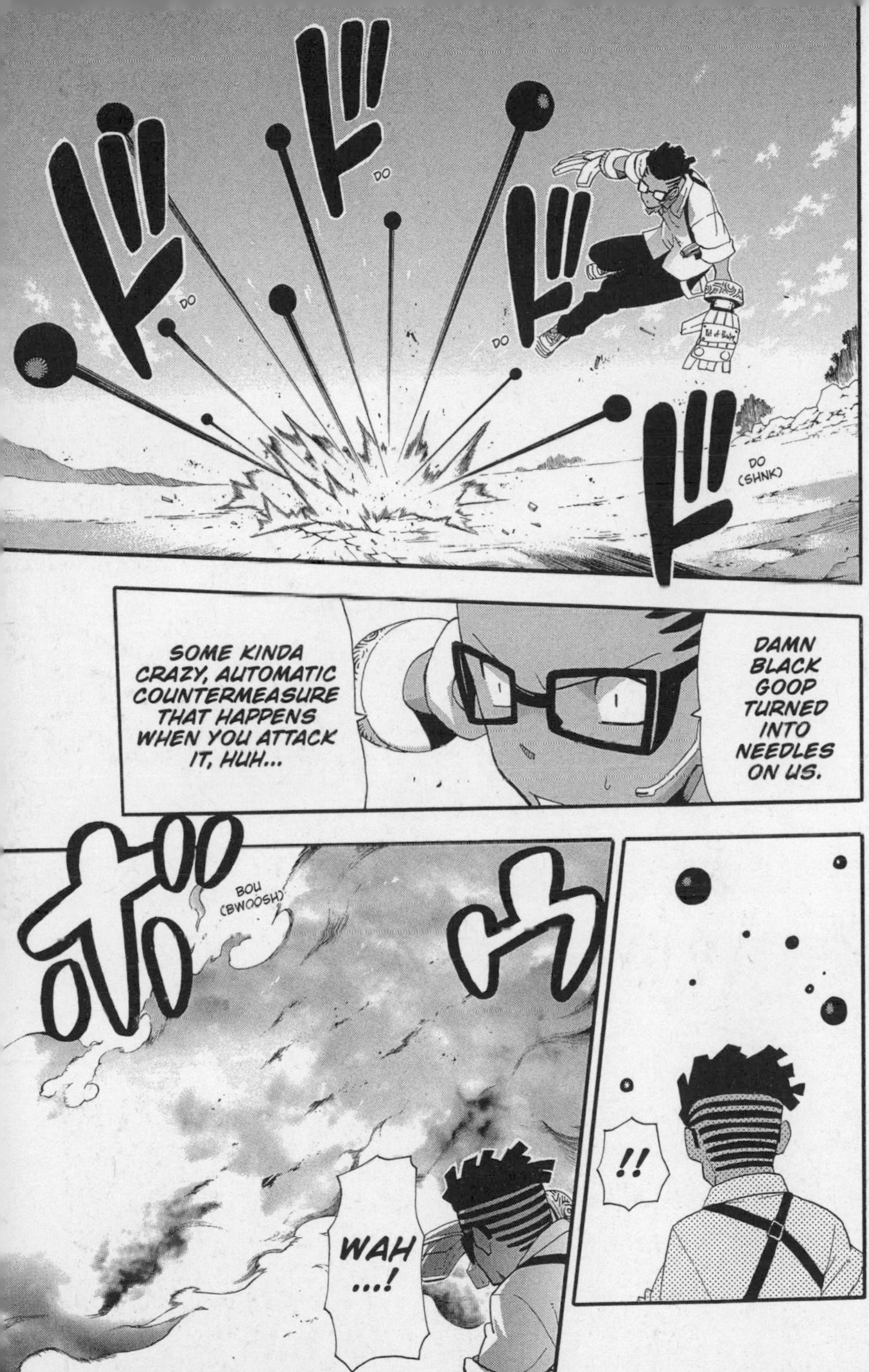
DO
(SHNK)
DO
DO
DO
DAMN BLACK GOOP TURNED INTO NEEDLES ON US.
SOME KINDA CRAZY, AUTOMATIC COUNTERMEASURE THAT HAPPENS WHEN YOU ATTACK IT, HUH...
!!
BOU
(BWOOSH)
WAH ...!

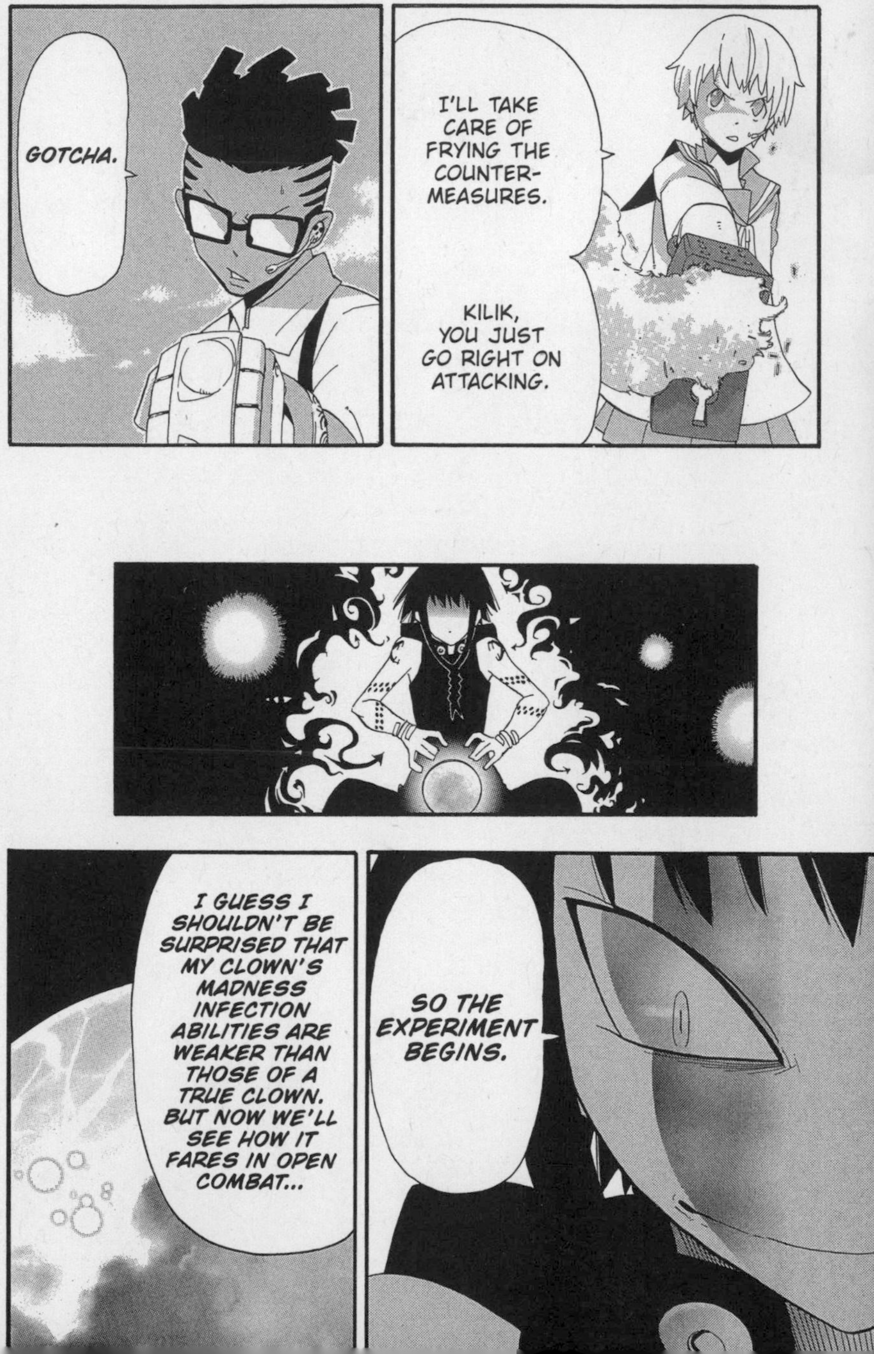
I'LL TAKE CARE OF FRYING THE COUNTER-MEASURES.
KILIK, YOU JUST GO RIGHT ON ATTACKING.
GOTCHA.
SO THE EXPERIMENT BEGINS.
I GUESS I SHOULDN'T BE SURPRISED THAT MY CLOWN'S MADNESS INFECTION ABILITIES ARE WEAKER THAN THOSE OF A TRUE CLOWN. BUT NOW WE'LL SEE HOW IT FARES IN OPEN COMBAT...

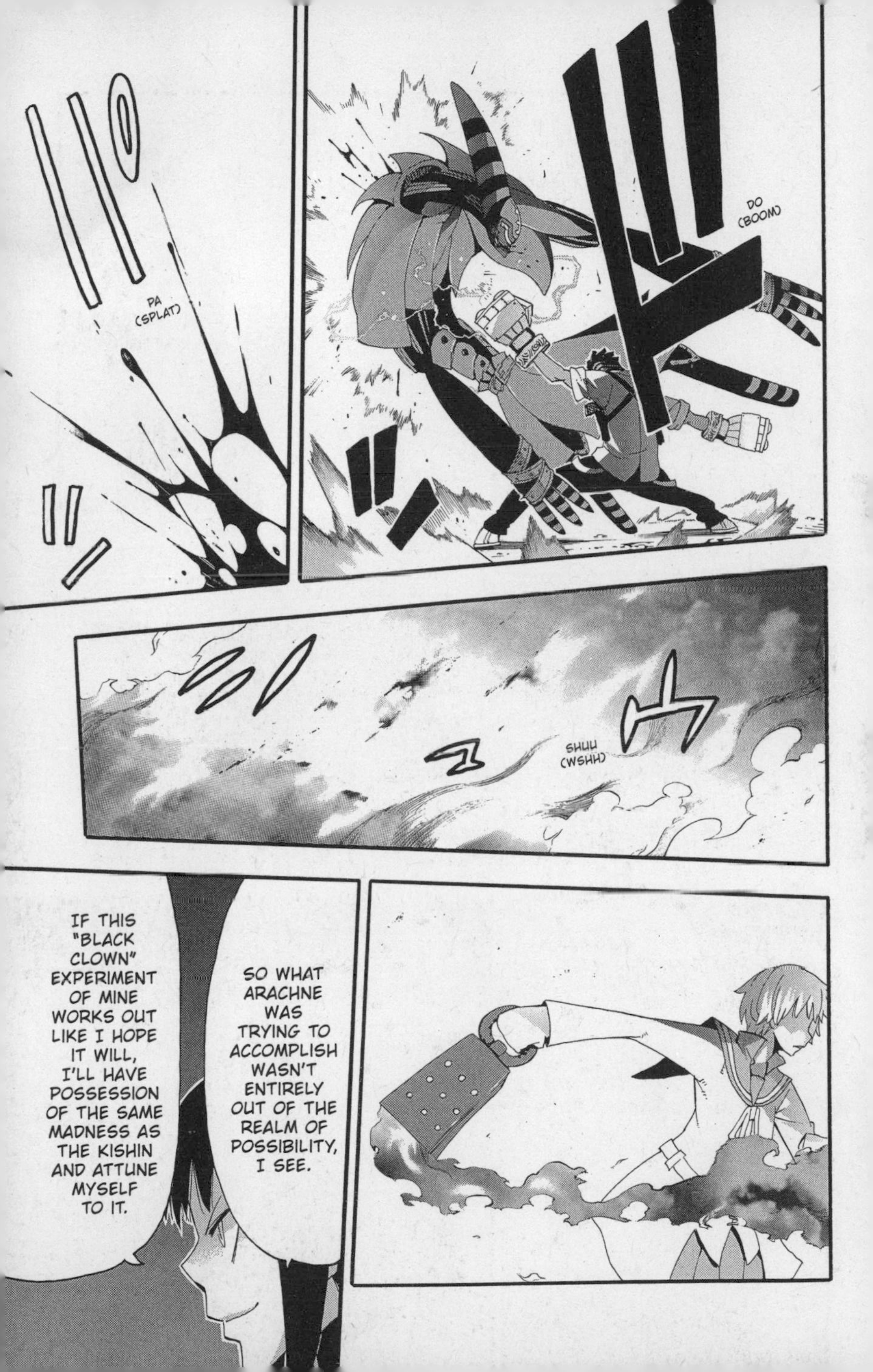
DO
(BOOM)
PA
(SPLAT)
SHUU
(WSHH)
SO WHAT ARACHNE WAS TRYING TO ACCOMPLISH WASN'T ENTIRELY OUT OF THE REALM OF POSSIBILITY, I SEE.
IF THIS "BLACK CLOWN" EXPERIMENT OF MINE WORKS OUT LIKE I HOPE IT WILL, I'LL HAVE POSSESSION OF THE SAME MADNESS AS THE KISHIN AND ATTUNE MYSELF TO IT.

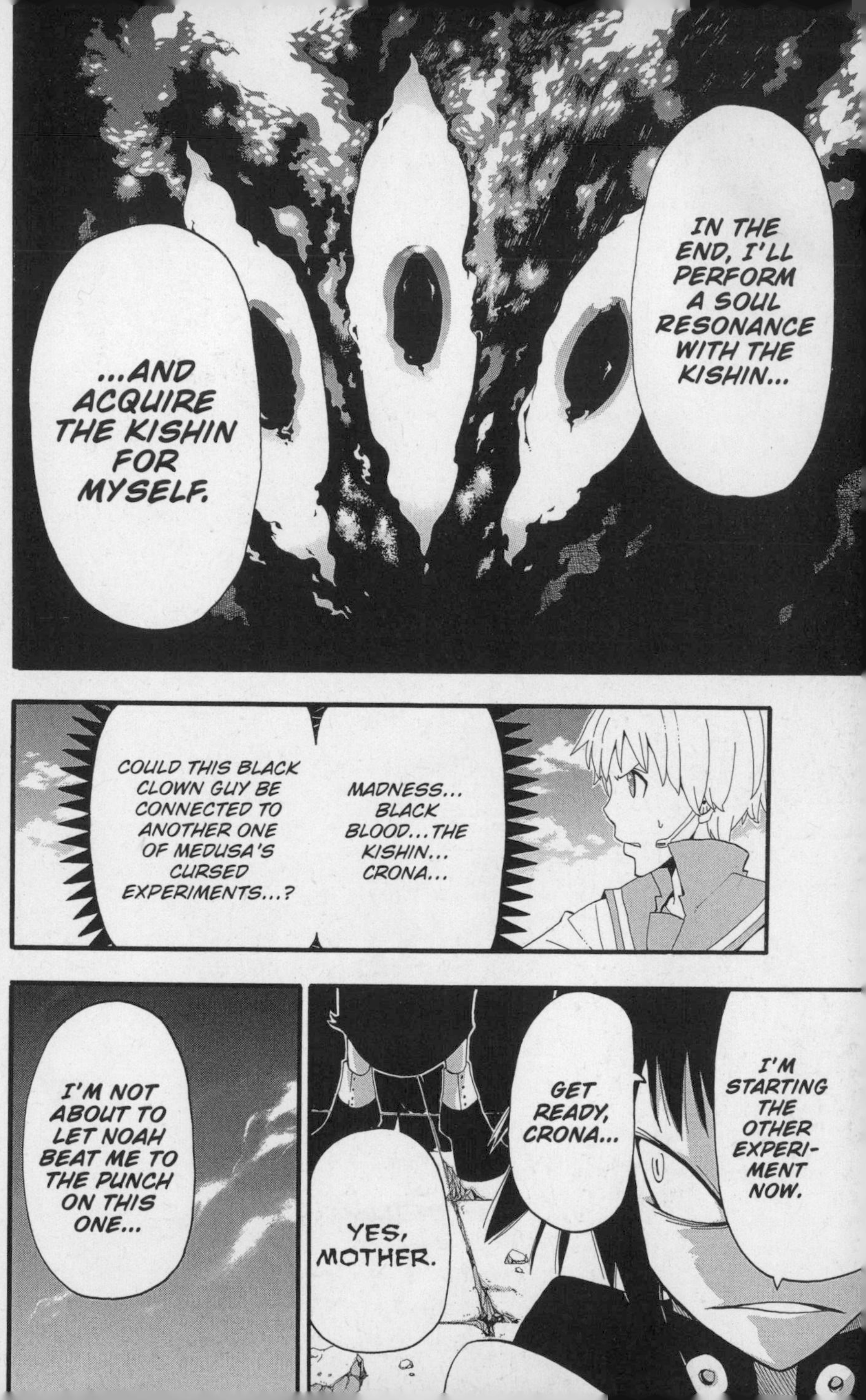
IN THE END, I'LL PERFORM A SOUL RESONANCE WITH THE KISHIN...
...AND ACQUIRE THE KISHIN FOR MYSELF.
MADNESS... BLACK BLOOD...THE KISHIN... CRONA...
COULD THIS BLACK CLOWN GUY BE CONNECTED TO ANOTHER ONE OF MEDUSA'S CURSED EXPERIMENTS...?
I'M STARTING THE OTHER EXPERIMENT NOW.
GET READY, CRONA...
YES, MOTHER.
I'M NOT ABOUT TO LET NOAH BEAT ME TO THE PUNCH ON THIS ONE...

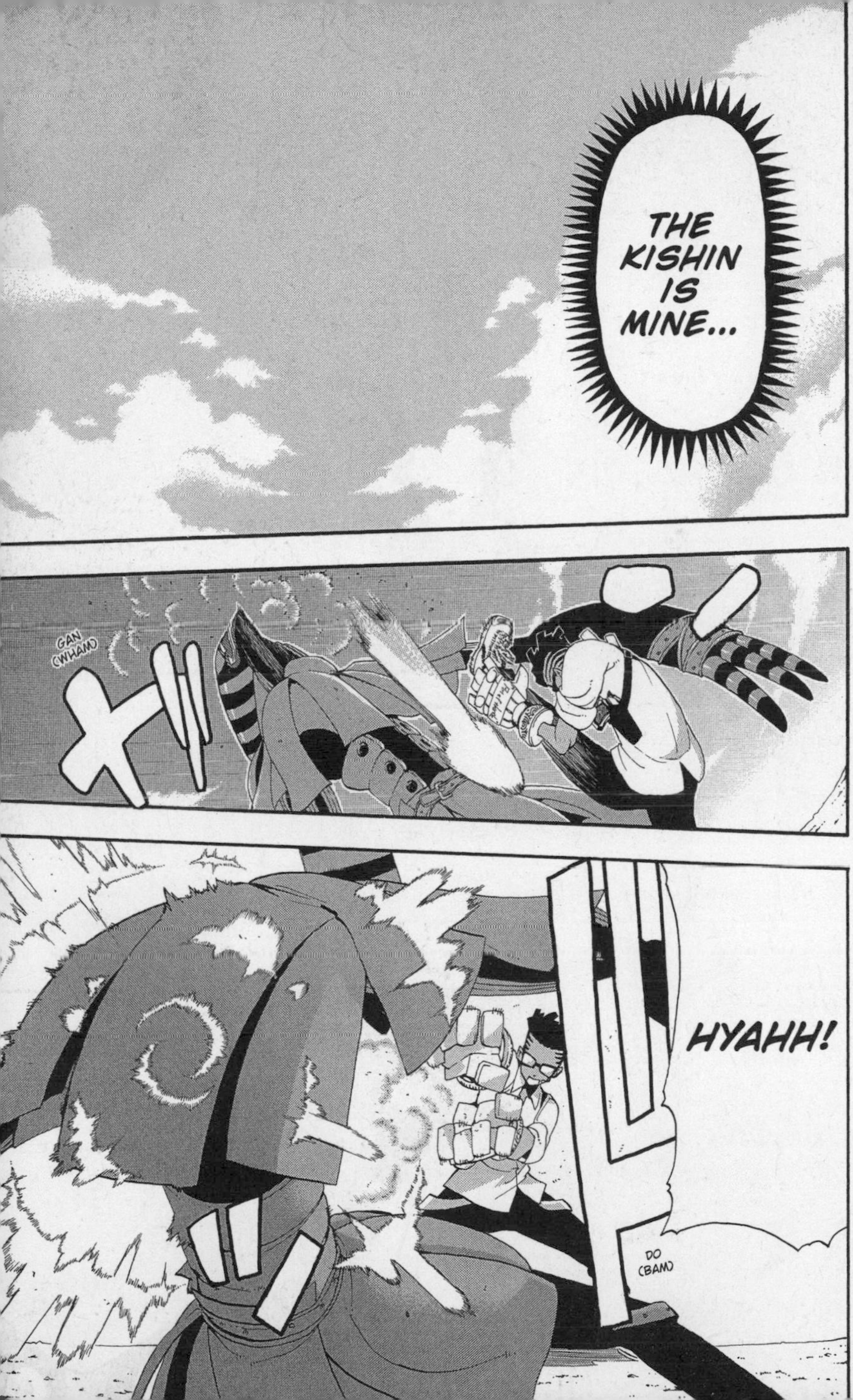
THE KISHIN IS MINE...
GAN (WHAM)
HYAHH!
DO (BAM)

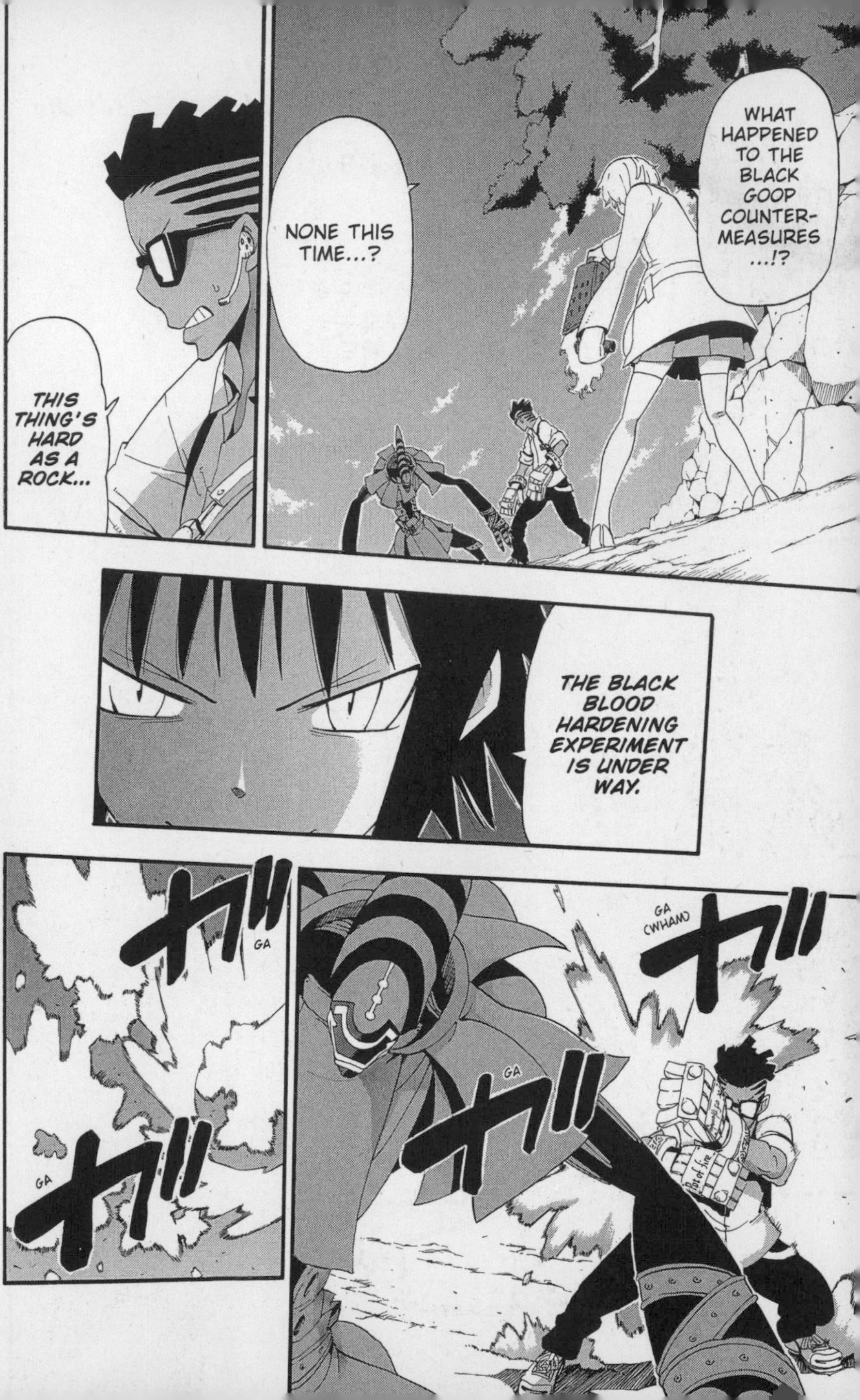
WHAT HAPPENED TO THE BLACK GOOP COUNTER-MEASURES ...!?
NONE THIS TIME...?
THIS THING'S HARD AS A ROCK...
THE BLACK BLOOD HARDENING EXPERIMENT IS UNDER WAY.
GA (WHAM)
GA
GA
GA

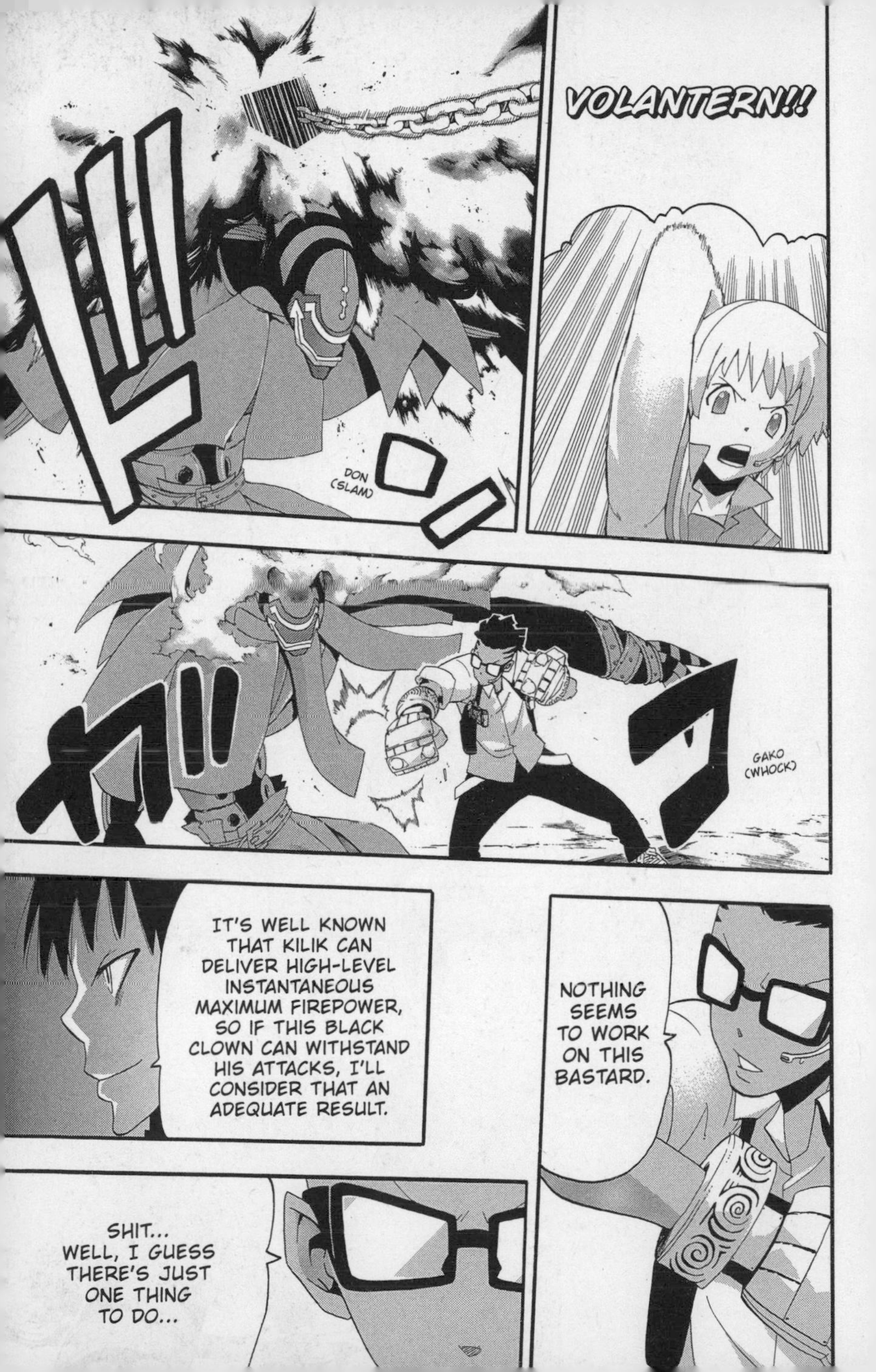
VOLANTERN!!
DON (SLAM)
GAKO (WHOCK)
NOTHING SEEMS TO WORK ON THIS BASTARD.
IT'S WELL KNOWN THAT KILIK CAN DELIVER HIGH-LEVEL INSTANTANEOUS MAXIMUM FIREPOWER, SO IF THIS BLACK CLOWN CAN WITHSTAND HIS ATTACKS, I'LL CONSIDER THAT AN ADEQUATE RESULT.
SHIT... WELL, I GUESS THERE'S JUST ONE THING TO DO...

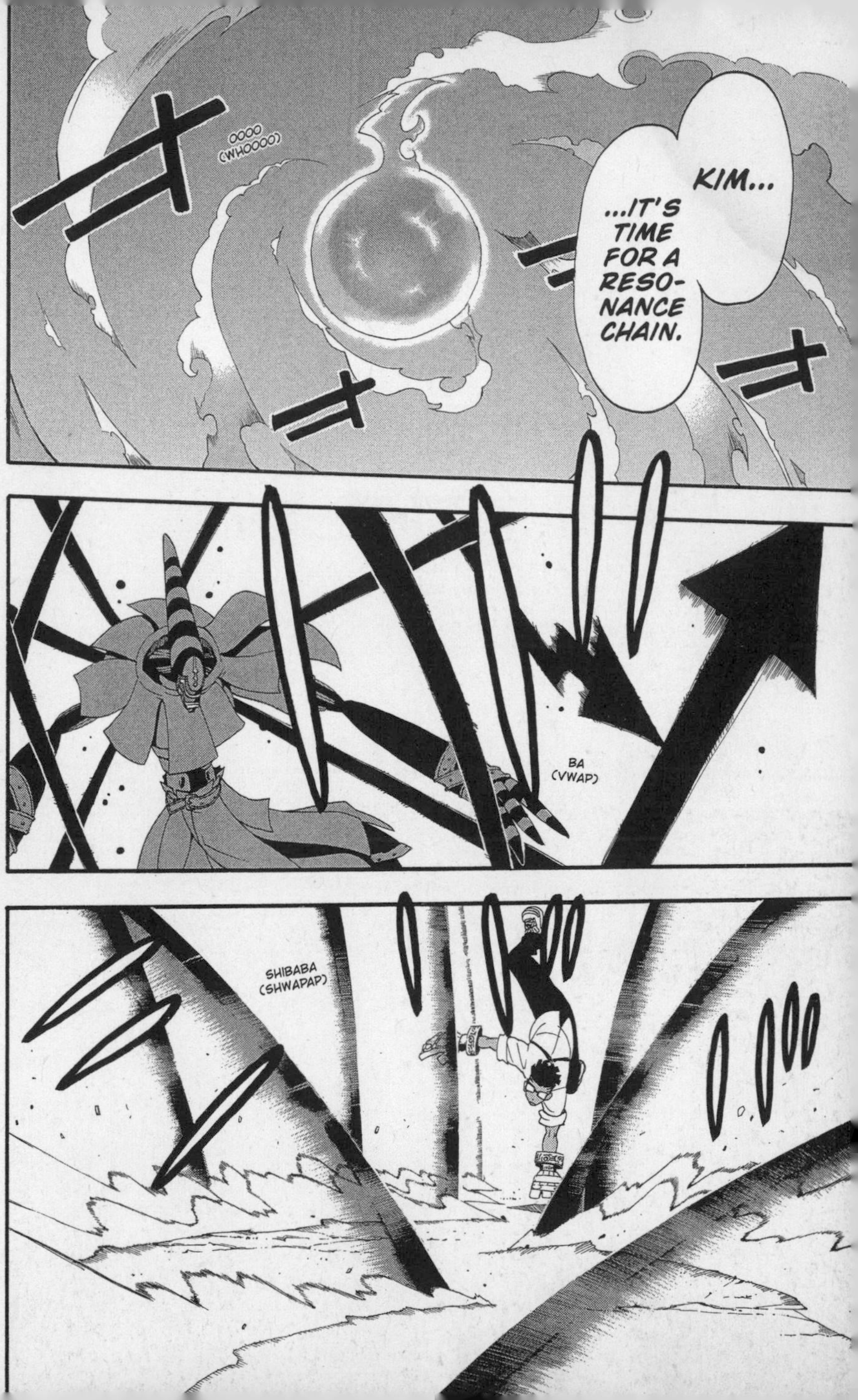
KIM...
...IT'S TIME FOR A RESO-NANCE CHAIN.
OOOO (WHOOOO)
BA (VWAP)
SHIBABA (SHWAPAP)

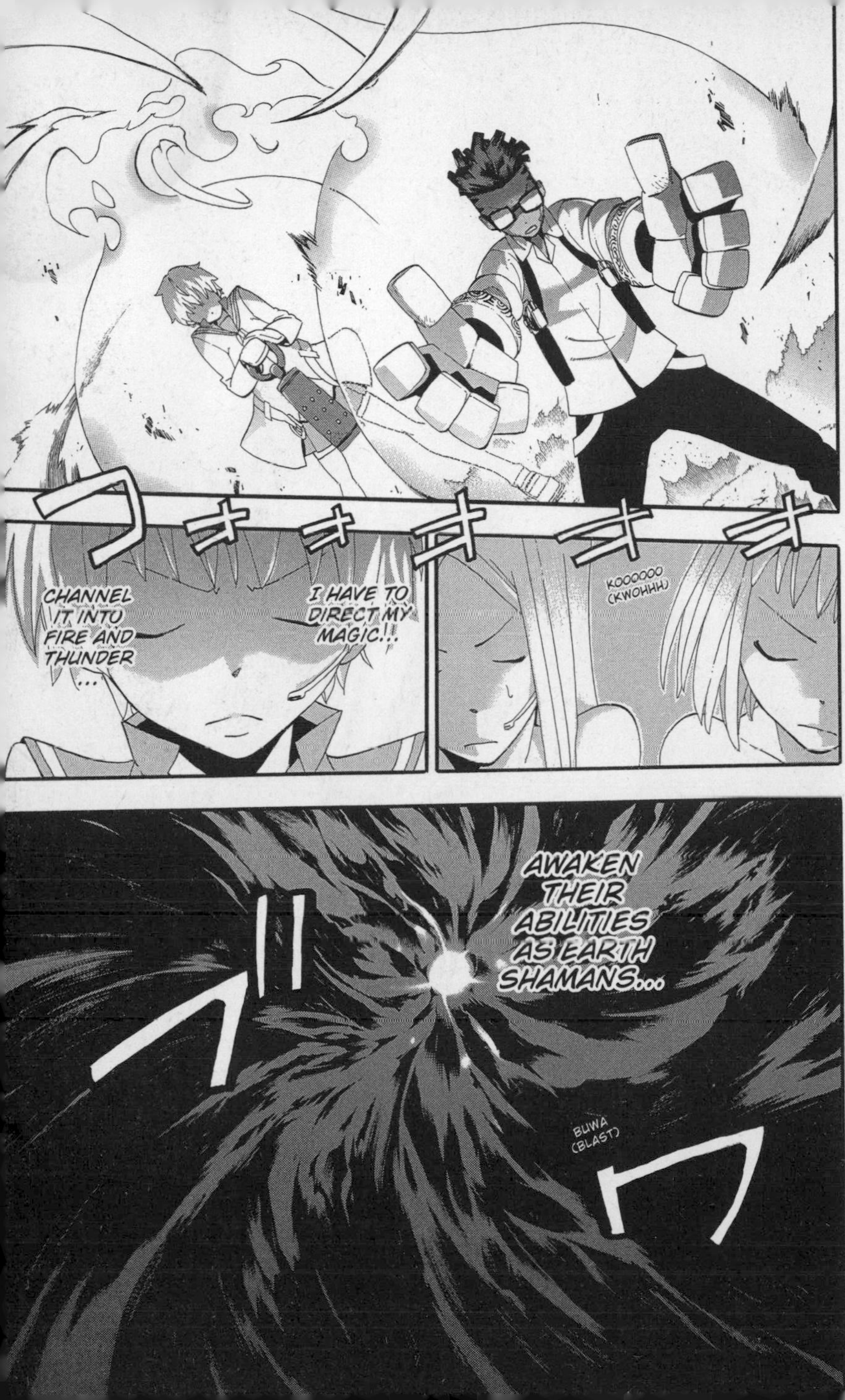
KOOOOOO (KWOHHH)
I HAVE TO DIRECT MY MAGIC!!
CHANNEL IT INTO FIRE AND THUNDER...
AWAKEN THEIR ABILITIES AS EARTH SHAMANS...
BUWA (BLAST)

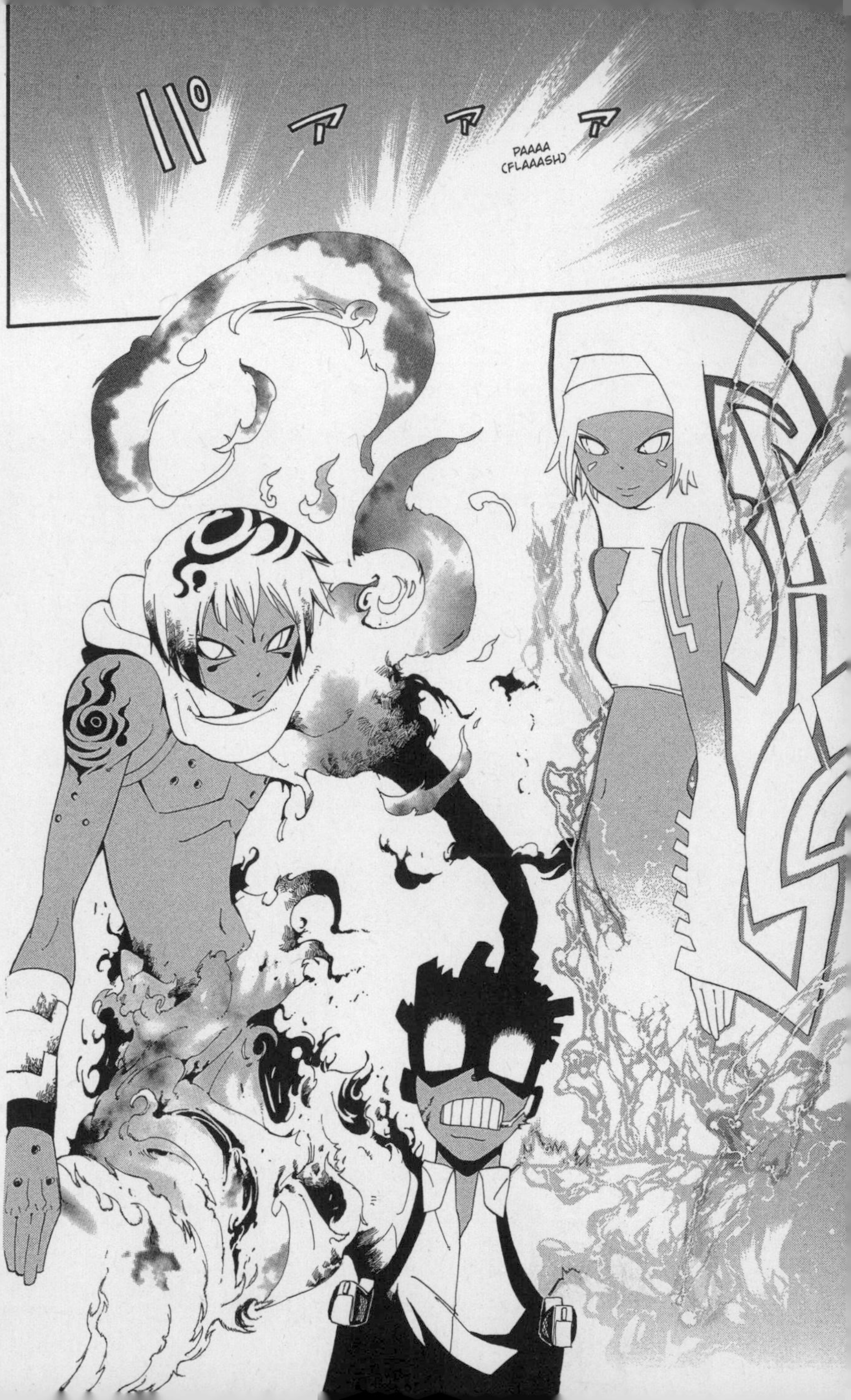
パァァァ
PAAAA
(FLAAASH)

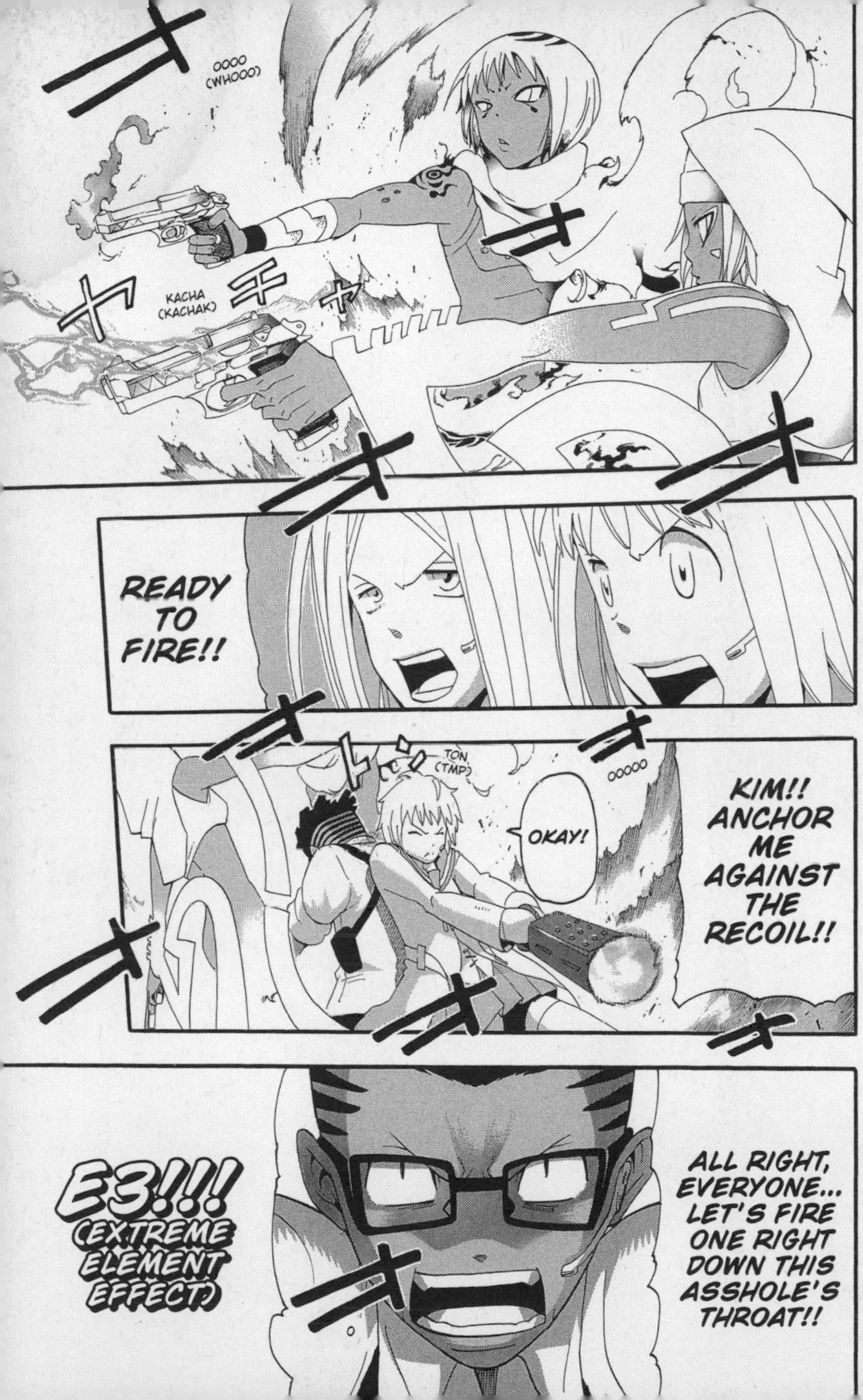
OOOO (WHOOO)
KACHA (KACHAK)
READY TO FIRE!!
KIM!! ANCHOR ME AGAINST THE RECOIL!!
OOOOO
OKAY!
TON (TMP)
ALL RIGHT, EVERYONE... LET'S FIRE ONE RIGHT DOWN THIS ASSHOLE'S THROAT!!
E3!!! (EXTREME ELEMENT EFFECT)

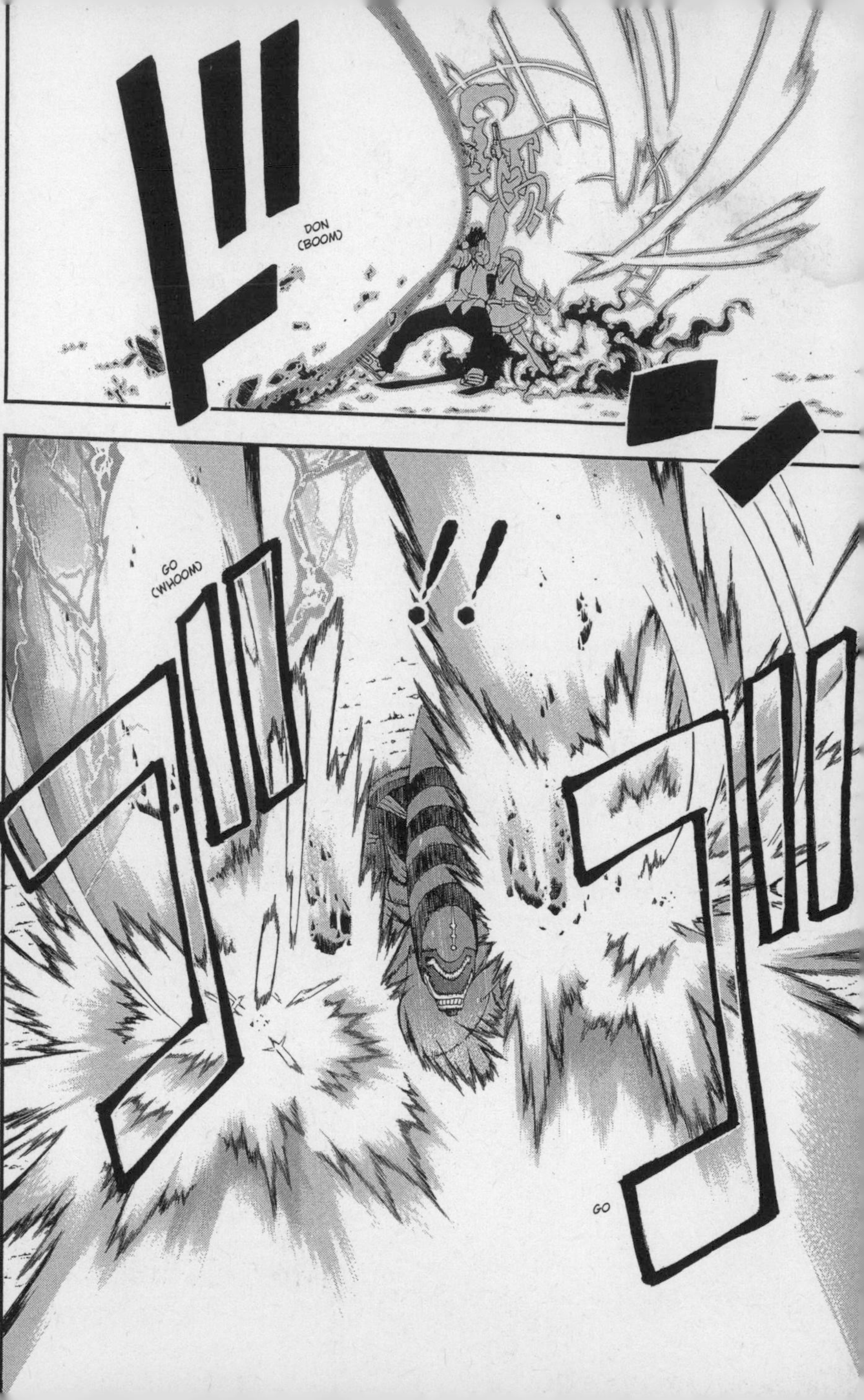
DON (BOOM)
GO (WHOOM)
!!
GO

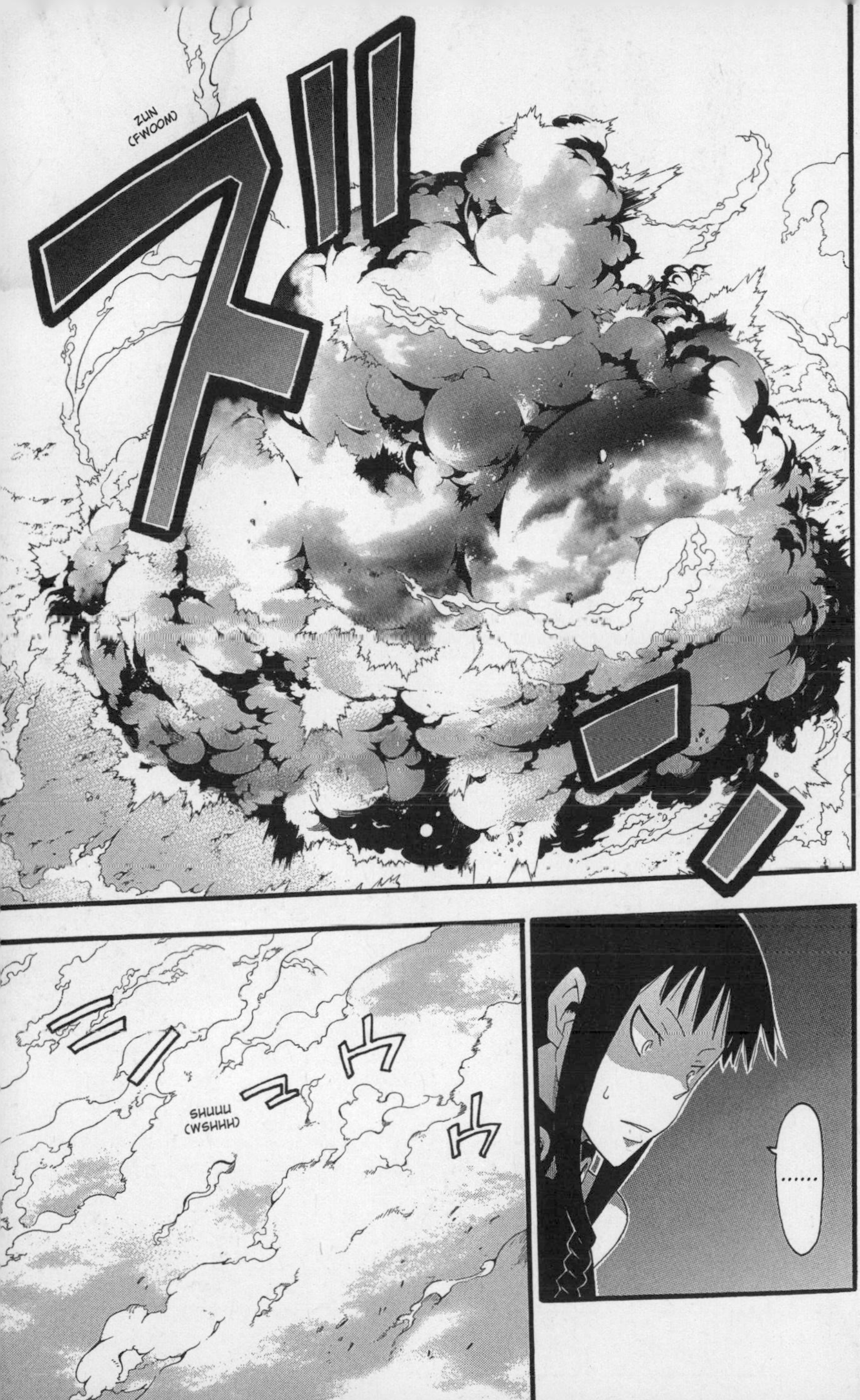
ZUN (FWOOM)
......
SHUUU (WSHHH)

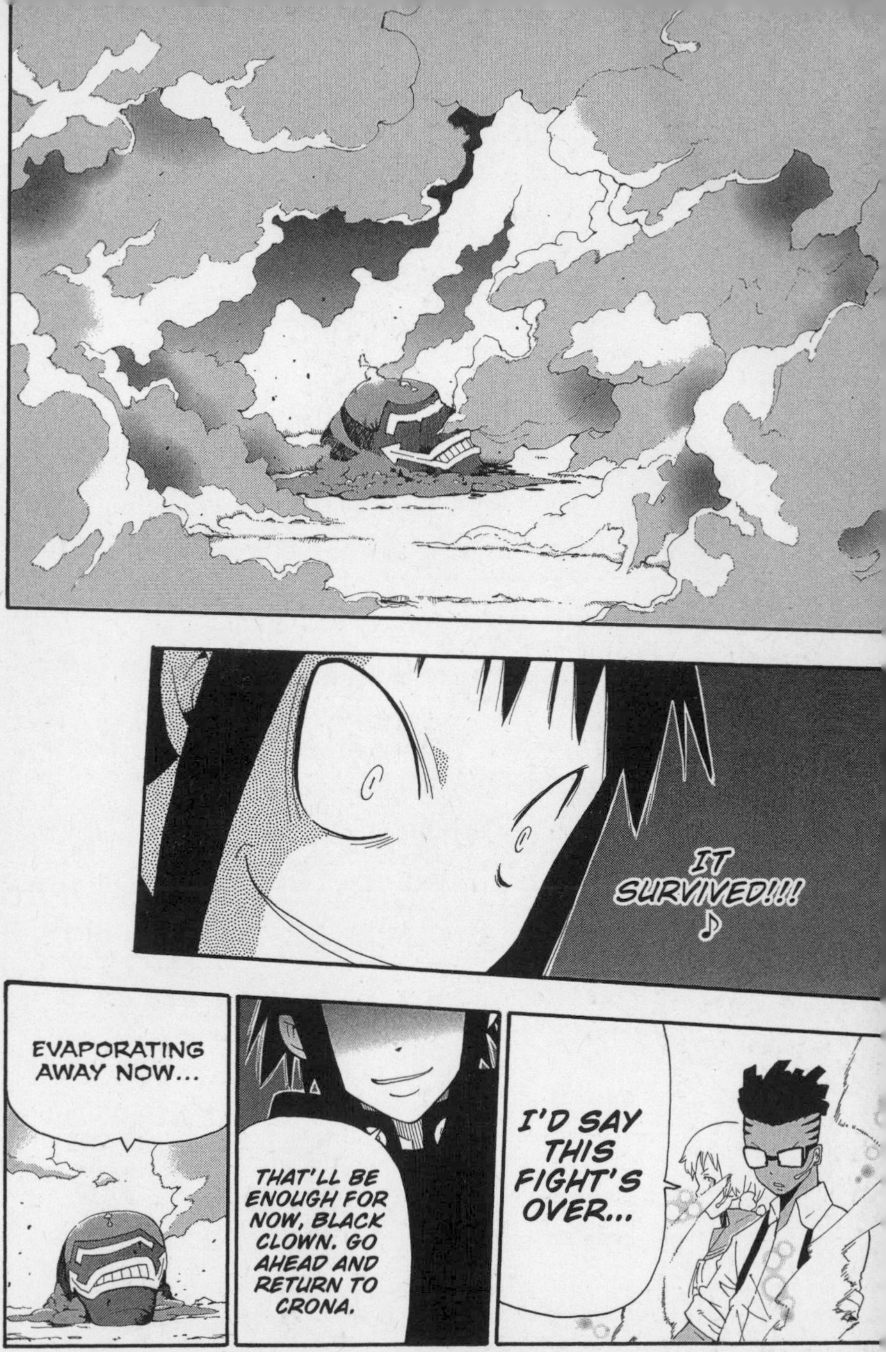
IT SURVIVED!!! ♪
I'D SAY THIS FIGHT'S OVER...
THAT'LL BE ENOUGH FOR NOW, BLACK CLOWN. GO AHEAD AND RETURN TO CRONA.
EVAPORATING AWAY NOW...

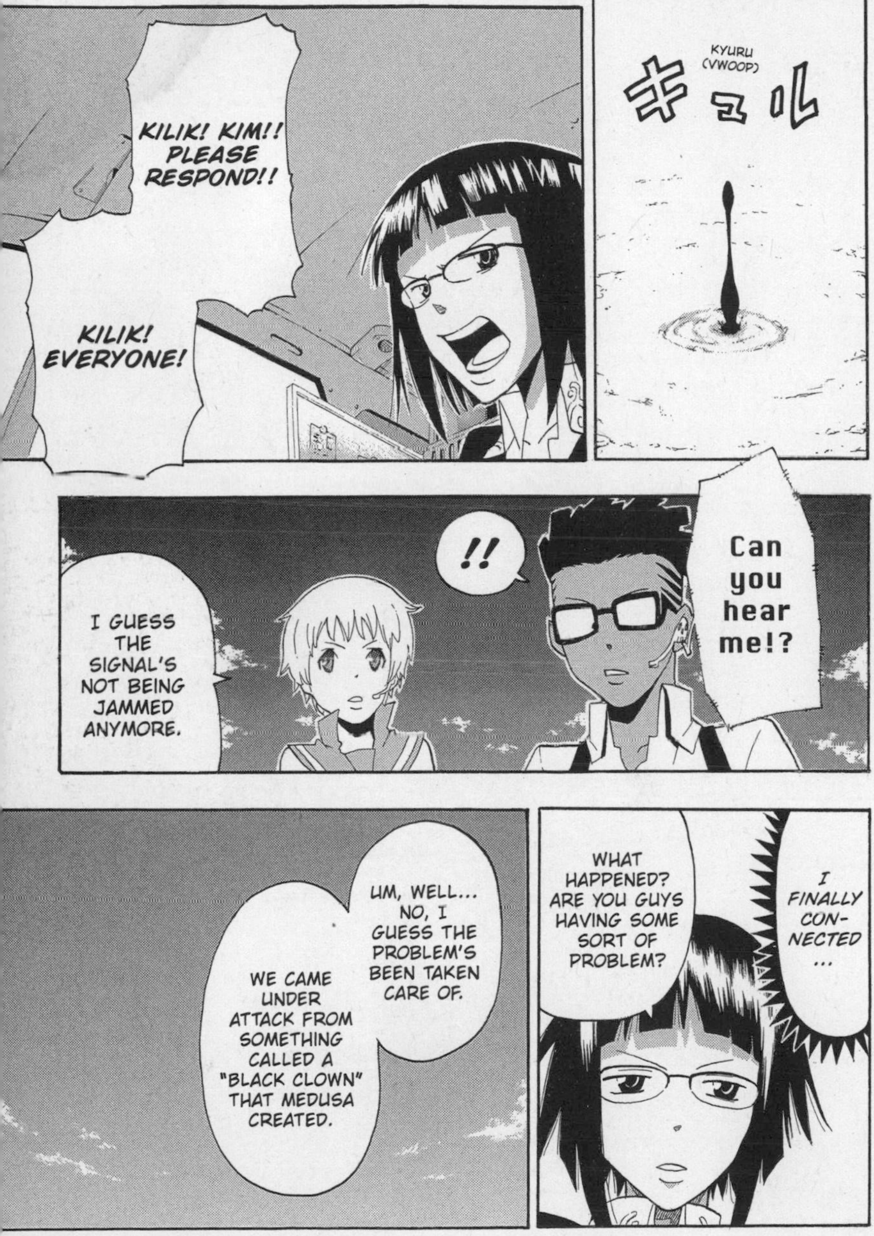
KYURU (VWOOP)
キュル
KILIK! KIM!! PLEASE RESPOND!!
KILIK! EVERYONE!
Can you hear me!?
!!
I GUESS THE SIGNAL'S NOT BEING JAMMED ANYMORE.
I FINALLY CON-NECTED ...
WHAT HAPPENED? ARE YOU GUYS HAVING SOME SORT OF PROBLEM?
UM, WELL... NO, I GUESS THE PROBLEM'S BEEN TAKEN CARE OF.
WE CAME UNDER ATTACK FROM SOMETHING CALLED A "BLACK CLOWN" THAT MEDUSA CREATED.

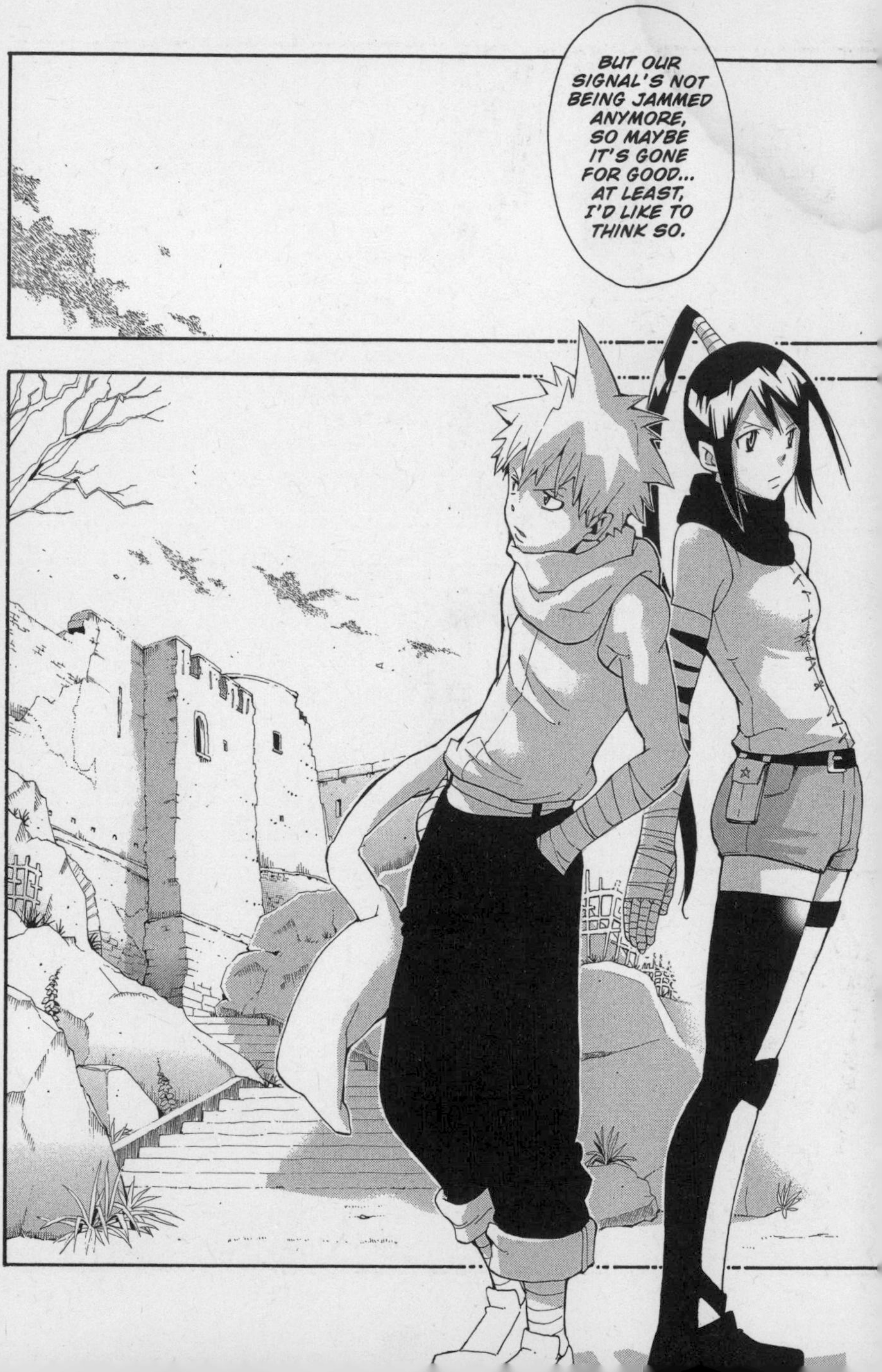
BUT OUR SIGNAL'S NOT BEING JAMMED ANYMORE, SO MAYBE IT'S GONE FOR GOOD... AT LEAST, I'D LIKE TO THINK SO.

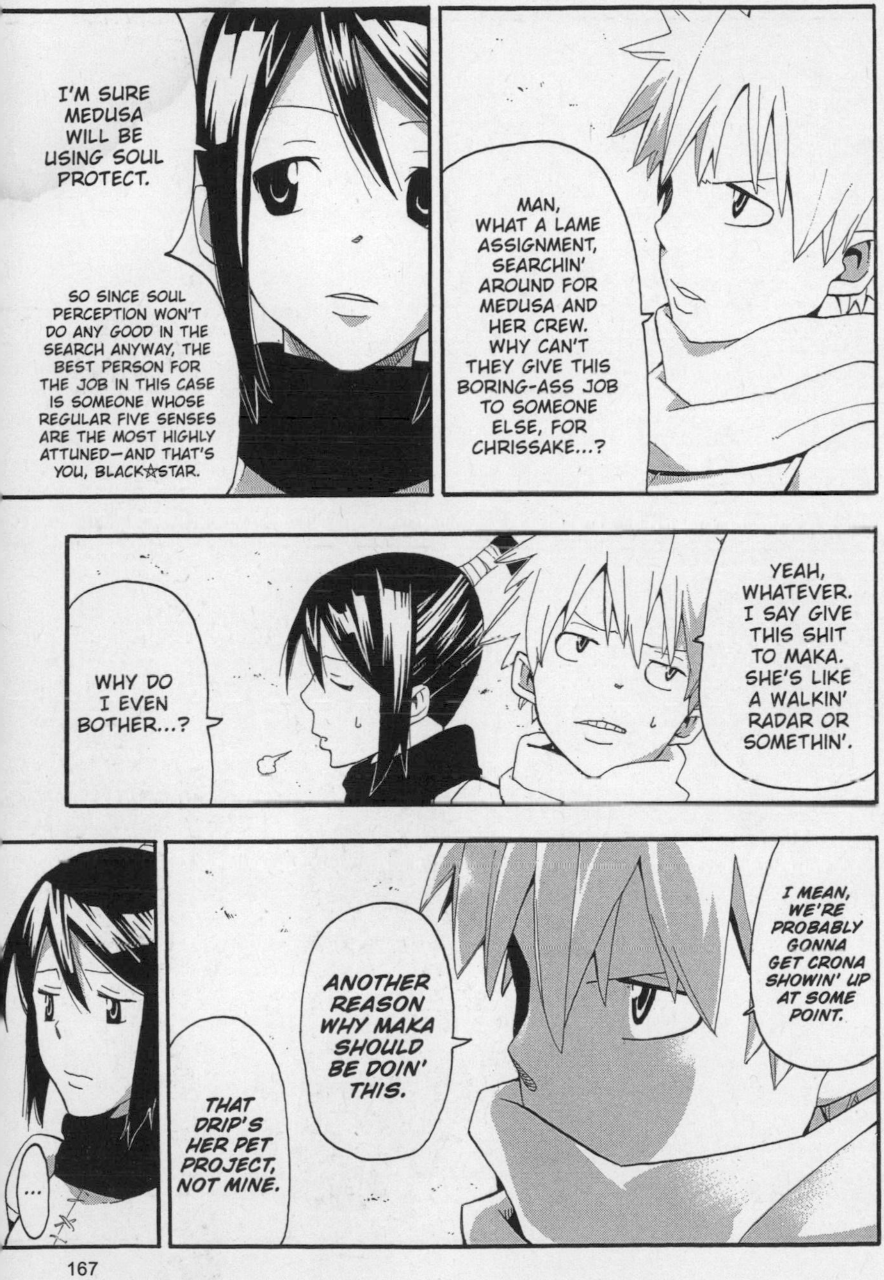
MAN, WHAT A LAME ASSIGNMENT, SEARCHIN' AROUND FOR MEDUSA AND HER CREW. WHY CAN'T THEY GIVE THIS BORING-ASS JOB TO SOMEONE ELSE, FOR CHRISSAKE...?
I'M SURE MEDUSA WILL BE USING SOUL PROTECT.
SO SINCE SOUL PERCEPTION WON'T DO ANY GOOD IN THE SEARCH ANYWAY, THE BEST PERSON FOR THE JOB IN THIS CASE IS SOMEONE WHOSE REGULAR FIVE SENSES ARE THE MOST HIGHLY ATTUNED—AND THAT'S YOU, BLACK☆STAR.
YEAH, WHATEVER. I SAY GIVE THIS SHIT TO MAKA. SHE'S LIKE A WALKIN' RADAR OR SOMETHIN'.
WHY DO I EVEN BOTHER...?
I MEAN, WE'RE PROBABLY GONNA GET CRONA SHOWIN' UP AT SOME POINT.
ANOTHER REASON WHY MAKA SHOULD BE DOIN' THIS.
THAT DRIP'S HER PET PROJECT, NOT MINE.
...

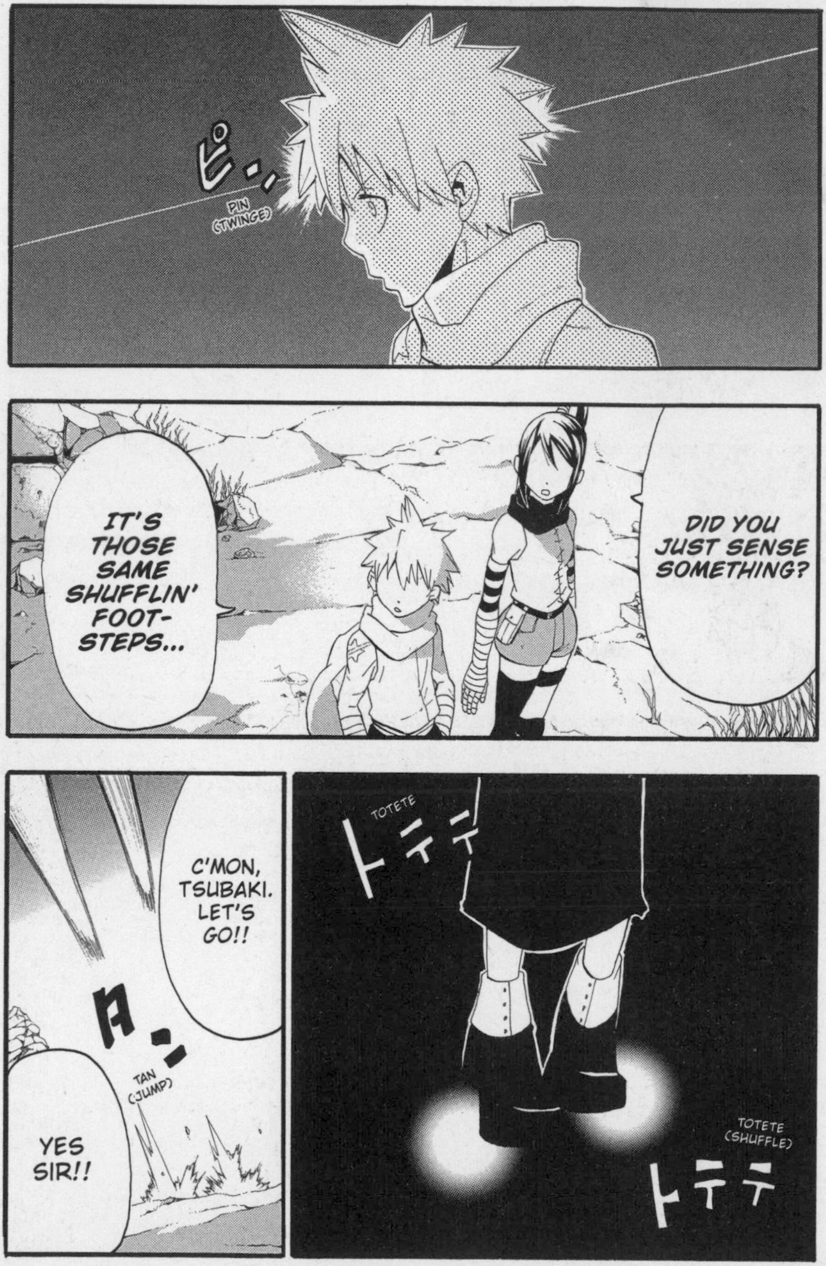
ピ
PIN (TWINGE)
DID YOU JUST SENSE SOMETHING?
IT'S THOSE SAME SHUFFLIN' FOOT-STEPS...
トテテ
TOTETE
トテテ
TOTETE (SHUFFLE)
C'MON, TSUBAKI. LET'S GO!!
タン
TAN (JUMP)
YES SIR!!

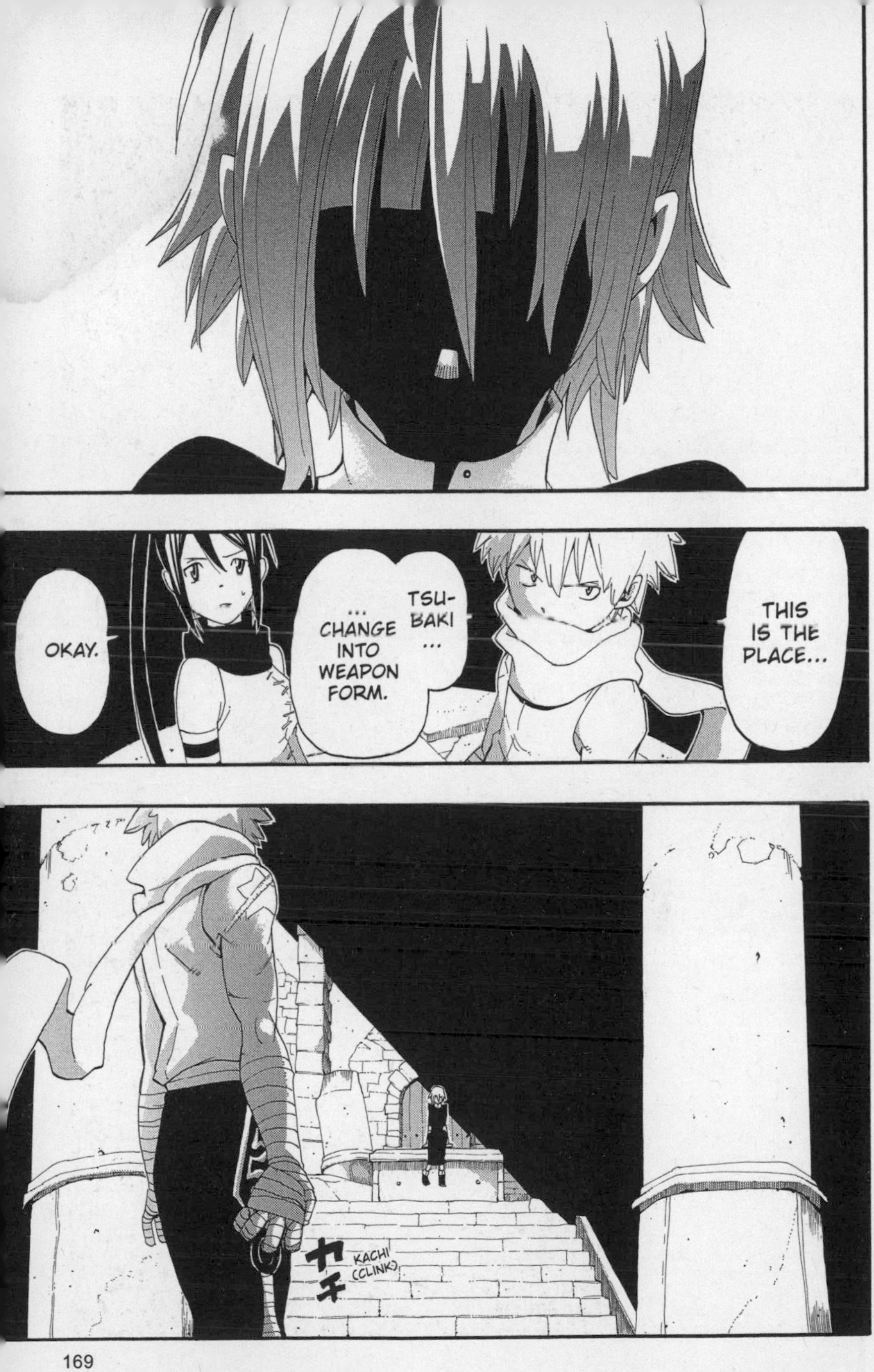
THIS IS THE PLACE...
TSUBAKI... ...CHANGE INTO WEAPON FORM.
OKAY.
KACHI (CLINK)

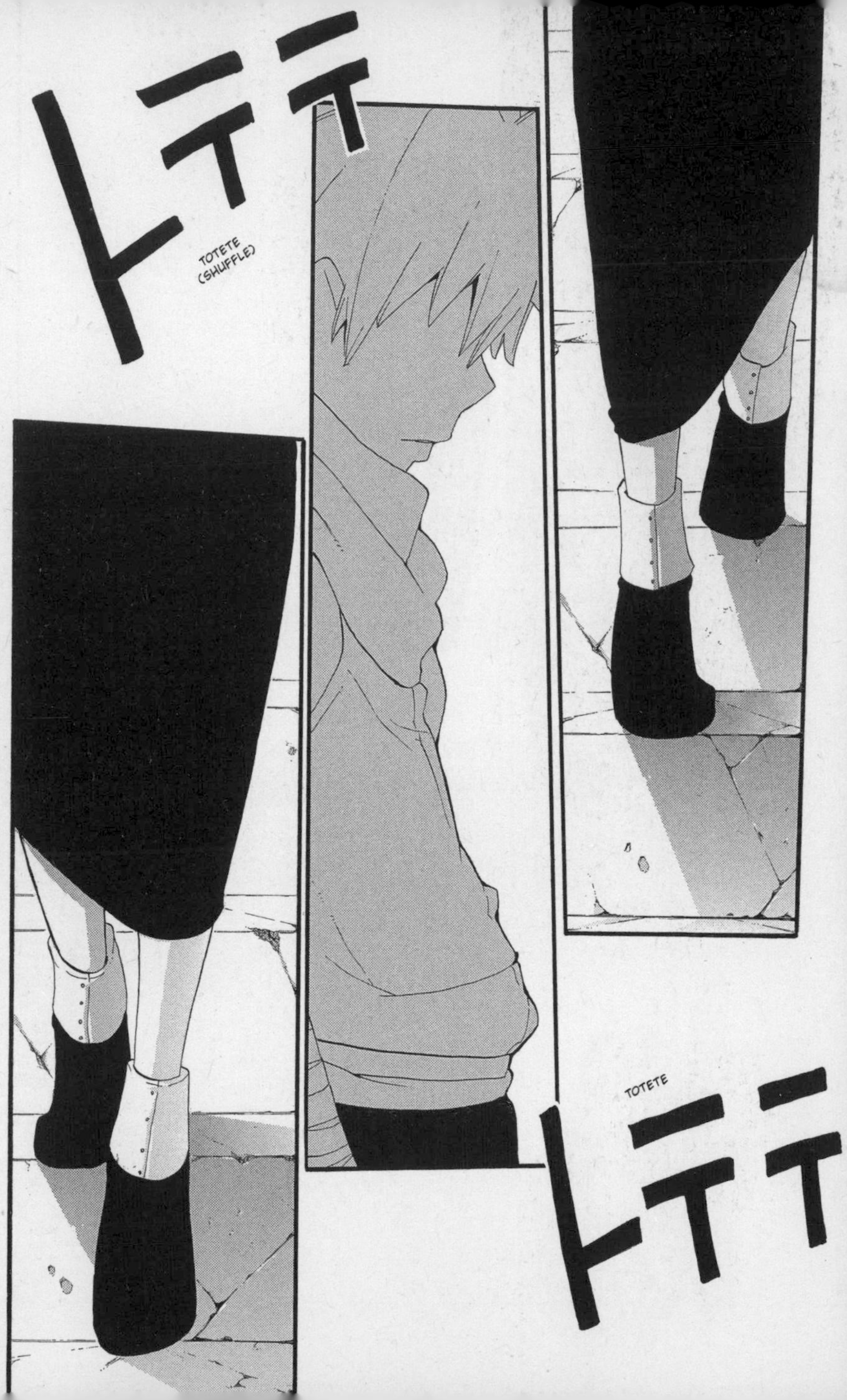
トテテ
TOTETE (SHUFFLE)
トテテ
TOTETE

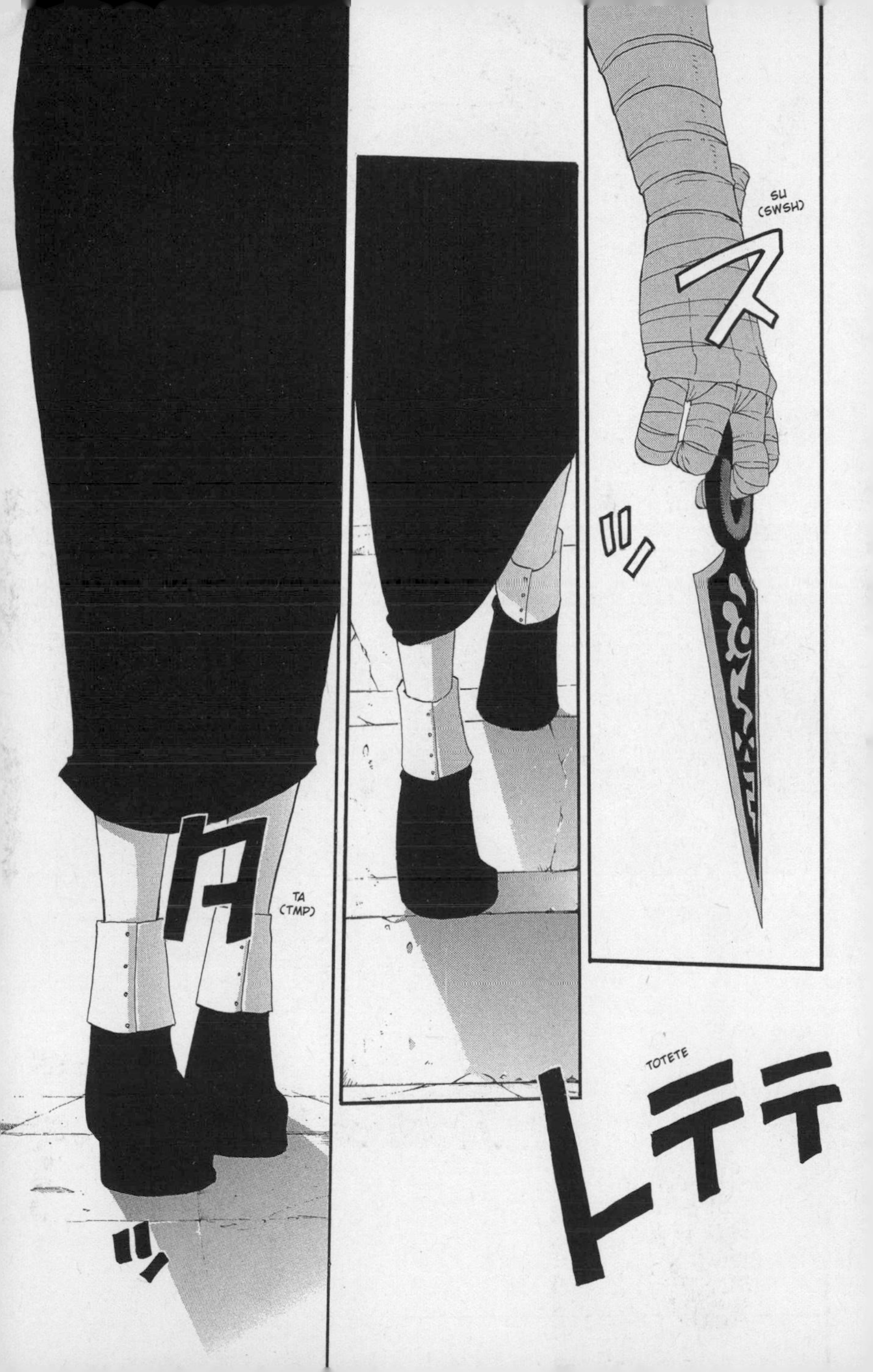
SU
(SWSH)
TOTETE
TA
(TMP)

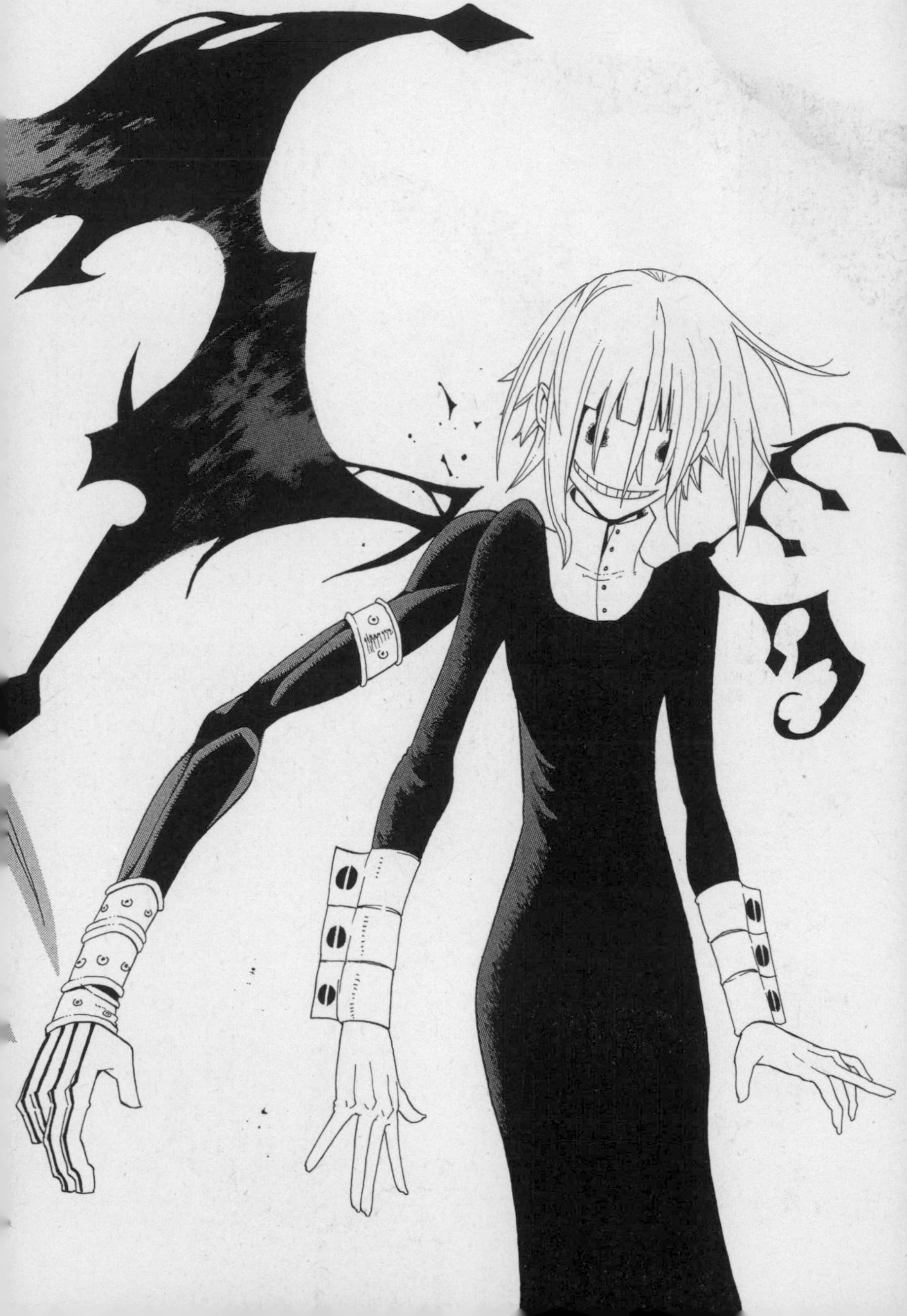

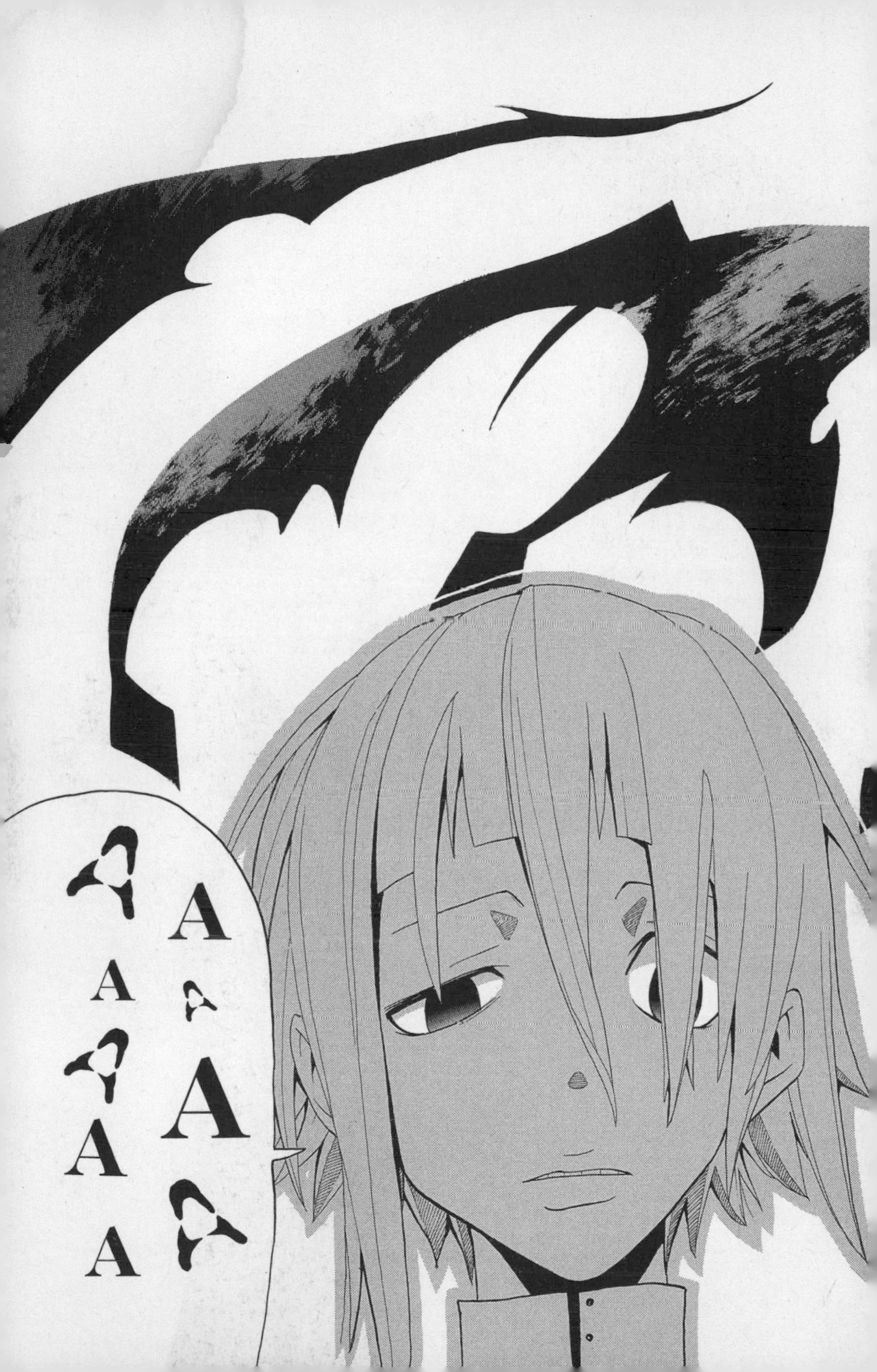
AAAAAAAAA

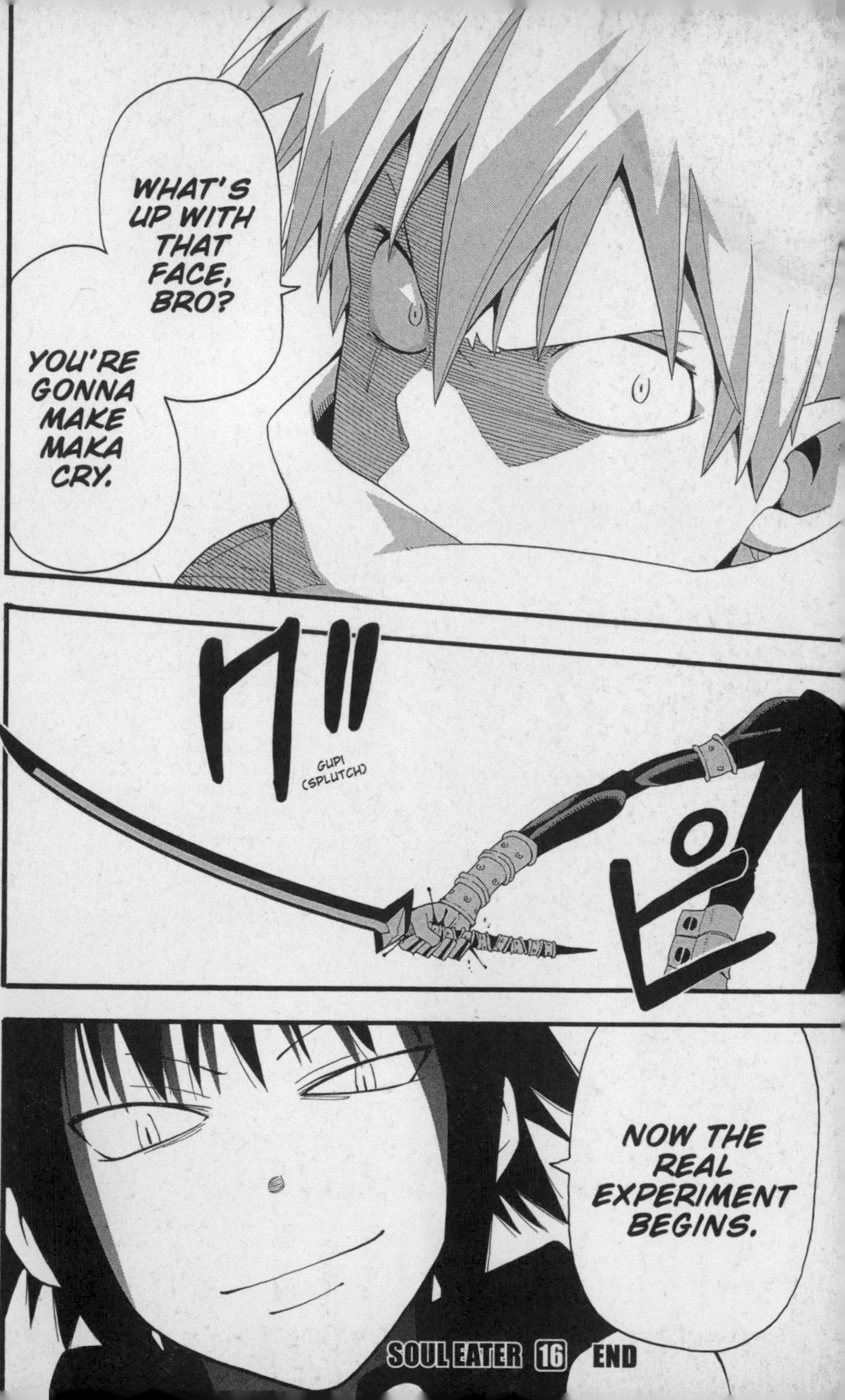
WHAT'S UP WITH THAT FACE, BRO?
YOU'RE GONNA MAKE MAKA CRY.
GUPI (SPLUTCH)
NOW THE REAL EXPERIMENT BEGINS.
SOUL EATER 16 END

SOUL EATER

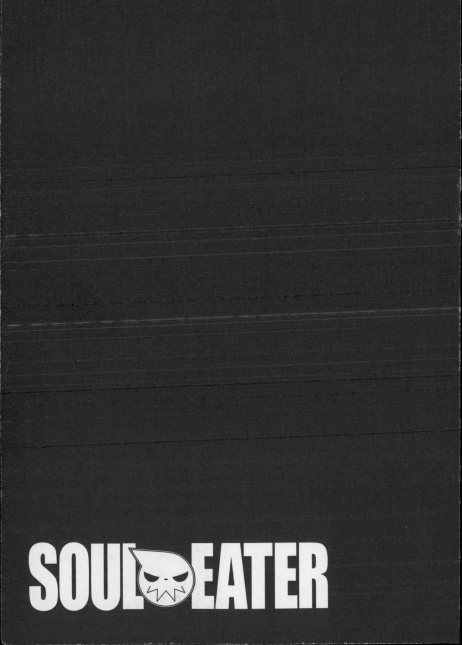

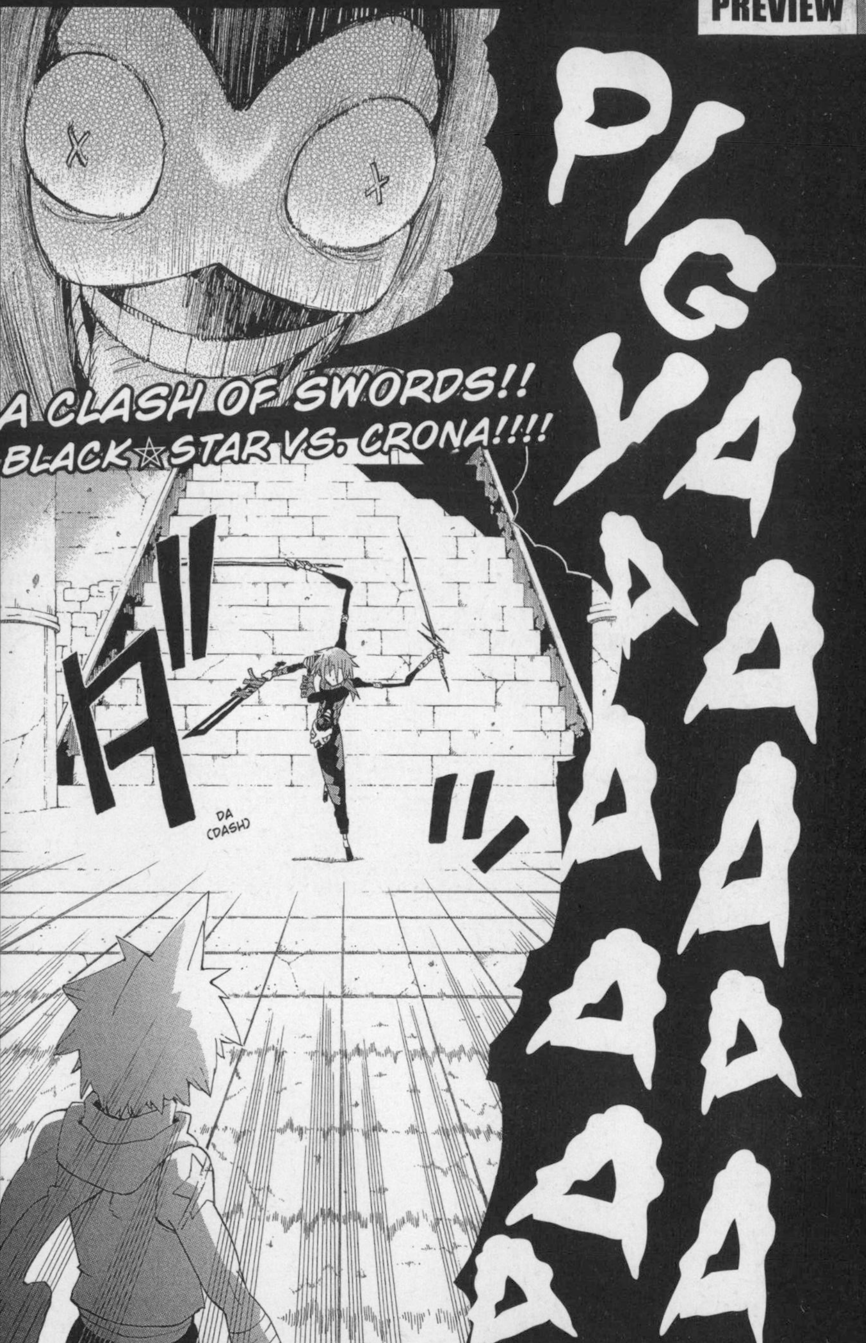
PIGYAAAAAAAAAAAAAAAA
A CLASH OF SWORDS!!
BLACK☆STAR VS. CRONA!!!!
DA
(DASH)

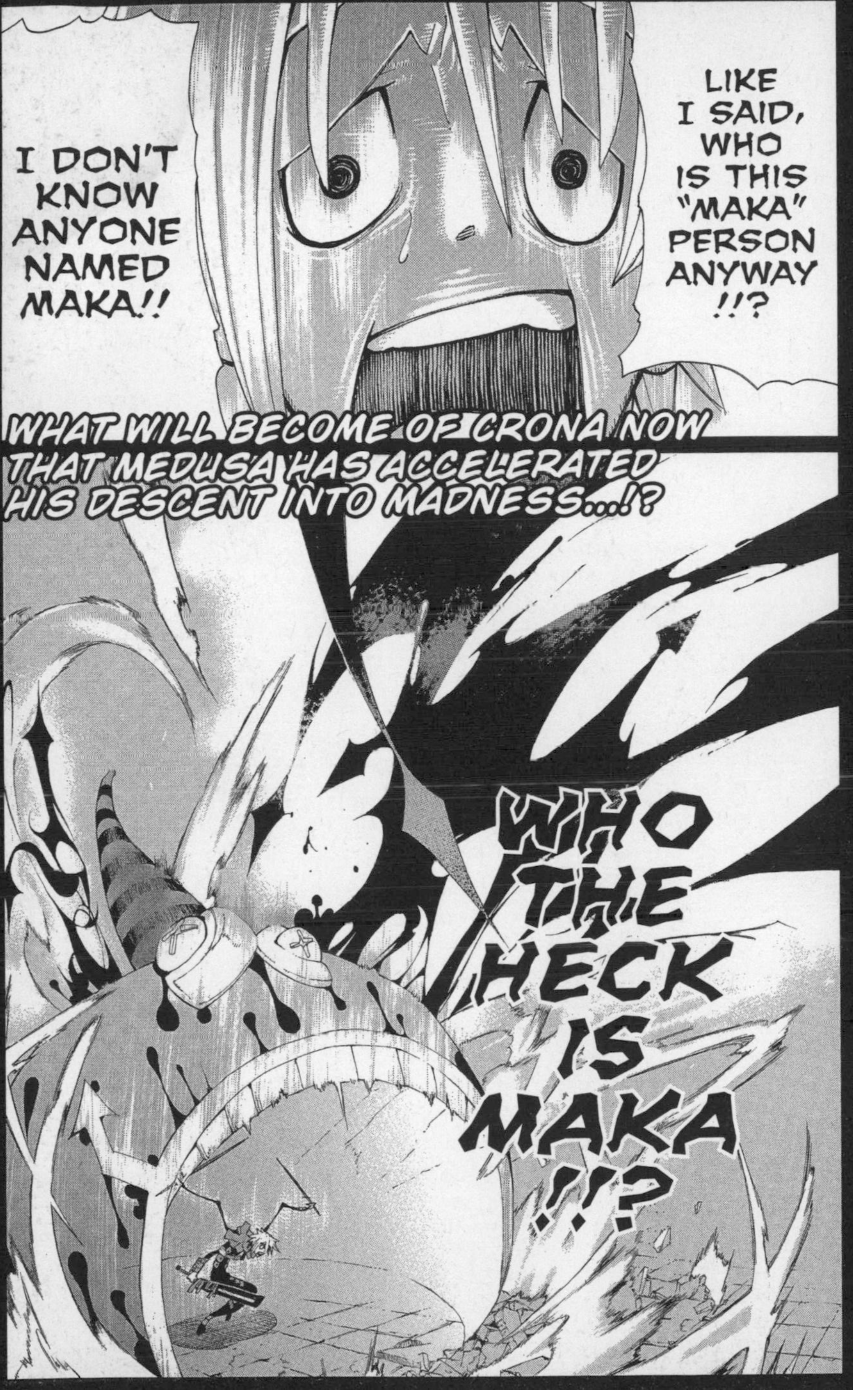
LIKE I SAID, WHO IS THIS "MAKA" PERSON ANYWAY !!?
I DON'T KNOW ANYONE NAMED MAKA!!
WHAT WILL BECOME OF CRONA NOW THAT MEDUSA HAS ACCELERATED HIS DESCENT INTO MADNESS...!?
WHO THE HECK IS MAKA !!?

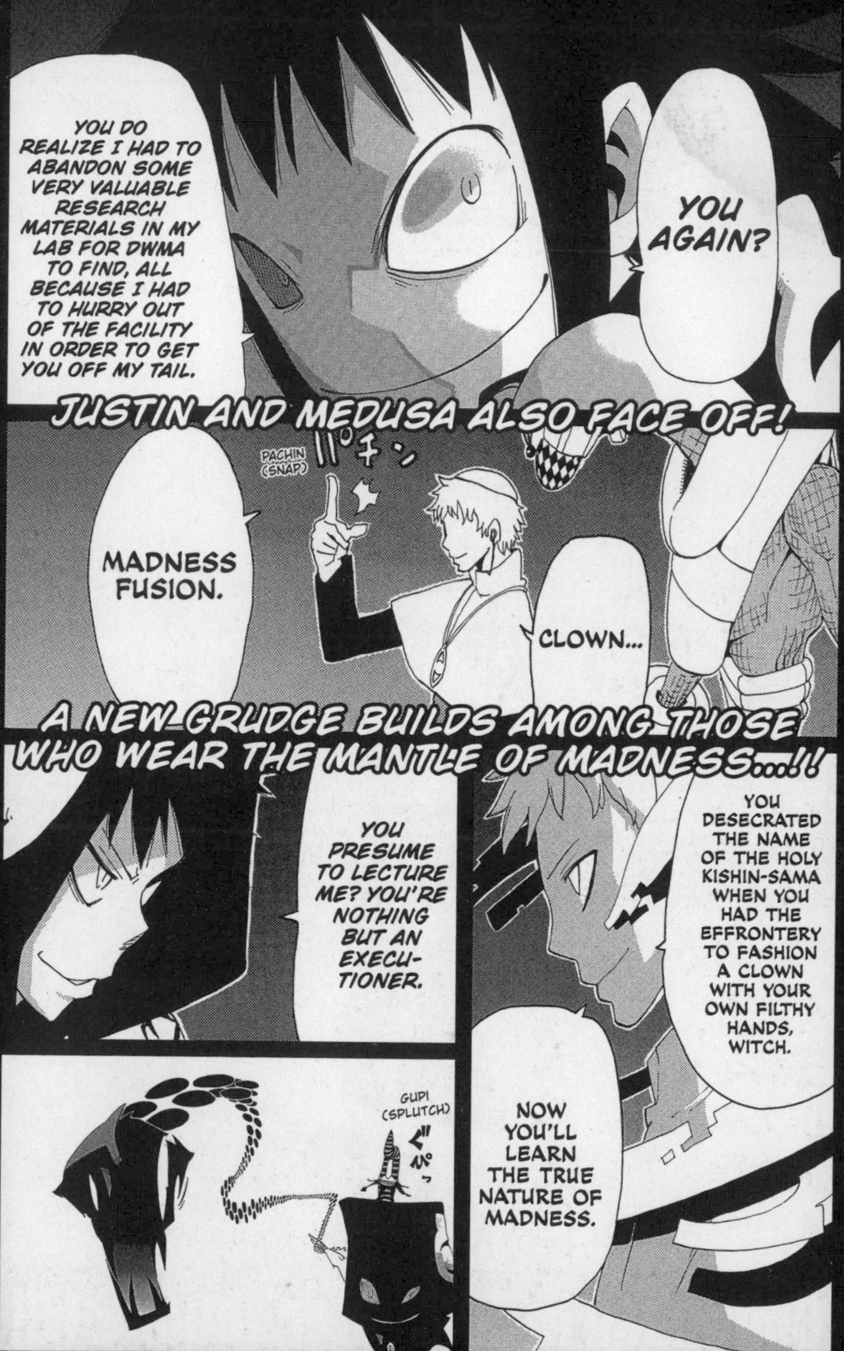
YOU AGAIN?
YOU DO REALIZE I HAD TO ABANDON SOME VERY VALUABLE RESEARCH MATERIALS IN MY LAB FOR DWMA TO FIND, ALL BECAUSE I HAD TO HURRY OUT OF THE FACILITY IN ORDER TO GET YOU OFF MY TAIL.
JUSTIN AND MEDUSA ALSO FACE OFF!
CLOWN...
PACHIN (SNAP)
MADNESS FUSION.
A NEW GRUDGE BUILDS AMONG THOSE WHO WEAR THE MANTLE OF MADNESS...!!
YOU DESECRATED THE NAME OF THE HOLY KISHIN-SAMA WHEN YOU HAD THE EFFRONTERY TO FASHION A CLOWN WITH YOUR OWN FILTHY HANDS, WITCH.
NOW YOU'LL LEARN THE TRUE NATURE OF MADNESS.
YOU PRESUME TO LECTURE ME? YOU'RE NOTHING BUT AN EXECUTIONER.
GUPI (SPLUTCH)

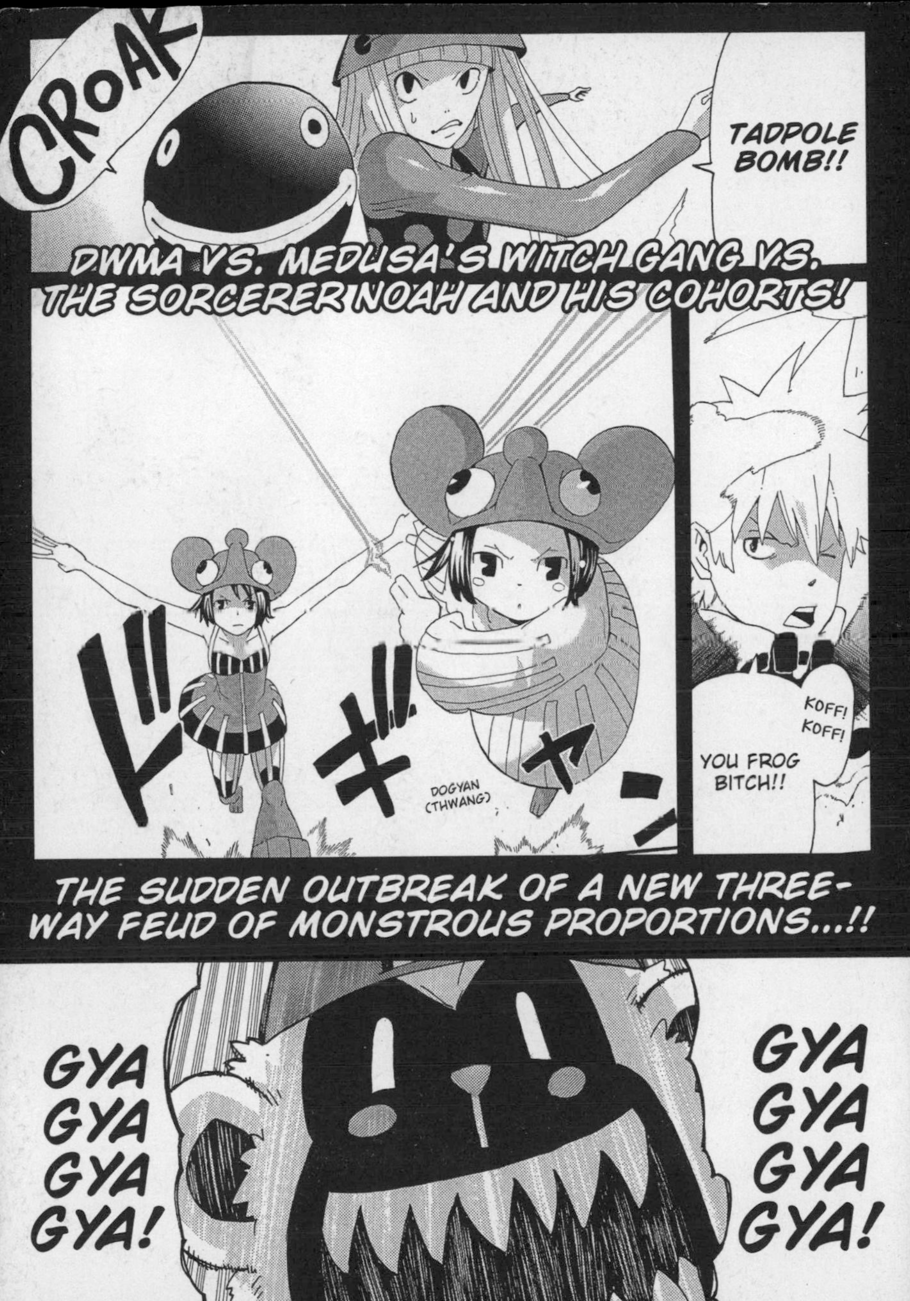
TADPOLE BOMB!!
CROAK
DWMA VS. MEDUSA'S WITCH GANG VS. THE SORCERER NOAH AND HIS COHORTS!
KOFF! KOFF!
YOU FROG BITCH!!
DOGYAN (THWANG)
THE SUDDEN OUTBREAK OF A NEW THREE-WAY FEUD OF MONSTROUS PROPORTIONS...!!
GYA GYA GYA GYA!
GYA GYA GYA GYA!

Continued in Soul Eater Volume 17!!

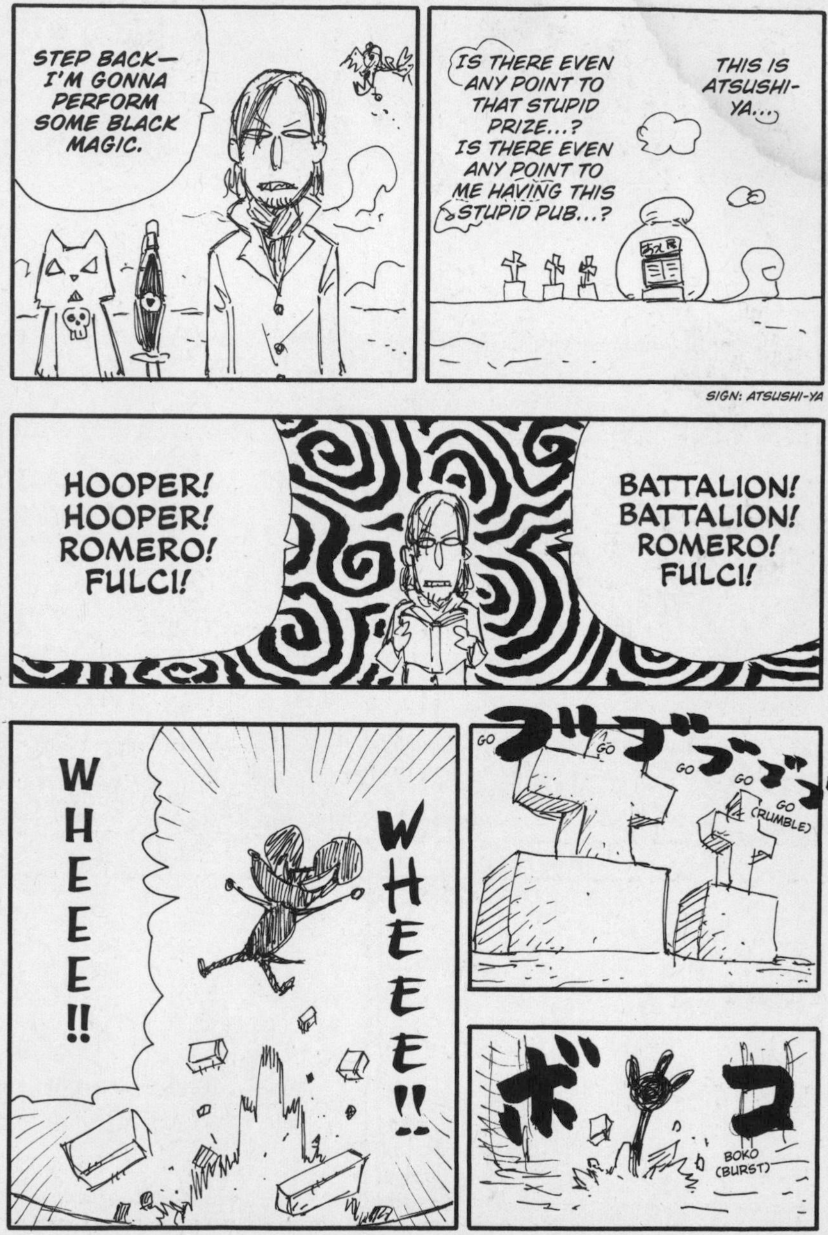

THIS IS ATSUSHI-YA...
IS THERE EVEN ANY POINT TO THAT STUPID PRIZE...? IS THERE EVEN ANY POINT TO ME HAVING THIS STUPID PUB...?
SIGN: ATSUSHI-YA
STEP BACK—I'M GONNA PERFORM SOME BLACK MAGIC.
BATTALION! BATTALION! ROMERO! FULCI!
HOOPER! HOOPER! ROMERO! FULCI!
GO GO GO GO GO (RUMBLE)
BOKO (BURST)
WHEEE!!
WHEEEE!!

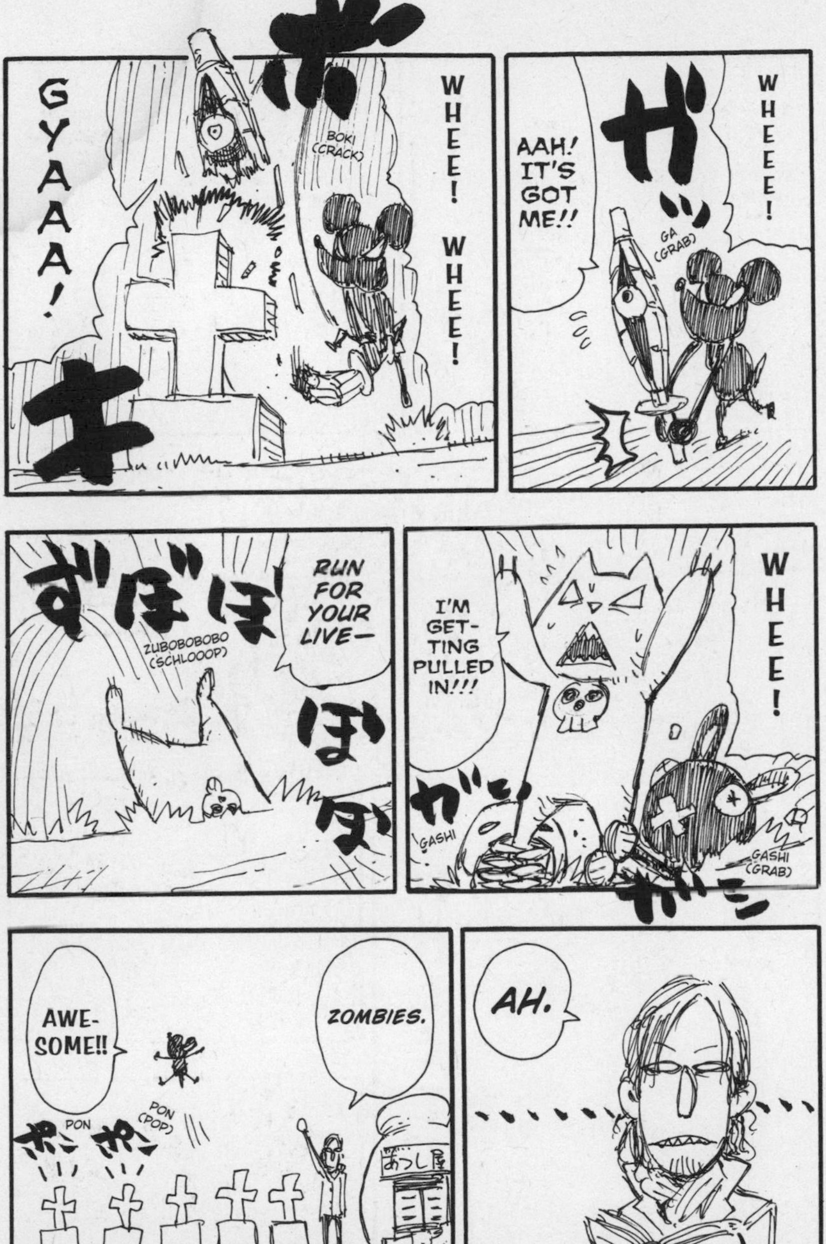
WHEEEE!
AAH! IT'S GOT ME!!
GA (GRAB)
WHEE! WHEEE!
BOKI (CRACK)
GYAAA!
WHEEE!
I'M GET-TING PULLED IN!!!
GASHI
GASHI (GRAB)
RUN FOR YOUR LIVE—
ZUBOBOBOBO (SCHLOOOP)
AH.
ZOMBIES.
AWE-SOME!!
PON (POP)
PON

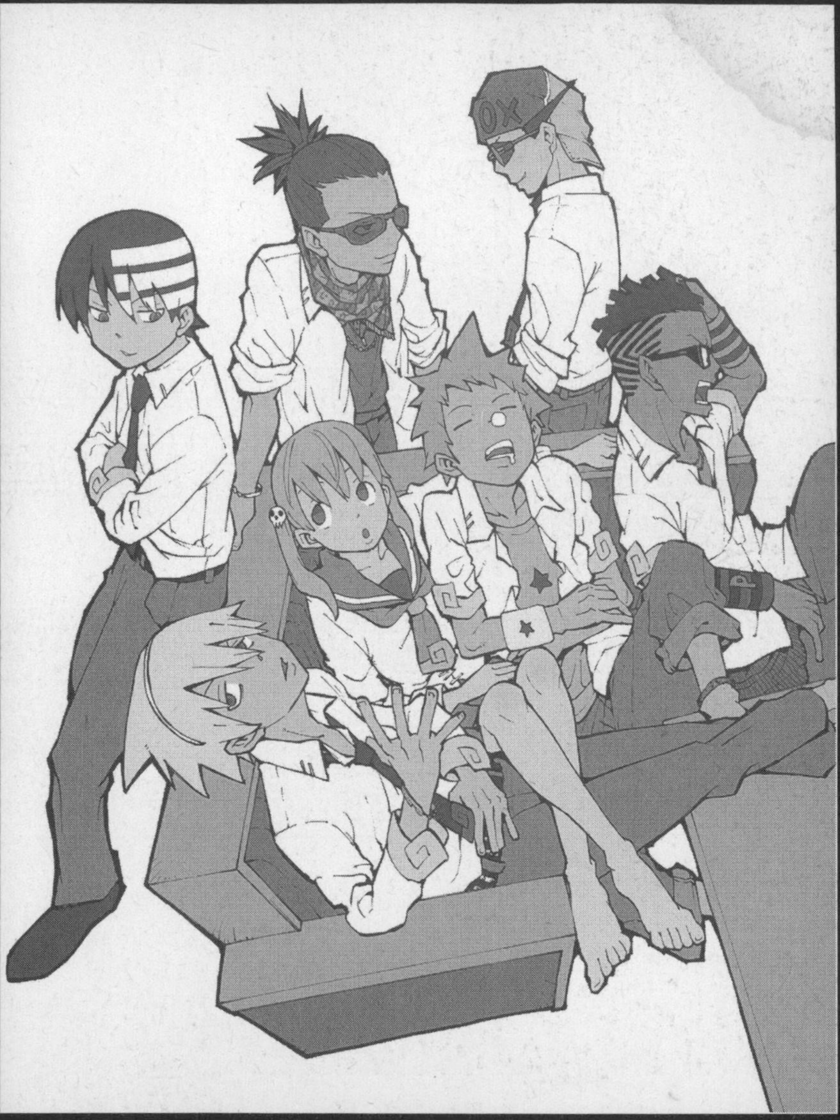
OX

SOUL EATER

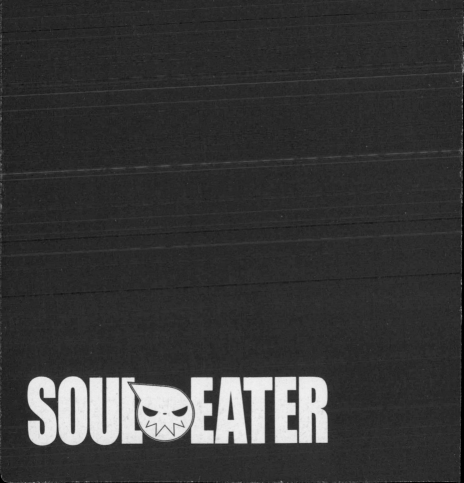

# Translation Notes

Common Honorifics

**no honorific**: Indicates familiarity or closeness; if used without permission or reason, addressing someone in this manner would constitute an insult.

**-san**: The Japanese equivalent of Mr./Mrs./Miss. If a situation calls for politeness, this is the fail-safe honorific.

**-sama**: Conveys great respect; may also indicate that the social status of the speaker is lower than that of the addressee.

**-kun**: Used most often when referring to boys, this indicates affection or familiarity. Occasionally used by older men among their peers, but it may also be used by anyone referring to a person of lower standing.

**-chan**: An affectionate honorific indicating familiarity used mostly in reference to girls; also used in reference to cute persons or animals of either gender.

**-senpai**: A suffix used to address upperclassmen or more experienced coworkers.

**-sensei**: A respectful term for teachers, artists, or high-level professionals.


PAGE 9

**"Grigori"** is a reference from a collection of apocryphal Jewish religious texts known as the Books of Enoch (of diverse provenance dating between the mid–first millennium BC and the mid–first millennium AD), where it refers to a group of fallen angels whose initial God-assigned role of watching over humanity was perverted by their lust for human women. (The word "grigori" itself is the Old Slavonic transliteration of the Greek *egregoroi*, "watchers"—which in turn translated the Aramaic word of similar meaning, *iyrin*—and comes specifically from the Second Book of Enoch, which survives mainly in Old Slavonic manuscripts. I've chosen this form of the word in translation because of its wider currency among angel enthusiasts in the English-speaking world. The actual Japanese spelling here indicates that Atsushi Ohkubo intended the Greek pronunciation for the Japanese audience.) According to the story, the watcher angels, prodded on by their leader, decided at some point to abandon their heavenly mandate and procreate with human women; the result was a race of beastly men known as the Nephilim, who devastated human society. (The Nephilim were also mentioned in the Book of Genesis as one of the reasons why God decided to bring about the Great Flood, from which only the pious Noah was spared.) The watcher angels also ran afoul of God's plan by teaching various dangerous practices and technologies to humans—such as how to cast horoscopes and how to make mirrors and various weapons—before humanity was ready for such things. Note, however, that all of this is probably entirely incidental from the viewpoint of the story in this manga. It seems that in the *Soul Eater* universe the word "grigori" is only meant as an oblique reference to angelic properties, such as having wings in the manner of Maka's soul.


PAGE 28

The suffix *-nyan* is a cutesy form of *-chan*, so this is equivalent to **"Azusa-chan."** Also recall that **Azusa's name** is a pun on *azusa yumi* "birchwood bow." In ancient Japan, bows were commonly made out of the wood of the Japanese cherry birch (Betula grossa), so much so that the phrase "*azusa yumi*" came to be used as a stock phrase in poetry for conjuring up images of pulling and twanging.


PAGE 30

Gopher

The name of Gopher, one of Noah's henchmen, may have been chosen specifically because of his connection to Noah, namesake of the biblical Noah. In the story of Noah's ark in the Bible (Genesis 6:14), Noah was required to build his ark out of something called "gopherwood" (*gofer* in Hebrew). Although the exact meaning of the word in the original Hebrew is unclear, many modern English translations of the Bible, such as the NIV, use "cypress" instead.

PAGE 40
**Maka's last name** may be a reference to Damon Albarn of the British pop groups Blur and Gorillaz.

PAGE 43
The **large numbers painted on the mountains** seen in this chapter are probably there for some sort of (i.e., who knows what) flight-training purposes, but it could be a fun and interesting challenge to see whether Atsushi Ohkubo may have buried any hidden messages in the numbers, à la the "42-42-564" (*shini-shini-goroshi*) of Shinigami-sama's mirror number. For example, the sequence "37514" on page 44 (scanned from right to left) could be read as *Mina koi yo*, "Come on, everybody" in Japanese.

PAGE 46
According to Greek myth, the legendary **Spartoi** were so named because they sprang from the earth after Kadmos, the founder of Grecian Thebes, sowed the teeth of a dragon (on the advice of Athena) that he had slain; he did so in order to replace his men, who were killed fighting the dragon in the first place. The Spartoi were very unruly, however, so Kadmos tossed some rocks into their midst (also on the advice of Athena) and the confused Spartoi, each thinking some other was throwing rocks, fought amongst themselves until only five remained. Some of the unsown dragon teeth were later given to Jason (of Argonauts fame) by King Aeetes, who offered to hand over the Golden Fleece if Jason could kill all the Spartoi that sprouted from the ground after scattering the teeth. A witch named Medea helped Jason get the Spartoi to kill each other instead of him.

PAGE 62
The so-called "42" flavors here is a joke along the same lines as Death the Kid's "Death Eagle .42" (seen in Volume 14, page 27): i.e., the "42" is chosen specifically because that number sequence can be pronounced *shini* ("death") in Japanese.

PAGE 101
The **kanji character** on the front of the demon tool paper that Justin uses to escape is a rare Chinese character meaning "divination"—specifically, casting the Yijing by counting yarrow straw sticks. Here, it is translated as "augur" in order to retain some of the exotic mystical flavor.

PAGE 117
The kanji used to write the "utility" part of **Utility Meister** literally means "all-purpose" (*bannou*), suggesting that "utility" is being used in the sense of "utility knife" or something along those lines. It seems that Kiriku has the versatility as a meister to synchronize with many different weapons.

PAGE 117
Kimial Diehl
Apparently **Kim's full name** is Kimial Diehl (Kimiaaru Diiru in Japanese), although she is almost always referred to as simply "Kim." Recall that her name may be a reference to Kim Deal, bassist and vocalist for the alternative rock band the Pixies (for example, she has an attack called "Change Pixie").

PAGE 118
The word ***incom*** is actually a Japanese-made abbreviation of the English word "intercom" that is used mainly in the radio, television and film industries in Japan. Interestingly, it doesn't refer to the entire voice communications system that we would see as the "intercom" natively in English, but specifically to the headsets used in voice communications among production staff. So the Japanese word is appropriately applied to the demon tool headsets in this case. On a side note, the kanji used to spell this word literally means "hidden meeting without (wires)."

**PAGE 119**
This **pun on the word "jam"** is not an artifact of translation—in fact, it was introduced by the manga author himself, using different kanji in each case to indicate to Japanese readers which meaning of "jam" (to play improvisationally or for a bullet to get stuck in a gun's chamber) was intended.

**PAGE 121**
Liz uses **-onee** (literally "big sister") as a weak honorific for Azusa (compare to Black☆Star's casual use of "Marie-*neechan*" for Marie), showing that she respects Azusa for her age and talent but looks on her more as an almost-peer than as an instructor or supervisor. This usage is similar to that of the more standard *onee-san* (same meaning), a common term of casual address for young to middle-aged adult women.

**PAGE 127**
Patty's **nickname for Azusa**—a shortened version of "Azusa-*san*." It goes without saying that this form of address is even less respectful than Liz's (see note above), but it shows that Patty looks on Azusa with camaraderie and affection.

**PAGE 159**
Volantern
The name of this **attack of Kim's** is a portmanteau of "*vol*" ("flight") and "lantern," suggested by the fact that the lantern (i.e., Jackie) flies during the attack, jetting toward a foe and exploding on impact.

**PAGE 182**
It was revealed in the bonus manga section of Volume 15 that *Soul Eater* was not chosen as the recipient of the **2009 Kodansha Manga Prize** (and Atsushi Ohkubo was a little disappointed about that).

**PAGE 182**
The names "Romero," "Fulci," and "Hooper" are instantly recognizable to horror movie buffs as references to legendary film directors **George Romero** (*Night of the Living Dead*, 1968), **Lucio Fulci** (*The Beyond*, 1981) and **Tobe Hooper** (*The Texas Chain Saw Massacre*, 1974), but *Battalion* may not be as easily understandable to English-speaking audiences. In fact, *Battalion* was the title given to the 1985 horror film ***The Return of the Living Dead*** in Japan, so this too is a reference to a classic name in the horror movie world.

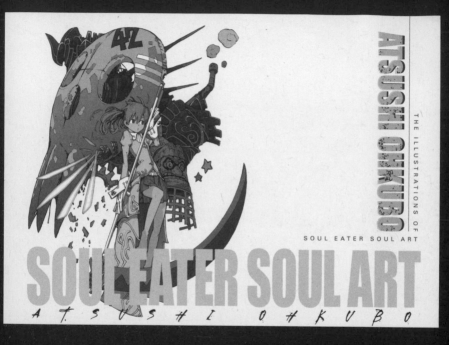

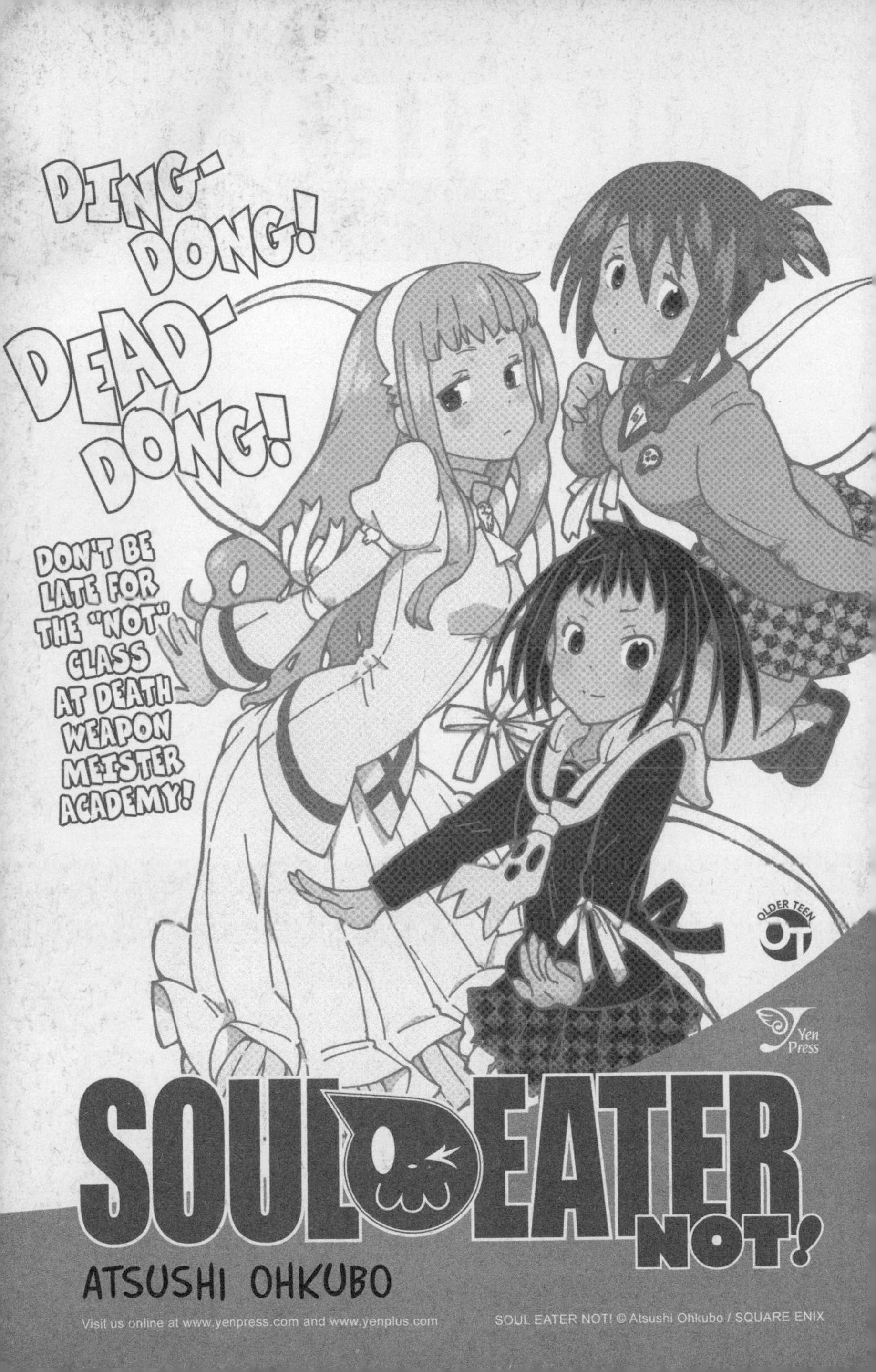
DING-DONG!
DEAD-DONG!
DON'T BE LATE FOR THE "NOT" CLASS AT DEATH WEAPON MEISTER ACADEMY!
OLDER TEEN OT
Yen Press
SOUL EATER NOT!
ATSUSHI OHKUBO
Visit us online at www.yenpress.com and www.yenplus.com
SOUL EATER NOT! © Atsushi Ohkubo / SQUARE ENIX

# SOUL EATER ⑯

### ATSUSHI OHKUBO

**Translation: Jack Wiedrick**

**Lettering: Alexis Eckerman**

Yen Press
Hachette Book Group
237 Park Avenue, New York, NY 10017

HachetteBookGroup.com
YenPress.com

Yen Press is an imprint of Hachette Book Group, Inc. The Yen Press name and logo are trademarks of Hachette Book Group, Inc.

First Yen Press Edition: September 2013

ISBN: 978-0-316-24431-2

10 9 8 7 6 5 4 3 2 1

BVG

Printed in the United States of America